The Best Bargain

FAMILY VACATIONS

in the U.S.A.

BY THE SAME AUTHORS

Innocents Abroad: Traveling with Kids in Europe

The Best Bargain
FAMILY
VACATIONS
in the U.S.A.

LAURA SUTHERLAND
and
VALERIE WOLF DEUTSCH

St. Martin's Press   New York

The authors have made every effort to ensure the accuracy of the travel information in this book, but readers should be aware that information does change. The authors and publisher cannot accept responsibility for any inconvenience or injury sustained by a traveler resulting from information obtained from this book.

Design by Judith A. Stagnitto

Library of Congress Cataloging-in-Publication Data

Sutherland, Laura.
    The best bargain family vacations in the U.S.A. /
Laura Sutherland and Valerie Wolf Deutsch.
        p. cm.
    ISBN 0-312-08704-7
    1. United States—Guidebooks.   I. Deutsch, Valerie
Wolf. II. Title.
    E158.S95   1993
    917.304'928—dc20   92-43174
                                            CIP

First edition: March 1993
10 9 8 7 6 5 4 3 2 1

CONTENTS

PREFACE

We are parents who rely on at least one yearly getaway for a special time together with our families. But like many families today, we need to stretch our vacation dollars as far as possible. Other guidebooks we consulted listed spectacular destinations that were fun to fantasize about, but most were too expensive for the average family. We started asking friends to tell us about their favorite "bargain" family vacations. We wanted to learn about different types of vacations—from secluded spots where we could leave our busy lives behind to places packed with activities to fill our days. Our criteria was "the best for less." Friends referred friends, who in turn referred their friends, and soon we found suggestions coming in from all over the country. The seeds of this book were sown.

When we could not visit recommended places personally, we interviewed recent visitors. We then collected the best low-cost, high-value destinations in this first edition of *The Best Bargain Family Vacations in the U.S.A.* All information about rates, types of accommodations, and special features were current at press time, but always confirm them when you call for a reservation. We hope they fit the bill.

ACKNOWLEDGMENTS

This book was inspired by our young traveling companions Madeleine, Walker, Silvie, and Rebecca, who continue to reinforce our motto: You *can* take them with you. Special thanks go to our supportive agent Vicky Bijur and our editor Anne Savarese. We are especially grateful to the many families who so eagerly shared their favorite bargain vacations and hideaways with us. And, of course, our heartfelt appreciation goes to our wonderful husbands, Lance Linares and Richard Deutsch.

INTRODUCTION

*I*magine your perfect family vacation. Is it lying on a warm beach with your children splashing in the waves, just steps from a cozy cottage? Or sitting high on horseback, riding through a grassy meadow on the way to a cowboy campfire cookout? Perhaps you prefer to relax in an Adirondack armchair by the lake, reading books and smelling the pine-scented mountain air while your kids chase frogs along the shore. Or what about a full-service resort with golf, tennis, fishing, boating, and swimming? If the perfect family vacation has remained a fantasy because you've thought it too expensive, read on. You'll be surprised that you don't have to give up your dream. We have uncovered many excellent vacation values and real bargains throughout the country and provide you with a broad range of choices, recognizing that one family's vacation wonderland is another's vacation wasteland.

Vacations are a chance to have fun together as a family, to rest, explore new places, gather new perspectives on the world around us and ourselves, and escape the distractions and pressures of everyday life. Even if your budget is modest you can enjoy vacations that will create a wealth of happy memories to relive as a family for years to come.

When vacation time finally coincides for everyone in your family, try to think hard and plan carefully. The most successful vacations are those that take everyone's needs and personalities into consideration. What does each member of your family realistically want in a vacation? Rest? Relaxation? Outdoor adventures? Art and music? Time around other children?

Is your family the active, outdoor type or one that prefers quieter pursuits? Are your family members fascinated with a certain topic, like the Wild West, dinosaurs, baseball, or life on the prairie? Thoughtful planning that involves the entire family will ensure a successful holiday.

If you and your spouse work long hours and look forward to vacation time as family time, a relaxing getaway along a lake or seashore where you can play together without a set schedule may work best. If you have young kids and never seem to catch up on your rest, a place with an exciting children's program will give you a break and the kids a chance to play with others their own age. You'll pay a bit more, but you will be more relaxed in the long run. If your kids drag their feet over washing the tiniest dish and the thought of one more week of fixing three meals a day makes you pale, look for a ranch, farm, or resort that offers an "American plan," which includes three meals a day in the price. If your children are preteens or teenagers and you want something physically or mentally challenging, try an adventure vacation where you can rush down the rapids of a river, or a learning vacation helping with an archaeological dig or assisting newly hatched sea turtles to race to the safety of the sea.

Each chapter covers a different type of vacation. Entries within each chapter are arranged by geographical region. To find entries in a specific state, consult the index at the back of the book.

EARLY PLANNING PAYS OFF

Advance planning and thoughtful research can save you hundreds of dollars on your vacation. Many of the best bargains in family travel are snapped up quickly. Make it your New Year's resolution to plan your summer vacation in January, February, or March. That way you'll have first choice at many of the bargain places listed in this book. If you're not boxed in by strict school schedules, travel off-season and avoid the crowds while you save 25 to 35 percent.

If you're driving to your destination, consider less expensive lodging along the way. We list family hostel information on pages 7–8 and budget hotel chains in the back of the book. Always ask about discounts and package deals before you make a reservation. And remember to book in advance; footloose-and-fancy-free ideas of traveling don't always apply when traveling with children.

Making your own meals, even if it's just lunch and an occasional breakfast or dinner, can save you lots of money in the long run. Eat at a picnic site, or even in your room, with food purchased at the supermarket instead of eating at restaurants for every meal. Do it the way the Europeans do,

with French bread, cheese, apples, and other finger foods. Bring a cooler.
Collect as much information as you possibly can about your destination
before you go. Get pamphlets, brochures, magazines, articles, and library
books. Write to state tourist offices for general ideas and city and town
chambers of commerce for more specific information. Involve the kids in
the planning process—get a map and show them your route. Let them
know what to expect, and let them know what you expect of them. Have
the kids pick out a few special toys, tapes, games, or books to take on the
trip and then pack these away until vacation time. Buy a few surprises,
too, and wrap them up, dispensing them every now and then on the trip
as needed.

If you're making a long drive, try to plan your stops at the most interesting places with the best overnight deals. If you're taking a driving
vacation, plan your stops around county fairs, local festivals, and other
special events, and vary your routes from the interstates to smaller roads
to take advantage of interesting off-the-beaten-track sites. By choosing
your stops in advance you can book early and be assured of a room. Many
budget hotels and motels do not charge for children. Before you go, be
sure to call several places to get the best price; then book it with a credit
card and ask for confirmation in writing.

Try to schedule a balance of activity and rest each day. Remember,
planning your day is like packing, so sit down with the family and make
a list of everything each person hopes to do. Then eliminate half of the
items on the list by concentrating on everyone's "can't miss" list. Above
all, be flexible; there's no need to stick to a prearranged schedule. Be
ready to make contingency plans depending on the weather.

YOUR TRAVEL BUDGET

To help you design your vacation budget, here are some common travel
expenses you should plan on. Remember, prices do change, so be sure
to check with your destination before finalizing your budget.

Transportation

Airplane, train, or bus fare (round-trip)
Airport-to-destination fare
Car rental
Public transportation
Gasoline
Car entertainment, new toys, audiotapes

Food and Lodging

Accommodations
Meals and snacks
Tips and service charges

Activities

Sports
Entertainment
Equipment rental
Excursions
Lessons

Miscellaneous

Souvenirs
New clothing and supplies
New luggage
Film purchase and development
Unexpected expenses

WHERE TO STAY

HOME EXCHANGES

Exchanging your home for someone else's can completely eliminate your lodging costs once you've arrived at your destination. If the family you exchange with happens to have kids similar in age to yours, you may get a houseful of appropriate toys and books, too. Home exchanges can be lined up for a few days or a week or a month; details are between you and the other party. To arrange, contact a home exchange service (see below), pay your fee, list your house, and write letters or call everyone with a home that appeals to you. Once you get a response, ask lots of questions (the exchange services give you a list) and ask for references of people who have used the home before. Try to provide the same for your home. The more carefully you work out the details, the more successful the exchange.

The two oldest and biggest home exchange firms in the United States are: **Vacation Exchange Club,** P.O. Box 650, Key West, Florida 33041,

telephone 800–638–3841; 305–294–3720. This club publishes four catalogs per year; if you join, your home is listed in each one. Listings cost
$50, or $62 with a photograph. **Intervac U.S.**, P.O. Box 590504, San
Francisco, California 94159, telephone 800–756–HOME and 415–435–
3497. This service charges $62 (seniors $55) for a listing in one of its
catalogs but you receive all three of its catalogs over the period of a year.
  Here are some additional tips:

- Some veterans recommend that you phone rather than write
  when you find a home you're interested in; the places with
  the best locations tend to go first.

- Discuss such details as trading cars, repair responsibilities,
  smoking policies, and your specific arrival and departure dates.
  Then put your arrangements in writing.

- It's a good idea for both parties to leave a notebook listing
  important phone numbers, information about the house's pe-
  culiarities and appliances, and some information about the
  neighborhood and town.

- Be sure to ask about tried-and-true baby-sitters, and get their
  phone numbers.

- Ask your neighbors to introduce themselves and make themselves available for questions or problem solving.

BUDGET MOTELS

No-frills budget motels generally offer little in charm and personality, but
the price is right and they are clean and comfortable. The industry's
criterion for "budget" is a single room rate of less than $50 per night;
many cost much less. Most major chains have toll-free phone numbers
and will send you a directory of motel locations free of charge.
  Well-priced "double doubles" (two double beds in one room) can easily
accommodate a family of four. Kids under twelve (and often under eighteen) usually are free, and cribs and rollaways are available at most motels
for a nominal fee or free of charge. Reservations are not always required,
but it is best to stop early for the night, especially in season. If you're
planning to use budget motels in resorts or popular tourist areas, definitely
reserve in advance.
  We list a number of the larger budget motel and hotel chains in appendix

I. You also can get a copy of the *National Directory of Budget Motels* from Pilot Books, 103 Cooper Street, Babylon, New York 11702.

ALL-SUITE HOTELS

One of the newest hotel trends and one that is beneficial especially to traveling families, all-suite hotels offer privacy, more space, and kitchen facilities. They vary from deluxe to budget. Most have two separate rooms, usually a bedroom and a living room (with kitchenette) that converts into a bedroom at night, with a door between them. Many even have television sets in each room and include a complimentary breakfast. Choice Hotels, Days Inn, and Travelodge are developing budget all-suite hotels. See appendix I for their toll-free numbers. The book *All-Suite Hotel Guide*, by Pamela Lanier, lists all-suite hotels throughout the United States and beyond. Contact Lanier Publishing, P.O. Box 20249, Oakland, California 94620-0429.

STANDARD HOTELS

Many hotels in major metropolitan areas offer special weekend packages to lure business during their slow time of the week. More of the larger hotel chains also have realized that family travel is a big movement in the travel industry and are creating packages just for them. Children usually stay free in the same room as their parents, and the savings can be substantial. Meals or meal discounts and use of sports facilities may be included in the rates.

STATE PARK CABINS AND RESORTS

State park cabins and resorts are one of the best-kept secrets in bargain vacation travel. More than twenty-five states have resort facilities and inexpensive cabins along rivers, lakes, and beaches throughout their state park system. The cabins range in style from rustic, which require you to bring your own linens and cooking equipment, to downright elegant, with every amenity included. Because state park cabins and resorts are set in protected areas of natural beauty, most of the parks have hiking trails, naturalist programs, swimming, boating, playgrounds, and picnic areas. Prices for extra recreational activities such as horseback riding and boat rentals tend to be far lower than those at private resorts and parks. We devote a chapter to state park cabins and resorts and list a few of the best throughout the book. Early reservations are *essential*, and each state has its own particular reservations system. Plan ahead and you will be richly rewarded.

BED-AND-BREAKFAST ESTABLISHMENTS

Staying in another family's home can offer travelers hospitality, local charm, and a healthy breakfast. Since many bed and breakfasts are furnished with antiques and delicate bric-a-brac, kids are not always welcome. Make sure to ask whether children are allowed; avoid those that state "well-behaved children welcome" or you'll spend your entire stay nervously hovering over your youngsters. Always ask if the B and B has a family rate and if children may stay in cribs or rollaways in their parents' room or you must rent a suite of rooms. If your children are young, find out if the B and B has a yard they can play in or if any toys or activities are provided for children. More and more B and Bs are opening their doors to families, but they have been quite slow to do so. Many of the excellent B and B guidebooks available indicate where children are welcome.

FAMILY HOSTELS

Does the term "youth hostel" conjure up images of a dingy, cavernous room jammed with bunk beds, sullen teenagers, dusty backpacks, and contaminated sleeping bags? Try this image instead: clean, private rooms for families in historic lighthouses, treehouses, farms, and lakeside inns. Family hosteling, long favored in northern Europe, is gaining popularity in the United States, and recently many American youth hostels have added family rooms so families can bunk down together. To keep costs low, hostelers provide their own food, bed linens, and towels. Many hostels offer kitchen facilities and some offer meals; bathrooms are shared. In addition, many hostels provide a variety of programs for guests, ranging from slide shows and programs on an area's natural history to walking tours of historic neighborhoods.

You do not need to be a member of the American Youth Hostel Federation to stay in a hostel, but nonmembers pay an extra $3 per person per night. If you plan to use more than one hostel in the course of a year you will find it more economical to join. Adult members can expect to pay from $6 to $12 per night, and children ordinarily pay half the adult rate.

We list hostels with family rooms that fit into our chapter categories, but there are many more to choose from. Members receive a complete listing of all facilities in the United States and Canada. Annual family memberships cost $35 per year and include parents and children under eighteen years of age. Besides discounts on rooms you'll receive the AYH handbook, *Hostelling North America*, which gives detailed listings on more than two hundred American Youth Hostels; a semiannual magazine called *Knapsack*, which provides updates on hostel openings and travel tips; and other miscellaneous travel discounts. Your membership card is good for AYH-affiliated hostels worldwide. For more information contact American Youth Hostels, Inc., P.O. Box 37613, Washington, D.C. 20013-7613, telephone 202–783–6161.

CAMPING

Some love it, others detest it, but with the exception of a home exchange, camping is certainly the best way to save money on accommodations. Campgrounds can be found in national parks, state parks, public recreation areas, and on private property. Facilities range from primitive sites to full-scale campground resorts with playgrounds, swimming pools, and launderettes.

Don't plan a long family camping trip with your kids without trying it out first close to home, or you'll end up like our friend Janice did, sleeping in the car with her frightened preschooler while her husband enjoyed the quiet of the tent—alone. And never arrive at the campsite past sunset, or you'll have to listen to tired and whiny kids while you fumble and grumble over the tent in the dark.

Most state travel offices provide a list of campgrounds; see appendix II for addresses. A wide selection of guidebooks are available on camping, too; check your local library or bookstore.

Kampgrounds of America (KOA) campgrounds are familiar to families vacationing on a budget, but noncampers might not be aware that most KOAs have what they call "Kamping Kabins," very simple cabins furnished with beds and sometimes a small table and a chair or two. Cabins have a barbecue grill, water supply, and picnic table in front. Campers must share the shower and toilet facilities, but this is a favorable option for those who want to enjoy the benefits of camping without pitching a tent.

GETTING THERE

BY CAR

Driving to a vacation destination with a large family is usually less expensive than buying airline tickets for the whole crew and renting a car once you've arrived. But don't forget to figure into your calculations that it always takes longer to get anywhere with kids. The wear and tear on your nerves can be a factor, too; listening to your young road warriors fight and whine on the drive home may diminish all of the relaxation benefits of your vacation. But traveling by car does give you the freedom to stop where you want and take interesting side trips along the way.

Plan on stopping and stretching every two or three hours, and build that extra time into your itinerary. If you're driving through a town, ask for the nearest school, park, or playground and pull off to let the kids swing, slide, and blow off steam. Don't try to drive too far in one day, or all of you will be too crabby and short-tempered to remember that you're supposed to be having fun. And if you try to drive straight through to save money on hotels, you'll probably end up like Robin, whose family drove from California to Nebraska, stopping only for gas and food. The three kids slept in the 1954 sedan en route—one on the floor, one on the seat, and Robin, the youngest, stretched out along the shelf below the back window. She recalls her family vacations with a cramped shudder.

Make sure your car is in top shape to avoid unexpected financial burdens along the way. Plan to have it checked and serviced by a reputable mechanic before you go. A well-tuned engine can save 3 to 8 percent on fuel. Be sure to take a basic tool kit, flares, flashlights, and gloves, just in case.

Here are some drive-time tips:

- Plan plenty of stops along the way. We can't emphasize this enough.

- Exchange seats several times each day for fresh perspectives and new seatmates.

- Bring outdoor activity toys and equipment, such as jump ropes, Frisbees, and inflatable balls, or play tag and run races.

- Pack a cooler instead of relying on quick-stop restaurants. In addition to saving you money, *you'll* be choosing what the kids will eat. Plus, snacks can be a real boredom fighter.

- Picnic outdoors as much as you can to allow the kids a chance to stretch and to keep the car a bit cleaner.

- Pack water instead of pop or juice to quench thirst; it cuts down on bathroom stops, as kids drink it only when they're thirsty, not because they like the taste. Give each child his or her own canteen or, better yet, a bicyclist's water bottle—they're the most dribble-proof containers we've found.

- Pack a broad selection of music and story tapes. Invest in separate Walkman-type tape players for each child if your kids are older or if they disagree on what they want to hear, and let each choose a few new tapes. Sneak in two or three quality books on tape to foist upon them when they're bored and vulnerable.

- Always end the day early.

BY AIR

If your time is limited and you want to travel a long distance, flying is the only way to go. There are a few ways to save money on airfare. Always shop around with several different airlines before buying your tickets. Don't assume that your travel agent will get you the very best deal; do some of the research yourself. Certain air routes have reduced rates at night; if you and your children are good sleepers, you might save money this way. Generally the best fares are offered off-season, but occasionally you can get great deals during the peak season if airlines are competing for travelers. If you fly often, join a frequent flyer club, especially one that lets children accumulate airline mileage. Many clubs have package deals that allow you to accumulate mileage by using their credit cards and affiliated businesses, from phone systems to hotel chains and car rental companies. Free airline tickets and upgrades are awarded depending on the number of miles you accumulate.

Summer travelers who wish to take advantage of reduced airfare packages should make sure their reservation plans mesh with their air dates. Reduced fares often require a midweek flight, while many housing and resort reservations run Saturday to Saturday or Sunday to Sunday.

BY RAIL

Train travel appeals to kids of all ages, and the extensive Amtrak system will take you almost anywhere you want to go. Most families we interviewed felt that shorter train trips worked best, as children tend to get fidgety on long trips. Train travel offers unlimited opportunities for enjoying beautiful scenery, but most kids couldn't care less about scenery. And unless you have the financial resources for a private sleeping compartment, you will be sleeping in your seats on the longer hauls. Bring your own extra blankets, pillows, and food, but do plan to eat at least one meal in the dining car to enjoy the white tablecloths and uniformed waiters. Amtrak's snack bar food is mediocre and expensive, and on longer trips it often runs out, so lay in a good store of provisions before you go.

Remember that once you arrive at your destination, you will need a rental car unless there is regular and reliable public transportation. Before you go, find out where your destination station is located (some "stations" are nothing more than a bench and an overhang) and what kinds of services are available there.

Amtrak offers a few family package deals that can save you money on tickets; these tend to change from season to season, so be sure to inquire when you're thinking of booking. Another package popular with families is the Air-Rail Travel Plan, which lets you travel one way by rail and one way by air for one round-trip price and allows up to three stops on the train journey. Zone pricing is offered, and off-peak travel times are less expensive than peak travel times. For more information call 800–USA–RAIL.

SOUVENIRS

If your kids are collectors, encourage them to search out lower-priced items, such as decals, pencils, plastic snow globes, pennants, or postcards. T-shirts make practical souvenirs, but give your kids a limit on the number you will buy throughout the trip. You will protect your pocketbook and the kids will choose only those they really like and plan to wear. Some families we know buy their children an item of clothing at every stop; each time the child wears the item throughout the next year they recall fond memories of their summer vacation. Other families give older kids their own spending money and let them budget for souvenirs. It's remarkable how tightfisted kids can be when they're spending their own rather than their parents' money.

HALF-PRICE DISCOUNT BOOKS

Coupon discount books can save you up to 50 percent on hotel bills, restaurant meals, and admission fees to entertainment and recreational activities. The largest publisher of directories and coupon books, Entertainment Publications, offers a book called *Travel America at Half Price,* along with individual city or region guides that include numerous two-for-one and 50-percent-off deals at hotels, motels, restaurants, and attractions. If you're traveling to a city these savings can add up. For example, families planning a beach vacation in St. Augustine, Florida, can pick up a discount book for the entire Jacksonville area and receive discounts to the Fountain of Youth, Ripley's Believe It or Not, and wax museum and historical tours; for more information call 800–477–3234. Discount books cost $30 to $42, depending on the area covered. A special book for teenagers called the *Gold C Saving Spree* covers a total of thirty-two different vacation destinations. Priced at $10, *Gold C* contains hundreds of two-for-one and half-price offers geared specifically to this age group.

DISNEYLAND AND DISNEY WORLD

Shrewd parents pad their wallets for trips to these American shrines, and no guidebook on budget family travel is complete without mentioning them. Costs to anticipate include transportation, lodging, food, admission, and souvenirs. There's not much you can do about admission prices, but you *can* whittle away at the other categories and still have a good time. Disneyland in Anaheim, California, is a much smaller complex than its Florida counterpart, and visitors can see most of the park in one day. Disney World and environs in Orlando, Florida, is enormous and can occupy visitors for close to a week.

Here are some money-saving tips for both parks:

- The least busy times of year are January, May, September, October, and early December. The busiest times are June through August and holiday periods. The busiest day of the week is Saturday and the parks are the most crowded from noon to 5 P.M.

- Stay in a motel with a kitchenette or a condominium and prepare your own hearty breakfast and dinner.

• Arrive at the park well before the doors open to get a good place in the ticket line. Go to the most popular rides first.

• Visitors are not supposed to bring in their own food, but sneak a few high-energy snacks (protein-enriched candy bars, nuts, and raisins) into your backpack or purse. That way you'll avoid buying expensive snacks and you can postpone lunch until after the peak lunch crowds have left. You'll have fewer people on the rides during the lunch hour and waste less time in lines. One family we interviewed ate an enormous breakfast at their hotel, snacked during lunch, and then splurged on a midafternoon dinner at the park. Back at the hotel Mom and Dad fixed a healthy evening snack before the group retired for the night.

• Discuss souvenirs with your children in advance. Many parents recommend buying an article of clothing, such as a T-shirt or sweatshirt; knickknacks, mouse ears (although they are a lot of fun), and other keepsakes will eventually collect dust.

• Check the travel section of your local newspaper for any package deals that might work for you, and compare the costs with a do-it-yourself arrangement.

DISNEYLAND

Unlike Disney World, California's Disneyland can be "done" in a day (two at the most), but you should plan a two-night stay somewhere near the park to fit it all in. That way you'll get a bright and early start (and won't have to fight Los Angeles commuter traffic) to beat the crowds to the park, and you can stay until it closes.

Where to Stay

If you want to combine a Disneyland visit with a trip to the beach and other Los Angeles sites, see page 201 for accommodation ideas in the Los Angeles area. We found the least expensive lodging near Disneyland to be the Motel 6 chain—low in ambience, but you'll be spending almost all of your time at the Magic Kingdom. Call reservation headquarters (505–891–6161) and ask for the Motel 6's in Anaheim, California. The one at 100 West Freedman Way is two blocks from Disneyland; the next closest is at 2920 West Chapman Avenue, two miles from the park. Motel 6's on North State College Boulevard and South Beach Boulevard are both about five miles away.

DISNEY WORLD

You could spend a month and your retirement nest egg visiting all of the intoxicating theme parks, amusement parks, water parks, shows, and tours in Orlando. You'll save a considerable amount of money if you limit your visit to Disney World and one other attraction, such as Universal Studios. These alone will take you nearly a week to explore.

Where to Stay

Many midrange motels and hotels offer free transportation to and from Disney World. These hotels charge more for rooms than those with no transportation service, but the cost is worth it if you don't have your own car; many shuttle companies charge $10 per person each way. If you have your own car, consider staying in a condominium within a short drive of the park. You'll have your own kitchen, laundry facilities in your room, more space, and a swimming pool. Condominium prices are surprisingly competitive with the hotels. Parking at Disney World is $4 per car.

Condo Lodge Vacation Villas, located between Disney World and the Orlando airport, has reasonably priced one- and two-bedroom condominiums that sleep two to six people for $70 to $90 per day, $475 to $625 per week. Tickets to Disney World and other attractions are available at the Guest Services Office when you check in. Address: 4145 West Vine Street, Kissimmee, Florida 34741. For inquiries: CondoLodge, 6105 Granby Road, Derwood, Maryland 20855. Telephone: 800–866–2660.

The best deals in budget motels are two Econo Lodges that offer good prices but no free transportation to the park. Children under eighteen stay free in their parents' room. Units with kitchenettes are not available, nor is there a swimming pool. Double rooms are $50 per night. Addresses: 5870 Orange Blossom Trail, Orlando (twelve miles from Disney World), telephone: 407–859–5410; 9401 South Orange Blossom Trail, Orlando (fourteen miles from Disney World), telephone: 407–851–1050.

Aside from campsites, the least expensive place to stay is in one of the KOA Kampground's thirteen "kamping kabins." If you don't mind staying in a single room with a double bed, bunk beds, and a shared bathhouse nearby, this place can really save you money. You can cook on the barbeque grill outside and eat at the picnic table next to it. Other features include free shuttles to Disney World, Epcot Center, MGM Studios, Universal Studios and Sea World, swimming pool, game room, shuffleboard, tennis, and petting zoo. Guests bring their own bedding and towels. Plan to pay $45 per night for a family of four. Spring and fall are the best times to stay in these cabins, as July and August are hot and humid. Address: 4771 West 192, Kissimmee, Florida 34746. Telephone: 800–331–1453 or 407–396–2400.

RESORTS

*A*ssemble a beautiful setting, a glimmering pool or lake, plentiful sports and games, and lively entertainment in one location, and you've got a resort vacation. Big bucks? Usually. But we've tallied an impressive number of resorts that offer good values or low prices. A number of them have supervised children's programs, perfect for parents who need a vacation both with *and* from their children.

Resort prices vary considerably. The more amenities the resort offers and the more the staff does for you, the more it will cost. Comparing prices for resorts can be a bit like comparing apples and oranges. American plan resorts include three meals a day in the price. Many others offer housekeeping cabins that allow you to cook your own meals. Some resorts charge for everything from canoes to shuffleboard equipment, but just as many offer guests the free use of all recreational facilities. The most economical choice will depend on your family and what they like to do. But beware: it's easy to make the same mistake that Sam did when he selected a resort with a dazzling array of activities, all with separate prices. It appeared less expensive than an all-inclusive package, and he thought he could offer his two *very* active preteen boys the choice of one special sport or game per day. The frustrated kids spent the vacation nagging and Sam spent the week nervously adding up receipts. This doesn't mean you should avoid resorts with separate fees for activities; just be realistic and calculate all of the various costs when you budget your vacation.

Some people we interviewed found it economical to share cottage resort accommodations or a condominium with another family. Larger units often cost much less per person than smaller ones, which can make the most desirable resorts affordable. In addition to the lower cost per family, families staying together have their own kitchen, playmates for their kids, and companions and built-in baby-sitters for themselves.

We list every type of resort, from enormous ones with a laundry list of diversions to serene lakeside places with a boat or two and a game of horseshoes. Take note of the state park resorts found in a number of lucky states. They offer excellent prices, numerous recreational facilities, naturalist programs, and magnificent settings. Because they are among the very best in bargain vacations, you must book as far in advance as possible. See pages 308–327 for more information on other states with resort parks. Many oceanfront resorts are covered in our beach chapter.

Here are a few questions to ask:

- Are there package deals for families?

- Are there seasonal discounts?

- What is and what is not included in the price?

- What about taxes and gratuities?

WEST COAST

RICHARDSON'S RESORT

Address: PO Box 9028, South Lake Tahoe, California 95731.
Telephone: 916–541–1801.

Get around on land by bicycle, horse, or roller blade skates, and travel over water via paddle-boat, kayak, or jet ski—all are available at this full-service resort on the south shore of Lake Tahoe. Choose from lakeside cabins, a hotel, condominiums, and campsites. Families visit in winter to enjoy the many downhill ski resorts nearby and in summer to take advantage of the Tahoe area's recreational activities. Richardson's sits on Forest Service land next to a nature center and several historic estates, all of which run programs during the summer months. The resort's restaurant and bar overlook a popular broad sandy beach. Tame geese have been known to frequent the beach, looking for an occasional handout.

Season: Year-round, but the best selection of cabins is available in July and August.

Accommodations: Cabins, which sleep between two and eight people, are the best value for families. Four-person rustic cabins, rented by the week, are open in the summer only; they provide fully equipped kitchens, all linens, porches, and small bedrooms, but no insulation or heat. Larger, more deluxe cabins also are available.

Special Features: Bike rental shop (the resort is on a bike trail), horseback riding rentals, Roller blade rentals, horseshoes, croquet, pool table, tennis, volleyball, hiking, ice-cream parlor, and playground are all part of the facility. A marina at the resort rents motorboats, paddleboats, kayaks, and jet skis and includes parasailing and a water-ski school. The sandy beach is public and can get crowded during peak use; other good beaches are nearby.

Cost: Rustic cabins $500 to $600 per week, deluxe cabins $850 to $950 per week. Bike rentals $5 per hour, horseback riding $16 per hour, Roller blades $12 per hour.

Nearby: Emerald Bay and Fallen Leaf Lake offer excellent mountain bike riding, and the Forest Service's Tallac Historical Estates, right next to resort property, has festivals, art shows, and concerts in the summer months. The Forest Service's visitors center is just down the road with an information display, guided nature walks and other naturalist programs, and amphitheater concerts. A "stream profile chamber" further down the road lets you observe trout and salmon through an underwater window. Erhman Mansion at Sugar Pine Point has tours of its allegedly haunted interior.

TRINITY ALPS RESORT

Address: Star Route Box 490, Lewiston, California 96052.
Telephone: 916–286–2205.

Kids can pan for gold in the river as much as they please with Trinity Alps Resort's gold-panning equipment; every summer several lucky children take home a nugget or two. Forty-three private cabins are tucked among the trees along both banks of the Stewart Fork River, with several bridges connecting the two sides. A sandy beach right next to the swimming hole in the river is centrally located to all of the cabins, and its gentle slope makes it safe for both toddlers and older children. Other favorite daytime activities include tubing down the river and trail riding. The resort's stable offers one- and two-hour trail rides, an all-day ride, and a special breakfast ride that should not be missed. When you're tired of cooking, visit the excellent restaurant, which serves dinner on a patio above the river.

Season: May 15 to September 30.

Accommodations: Cabins have equipped kitchens, dining areas, outdoor barbecues and picnic tables, and private bathrooms. Most of them also have a covered outdoor sleeping veranda overlooking the river. Cabins along the far side of the river are the most private. This resort has been in continuous operation for seventy years, and many families book for the following year before they leave. May, June, late August, and early September are the easiest times to get reservations.

Special Features: The resort has a small general store, a soda fountain, and a community center that offers complimentary family movies, square dancing, and talent shows in the evening. On the grounds are tennis, badminton, volleyball, horseshoes, gold panning, Ping-Pong, tubing, bonfires, and sing-alongs.

Cost: Cabins and apartments sleeping four $395 to $435 per week. Larger cabins sleeping six $545 to $715 per week. Bring your own bed linens or rent them for $15 per week per bed. Bring your own towels.

Guided horseback rides for one hour $15, two-hour rides $25, and breakfast rides $35 per person. All-day rides into the Trinity Alps Wilderness Area $60, lunch included.

Nearby: Trinity Lake is one and a half miles away. Golf courses and numerous hiking and bike trails are a short distance from the resort.

KONOCTI HARBOR RESORT AND SPA

Address: 8727 Soda Bay Road, Kelseyville, California 95451.
Telephone: 800–862–4930; 707–279–4281.

Parents can pamper themselves at Konocti's health spa while the kids make friends their own age at the daily children's program. Activities for youngsters ages five to fourteen run from 10 A.M. to 4 P.M. and then start up again at 5 P.M., ending at 10 P.M. Konocti is known for its concert series by Clear Lake, with a full spectrum of entertainers that have included Crystal Gayle, Tony Bennett, B. B. King, and Eddie Money. The evening children's program is timed so that parents can attend the first show of the night. Concert ticket holders get reductions on room rates. There's plenty for the family to do together, too, with two Olympic-size swimming pools, tennis courts, miniature golf, and rides on Clear Lake in a sixty-five-foot paddle wheeler.

Accommodations: Standard rooms have two double beds. Family units have a double bed and a set of bunk beds in the bedroom and a couch, desk, chair, and TV in a small sitting room. Apartments contain two full-size beds, a queen-size sofabed, kitchen, and barbecue area.

Special Features: Two swimming pools (lessons are available), two wading pools, playground, miniature golf course, sixty-five-foot paddle wheeler rides, golf, shuffleboard, badminton, basketball, horseshoes, vol-

leyball, Ping-Pong, and tennis. The children's day camp operates from 10
A.M. to 4 P.M. with arts and crafts, miniature golf, swimming, tennis, and
lunch. An evening children's program runs from 5 to 10 P.M. with movies,
miniature golf, and more. The health spa has a sauna, Jacuzzi, aerobics
classes, weights and exercise equipment, and a lap pool. Massages are
available for an extra charge, and a beauty shop is next door.

Cost: Children under twelve stay free in parents' room; teens $10 per
night. Standard rooms and family units $72 per night; apartments start at
$130 per night. Children's program $15 per child per day session and
$15 per child per night session. Miniature golf $2 per person; tennis
$8 per hour plus $2 for night lighting. Use of the health spa $7.50 per
day.

KA-NEE-TA VACATION VILLAGE

**Address: 100 Main Street, PO Box K, Warm Springs, Oregon 97761
(seventy miles from Bend).**
Telephone: 800–831–0100; 503–553–1112.

This full-service resort offers all kinds of accommodations, from hotel
rooms to camping, but your kids might never forgive you if you don't stay
in one of the brightly painted canvas tepees. Big enough to sleep six to
eight people, the tepees are set on cement bases and have a built-in picnic
table and a fireplace in the center. This experience isn't luxurious resort
living, but it's one your children are not likely to forget. Ka-Nee-Ta has
numerous recreational facilities, all for an extra fee. A river runs through
the property for exploring, fishing, and rafting; there is also horseback
riding, an eighteen-hole golf course, a large swimming pool, bike rental,
and much more.

Season: Year-round.

Accommodations: Choose from the tepees, cottages, hotel rooms, or
primitive tent camping. Tepees have eighteen square feet of enclosed
space and use bathhouse facilities nearby. Bring foam pads and sleeping
bags, and food. One-bedroom cottages sleep up to three people and do
not have kitchens. Two-bedroom cottages have fully equipped kitchens;
lodge rooms range from doubles to deluxe suites.

Special Features: Pool, horseback riding, golf, hiking trails, badminton,
volleyball, horseshoes, fishing, tennis, kayaking; laundry facilities, snack
bar, restaurant.

Cost: Tepees $50 per night for up to five people; $10 per person above
that. One-bedroom cottages $85 per night for two people; two-bedroom
cottages $100 per night for two. Each additional person age six and up
$12 per night. Tent camping $15 per night; lodge rooms $95 to $235 per

night. Cottage and lodge accommodations include free use of the swimming pool.

Rental bikes $6 to $10 per hour; guided horseback rides $20 per hour; tennis $10 for ninety minutes; kayaking $15 per three-mile trip.

Nearby: A reindeer and llama farm are ninety minutes away near the town of Sisters.

ROCKY MOUNTAINS AND SOUTHWEST

YMCA OF THE ROCKIES

Address: Membership Office, Schlessman Center Executive Offices, Estes Park, Colorado 80511-2800.
Telephone: 800–777–YMCA.

People have been coming to the YMCA of the Rockies for three and four generations to enjoy one of the best-loved family vacation destinations. It is popular in winter months for skiing, ice-skating, snowshoeing, and sledding. During the summer families can take advantage of swimming, hiking, hayrides, horseback riding, and a supervised children's day camp. The YMCA of the Rockies has facilities in two locations in Colorado: Snow Mountain Ranch, built in the 1960s near Winter Park, is the newer facility. Estes Park, about twenty-five miles away, is adjacent to the Rocky Mountain National Park and has been in operation for more than eighty years.

Snow Mountain Ranch

An absolutely breathtaking setting on over four thousand acres filled with lodgepole pines and spectacular views of the Indian Peaks and Gore ranges, Snow Mountain is a popular downhill and cross-country ski center in winter and has many exciting summer activities as well. Recreational and athletic pursuits include mountain biking, swimming, and horseback riding, and a youth day camp runs from 8:30 A.M. to 3:30 P.M. The program is supervised by college-age counselors trained by the center, and activities for children are divided and organized by age group. Kids hike, take nature walks, play games, swim, play miniature golf, and do arts and crafts projects.

Address: PO Box 169, Winter Park, Colorado 80482.
Telephone: 303–887–2152.

Accommodations: More than forty cabins have kitchens and fireplaces and sleep five to twelve people. Four different lodges have rooms sleeping four or five people, and most have private baths. Many lodge rooms have a double bed and a set of bunk beds. Campsites and RV hookups also are available.

Special Features: In summer select mountain biking, hiking, horseback riding, pony rides, swimming in an Olympic-size indoor pool, a crafts center, miniature golf, and hayrides. In the evenings there are campfires, movies, and square dancing. During the winter a ski rental shop is on the premises, downhill skiing is nearby, and there are sleigh rides and snowshoeing.

The children's program runs during the summer from 8:30 A.M. to 3:30 P.M. Half-day rates are an option, and child care can be arranged during lunch.

Cost: Two-bedroom cabins $97 to $184. In the Blue Ridge lodge unit, a room that sleeps five in bunks and a twin bed with a half bath and shared showers, $28 per night. Aspenbrook Lodge rooms, two double beds and one set of bunks, full bath, and phone, $54 per night. Discounts of up to 25 percent available for cabins and lodge rooms in early December and from April through mid-May.

Children's program $10 per day for the full-day program, $5 for half day. Horseback riding $15 per hour; white water rafting about $50 for a half-day raft trip; mountain bike rental $10 for two hours.

Nearby: Downhill skiing is available at the Winter Park and Silver Creek ski areas. Grand Lake, Shadow Mountain Lake, and Lake Granby are a few miles away for fishing, sailing, and other water sports.

Estes Park Center

Estes Park is at a higher elevation (8,010 feet) amid mountain peaks, and hiking is popular here on trails that head into Rocky Mountain National Park next door. Other recreational options exceptional for their prices include horseback riding, swimming, and tennis, to name a few. In summer the children's program for ages three through fourteen is a big draw with arts and crafts, swimming, riding, miniature golf, and an overnight camping trip. Teens plan their own activities with an emphasis on outdoor adventure. White water trips and guided hikes into the national park can be arranged.

Address: 2515 Tunnel Road, Estes Park, Colorado 80511-2550.

Telephone: 303–586–3341.

Season: Year-round.

Accommodations: Two hundred housekeeping cabins are available. Many two- and three-bedroom housekeeping cabins have kitchens and fireplaces and sleep four to ten people. Four different lodges have rooms sleeping three to six people, all with private baths. Each lodge has a lounge with a stone fireplace where families can gather.

Special Features: Horseback riding, hayrides, hiking, indoor swimming pool, miniature golf, square dancing, tennis, arts and crafts, cross-country skiing, ice-skating, sledding, summer concerts. The children's program operates during the same hours as those of Snow Mountain, above.

Cost: In peak season, cabins $46 to $190 per night. Simple two-bedroom family cabin (with complete kitchen and fireplace) that sleeps five $85 per night. Rooms that sleep five in the Eastside Lodge $38 per night for two sets of bunks and a twin bed. Five-person rooms in the Wind River Lodge $74 per night. Discounts of up to 25 percent available off-season.

Children's program $5 per day for preschool age, $10 for kindergarten through eighth graders. Horseback riding $15 per hour; white water rafting $40 to $50 per half-day trip.

Reservations: Estes Park Center uses a system of priorities in making reservations. "Cabin donors," people who have contributed the cost of a cabin, get first priority. "Partner" members, who pay a family membership fee of $300 per year, get second priority. Third priority goes to regular members, who pay $75 per year per family. Reservations are then open to nonmembers. Most requests are for July and August, so if you can plan your vacation for another time of year you will improve your chances of getting what you want. Be as flexible as you can by requesting either location and several options for dates and cabin types. If you plan to stay for two weeks or more it is well worth making the extra contribution to ensure your request. Reservations are accepted by mail in order of date postmarked, so a prompt reply makes a difference.

Nearby: Both camps adjoin Rocky Mountain National Park; see pages 114–115 for more on this area.

HOMESTEAD

Address: PO Box 99, North Homestead Drive, Midway, Utah 84049.
Telephone: 800–327–7220; 801–654–1102.

Located just minutes away from downhill ski resorts such as Snowbird and Alta and thirty minutes from Park City, Deer Valley, Sundance, and Park West, the Homestead is a country resort with big appeal in winter. Ski packages for families are reasonably priced and include car rental. Summer activities are plentiful, too: golf, horseback rides, swimming, mountain biking, tennis, and recreational games. Package deals come up throughout the year; be sure to inquire when booking.

Season: Year-round.

Accommodations: Guest rooms and condominiums are available;

guest rooms have one or two double beds and a private bath, and are less expensive. Condos have kitchens and house up to eight people.

Special Features: Eighteen-hole golf course, hayrides, buggy rides, mountain bike trails, indoor and outdoor pools, sauna, hot tub, Jacuzzi, lighted tennis courts, horseshoes, croquet, volleyball, shuffleboard, badminton.

Cost: Guest rooms $65 to $95 per night. Children under two are free and kids over two cost $10 each per night. Some of the lowest-priced rooms have two double beds, suitable for three or four people, and can be had for the price of a double if they are available; be sure to ask. Pricey condos start at $175 per night. Mountain bikes rent for $5 to $10 per hour; guided horseback rides $12 per hour.

Nearby: Boating, waterskiing, fishing, hiking.

PAH TEMPE HOT SPRINGS RESORT

Address: 825 North 800 East, Hurricane, Utah (forty minutes from Zion National Park, two hours from Las Vegas).
Telephone: 801–635–2879.

Ten warm and shallow natural grotto pools line the steep-sided Virgin River canyon right next to this resort. Originally used by the Paiute Indians as a source of sacred healing, the geothermal water still flows from the riverbed into rock grotto pools along the sandy river bottom and tumbles over waterfalls. Guests can soak in pools of all different temperatures; some mix with the cooler river water, and some don't. Farther upstream are four more pools. A naturally heated, shaded swimming pool is available to all guests who stay in a bed-and-breakfast motel, large retreat center, or campground area.

Season: Year-round.

Accommodations: Seven bed-and-breakfast rooms can accommodate families in connecting rooms or by adding comfortable sleeping mats to larger rooms. The Rock House retreat center sleeps a minimum of ten people; with five double beds and extra rooms for pads and sleeping bags, it's housed as many as thirty. You can rent it with or without use of the kitchen. Many guests use it for family reunions.

Special Features: Shaded, naturally heated outdoor swimming pool, seven soaking tubs along the riverbank, vegetarian restaurant, massage therapy, nature walks, yoga classes, water aerobics. No smoking or alcohol allowed. RV hookups and camping are on the premises.

Cost: Bed-and-breakfast rooms, or a duplex with two double beds and a private bath, $80 to $110 per night for four people; includes breakfast and use of the swimming pool and water canyon pools and tubs. The Rock

House, with kitchen, $275 per night for the first ten people, $20 for each additional person; without the kitchen, $225 per night. Day use of pools and river area $5 for adults, $3 for children six to twelve, $1 for children five and under. Restaurant lunch and dinner $3.50 to $7.50. Camping sites $25 for two people.

CHAIN-O-LAKES

Address: PO Box 218, Romayor, Texas 77368.
Telephone: 713–592–2150.

Twelve lakes with names including Camp Lake, Swim Lake, Skillet Lake, Corral Lake, and Crystal Lake offer some of the best family swimming and boating in the Lone Star State. The kids will want to spend most of their time at Swim Lake, a three-and-a-half-acre spring-fed lake with inner tube rentals and a slick, steep water slide called the Rampage. Boats and canoes can be rented for use on the other lakes, and the facility also has guided horseback rides, nature trails, and excellent fishing. Low-priced cabins let you do your own cooking, or you can eat at the hilltop restaurant. Campsites and RV hookups are scattered throughout the lake areas. Tame alligators in the lakes can be spotted and love to be fed marshmallows.

Season: Year-round.

Accommodations: Three types of cabins are available; all have kitchens, air-conditioning, full baths, and all linens except beach towels. Older rustic cabins do not have dishes or utensils and are a bit tired, but are well priced; each accommodates up to six people. Duplexes can accommodate six people in one large room with two double beds and one set of bunks; the kitchenette contains dishes and utensils. Log cabins are pleasantly decorated and popular, especially on weekends. Wilderness campsites, RV hookups, and campsites with water and electricity are available as well. Because the various accommodations at this resort are spread out among twelve different lakes, it never feels as crowded as you might expect.

Special Features: An immense swimming lake, water slide, guided trail rides, pony rides, hayrides, golfing, horse-drawn carriage rides, boat and tube rentals, restaurant.

Cost: Rustic cabins $45 to $90 per night; duplex cottages $60 per night; log cabins $100 to $140 per night in peak summer months, slightly less the rest of the year. Reservations required for all accommodations and for the restaurant. Guided trail rides $10; waterslide $3 per day (unlimited use); canoe and boat rentals $12.50 for four hours, $16.50 per day, $22 for twenty-four hours.

CENTRAL UNITED STATES

VILLAGE RESORTS

Address: PO Box OR, Spirit Lake, Iowa 51360-0645.
Telephone: 800–727–4561; 712–337–3223.

The Village Resorts complex includes Village West Resort, Manhattan Beach Resort, Village East Resort, and Oaks Resort on opposite shores of West Lake Okoboji; a Village Express Fun Bus provides free transportation between them. Guests can use all facilities free of charge, regardless of where they stay, and two different children's recreation programs run throughout the summer months. Families can even take a boat ride across the lake to an amusement park for a few hours and pick up the boat again for the trip back. Accommodations range from deluxe townhouses to rustic cabins. A Family Frolic Package is available on summer weekends.
Season: Year-round.

Village West and Manhattan Beach (west side of lake)

Accommodations: Village West has luxury townhouses and rustic cabins. The cabins are air-conditioned and have private baths and small kitchenettes with stovetop, refrigerator, and dishes, but no phones or TVs. They sleep six to nine people in two to four bedrooms. Manhattan Beach has apartment units that include kitchenettes and sleep four to six people. The apartments and cabins are available late spring through early fall only; townhouses are available year-round.

Special Features: Indoor pool and spa, miniature golf, sandy beach on lake with roped-off swimming area, tennis, restaurants, and ice-skating in winter. Each week during the summer a list of organized children's activities is made available to guests, and families can select as few or as many as they wish.

Cost: From late May to early September cabins accommodating seven $750 to $812 per week, $104 to $135 per day. In April and early May $380 to $425 per week, $55 to $70 per day. Townhouses $1,500 per week in July and August, $950 per week the rest of the year. Manhattan Beach rentals in July and August $686 to $1,000 per week.

Village East and East Oaks

Accommodations: Village East has a hotel, and children sixteen and under stay free if they share their parents' room. East Oaks has rustic cabins, some with kitchenettes, that sleep two to six people; motel rooms; and motel efficiencies with kitchenettes. Village East is open year-round; East Oaks is open late spring through early fall only.

Special Features: Village East has an indoor pool and spa and an athletic club with indoor racquetball and tennis, a fitness clinic, outdoor tennis courts, aerobics classes, organized children's activities, an indoor walking track, a championship golf course, and restaurants.

Cost: Motel units start at $350 per week, $52 per night. Motel efficiencies start at $425 per week and $62 per night. Cottages $413 to $550 per week, $65 to $85 per night.

Family Frolic Package

This bargain package allows families of four (with kids sixteen and under) to stay for three days and two nights at either Village East or Village West. The cost per family of $300 to $350 includes dinner and breakfast for two at several restaurants, a ride around the lake on a fifty-four-foot yacht, four all-day passes to a nearby amusement park, supervised children's activities, and recreational programs for the entire family.

Nearby: A marina rents all kinds of boats; cruise to Arnolds amusement park and back.

POTAWATOMI INN

Address: No. 6 Lane 100 A, Lake James, Angola, Indiana 46703.
Telephone: 219–833–1077.

Families stay busy here in summer or winter at Pokagon State Park, on the shores of Lake James and Snow Lake. Warm weather means swimming, hiking, fishing, boating, horseback riding, tennis, and the park's cultural arts programs. In winter you can ice-skate, cross-country ski, or try the fast and thrilling 178-foot twin toboggan run. A full-time naturalist staff conducts activities throughout the park year-round. The Potawatomi Inn complex has motel rooms, cabins, and inn rooms in several adjacent buildings.

Season: Year-round.

Accommodations: All units are air-conditioned and have private baths. Cabins, motel rooms, and inn rooms all have one or two double beds. Cabins are set in a wooded area; the three-story inn has an indoor pool and restaurant, and the motel units open on the parking lot. No accommodations have cooking facilities, but there is a full-service restaurant in the inn for all guests.

Special Features: An indoor swimming pool is available for inn and cabin guests only. A lakeside swimming beach with diving boards and floats is supervised by lifeguards. The park's other amenities include tennis courts, playgrounds, picnic areas, hiking, fishing, ongoing naturalist programs, and boat and horseback riding rentals. The toboggan slide operates from Thanksgiving through February.

Cost: Weeknight rates $40 to $60 per room; weekends $45 to $65 per night. Cribs and rollaway beds available for a small charge. Trail rides $10 per hour; rowboats $1.75 per hour; paddleboats $4 per hour; life jackets $1 per hour.

CRYSTAL MOUNTAIN RESORT

Address: Thompsonville, Michigan, 49683.
Telephone: 800–968–7686; 616–378–2000.

This family ski resort turns into a full-service resort in summer with a children's program, twenty-seven-hole golf course, tennis, and mountain bike rental and trails. Kids under seventeen stay free in parents' room from April through October. The children's program operates during the day and again in the evening three days a week during the summer months.

Accommodations: Basic motel rooms, motel units with kitchens, condominiums, and private homes. Motel rooms have two queen-size beds. Cots are available at no extra charge.

Special Features: Indoor pool and fitness center, outdoor pool, hiking and mountain bike trails, restaurant, chairlift rides, and horse-drawn carriage rides around the golf course and grounds. The children's program, offered from 10 A.M. to 4 P.M. and from 5 to 9 P.M. on Monday, Wednesday, and Saturday, includes arts projects and environmental activities, hikes, scavenger hunts, pond explorations, and local beach trips. Children between ages eight and thirteen can go on an overnight campout, leaving at 6:30 P.M. and returning the next morning.

Cost: Motel rooms $85 on Friday and Saturday nights, $72 during the week; higher in winter during ski season. Motel rooms with kitchens $99 on weekends, $89 during the week. One-bedroom condominiums $145 during the weekend, $127 during the week. Day camp $21 for the daytime session (includes lunch), $14 for the evening session. Overnight campouts $19 to $25. Mountain bikes $4 an hour; half- and all-day rates available. Tennis courts $5 per hour; horse-drawn carriage rides $12 per family.

Nearby: Sleeping Bear Dunes is about forty-five miles away, Lake Michigan is seventeen miles away, and Crystal Lake is twelve miles away. Horseback riding and river rafting are about thirty minutes away.

VILLAGE INN RESORT

Address: PO Box 98, Lutsen, Minnesota 55612.
Telephone: 800–642–6036; 218–663–7241.

Originally a downhill and cross-country ski resort, the addition of an eighteen-hole golf course and alpine slide has turned this action-packed resort into a four-season destination. Week-long stays in two-bedroom townhouses offer the best value, giving families enough time to enjoy the many activities on the resort grounds as well as visit the nearby Boundary Waters Canoe Area and charming town of Grand Marais. The alpine slide is undisputably the favorite with kids, and many adults, too; you can't ride it just once. A free children's program for three- to twelve-year-olds runs during summer afternoons.

Season: Year-round.

Accommodations: Three types of accommodations are available. Two- or three-bedroom townhouses sleep four to ten people and come fully equipped with all kitchen essentials and linens. Condominiums range from a one-room efficiency unit that sleeps four to a one-bedroom unit that sleeps six with loft, kitchen, fireplace, deck, and two full baths. The resort's inn has the atmosphere of a bed-and-breakfast establishment, with each room decorated differently.

Special Features: In summer recreational amenities include the alpine slide, indoor pool, whirlpools, sauna, tennis, miniature golf, volleyball, eighteen-hole golf course, hiking trails, and mountain bike rental. A free children's program includes arts and crafts, nature talks and hikes, and boating. Bonfires are held four nights a week. Downhill and cross-country skiing and sleigh rides are available in winter.

Cost: Week-long stays in two- and three-bedroom townhouse units $400 to $650, depending on size and season; two-bedroom townhouse in peak summer season $540 per week. Nightly stays $110 to $165. The condominiums are better choices for short stays, $65 to $150 per night, depending on size, time of year, and day of week. Inn rooms $97 per weekend night and $72 per weeknight. Alpine slide: single rides $5; six-ride books, adults $20, kids $15. Horseback riding $15 per person, $29 for two people per hour. Pony rides for children under seven $5.

BAREFOOT BAY

Address: PO Box 0, Elkhart Lake, Wisconsin 53020.
Telephone: 800–345–7784; 708–540–9300 (reservations office); 414–876–3323 (resort).

If your ideal vacation is to lounge around the pool or beach with a great novel while the kids are off having fun with others their own age, this could be the place for you. Barefoot Bay has a supervised kids' program with activities from 10 A.M. to 11 P.M. each day. Three meals a day and all recreational activities except boating are included in one low price. Children stay free in parents' rooms, paying only for meals.

Season: Memorial Day to Labor Day.

Accommodations: Standard, superior, and deluxe rooms are available, all with air-conditioning and private baths. Standard rooms have one or two double beds; the larger standard rooms can hold a cot or a crib. Superior rooms, a little larger than standard rooms, usually have two double beds and a sofabed or room for a cot or crib. Deluxe rooms, in the newest building near the pools, have two double beds and plenty of room for a cot or a crib. Barefoot Bay has a total of 150 rooms.

Special Features: Indoor and outdoor swimming pool, lake swimming, tennis, miniature golf, family theme nights, entertainment, aerobics classes, softball, volleyball, croquet, horsehoes, shuffleboard—all are included in the rates. Waterskiing, jet skis, pontoons, tubes, paddleboats, mini-speed-boats, and canoes are available at an additional charge.

The children's program is divided by age group with separate counselors for each one: turbo tykes (three to five), happy campers (six to eight), tweens (nine to twelve), and teens. Activities vary by age group but generally include stories, games, nature walks, arts and crafts, field games, and swimming at the beach.

Nightclub shows run every evening, and children three and over are supervised in an evening program until the show's end. Shows vary throughout the week, and musical theater performances are a staple of the resort.

Cost: Several packages are available for two, three, five, or seven nights. Seven-night stay for adults $555 to $720 per week per person. Two-night, three-day stays midweek $175, weekends $185. Rates for children sharing a room with parents include three meals and the recreational program: thirteen to seventeen $18, eight to twelve $15, three to seven $12, two and under free. Discounted rates available at certain times of the year; inquire when booking.

Nearby: Eighteen-hole golf course.

QUARTZ MOUNTAIN RESORT

Address: Lonewolf, Oklahoma, 73655 (twenty miles north of Altus). Telephone: 405–563–2424.

An endless selection of diversions awaits families at this sprawling state park resort. Choose from indoor or outdoor swimming, boating, tennis, miniature golf, hiking, lawn games, a thrilling water slide, and kiddie rides, to name just a few. Kids eighteen and under stay free when sharing their parents' lodge accommodations; families also can stay in comfortable one- or two-bedroom cabins. During the summer in-park naturalists and recreation staff offer organized activities including nature hikes, bird watches, scavenger hunts, dances, movies, arts and crafts activities, water aerobics, evening storytelling, ice-cream socials, and marshmallow roasts around the campfire.

Season: Year-round.

Accommodations: Lodge rooms sleep two to three people and one- and two-bedroom cabins sleep four to six. They provide full kitchens (with microwave instead of conventional ovens) and all linens, but you must provide your own cookware and dishes. A dormitory unit for family reunions and other large groups has a kitchen and living room and can sleep sixty-four people.

Special Features: Many of the recreational activities are free; boat rental, the fun park, water slide, and miniature golf require a nominal fee (see below). Ping-Pong, badminton, tennis, basketball, archery (with supervision), fishing, paddleboating, go-carts, and other activities also are available.

Cost: Two-bedroom cottages $80 to $90 per night, depending on size; rates are lower before May 15 and after September 15. Lodge rooms $60 per night; suites $125 per night. Family reunion lodge $640 per night. Paddleboats and canoes $2.50 for thirty minutes; go-carts $4 for six minutes; kiddie bumper boats $3 for five minutes; eighteen-hole miniature golf course $2.25 per person; water slide $3 for thirty minutes.

Outdoor Adventure Vacation Packages vary from year to year but can be very economical, so inquire when you book. The resort is booked by the Oklahoma Arts Institute for special student programs through most of June.

Nearby: Museum of the Western Prairie in Altus, Wichita Mountains Wildlife Refuge, Anadarko's Indian City.

THE SOUTH

GASTON'S WHITE RIVER RESORT

**Address: No. 1 River Road, Lakeview, Arkansas 72642.
Telephone: 501–431–5203.**

No one ever leaves empty-handed after fishing on a stretch of the White River, known for its prolific rainbow and brown trout. Gaston's resort, situated on several hundred acres in the Ozark Mountains of Arkansas, is paradise for any family that likes to fish, swim, or float along the water. Bull Shoals Lake, a short distance away, offers small- and largemouth bass fishing. When you tire of reeling in the big ones, head to the swimming pool, tennis court, or playground. Comfortable rustic cabins have kitchenettes and housekeeping service, and a restaurant serves delicious home-cooked meals when the family chef needs a break.

Season: Year-round.

Accommodations: Motel rooms have two double beds and a private bath; studio units are one large room with two double beds and a small kitchen area. A typical two-bedroom family cabin has a private bath, fully equipped kitchen, and living room with fireplace. All couches in cabin accommodations convert into double beds. Children under six stay free.

Special Features: Activities center on trout fishing; there is also a nature trail, swimming pool, tennis court, playground, game room, restaurant, gift shop, and sporting goods shop. Fishing guides can be hired for half- and all-day boat trips.

Cost: Motel rooms $60 for double. Studios $70. Two-bedroom family cabin $85 for double; each additional person $10 per night. Cabin prices include use of a twenty-foot-boat and all other facilities. You can rent a motor for the boat for $40 per day.

Nearby: Pontoon boat rental and tubing.

F. D. ROOSEVELT STATE PARK

**Address: 2970 Highway 190 East, Pine Mountain, Georgia 31822.
Telephone: 404–663–4858.**

Choose from stone cottages on a picturesque ridge or cottages perched along sparkling Delano Lake for your stay. Water sports enthusiasts can swim in the large pool or explore and fish in two different lakes. Beginning and advanced riders can take guided trail rides on gentle mounts. Thirty-five miles of hiking trails and interpretive walks wind through the park. The popular Callaway Gardens is a short drive away.

Season: Year-round.

Accommodations: Twenty-one cottages with one or two bedrooms are available. All are equipped with complete kitchens and heat. All of the two-bedroom units and four of the one-bedroom cottages are air-conditioned. One-bedroom cottages sleep up to six people; two-bedroom cottages sleep up to eight people.

Special Features: Swimming pool, ball fields; a naturalist program operates during the summer with programs including family campfires, nature talks, and a hands-on junior ranger program with crafts; trips to lakes, streams, and tributaries; walks in the woods; and bird and reptile identification. Most of the programs are free or have a very minimal charge.

Cost: One-bedroom cabins $45 per night Sunday through Thursday and $55 Friday and Saturday nights. Two-bedroom cabins $55 per night Sunday through Thursday, $65 Friday and Saturday. Reservations are taken two years in advance, by the week only, but those who call thirty days in advance often can find cancellations. Flat-bottom fishing boat rental $3 per hour; and horseback riding $15 per hour.

Nearby: Callaway Gardens has world-renowned rhododendron and azalea gardens, a butterfly center where visitors can walk amid the colorful flying insects, golf courses, exhibits on horticulture, and a vegetable and herb garden. Six Flags Over Georgia amusement park is nearby, and Atlanta is just over an hour away.

BLUEWATER BAY

Address: PO Box 247, Niceville, Florida 32588-9981.
Telephone: 800-874-2128 (outside Florida); 800-897-3613 (in Florida); 904-897-3613.

A low-priced Family Vacation Summer Fun Package makes Bluewater Bay on the Gulf coast one of the most economical of all full-service family resorts. This gigantic development includes condominiums, permanent residences, and villas for rent, and it has been rated by *Family Circle* as one of the best family resorts. A children's program, which operates as part of the Summer Fun Package, has special activities for preschoolers, school-age children, and teenagers during the day and certain evenings. Golf and tennis enthusiasts should look into special package arrangements that combine golf or tennis with lodging and other recreational options.

Season: Year-round.

Accommodations: The family package houses guests in two- or three-bedroom condominiums with all linens and full-size, fully equipped kitchens.

Special Features: Three championship nine-hole golf courses, twenty-one tennis courts with three different playing surfaces, playgrounds, private bayside beach, five swimming pools, nature and bike trails, playgrounds, fishing, deep-water marina with boat rental, bike rental, five restaurants.

Cost: Family Vacation Summer Fun Package, $729 per seven-day week, includes two-bedroom condominium, daily supervised activities for children, free weekly golf and tennis clinics, reduced court and green fees, and tickets to the Monday night family mixer. Three-bedroom units $829 per week.

CUMBERLAND FALLS STATE RESORT PARK

Address: 7351 Highway 90, Scorbin, Kentucky 40701.
Telephone: 800-325-0063; 606-528-4121.

Cottage and lodge accommodations are within an easy half-mile walk of Cumberland Falls, where a spectacular waterfall sixty feet high and twenty-five feet wide cascades into a misty curtain as it crashes down on the rocks below. It produces a "moonbow" on clear nights during a full moon, one of only two waterfalls in the world to do so. Families can swim in the river a short distance from the falls or in an Olympic-size pool; they also can ride horses, play tennis, fish, hike, or participate in various planned nature and recreational activities during the summer. The Cumberland Falls Rainbow Mist Ride offers boat rides near the waterfall.

Accommodations: Comfortable lodge and duplex rooms have two double beds. One- and two-bedroom cottages have all linens and fully equipped kitchens.

Special Features: Seventeen miles of hiking trails, fishing, horseback riding, river rafting, tennis courts, shuffleboard, horseshoes, small museum and nature center, dining room, coffee shop, picnic shelters, grocery store, planned recreation, square dancing.

Cost: Lodge rooms with two double beds $54 to $70 per night, depending on time of year; summer is the most expensive. One-bedroom cottages $70 per night; two-bedroom cottages $80 per night. Children under sixteen stay free in parents' room.

Nearby: The town of South Fork, thirty minutes away, has a scenic train ride that takes visitors through a gorge to a restored coal-mining community.

LAKE CUMBERLAND STATE RESORT PARK

Address: 5465 State Park Road, Jamestown, Kentucky 42629.
Telephone: 800–325–1709; 502–343–3111.

Fifty thousand acres of water and miles of shoreline makes this one of Kentucky's finest fishing and pleasure boating areas. Its marina rents houseboats, ski boats, and pontoons and a stable on the park grounds runs guided trail rides through the woods and meadows. Deer and raccoons wander through the resort regularly, and the squirrels are so tame you can feed them a biscuit by hand. A planned recreation program with guided nature hikes, movies, arts and crafts, and water games runs from Memorial Day to Labor Day.

Season: Year-round.

Accommodations: Wildwood Cottages have woodland settings. Most have one or two bedrooms with a double and a single bed in each, a fully equipped kitchen, living and dining areas, air-conditioning, and a back porch with an outdoor grill. Linens are provided. Lure Lodge has sixty-three rooms, each with two double beds, a private bath, and a spectacular view of the lake from a private balcony.

Special Features: Indoor and outdoor swimming pool, exercise room, hot tub, game room, dining room, gift shop, convention center, marina with one hundred open slips, fishing, a nine-hole par-three golf course, miniature golf, tennis courts, horseback riding, four miles of hiking trails, planned recreation, nature center, grocery store, picnic shelters.

Cost: Lodge rooms $65; children sixteen and under stay free in parents' room. One-bedroom cottages $80, two-bedroom cottages $90 per night in the summer, lower the rest of the year. Miniature golf $1.50 per game; nine-hole golf course $6 for all-day play (club rentals available); horseback riding (Memorial Day to Labor Day) $8 per hour-long guided trail ride. Houseboats that can accommodate eight people $660 per weekend (Friday afternoon to Monday morning), $710 midweek (Monday afternoon to Friday morning). Pontoons that hold eight to ten people $105 per day; ski boats $200 per day.

Nearby: Dam tours and fish hatchery with rainbow trout.

GULF STATE PARK RESORT

Address: 20115 State Highway 135, Gulf Shores, Alabama 36542.
Telephone: 205–948–PARK for cabin information and reservations;
800–544–GULF or 205–948–4853 for resort hotel information
and reservations.

One of six of Alabama's state resort parks, Gulf has the warm salt waters of the Gulf of Mexico on one side and a large freshwater lake on the other. The resort hotel facility borders the white sand beach of the Gulf of Mexico, and every room has a private balcony overlooking the water. Cabin accommodations across from the resort overlook the lake. A number of rooms in the resort have kitchenettes; other facilities include a swimming pool, fishing pier, tennis courts, restaurant, and poolside bar serving drinks and snacks. Across the street on the lake side, guests can enjoy an eighteen-hole championship golf course, tennis courts, a swimming beach, boating, and biking. Special programs for children operate during the summer with nature talks, story time, sand castle building, fishing, beach walks, lake studies, and a junior ranger program. Guests can check out recreation equipment for lawn games free of charge.

Season: Year-round.

Accommodations: Standard rooms in the resort hotel have two double beds; kitchenette units have one double bed and a small kitchen; two-room suites have a kitchen. All have private balconies overlooking the Gulf. Modern cabins on Lake Shelby have fully equipped kitchens, two or three bedrooms, and a sofabed; all linens are supplied. Rustic cabins, built in the 1930s, are in the woods and include one big room with a kitchen area, heat, and air-conditioning. Campsites and a group lodge are available.

Special Features: Two and a half miles of white sand beaches, an 825-

foot fishing pier, a swimming pool, and a 500-acre freshwater lake, with fishing, boating, and swimming; tennis, golf, nature center, playground, bicycling, hiking.

Cost: All hotel and cabin guests have access to lake fishing and boat launching, swimming pool, beach area, and tennis courts.

Resort: children twelve and under stay free; each child over twelve $5 additional per night. In peak summer season standard rooms and one-room kitchenette units $91; suites (which sleep six to eight people) $175. In spring and fall standard rooms and one-room kitchenette units $65, suite $125. In winter standard rooms and one-room kitchenette units $49, suite $95 per night. Rollaways $5 per night.

Cabins: in peak season rustic cabins $36 to $50 per night, modern cabins $70. Larger cabins accommodating up to eight people in three bedrooms $91. Off-season rates are lower, usually $36 to $45 for rustic and modern cabins. Note that cabins fill faster than resort rooms.

Canoes and johnboats $7 per day; green fees for eighteen holes of golf $17 per person per day, $20 with a golf cart; bike rental $1 per hour or $7 per day (adult-size bikes only); fishing on the pier $3; sightseeing on the pier $1 per person. You need a fishing license to fish, which you can buy at the pier or the boathouse.

HICKORY KNOB STATE RESORT PARK

Address: Route 1, Box 199-B, South Carolina 29835.
Telephone: 803–391–2450.

Guests at this well-priced resort have the advantage of golfing on an eighteen-hole championship course; fishing in Strom Thurmond Lake for bass, yellow perch, and crappie; and using a swimming pool, archery course, and playground. Lodge rooms, cabins, campgrounds, or the historic Guillebeau House can accommodate guests, but families will find the cabins the most economical and best suited to their needs. A staff "recreator" on the year-round recreation staff organizes children's activities throughout the summer; these include Frisbee golf, birdhouse construction, nature walks, and various arts and crafts activities.

Accommodations: Lodge rooms have two double or two single beds. Suites have small kitchens and sleep up to four in a bedroom and a living room. Cabins, which accommodate up to six people with two double beds and a sofabed in the living room, have fully equipped kitchens and all linens are provided. One-week rentals are available June through August only. The two-bedroom historic Guillebeau House, a log cabin built in the 1700s, has one bedroom downstairs and one upstairs, two baths, a living room, and a front porch and accommodates four people.

Special Features: Swimming pool, putting green, playground, nature trail, badminton, horseshoes, volleyball, skeet range, summer activities for kids, stickball, Frisbee golf, archery, tennis, restaurant, gift shop.

Cost: May through August, lodge rooms $40, suites $80 per night. September to April, rooms $36, suites $72 per night. Rollaway beds $2 per night. One-bedroom cabins $50 per night, $300 per week. Guillebeau House $80 per night, $480 per week. Children under twelve stay free in their parents' rooms. Green fees for golf $12 to $16, depending on season. Johnboats $5 per day.

Reservations open in January for the following year, but cancellations can make space available at the last moment.

HIGH HAMPTON INN AND COUNTRY CLUB

Address: 640 Hampton Road, Cashiers, North Carolina 28717.
Telephone: 704–743–2411.

Well-priced for a full-service American plan resort, High Hampton offers a children's program during June, July, and August. Parents who want a vacation that combines togetherness with time alone will enjoy an eighteen-hole golf course, tennis, hiking, sailing, boating, or swimming while the kids keep busy with others their own age. The children's program for ages four to twelve runs from 9 A.M. to 2 P.M. and 6 to 9 P.M. Supervised daytime activities include games, arts and crafts, nature walks, swimming, boating, donkey cart rides, and more. The evening program includes dinner followed by a hayride, games, stories, or a movie. June is the most economical month to visit, as room prices are discounted.

Season: April through November.

Accommodations: Guests stay at the inn or rent rooms in cottages scattered around the grounds. All have private baths. Children can share rooms with their parents for reduced fees. Most inn rooms have two double beds. Cottages, rented by the week, have fully equipped kitchens and two baths; they sleep six in two bedrooms and a sleeping loft. Rollaway beds and cots are available.

Special Features: Eighteen-hole golf course, eight tennis courts, lake swimming (with small sandy beach and playground nearby), sailing, canoeing, rowboating and paddleboating, fishing, hiking trail, fitness trail, bird watching, croquet, badminton, darts, volleyball, archery.

Cost: Inn rooms include three daily meals and all tips. On Friday and Saturday, rooms sleeping four $80 per person per night for the first two people, $54 per person per night for the third and fourth person. Sunday through Thursday $73 per person per night for the first two people, $49 per person per night for the third and fourth person. Children under six in room with two adults $43 per night. Cottages $1,400 per week in July, August, and October; $1,100 per week April through June, September, and November.

Children's program $2 per child per hour. Golf course $20 per day per person; tennis $4 per person per hour. Paddleboats cost $3 per hour; canoes and rowboats $2 per hour; Sunfish $4 per hour.

Nearby: Waterfalls and excellent antiquing.

OGLEBAY RESORT

Address: Wheeling, West Virginia 26003.
Telephone: 800–624–6988; 304–242–3000.

Oglebay is an enormous resort in the Appalachian foothills of northern West Virginia, with a three-acre lake, indoor and outdoor swimming pools, hiking and jogging trails, a children's zoo, a colorful model train display, three golf courses, and eleven tennis courts, among other options. Families can stay in its 204-room lodge or opt for one of its thirty-four comfortable cabins. Oglebay has many package deals throughout the year, and smart shoppers should always ask what special deals are available when they call.

Season: Year-round.

Accommodations: Lodge rooms and two types of cabins are available. The standard four-bedroom family cabin sleeps up to twelve people and has a fireplace, fully equipped kitchen, phones, and one bath. The Oglebay family deluxe cabins sleep ten to twenty-six people and include a fully equipped kitchen, spacious living and dining area, fireplace, air-conditioning, and color television.

Special Features: Oglebay has golf, tennis courts, swimming pools, Jacuzzi, paddleboating, a children's zoo, miniature golf, a nature center, hiking, fishing, riding lessons, a train, summer stage entertainment, and an arboretum. Lodge guests and those who purchase package deals get free or reduced admission to some activities, and cabin guests have free use of the swimming pool.

Cost: Oglebay has many package deals throughout the year, but one of the most popular with families is the weekday Summer Package: adults pay $57 to $75 per night and get free tennis, miniature golf, par-three golf, paddleboating, zoo admission, swimming, and $10 worth of food and beverage coupons. Kids stay free in their parents' room. Activity packages $5 per child per day.

Standard cabins with four bedrooms sleeping twelve people $515 (September through May) to $585 (June through August) per week. Deluxe cabins with two bedrooms sleeping ten $475 (September through May) $550 (June through August) per week. Lodge rooms with two double beds $80 to $95 per night in peak summer season. Children stay free in parents' rooms. Lodge rooms include $20 in food and drink coupons to use at Oglebay, and all activities are free for the first two people per room. Activity books for kids $5 each.

CACAPON RESORT

Address: Berkeley Springs, West Virginia 25411.
Telephone: 304–258–1022.

Families and family reunion groups come back again and again to this well-appointed state resort park with a range of well-priced accommodations. Its 6,115 acres of open fields, mountains, and lake offer endless recreational opportunities. An eighteen-hole golf course and excellent tennis courts keep many parents amused, while children enjoy swimming at the lake under the watchful eye of a lifeguard. A summer naturalist and recreation director keeps the kids busy with nature hikes, arts and crafts, organized sports, and a junior naturalist program. Families can rent rowboats or paddleboats and try a little fishing, ride horses, or explore the ridges and valleys of this magnificent natural setting.

Season: Year-round; some cabins are available only in summer.

Accommodations: Three types of accommodations are available: cabins, the Cacapon Inn, and a motel-like lodge. Three styles of cabins can be rented: eleven "deluxe cabins" have large living rooms, fireplaces, fully equipped kitchens, heat, all linens, and two or four bedrooms. Thirteen older "Standard cabins" have lofts or two bedrooms, fireplaces, heat, and fully equipped kitchens. Six one-room "efficiency cabins" have a small kitchen area equipped with all cookware and dishes, built-in bunk beds, a small bath with a shower, and a screened porch. The Cacapon Inn, built in the 1930s, has eleven double rooms with private or shared baths and is comfortable for families with older kids staying in a room separate from their parents. A group kitchen can be used by all inn guests. The lodge has forty-nine comfortable motel rooms with private baths and a restaurant.

Special Features: Lake swimming with lifeguards on duty, rowboat and paddleboat rentals, golf, fishing, tennis, horse rental, tennis, shuffleboard, volleyball, croquet, hiking trails, arts and crafts center, year-round nature and recreation program.

Cost: Deluxe cabins $475 per week for four people, $535 per week for eight people from April through October; nightly rates $50 to $85, depending on size and day of week. Standard cabins $285 per week for two to $450 per week for six from April 15 through October; nightly rates $42 to $75. Economy cabins $230 per week for four people from Memorial Day weekend through Labor Day; nightly rates $30 to $45, depending on day of week. Cacapon Inn rooms $28 to $35 per night. Motel rooms $55 per night for two, $70 for four people. Reservations are taken up to a year in advance, and summer weekend cabin rentals are especially popular.

Guided horseback rides $12 per hour; golf $11 for nine holes and $18 for eighteen holes; rowboat and paddleboat rentals $5 per hour or $2.50 per half hour; croquet $1 per hour; tennis $2 per hour for a court and 50 cents per hour for rackets. Lake fishing requires a license, which you can buy from the park office.

THE NORTHEAST

YMCA SILVER BAY ASSOCIATION

Address: Silver Bay, New York 12874 (ninety minutes from Albany). Telephone: 518–543–8833.

Amid the forests and wide green lawns along Lake George, Silver Bay has long captivated vacationers with its pristine beauty. Guests originally arrived by steamboat, and their luggage was transported by horse-drawn carriage to their lodgings. Many of the original native Adirondack wood and stone buildings remain and are listed on the National Register of Historic Places. Silver Bay's recreational options rival those of the most costly resorts. You must join the Silver Bay Association in order to use the facilities and participate in programs. Silver Bay books conferences throughout the summer, but families may stay when there is extra space, and the last two weeks in August are set aside just for families.

Season: Year-round.

Accommodations: An inn, twelve lodges, and twenty-three cottages provide sleeping accommodations for eight hundred people.

Special Features: Two gymnasiums, art center, boating (sailboats, rowboats, and canoes), library, crafts center, chapel, six tennis courts, two beaches, swimming, basketball, field and water sports, lawn bowling, aerobics, volleyball, weight training, archery, boat cruises, and supervised age-group programs for babies through teenagers (summer only), shuffleboard, hiking; ice-skating, cross-country skiing, snowshoeing in winter.

Cost: Family membership in the Silver Bay Association $50 per year. Housekeeping cottages (with kitchens) $336 to $675 per week; includes program fees. When more than five people occupy a cottage in summer, $30 additional per person per week. American plan (includes room, meals, and program fees) $476 per adult to $259 per child three to twelve, per week; children under three free. A first-timer plan allows you a 20-percent discount on room and board rates if you have never visited before.

CANOE ISLAND LODGE

Address: Box 144, Diamond Point, New York 12824.
Telephone: 518–668–5592.

Located on Lake George with its own private island less than a mile away, Canoe Island Lodge has excellent swimming, boating, and a European Alpine atmosphere. A huge flotilla of boats takes guests to the gentle, sandy beach at the island or runs them around the lake. If you want a relaxing ride choose the slow, forty-person flat-bottom passenger boat, or if the wind is up try one of the new thirty-foot sailboats. Thrill seekers will want a turn waterskiing behind the ski-nautique boat. A two-hundred-foot beach on the mainland has excellent swimming, and a gently sloping sandy beach on the island is perfect for young children. Families can stay in chalet-type lodgings or quaint log cabins; one family has come back year after year for five generations to relax at this warm and friendly American plan resort.

Season: Mid-May to mid-October.

Accommodations: Most of the accommodations are chalet or bungalow rooms with private baths and windows on three sides. Many rooms have two twin-size and a queen-size bed and are spacious for families. Families with older children may prefer two rooms with a connecting bath. Two-bedroom log cabins with a fireplace and small kitchen area are perfect for four or five people. There is a three-night minimum.

Special Features: Four large sailboats, cruise boats, and aluminum boats are at the guests' disposal (a staff member drives); tennis courts, Ping-Pong, waterskiing, square dance, variety show, social dancing, fishing on the lake. Directed children's programs include arts and crafts and nature experiences. One night each week, usually Thursday, the island has a barbecue for all guests.

Cost: Peak season rates from July to Labor Day include lodging, breakfast and dinner, and all activities. (Off-season, lunches also are included.) Adults $460 to $879 per person per week, depending on type of accommodations. Family rate: first two people in a room pay the full rate, usually $85 to $90 per person per night. Children two and under $12 per day, $86 per week; children three to six $26 per day, $170 per week; seven to twelve $38 per day, $255 per week. A third adult in a room pays three-quarters of the regular rate.

Family log cabins $82 per adult per night, $530 per week. Children's rates same as above.

FIELDSTONE FARM

Address: PO Box 528, Cooperstown, New York 13326.
Telephone: 800–336–4629; 315–858–0295.

Friendly informality describes Fieldstone Farm's atmosphere, and judging by the number of repeat guests, the staff definitely is doing something right. You can turn the kids loose to explore its 170 acres of fields, ponds, and forests. City children enjoy catching frogs and boating around the seven-acre pond on the property and swimming in the pool. Parents enjoy the scenic beauty and safe, rural atmosphere; parents and kids both like the fact that it's just minutes from the Baseball Hall of Fame in Cooperstown. Wildlife roams through the area, wild geese nest in the pond; guests can spot deer and turtles, play games, and take hikes.

Season: Accommodations can be booked year-round, but most of the activities are available from mid-May to mid-October only.

Accommodations: Six apartments and eleven cottages have complete kitchens and range from studios to three-bedroom units sleeping eight. Week-long guests supply their own linens. Linens can be supplied to nightly guests for an additional charge. Most units are set up for families with a combination of double and twin beds.

Special Features: Outdoor swimming pool, two stocked ponds for fishing and frog hunting, paddleboats and rowboats, kayaks, tennis, shuffleboard, playground, grassy games area, basketball, volleyball, Ping-Pong, indoor game room with bumper pool, foosball, and more (no video games).

Cost: During the peak season, June 15 through Labor Day, one- to three-bedroom apartments or cottages $55 to $100 per day, $325 to $550 per week. Weekly stays only are accepted during the summer, although if there are last-minute openings, the policy is flexible. Boat rental $4 per hour.

Nearby: National Baseball Hall of Fame (see pages 299–300).

TIMBERLOCK

**Address: Indian Lake, Sabael, New York 12864 (summer);
RR 1, Box 630, Woodstock, Vermont 05091 (winter) (ten miles south
of Indian Lake Village, five hours from New York City, five-plus
hours from Boston).
Telephone: 518–648–5494 (summer); 802–457–1621 (winter).**

With cabins along a half-mile stretch of pristine Indian Lake, Timberlock
is surrounded by the Adirondack Forest preserve. Seventy-five percent of
its guests return year after year for the unpretentious atmosphere, good
food, and myriad water sports. In summer the dining room is a covered
porch with views of the lake; meals are simple, hearty, and healthy. Cabins
are lit by gas lamps and heated by wood stoves. Nightly campfires, a player
piano, and moonlight canoe rides are favorite evening activities. The large
log lodge has a huge stone fireplace, games, puzzles, and a small library
for guests. A children's lodge keeps youngsters busy with Ping-Pong, table
soccer, games, and meeting new friends.

Season: Late June through Labor Day.

Accommodations: There are ten cabins right at the water's edge. One-
room cabins are available with or without baths. A family cottage with
two to three bedrooms is available for larger groups. Linens are provided
for all units, which have comfortable beds, screened porches, and wood
stoves, but no electricity.

Special Features: The sandy beach along the lake is perfect for building
sand castles, and guests can swim out to a raft. Canoes, sailboats (lessons
are available), rowboats, kayaks, and fishing motorboats can be rented.
There are facilities for tennis, badminton, archery, horseshoes, volleyball,
and basketball. Waterskiing is free on Sunday afternoon; otherwise a fee
is charged. Fishing is excellent for rock bass, perch, northern pike, and
lake trout. Staff can be hired to baby-sit in the evenings but not during
the day. With enough advance notice, daytime baby-sitting on site can be
arranged with a town resident.

Costs: American plan, per person per week: adults $550 in family cottage
or one-room cabin with bath, $500 in one-room cabin without bath.
Childen twelve to fourteen or the third or fourth adult in a cottage $450;
ages eight to eleven $375; four to seven $275; two to three $225; under
two free. Nightly, $80 to $95 per adult; two-night minimum stay.

English or western riding $15 per hour; rides offered daily except Sat-
urday. Staff will meet buses in Indian Lake Village.

Nearby: Storytown, ice caves at Chimney Point, beaver pond.

CHALFONTE

**Address: 301 Howard Street, Cape May, New Jersey 08204
(located at the lower end of the Atlantic Peninsula, three and a half
hours from New York City).
Telephone: 609-884-8409.**

The mix of ingredients at the Chalfonte is uncommon: a Victorian landmark
hotel in one of the oldest seashore resorts on the Atlantic coast, famous
Southern soul-food cooking, dinner theater and classical music concerts,
and a children's workshop series that runs for three weeks during the
summer. It all blends together to make one memorable vacation, rich in
cultural exposure for young and old and deliciously rich in calories. The
entire town of Cape May, noted for its gingerbread Victorian architecture
and famous lighthouse, is on the National Register of Historic Places, and
the Chalfonte is one of its liveliest places for families to stay. Room rates
include dinner and breakfast, and children stay free in parents' rooms,
with an additional charge only for meals. Dinner might be deviled crab à
la Chalfonte or southern fried chicken, and the breakfast table is often
laden with spoonbread, homemade biscuits, eggs, fresh fish, bacon, juice,
and coffee. A separate dining room for children six and under allows
adults to enjoy their meals in peace. After the children finish eating, they
can play in the backyard playground under the watchful eyes of enthu-
siastic college-age staff. The children's workshops in late July and early
August include theater, creative movement, mime, storytelling, and music.
Cape May's beach is two short blocks away.

Season: May through October.

Accommodations: Simple accommodations are old-fashioned but clean
and comfortable; some rooms even have a washbasin. Guests can stay in
the main building, built in 1876, or one of three cottages. Most rooms
share a bath with several other rooms. One cottage has a kitchen, living
room, and lovely porches, while another eight-bedroom cottage is reserved for families with children under the age of six.

Special Features: Live theater performances take place five nights a
week, and classical music concerts are held one night a week. The concerts
are free, but theater tickets must be purchased; guests get a discount.
Children's workshops are for ages five and up; baby-sitting is available for
younger ones. In addition to the children's program, a series of workshops
on watercolor and various crafts is held each summer for adults.

Cost: Double room with breakfast and dinner $75 to $130 in midweek,
$84 to $135 on weekends. Children stay free in parents' rooms but are
charged for meals: under one year $3, two to six years $6, seven to ten
years $11, eleven to fourteen years $15, fifteen years and over $25 per
night. In-season rates vary, and higher prices apply mid-July through

August. The following gratuities are required and are added to your bill: adults $6 per day, children $4 per day. Weekly, monthly, and group discounts available.

Nearby: Amusements are found throughout the city. Walk the promenade, rent a boat, take a trolley or a walking tour of the town. The nearby Historic Coldspring Village, a nineteenth-century southern Jersey farm village, has a petting zoo and a working farm, and tennis and golf are close.

RODGERS DAIRY FARM VACATION

Address: RFD 3 Box 57, West Glover, Vermont 05875.
Telephone: 802–525–6677.

A winner of the *Family Circle* Resort of the Year Award, this working dairy farm gives children the opportunity to entertain themselves by playing with kittens and puppies, watching goats, gathering eggs, milking a cow, and exploring the barn. Children can ride a horse or pony, go on a hayride, play on the swing set and in the sandbox, or swim at Shadow Lake about four miles away. Some families never leave the farm during their visit, while others use it as headquarters to explore the area. Three healthy meals are served daily.

Season: June to November.

Accommodations: Five guest rooms house two to three people each and have shared baths. Families with older kids can take more than one room.

Cost: American plan, adults $240 per week, $40 per night; children under twelve $135 per week, $25 per night. Includes three meals a day. Bed-and-breakfast rates (breakfast only): adults $30 per night, children under twelve $15 per night.

TWIN LAKE VILLAGE

Address: 21 Twin Lake Villa Road, New London, New
Hampshire 03257 (one hundred miles from Boston).
Telephone: 603–526–6460.

Located on two hundred acres of sweet-smelling woods and gently rolling hills, Twin Lake Village offers a little something for everyone: nine-hole golf, tennis, water sports, and a baby-sitting program in the morning for two- to five-year-olds so parents can have some time to themselves. The waterfront area at this family-oriented American plan resort has a shallow, sloping beach and a large dock where teens and adults can sunbathe, plus canoes, rowboats, and kayaks for guests to use whenever they wish. More than 80 percent of guests return for the gracious atmosphere, excellent prices, and range of diversions for all ages.

Season: The American plan season runs from late June through Labor Day; some housekeeping cottages can be rented by the week from mid-May to late June.

Accommodations: Cottages, apartments, and hotel rooms are available. The Victorian-style cottages, built in the 1920s and 1930s, have two to seven bedrooms, a living room, and a fireplace; some also have a kitchen. Apartments have two or three bedrooms, and there are private rooms in the main hotel. Most families stay in two- or three-bedroom cottages.

Special Features: A small raft is moored near the shore and a sunbathing dock is nearby. Other recreational activities include softball, shuffleboard, fishing, children's dances, bingo, tennis courts, and a supervised children's playhouse, which operates every morning except Saturday. Sailboats are available for an additional fee.

Cost: For four people sharing a two-bedroom suite, $325 per person per week; children two to five 15 percent less, children under age two $50. Rates include three meals a day; use of all facilities, including tennis courts, rowboats, canoes, kayaks, supervised children's playhouse, nine-hole golf course, and housekeeping service. Sailboats $16 for a half day. Housekeeping cottages $750 per week from mid-May to mid-June. Tips, not included in the rates, are strongly suggested.

LOCH LYME LODGE

Address: RFD 278, Route 10, Lyme, New Hampshire 03768.
Telephone: 800-423-2141; 603-795-2141.

Families have been coming to Loch Lyme for the past seventy years to enjoy the blue water, green fields, flickering of fireflies, and whispering of the wind in the pines. Without any noisy interruptions from televisions, telephones, or video arcades to distract your kids, you can all enjoy the wholesome pleasures of an old-fashioned family vacation. Even the most active of kids will be happy with the full spectrum of sports and games available here, and the most sedentary of parents will be immensely satisfied, watching the world go by from the comfort of the Adirondack chairs along the lake.

Accommodations: There are three types of accommodations. Four bed-and-breakfast rooms in the main lodge have shared bathrooms. Housekeeping cabins have fully equipped kitchens. Twenty-four modified American plan (breakfast and dinner) cabins have living rooms, fireplaces, porches, and one to four bedrooms. Housekeeping service provided daily for the bed-and-breakfast rooms and modified American plan cabins, weekly for housekeeping cabins.

Special Features: A shallow beach is perfect for toddlers, and more accomplished swimmers enjoy diving off a float into deep water. Boats, canoes, and sailboards are available at no extra charge. A croquet field, tetherball, badminton, clay tennis courts, and good fishing are near the lodge. If you miss the 8 to 9 A.M. breakfast, a continental breakfast is served between 9 and 10:30. This is a very popular resort that has been enjoyed by multiple generations of families, many of whom book a year in advance.

Cost: Housekeeping cabins $450 (accommodate four to five people) to $600 (slightly larger cabins) per week. Cabins with modified American plan $55 per person for the first and second adult, $45 for the third and fourth adult; $30 children five to fifteen staying in a regular bed, $22 on a cot or daybed per night. Lodge rooms with modified American plan $43 per person per day. Children four and under stay free. Ask about Loch Lyme Lodge's many discounts and packages for further reductions.

ROCKYWOLD-DEEPHAVEN CAMP

Address: PO Box B, Holderness, New Hampshire 03245.
Telephone: 603-968-3313.

Tucked along the shore of Squam Lake, the Rockywold-Deephaven family vacation camp has been open to people of all ages since 1897. Its sixty cottages and two lodges accommodate from two to fourteen guests each. A daily schedule of organized activities, which might include mountain climbs, talent shows, square dances, water sports competitions, or capture-the-flag games, is posted near the dining halls. A supervised morning program for children ages three to five operates during July and August. The camp's serenity and respect for nature bring families back year after year.

Season: June to Labor Day.

Accommodations: Each cottage has a living room with fireplace, screened porch, private dock, and icebox, where ice harvested from Squam Lake is delivered. Cottages are rented by the week only and sleep two to fourteen people. Rooms have one or two twin beds, and living rooms have daybeds. Lodge facilities for single or double occupancy can be rented by the day. All have daily housekeeping service.

Special Features: Eight tennis courts are spread throughout the camp, along with an athletic field, reading rooms, and a library. Kids enjoy the wading beaches, toddler playground, recreation hall, indoor play areas, and miles of hiking trails. Games and outings are organized for all ages, and baby-sitting is easily arranged with advance notice. Canoes, rowboats, sailboats, and kayaks can be rented.

Cost: Weeks run Saturday to Saturday, and cottages are priced according to the number or people assigned to them. Two-person cottages (which sleep four) $1,351 per week for two adults; includes all meals and activities except boating. Extra guests in any cottage $364 per person per week; $182 for two- to five-year-olds; children under two stay free. Four-person cottages (which can sleep six to eight people) $2,254 per week.

Canoes and kayaks $15 per day, $60 per week; rowboats $20 per day, $80 per week; sunfish sailboats $35 per day, $140 per week. Limited private sailing, tennis, and swimming lessons are available.

FRANCONIA INN AND HILLWINDS LODGE

Address: Franconia Inn, Easton Road, Franconia, New Hampshire 03580. Hillwinds Lodge, Route 18, Franconia, New Hampshire 03580. Telephone: 800-473-5299; 603-823-5542 (Inn); 603-823-5551 (Lodge).

Spend the lazy days of summer in this gracious country inn, which has facilities for swimming, hiking, riding horses, and bicycling through forests and meadows. If your budget is particularly tight, opt for the Franconia's sister lodging, the Hillwinds Lodge, which is more like a no-frills motel. Guests have use of recreational facilities at both places, regardless of where they stay. The location is perfect for invigorating outdoor fun in adjacent Franconia Notch State Park, and the area is filled with such vacation musts for kids as alpine slide rides, the Mount Washington Cog Railroad, Santa's Village, and Story Land. The inn offers a modified American plan (rates include breakfast and dinner), a bed-and-breakfast arrangement, or a European plan (lodging only). The Hillwinds Lodge provides motel rooms only.

Season: Year-round except April and early May.

Accommodations: The Franconia Inn has thirty-five guest rooms, all with private baths. Several rooms have a double and a single bed, and larger families can use the family suite of two bedrooms connected by a common bathroom. The inn has two porches, one situated for watching the sunrise, the other for viewing colorful sunsets. The plain and simple Hillwinds Lodge has thirty rooms with private baths and two double beds, a restaurant, and a lounge. Rollaway beds are available at both.

Special Features: Most of the leisure-time amenities are at the inn: clay tennis courts, riding stable, library, nightly movies, board games, heated outdoor pool, hot tub, trout fishing, croquet, bicycling, fifty kilometers of hiking trails; in winter, horse-drawn sleigh rides, ice-skating, cross-country skiing on the premises, and downhill skiing nearby.

Cost: Rates include use of tennis courts and equipment, swimming pool, bicycles, hot tub, croquet, golf course, badminton, movies, cross-country trails ticket. Inn: standard double rooms $85; $95 bed and breakfast; $150 modified American plan. Children three and under stay free; four to eleven $5 additional; over eleven $10. Rollaways and cribs are available free of charge. Lodge: rooms with two double beds $42 for up to four people. Horseback riding $20 per person per hour; thirty-minute sleigh ride $10 per adult, $5 per child age two to eleven.

Nearby: Golf, alpine and water slides, Santa's Village, Story Land, Mount Washington Cog Railway, Appalachian Mountain Club hiking trails.

INN AT EAST HILL FARM

Address: Troy, New Hampshire 03465.
Telephone: 603–242–6495.

With cows to milk, eggs to collect (young guests can put their names on the eggs they collect and have them cooked for breakfast), and ponies to ride, the Inn at East Hill Farm has kids persuading their families to return year after year. Water recreation for all ages includes swimming pools, a pond with paddleboats, a toddlers' wading pool, and an outdoor beach party with waterskiing. Other options include lawn games, hiking trails, and animals to pat and feed. Families with preschool age or young school-age children particularly enjoy this resort, and parents appreciate the adult swimming hours, the nightly bring-your-own cocktail party, and the healthy food selections.

Accommodations: Simple cottages have two or three bedrooms and a bath; some also have a living room. Motel-type units are comfortable but not fancy. A "deluxe" unit with air-conditioning is available. There are a total of sixty rooms.

Special Features: Two outdoor pools, indoor pool and sauna, and tennis court. Barns with goats, chickens, pigs, bunnies, ducks, turkeys, a donkey, cows, sheep (baby pigs, cows, and bunnies in the summer). Horse-drawn hayrides with ice-cream parties take place weekly. Pond with paddleboats, beaver house, swings, sandbox, and wading pool. Summers and winter holidays have at least one organized children's activity; a list is posted each morning. Selections might include games on the lawn, arts and crafts, mountain climbing, nature hikes, swimming, or story time. Guests can take their own cars to Silver Lake, seven miles away, where they can use rowboats or canoes. Waterskiing is offered several times a week; instructors are available. In winter guests can cross-country ski, go snow sliding, ice-skate, or swim indoors.

Cost: Nightly, adults $58, children five to eighteen $41, two to five $21, under age two free. Rates include all meals and activities. High chairs and cribs provided free of charge.

ROCKHOUSE MOUNTAIN FARM

Address: Eaton Center, New Hampshire 03832 (six miles south of Conway).
Telephone: 603–447–2880.

Rockhouse's private beach on Crystal Lake in the foothills of the White Mountains has sailboats, canoes, and rowboats available to all guests. Once a week a lunchtime barbecue is held along Swift River so guests can swim in the river and slide down the gentle waterfalls. Farm animals including horses, cows, pigs, ducks, geese, dogs, and cats can be petted and fed, and swings hang from the rafters of the barn. A recreation room has Ping-Pong; guests can take hayrides and explore 450 acres of hillside and fields. Fall foliage is exceptional here.

Season: Mid-June through October.

Accommodations: Stay by the week in June and July or by the night the rest of the season. Families stay in an old New England farmhouse in small or medium-size rooms with shared or private baths. Children six and over can stay in a special bunk room just for them.

Special Features: Families can join in farm activities such as milking cows or haying, and kids love to feed the fish in the ponds. There are llamas and peacocks in addition to all of the farm animals, and delicious home-cooked meals.

Cost: Rates for children staying in parents' rooms or in bunk room are discounted; if they stay in their own room they pay the regular adult rate. Daily adult rate double occupancy, $50 with shared bath, $60 with private bath. Kids' discount twelve and up $34 per day, six to eleven $30 per day.

ALDEN CAMPS

Address: RFD 2, Box 1140, Oakland, Maine 04963.
Telephone: 207–465–7703.

Quaint cottages are scattered in a sweet-smelling pine grove along the cove of a lake where waterskiing, fishing, and canoeing are a regular part of each day. Meals are served in an old farmhouse in an open area near meadows and fields. Alden Camps, known for its outstanding food, employs a special chef, an assistant chef, and a pastry cook. A changing menu includes six to ten entrées. The resort is small enough so that everyone is friendly and cordial, but privacy is respected if you want to get away and quietly read a book. The resort has been in business for eighty consecutive years, and parents who once brought their children now have grandchildren along.

Season: Memorial Day to Labor Day.

Accommodations: Eighteen rustic cottages on the shore of the lake range in size from one to three bedrooms; all have private baths and screened porches facing the lake. Two-bedroom cottages have either a double bed in one bedroom and two twin beds in the other or two twin beds in each. Bed linens, towels, and daily housekeeping service are provided. Cribs are available on request. Cottages are heated by wood-burning stoves, and firewood is supplied.

Special Features: East Lake, known for its excellent fishing, has a gently sloping sandy beach perfect for youngsters and a dock and float for sunbathers. Waterskiing, tennis, Ping-Pong, shuffleboard, a swing set, croquet, horseshoes, volleyball, badminton, tetherball, and beautiful hiking trails are available. Small fishing boats and canoes can be rented at the resort, and sailboat and sailboard rentals are available nearby.

Costs: Two-bedroom cottages $75 per adult per night, $450 per week. Infants $10 per day, $60 per week; children one to three $20 per day, $120 per week; four to six years $30 per day, $10 per week; seven to nine $40 per day, $240 per week; ten and eleven $50 per day, $300 per week. Fifteen-percent tip strongly encouraged. Daily boat rental $10 for boat, $15 for motor; reduced rates for weekly rental.

OAKLAND HOUSE AND FAMILY COTTAGES

Address: Sargentville, Maine 04673
Telephone: 800–359–RELAX; 207–359–8521.

Jim Littlefield's family has owned this property since the 1770s, and his great-grandfather was the first to take in guests in July 1889. The resort property, which extends a quarter of a mile on a strip of land that separates a lake from the ocean, offers water recreation on both fresh and salt water. A lakeshore swimming beach is perfect for families with small children, and rowboats are available on the lake and seashore at no extra charge. Sailing is excellent on the island-studded saltwater bay.

Oakland House particularly welcomes families with children in the summer; a special family dining room allows parents and kids to eat with others their own age. It's a perfect blend of informality and elegance, with silver candlesticks and white tablecloths but no shirt-and-tie dress code. Hot-air balloon rides are available during July and August; the tethered balloon is inflated on the property and floats skyward to two hundred feet, where passengers can see the entire bay as the sun sets.

Season: Oakland House is open from early May through October. Summer season runs from mid-June to Labor Day.

Accommodations: The least expensive accommodations are in the

Acorn building, originally constructed as a giant icehouse to supply sailing vessels coming into the area. It's simple and old-fashioned, roomy enough for a family of five on the first floor and seven on the second. The ground floor has a living room with a fireplace, three bedrooms, and a bath. The two upper floors, which have four bedrooms and a bath, are rented as one unit.

Other family accommodations are in separate cottages, usually with a living room with fireplace along with kitchenette, porch, and bedrooms. Several are suitable for two families to share. Each cottage has a small kitchenette with a minimum of a refrigerator, hot plate, toaster, dishes, electric fry pan, and sink; some cottages have complete kitchens. All ten cottages have views of the ocean.

Special Features: Guests play badminton and croquet on the expansive Oakland House front lawn, and scenic hiking trails lead in many directions. A lobster picnic is served on the beach each week. Boat moorings are available to guests free of charge.

Cost: During the peak season (mid-June to Labor Day), when the resort serves breakfast and dinner to all guests, rates for children ages two to five are half price, ages six to eleven two-thirds price, infants to two years $42 per week. Acorn's rooms $225 to $315 per adult per week in high season, depending on precise date. Weekly cottage prices depend on location and interior finish: a typical cottage for four people $378 to $623 per adult and more elegant cottages up to $763 per adult. Lunches available for additional $28 per week. Cottage guests can get 40 percent off for the first two weeks and the last ten days of the peak season. Rates include use of rowboats and recreational facilities.

Nearby: Deep-sea fishing trips can be arranged, and a golf course is twelve miles away.

DUDE RANCHES

*G*iddyup, Old Paint! Your cowboys and cowgirls can ride the range every day, do-si-do and swing their partners, and croon ballads of the Old West by the campfire during a week-long stay at a dude ranch. Both guest ranches and working ranches take in visitors, and most of them offer families a complete package that combines good old-fashioned hospitality with lodging, horseback riding, and three hearty meals a day. Extra activities such as swimming, hayrides, fishing, river rafting, chuck wagon dinners, and campfire gatherings are regular features at many. Guest ranches offer the most complete vacation packages. Nestled at the base of majestic mountains or set alongside creeks and rivers, many have been run by the same family for years. Working ranches, where guests can help with daily chores, give families a vivid picture of the lives of modern cowboys and ranch families. They are often less elaborately equipped than guest ranches as well as lower in price. The majority of dude ranches are in Colorado, Wyoming, and Montana, but they can be found throughout the rest of the country, too. Some host one or two families while others can accommodate more than one hundred people at a time.

Most ranches offer two rides a day, one in the morning and one in the afternoon. No experience is necessary; instruction on horse care and riding is given at the beginning of a guest's stay. Children under six usually ride with supervision in a corral or are led around on ponies while older kids and adults go trail riding. Some ranches allow young children to ride in the front of a parent's saddle on trail rides. Be sure to bring proper riding boots; tennis shoes and sandals won't do.

This chapter is divided into three sections: section I describes ranches with all-inclusive packages; section II describes those that provide lodging and meal packages but charge extra for riding; and section III lists ranches that offer housekeeping cabin rentals and riding for an extra fee. Families that want to ride several times a day and eat hearty home-cooked meals three times a day should opt for an all-inclusive package. Those who don't plan to ride much can save money booking one of the other options.

Our price criteria for all-inclusive ranches has been established using an imaginary family of four people: two adults and two children ages eight and ten. Listed are ranches that cost less than $2,500 for a full week of horseback riding, lodging, meals, recreational activities, and in some instances a supervised children's program. Many of them cost less than $2,000 per week. This might sound expensive, but it's actually quite a bargain when you add up the cost of lodging, three meals a day, twice-daily guided horseback rides, breakfast rides, barbecues, swimming, fishing, square dancing, western music shows, sports, games, and more. Best of all, unlike a do-it-yourself vacation, someone else is planning the activities and making the decisions.

Shop around for the ranch that suits your family's ages and interests, as prices vary considerably from ranch to ranch. Some offer a special teenagers' rate, while others consider anyone over twelve an adult. Prices for younger children also can vary from ranch to ranch by hundreds of dollars a week. If you're bringing a baby or a toddler, select a ranch that has no charge for children under two or three. Amenities and extras vary as well. Some ranches include supervised children's programs in the price; others have no such programs. Some are located on lakes with boats available or on rivers with tubing and rafting included in the price. Some offer an overnight pack-trip ride for a fee; others include it in the price.

If you are flying to your destination, inquire about fees for airport pickup and delivery. Some ranches offer complimentary transportation, while others request a payment that can be nominal or hefty. Most ranches require week-long stays, although some have nightly or half-week rates. Many ranches add a 10- to 15-percent gratuities fee to your bill, while some include it in the quoted price. Still others strongly suggest that you leave a tip of that size for the staff. Be sure to inquire when booking. A number of ranches offer better deals in May, early June, September, and October. If this fits your schedule you can save even more.

In selecting a ranch that fits your budget, ask:

- Is there unlimited riding? How many trips are planned each day? How long are they?

• What is the minimum age for trail riding? What do little ones do when the adults are on a trail ride?

• Will the ranch provide guests' names for reference?

• Does the week run Sunday to Sunday or Sunday to Saturday? (Keep this in mind when you compare prices, as you might be getting one less day's worth of meals and activities.)

• What is and is not included in the price?

• What about taxes and gratuities?

If you are just "passing through" and want a short stopover, the Montana Department of Agriculture publication *Montana Ag Tours* lists farms and ranches that host day tours and overnight bed-and-breakfast stays. Most of these are mom-and-pop operations with excellent values. Write to State of Montana, Department of Agriculture, Agricultural Development Division, Agriculture/Livestock Building, Capitol Station, Helena, Montana 59620-0201.

The Dude Ranch Association has a magazine-directory available for $2 that describes all of its member ranches. Many of them are well above our price limit, but it's a fun publication to peruse. We include a few of their lower-priced ranches. Contact *Dude Rancher Magazine*, PO Box 471, LaPorte, Colorado 80535.

SECTION I
Ranches with all-inclusive packages

WEST COAST

GREENHORN CREEK GUEST RANCH

Address: 2116 Greenhorn Ranch Road, Quincy, California 95971-9204.
Telephone: 916–283–0930.

A comfortable, casual atmosphere and a magnificent setting along a sparkling lake in the Sierras keeps families coming back to Greenhorn Creek

Ranch year after year. Its prices are low and everything's included: two rides per day, horseback riding instruction for greenhorns, separate rides for beginners and experienced riders, pool and pond fishing, and the "rainbow ballet" at sunset, when the lake starts to vibrate with jumping fish. Children ages three to five are entertained in the Kiddie Corral program from 9 A.M. to 4 P.M. by a special "wrangler," usually a preschool teacher. They enjoy brushing the horses, pony rides, arts and crafts projects, nature hikes, and games. Kids age six and over can go on trail rides or participate in special supervised activities including scavenger hunts, fishing tournaments, volleyball games, and capture the flag.

Season: Year-round.

Accommodations: Couples and small families stay in one of twelve lodge rooms, which accommodate one to three people. Larger families opt for one of fourteen one- and two-room cabins with front porches and swings. One-room cabins have a double or queen-size bed and bunk beds or two twins; two-room cabins accommodate up to six people. All rooms have daily housekeeping service and private baths.

Special Features: Fishing and swimming in the front yard creek or pond; swimming pool; hayrides; weekly evening bonfire; several cookouts; hiking; minirodeo with barrel races, sack races, egg tosses, and such; square dancing; frog race; horseshoes; volleyball; Ping-Pong. The children's program operates during the summer.

Cost: Weekly rates vary according to season. In peak season, June 20 through August, adults $620, teens thirteen to eighteen $545, children three to twelve $515. Rates are lower in early to mid-June and lower still for the rest of the year. A 12-percent gratuities fee is added to your total bill. Discounts are available if you pay your bill a full month in advance.

Nearby: Golf course, boating.

HUNEWILL CIRCLE H GUEST RANCH

Address: PO Box 368, Bridgeport, Mono County, California 93517 (summer); 200 Hunewill Lane, Wellington, Nevada 89444 (winter).
Telephone: 619–932–7710 (summer); 702–465–2325 or 702–465–2201 (winter).

This forty-five-hundred-acre ranch borders a range of mountains, giving guests many choices of trails to follow through the rolling foothills and scenic mountain valleys. Children under ten are half price, making Hunewill a good buy for families with several young children. Several crystal-clear streams that run through the ranch are ideal for swimming and splashing on hot days. Kids over six can go on trail rides, and a special children's wrangler is available for lessons and rides appropriate to their

ability. Free child care for kids under six is offered during riding times.
Season: Late May to mid-September.
Accommodations: Twenty-four white cottages each have a private bath
and separate entrance. Most have a porch and two twin beds or a queen-
size bed; families take units with connecting doors. The main ranch house
was built at the turn of the century, when Bridgeport was being settled
by gold miners seeking their fortune.
Special Features: Two rides per day. A special breakfast ride and all-
day trip are offered each week; children take a shorter day-trip ride.
Between rides, guests can spend time playing horseshoes, Ping-Pong, and
volleyball, hunt for rocks and arrowheads, hike, fish, folk dance, and square
dance. Campfires are held on many evenings, and there is a weekly hayride.
Cost: Rates include three meals a day, lodging, private saddle horse,
twice-daily rides, and all activities and facilities. Adults $660 to $780,
depending on room and time of season; children under ten half price.
Nearby: Ghost towns of Bodie, Aurora, and Lundy, Mono Lake.

BAR-M-RANCH

**Address: Route 1, Box 263, Adams, Oregon 97810-9704
(thirty-one miles east of Pendleton).
Telephone: 503–566–3381.**

In operation by the Baker family for more than fifty years, Bar-M-Ranch
is for families with children age six or older. The ranch was originally a
stagecoach stop in the 1800s, and you can still see the markings from the
old stage road that traveled through the hills just above the ranch. Riding
instruction is offered to beginners, and kids are expected to learn to curry
and saddle their own mounts. Trail rides take you through the Blue Mountains and into many wilderness areas. There's trout fishing on the Umatilla
River, and the clear waters of a large swimming pool are warmed by a
hot geothermal spring. If you visit between mid-July and mid-August, enjoy
the Bakers' spectacular raspberry crop in the delicious home-cooked
meals.
Season: May through September. .
Accommodations: Thirty-two riding guests can be housed in several
different facilities. The main lodge, built during the Civil War, has rooms
with shared bathrooms. The Homestead building has four two-room apartments with private baths, each with a queen-size bed in one room and
two twin beds in the other. Two large three-room cabins accommodate
up to six people. Laundry facilities are available.
Special Features: Swim in the forty-by-sixty-foot naturally heated swimming pool or fish and swim in the river nearby. A private fishing pond is

stocked for kids under fourteen, and there is volleyball, square dancing, hiking, and birdwatching.

Cost: Adults $615 per week in rooms with private bath, less for lodge room. Children eight to fifteen $500, under eight $395. Prices include lodging, riding, meals, and all ranch activities. Campouts $25 extra per person per night. Transportation from Pendleton $50 per family. Try to book by February for the summer season.

ROCKY MOUNTAINS AND SOUTHWEST

CANYON RANCH

Address: 9820 Transfer Road, Olathe, Colorado 81425
(thirteen miles south of Delta).
Telephone: 303–323–5288.

This comfortable, rustic ranch operated by the friendly Mrs. B. B. Frisch has the lowest prices of any we found. Guests have plenty of opportunities to ride, hike, fish, explore, search for Indian arrowheads, or hunt for frogs in the pond. People come back year after year to enjoy the simple beauty of the surrounding area along with Mrs. Frisch's hospitality and good home cooking. A canal a short hike away has swimming and tubing, and kids love to splash and wade in the "crik." One or two rides are offered each day, according to the guests' preferences. Parents can take younger children on the front of their saddle or lead them around on a gentle pony.

Season: Year-round.

Accommodations: Families of three to four stay in the Wickiup, a log house divided to accommodate two parties. One side has a large room with a queen-size bed, a sofabed, and a single bed. The other side has a double bed and sofabed. Each side has a private bath. Larger families can sleep in the eight-bed log bunkhouse; a bathhouse is just outside the door. Home-cooked traditional meals are served in the main house; a typical dinner is roast beef, mashed potatoes, rolls, green salad, and apple pie. The beef is raised on the ranch with no added hormones.

Special Features: Cattle, geese, chickens, peacocks, guinea hens, and dogs roam the ranch. Activities include cookouts in the mountains, horseshoe games, apple picking in season, and observation of deer, marmots, and eagles.

Cost: Weekly, adults $350, children under twelve $300. Includes three meals a day and all riding and ranch activities.

Nearby: Indian caves and artifacts are within walking or riding distance.

The Black Canyon of the Gunnison, Grand Mesa, and the hot springs of Ouray are all nearby.

COULTER LAKE GUEST RANCH

Address: PO Box 906, Rifle, Colorado 81650.
Telephone: 303–625–1473.

Located on the scenic western slopes of the Rockies with a sparkling blue lake for swimming, fishing, and boating, Coulter Lake Guest Ranch has eight cabins scattered along the lakefront and among aspen trees. The owners were annual guests at this ranch for eight years before buying it twelve years ago. Twenty-eight hours of horseback riding are offered each week, along with square dances, bonfires, corral games, and sing-alongs. The trout-stocked lake has rowboats available to guests, and kids can jump into the lake from a dock. Any trout you catch you can eat for dinner.

Season: Riding season is June through early October; the ranch is open the rest of the year for snow sports.

Accommodations: Eight different-size cabins, all with private baths, sleep from two to eight people. Three of the cabins have individual bedrooms and are best for smaller families, while one large cabin can sleep eight people in three bedrooms.

Special Features: Daily rides (except Sunday), square dancing twice a week, cookouts, a twilight ride, two all-day rides, sing-alongs, horseshoes, hiking, four-wheel-drive trips.

Cost: Sunday to Sunday, two or more people per cabin $675 per person; children five to eleven $435 to 465, two to four $100, under two $25. Rates include meals, housekeeping service in summer, riding, horseshoes, lake fishing and swimming, use of rowboats, and all other activities. Airport pickups $90 round-trip from Grand Junction, $50 round-trip from Glenwood Springs Amtrak station. Three-day minimum stays with reduced rates available in June and September.

Nearby: Golfing, ice caves.

BLACK MOUNTAIN RANCH

Address: PO Box 607, McCoy, Colorado 80463 (between Steamboat Springs and Vail at an elevation of 8,250 feet).
Telephone: 303–653–4226.

When you arrive at Black Mountain Ranch, one special horse is selected just for you based on your riding ability, and that will be your mount throughout the week. Individual and group riding instruction are available for novices, and trail rides go out each morning and afternoon. Every Wednesday an all-day ride into the backcountry includes a picnic lunch. Children and adults are encouraged to participate in saddling and grooming the horses, mending fences, and moving cattle. Children old enough to ride their own horse can join the trail rides with the adults, or they can participate in a supervised children's program with nature hikes, fishing lessons, swimming, and riding.

Season: May through September.

Accommodations: Six large two-bedroom cabins have queen-size beds for parents and bunk beds for the kids, private baths, and living rooms with fireplaces. Two four-plex units each have two ground-floor apartments and two second-floor apartments. Bottom units have two bedrooms with a living room; top-floor units have one bedroom and a sleeping loft. Four-plex units have sofabeds in the living room and can sleep up to six people.

Special Features: Excellent hiking and backpacking opportunities lead to hand-hewn homestead log cabins. Children can learn to fish in the stocked fishing pond on the ranch. Other activities include trap shooting, volleyball, square dancing, old movies, and hot tubs. Kids also have a hayride, picnics, hikes, skits, sing-alongs, and games. If you catch a fish, the staff will prepare it for your next meal. Meals are family-style and hearty, with homemade desserts and freshly baked bread.

Cost: Weekly family rate $595 per person for the first two family members, $525 per week for each additional person. Children under six $256 per week. Includes meals, daily housekeeping service, children's activities, and all other activities except river rafting ($25 to $40 per person for half- or full-day trips) and overnight pack trips ($25 per person). Ten-percent discount available late May to mid-June and late August to early September. Gratuities not expected but greatly appreciated. Guests can arrange to be picked up at the Vail Transportation or the Amtrak center in Glenwood Springs, $25 for the first person and $5 per additional family member. This popular family ranch begins booking for summer by the first of the year.

PINES RANCH

Address: PO Box 311, Westcliff, Colorado 81252 (Colorado Springs is two hours away).
Telephone: 719–783–9261.

At an elevation of eighty-seven hundred feet, trail rides wind through breathtaking alpine terrain thick with forests, meadows, and streams; vistas can stretch for ninety miles. All children eight and under begin their riding instruction in the children's program, which meets each morning in the

Gingerbread Playhouse. They learn to ride on gentle horses and ponies in a separate arena; wranglers try to advance seven- or eight-year-olds who are competent riders to accompany their parents on longer trail rides. When they're not riding, kids enjoy arts and crafts, nature hikes, games, or a trek to the Short Creek Hideout, a rough-hewn two-story playhouse in an aspen grove next to a stream. Parents pick up kids for lunch and then drop them off again before the afternoon trail ride. A guest ranch has operated at this location for nearly one hundred years.

Season: May 1 to September 30.

Accommodations: Several types of accommodations are available: three large duplex-type cabins have two bedrooms on either side with private baths and a shared living room. One duplex cabin has two bedrooms and a living room on each side. A lodge has four bedrooms and is available for big families or two families that know each other. All rooms are heated, as the evenings can be chilly at eighty-seven hundred feet.

Special Features: Each guest is assigned his or her own horse for the week-long stay. Two rides are offered daily, with an all-day ride once a week and a "horses' holiday" on Sunday. There are breakfast rides, a Saturday rodeo, rodeo practices, workouts, and trail blazing. Other activities include horseshoes, hiking, square dancing, sing-alongs, cookouts, hayrides, and buggy rides. Several chilly ponds and streams are on the property, but the hot tub gets more use than the ponds. Coin-operated washers and dryers are available for guests, along with a snack bar, general store, and video game parlor.

Cost: Weekly, adults $650 to $750; children seven to twelve $540, three to six $450, two and under $300. Rates include meals and all riding and ranch activities except overnight pack trip ($50) and river rafting ($25 to $60 per person, depending on length of trip). Off-season rates for May and September $540 to $650 for adults; children ages seven to twelve $450, children three to six $380, two and under $300. Airport pickups can be arranged for $40 from Colorado Springs and $30 from Pueblo.

Nearby: Royal Gorge, with the world's highest suspension bridge; Bishop's Castle; and Buckskin Joe's, an old western town with hourly staged gunfights.

LAZY L AND B RANCH

Address: Route 66, Dubois, Wyoming 82513 (sixty-eight miles west of Riverton, in the east wing of the Wind River next to the Wind River Indian Reservation).
Telephone: 307–455–2839.

The East Fork of the Wind River winds through this ranch, offering tube-floating opportunities early in the season when the water is deep and excellent swimming in large swimming holes throughout the guest season. The hundred-year-old ranch, operated by Leota (the L) and Bernard (the B) Didier, has unlimited rides to old frontier homesteads, across prairies, and into the high country. Kids can create original works of art with stones in the lapidary shop, go on a hayride, swim in the pool, or learn to square dance if they tire of riding. An overnight ride lets guests sleep under the stars.

Season: Late May to early September.

Accommodations: Eleven modern log cabins, all with private baths, are situated around a common yard. Most cabins have porches or decks and simple interiors with a small sitting area. Cabins can accommodate one to eight people.

Special Features: Heated pool, tubing on the river, lapidary shop, rifle range, fishing, hiking, hayrides, cookouts.

Cost: Sunday afternoon to Saturday morning, adults $675 per person (double occupancy); children twelve and under $495 per person. Round-trip airport pickup in Jackson Hole or Riverton $50 per adult, $30 per child twelve or under. Book three to four months in advance.

Nearby: Old miners' ghost town of Atlantic City; Sacajewea's grave; Jackson Hole, the Grand Tetons, and the gateway to Yellowstone are an hour away.

TRIANGLE C RANCH

Address: PO Box 691, Dubois, Wyoming 82513 (seventy miles from Jackson Hole).
Telephone: 307-455-2225.

This ranch allows people to visit on a three-day plan, making a shorter trip affordable for families unable to swing the seven-day price. Located along the Wind River in the Shoshone National Forest, with towering mountain peaks as a backdrop, Triangle C offers a package deal that combines cabin accommodations, riding, and three square meals with white water rafting, fishing, hunting for Indian petroglyphs, airport pickup, and more. Horse-drawn hayrides, marshmallow roasts, campfires, and sing-alongs will thrill any city kid. Plenty of wildlife can be seen in the area— riders regularly come across bighorn sheep, moose, deer, chipmunks, and geese.

Season: Year-round.

Accommodations: All cabins overlook the Wind River. Eight cabins have modern baths and can sleep four to six people. Some of the larger cabins have two rooms with two double beds and two twin beds; four-person cabins have bunk beds and a double bed.

Special Features: Riding program for all abilities, western dances, white water rafting, volleyball, horseshoes, hiking, campfire sing-alongs, Yellowstone day trip. There is no minimum age for riding; kids under six can either ride with their parents, or stay behind for supervised activities. The sandy riverbank offers safe (but chilly!) swimming. The closest airport is in Jackson Hole; transportation to and from the airport is included in the price.

Cost: Adults $650 per week, double occupancy; children eight to seventeen $600, three to seven $550, two and under free. Three-day plan: adults $390, double occupancy; kids eight to seventeen $360, three to seven $325.

RAFTER Y RANCH

Address: Banner, Wyoming 82832 (twenty-three miles south of Sheridan).
Telephone: 307–683–2221; 904–437–6934 (December through March).

Riding is naturally the big attraction here, but children also love to play in the creek that runs through the ranch and splash in the crystal-clear dammed swimming area complete with waterfall. This working one-thousand-acre ranch has hosted guests by the week or by the half week since 1947. If a week's stay is not within your family's budget, try a four-day stay. You'll still enjoy riding, three home-cooked meals each day, swimming in the swimming hole, tennis, hiking, and fishing. You also can ride along country roads, into the forest, along the mesa near the ranch, and through the foothills of the Bighorn Mountains. Deer frequently are spotted in front of the cabins, and riders often see antelope, birds, wild turkey, and pheasants.

Season: Late June, July, and August.

Accommodations: Three log cabins sleep four or five people each. All have living rooms, fireplaces, private baths, and porches along Little Piney Creek. An authentic Basque sheepherder's wagon with bunk beds sits next to one of the cabins; children love to use it as an extra bedroom. A guest room in the main house has two twin beds, a private entrance, and a private bath.

Special Features: Horseback riding is the main activity, with horses and terrain to suit all abilities. Kids and adults can take separate trail rides or go all together. Each day begins with a morning ride after breakfast; afternoon rides also can be arranged.

Cost: Adults $640 per week, $95 per day (four-day minimum, although shorter stays can sometimes be arranged). Children under twelve $430 per week, $65 per day; children under three free. Airport pickup in Sheridan is included in the price.

Nearby: Fort Phil Kearney, Wagon Box Indian site, and Bighorn Equestrian Center, which has polo games on summer weekends.

CROSS MILL IRON GUEST AND CATTLE RANCH

Address: Crowheart, Wyoming 82512.
Telephone: 307–455–2414.

Cross Mill is not a resort ranch—it is a working cattle ranch where guests can help with any and all ranch activities. Days are structured and informal, with unlimited riding being the main activity; a selection of horses and terrain match all abilities. Experienced riders explore hilly areas and inexperienced riders travel over more gentle terrain with a wrangler. The nearby Wind River has fishing and agate and rock hunting. Delicious home-cooked meals are served country-style in the main lodge.

Accommodations: Six log cabins each have one double bed and a private bath; rollaway beds can be added. For older kids, a "bunkhouse" is in the main lodge, with six beds and a shared bath on each side.

Special Features: As this is a small operation, the riding program is tailored to each group and guests can take all-day rides or shorter rides. The river is on the property; kids find swimming holes and splash along the banks. Meals include homemade rolls and desserts. People start out eating light, but as the week goes on they work up big appetites after galloping in the sun.

Cost: Adults $525 per week, $85 per day. Children three to nine $425 per week or $70 per day. Overnight pack trips $25 extra. Round-trip airport pickup at Jackson can be arranged for $60 per party, $40 from Riverton.

Nearby: Many guests take trips to a nearby Indian reservation and search for petroglyphs.

RIMROCK DUDE RANCH

Address: 2728 North Fork Route, Cody, Wyoming 82414 (twenty-six miles west of Cody and east of Yellowstone's east gate).
Telephone: 307–587–3970.

You'll ride with the cowboys at Rimrock, with plenty of time to master all of the gaits in western riding. Guests can ride twice a day or opt for the all-day ride with a pack mule carrying their lunch. Rimrock's rates include riding, river float trips, tickets to the Cody Nite Rodeo (see page 273), breakfast rides, and a tour of Yellowstone National Park. Three hearty meals are served daily, and you can say "Please pass the potatoes" as many times as you wish. Many guests return each year, so reserve early.

Accommodations: Nine log cabins with western decor have private baths and daily housekeeping service. Most have two queen-size beds or a queen and single. Four-room cabins accommodate eight people and have two baths.

Special Features: At least two rides are offered per day. Other activities include rodeo trips, fishing in the pond on the ranch or in nearby streams, half-day float trips, hiking, tours of Yellowstone, ranch entertainment, square dancing, Ping-Pong tournaments, shuffleboard, and movies. The minimum riding age is five, and a wrangler takes children on special picnic and trail rides.

Cost: Seven-day minimum stay. Two people $94 each per day, three people $90 each, four people $87 each, more than four $55 each per day. Kids under four stay free. All-inclusive rates cover pickup at the Cody airport or bus station. Discounts available for two- and three-week stays.

TWO BARS SEVEN RANCH

Address: Virginia Dale, Colorado 80548; Tie Siding, Wyoming 82084 (the ranch sits right on the Colorado-Wyoming border, twenty-seven miles south of Laramie and I-80).
Telephone: 307–742–6072.

The hosts raise and train their own saddle horses at this seven thousand-acre working ranch made up of meadows, streams, and lakes. The week begins with a basic orientation to the horses, since many guests have had no riding experience. Two rides are offered each day, and depending on the time of year, guests can help with ranch chores such as moving cattle, taking out salt, and mending fences. In the evening head for a beaver dam and watch them busily gnawing down aspen trees, enjoy a hearty ranch-style barbecue, or take an overnight trail ride.

Accommodations: Six of the fourteen lodge rooms have private baths; others share a bathroom. Rooms and baths are heated and have outdoor entrances. Families of four or five often stay in two adjoining rooms with two baths.

Special Features: Two rides are offered each day. Children must be six years old to ride their own horse on the trail; little ones can sit in the front of their parents' saddle. Four nearby lakes are stocked with trout; the lake nearest the ranch has brook trout. You'll see plenty of wildlife in summer, including deer, marmots, prairie dogs, 160 different species of birds, badgers, and porcupines. Breakfast is ranch-style with pancakes, hash browns, and eggs; the afternoon meal is heavier than guests might be used to, but after they've been out riding they welcome a big lunch and dinner. Book early in the year for July.

Cost: May through November, adults $650 to $675 each per week (nonriding adults deduct 25 percent); kids eleven to fifteen $550, six to ten $525. Daily rates available, with a three-night minimum stay: adults in double room with bath $105 each; children eleven to fifteen $78, six to eleven $74, two to five $49. Fifteen-percent discounts offered in May and November; 10-percent discounts available June 1 through June 15 and Labor Day through October 31. Hosts are flexible in booking arrangements and will pick up guests at the Laramie airport free of charge.

SWEET GRASS RANCH

Address: Melville Route, Big Timber, Montana 59011 (summer); Otter Creek Ranch, Melville Route, Big Timber, Montana 59011 (September to June) (west of Melville, forty miles from Big Timber and 120 miles from Billings).
Telephone: 406–537–4477 (summer); 406–537–4497 (winter).

Warm and gracious hosts Bill and Shelly Carioccia encourage guests to get involved in the way of life on their ranch. The Carioccias particularly love to host families, people who help work the cattle, break colts, and do farm chores. The kids can feed the calves, pigs, and horses and learn to milk cows; fresh milk is served at every meal. When you tire of ranch activities, relax around the ranch, swim in the creek, go fishing, or watch the local beavers go about their business. The Sweet Grass River runs through the ranch, located in a valley in the foothills of the Crazy Mountains. Horseback rides take you up into the mountains, where you'll catch expansive three-hundred-mile views, or down into the lower, flatter open country. The hospitality at this ranch simply cannot be beat.

Accommodations: Guests are housed in rustic log cabins or in the main ranch house. There are cabins with two twin beds and a bathhouse less than a hundred yards away, and one- or two-bedroom cabins with private baths, some with living room and fireplace. Four bedrooms are upstairs in the main house; large families can use the entire unit, which includes a living room and bath. Most rooms have double beds, with the exception of the two-bedroom cabins, which have a double in one room and bunks in the other.

Special Features: Daily morning and afternoon rides take a wide variety of trails; two all-day rides also are available to guests. The horses rest on Sunday. There is no minimum age for riding; if parents aren't comfortable riding with little ones in the front of their saddle, the wranglers will take them. The Sweet Grass River is suitable for fishing (with lots of trout in the chilly waters) and swimming. There are beaver ponds near the lodge. More swimming holes and five mountain lakes are above the ranch, about a three-hour horse ride away.

Costs: Cabins without bath $500 per person. Two-bedroom cabins with private bath and fireplace $580 per person when four share it, $600 per person for three. Children three to five $250 unless they require a separate horse, children under three free.

Overnights $25 extra per person per night. Pack trips can be arranged for $25 extra per person per night. Airport pickups at Billings or Bozeman (both are about two and a half hours away) $90 per car, divided between the group dropped off and the group picked up; round-trip for a family generally costs about $45.

Nearby: Rodeos and ghost towns, float fishing on the Yellowstone River.

GILA WILDERNESS LODGE

Address: Beaverhead Route, Magdalena, New Mexico 87825 (two hours west of Truth or Consequences).
Telephone: 505–772–5772.

One group at a time stays at the Gila Wilderness Lodge, so if it's privacy you want, this is the place. Guests stay in a three-room modern bunkhouse that can house up to twelve people. Surefooted and gentle horses take you through box canyons and along the Gila River; you design your own riding program and your guide will take you out as often and for as long as you wish. Young children can ride in the saddle with their parents. Elk and deer can be seen near the lodge early and late in the day. Reservations are accepted by the day or by the week.

Season: Year-round.

Accommodations: The bunkhouse has two bedrooms with twin beds, a bunkhouse room, also with twin beds, and a private bath. Electricity is by generator.

Special Features: A little lake about a mile away has a small boat and excellent fishing. In addition to riding and hiking, guests can play horseshoes, croquet, volleyball, and badminton. The main lodge has a kitchen, dining area, and sitting room.

Cost: Adults $70 each per day and $400 per week (double occupancy). Children under twelve are half price, under five free. Picnic lunches provided if you want to hike.

Nearby: Indian ruins are within hiking distance.

SILVER SPUR GUEST RANCH

Address: PO Box 1657, Bandera, Texas 78003 (about an hour's drive from San Antonio).
Telephone: 512–796–3037.

Host Texas Tom calls his part of Texas cowboy country, and his ranch is just that. Activities include horseback riding, hayrides, horseshoes, and outdoor barbecues with brisket, chicken, and ribs. The ranch's twenty-three-hundred-foot elevation keeps it cooler in the summer than other spots in Texas. Horseback trail rides often go into the five-thousand-acre state park next door. Childen ten and over can go on trail rides, while little ones stay behind with a wrangler and ride safely in the corral.

Season: Year-round.

Accommodations: Three duplex stone cottages and a main lodge with twelve rooms are available for families. Each has a king-size and a double bed, a sofabed, a private bath, and air-conditioning.

Special Features: Inexperienced riders are offered instruction before heading out on hour-and-a-half trail rides. A three- or four-hour ride into the state park is available for experienced riders. Week-long guests have three trail cookouts, a cowboy cookout, and an evening hay wagon cook-out and ride. The ranch has a playground, trampoline, volleyball, Ping-Pong, horseshoes, and an Olympic-size pool with a large shallow end.

Cost: Adults $68 per day; children eleven to fifteen $58, seven to ten $48, four to six $30, one to three $5 per day. Minimum stay two days; weekly stays include seventh night free. Ten-percent discounts off-season.

Nearby: Bandera is a cowboy town with western dances accompanied by live music three times a week. San Antonio, about an hour to the southeast, has much to offer, and tubing, canoeing, and fishing are nearby.

MAYAN RANCH

Address: PO Box 577, Bandera, Texas 78003 (forty-five miles northwest of San Antonio).
Telephone: 512–796–3036.

The Mayan has entertained city slickers for more than forty years with a low-priced package deal that includes two rides a day, tubing down the river, swimming in an Olympic-size pool, and a complimentary children's program during the summer months. Cowboy cookouts take place every day except Sunday. Rates for children are lower than at many other ranches, and the proximity to San Antonio allows families to spend a week or so at the Mayan and a few days exploring one of Texas's most interesting cities.

Season: Year-round.

Accommodations: Thirty-four individual stone cottages sleep one to four people. The Mayan Lodge is a motel-like unit with adjoining rooms. All rooms are air-conditioned and heated.

Special Features: Two trail rides are offered daily, with horseback-riding instruction for beginners. Other activities include hayrides, cookouts, tennis courts, volleyball, fitness room, shuffleboard, tubing along the river, swimming, fishing, and hiking. A children's program and nightly entertainment are offered during summer months.

Cost: Adult $600 per week; children under twelve $255, twelve to seventeen $335.

CENTRAL UNITED STATES

TRIPLE R RANCH

Address: Box 124, Keystone, South Dakota 57751.
Telephone: 605–666–4605.

Originally an old mining camp, the Triple R Ranch welcomes guests interested in exploring the Black Hills of South Dakota on horseback. It is located in the middle of the Norbeck Wildlife Preserve, where deer, elk, wild turkey, mountain goats, and sheep are regularly spotted. Adults and children age seven and older take trail rides through the pristine Black Elk Wilderness Area, next door. There is no riding program for younger ones, but baby-sitting can be arranged. Lakota Lake and Iron Creek, adjacent to the ranch, offer excellent fishing and swimming. Guests also can swim and sun by the pool back at the ranch. Horse-drawn wagon rides and trips to the lighting ceremony at Mount Rushmore eight miles away provide happy memories for children.

Accommodations: Duplexlike cottages sleep four and have small kitchenettes. Small cabins can sleep five to six in separate bedrooms and a living room. The ranch can accommodate fifteen to twenty guests at a time.

Special Features: Swimming pool; fishing in the lake next door; hearty family meals; laundry; two rides a day, including a breakfast ride and an all-day ride; cookouts; entertainment; wagon rides, car trips to see a buffalo herd and the lighting ceremony at Mount Rushmore.

Cost: When three or four occupy the same cabin with two double beds, $625 per person. Includes daily housekeeping service, meals, horse rides.

Nearby: Side trips can be arranged to the Badlands National Park and Deadwood.

FLINT HILLS OVERLAND WAGON TRAIN

Address: PO Box 1076, El Dorado, Kansas 67042.
Telephone: 316–321–6300.

Ride in an authentic wagon or stagecoach through the Flint Hills with other "pioneer" families on this overnight wagon train experience. Since these trips are short, leaving at 10 in the morning and returning at 1 P.M. the following day, the cost is relatively low. You'll eat hearty pioneer-style meals—a chuck wagon lunch is served at noon on the first day, a cowboy-style dinner is cooked over an open fire at the evening campsite, and a huge breakfast and light lunch are served on Sunday. Transportation is in 1870s-style wagons. You'll either camp out under the stars (bring your own sleeping bags—and tents, if you want to be under cover) or sleep under the wagons. Cowboy music, sing-alongs, and tall tales about the early days are all part of the evening entertainment. Six trips are offered each season.

Season: June through September.

Cost: For one night and two days, adults and children age twelve and over $125 each, children under twelve $75. If you wish to go for one day you can participate until after the evening campfire and entertainment for 20 percent less.

WOODSIDE RANCH

Address: Mauston, Wisconsin 53948 (two and a half hours from Milwaukee).
Telephone: 608–847–4275.

With eighty-five head of horses, this fourteen-hundred-acre ranch perched on the side of a pastoral river valley has a steed to match any riding ability. After the morning ride when the horses are resting, guests can paddle boats and canoes around the fishing pond, swim, go on a hayride or surrey ride, or play a game of croquet. A supervised children's activity program runs during the summer months, so parents can ride while their young ones are safely entertained. Each morning or afternoon the kids can be dropped off at the little red school house for activities that include arts and crafts, games, stories, sports, and swimming.

Accommodations: Twenty-two log cabins and cottages with one, two, or three bedrooms all have private baths and fireplaces and house two to ten persons. Twelve rooms in the main ranch house can accommodate two, three, or four people. All units are air-conditioned in summer and heated in winter (firewood is provided). Bedding is provided but you must bring your own towels.

Special Features: Two or more trail rides are offered daily, and there is pony riding in a ring for small children. The minimum age for trail riding is about nine, depending on the child's ability to control a horse. The supervised play school for children has morning and afternoon sessions. Other features include a swimming pool, game room, outdoor cookouts, tennis, croquet, badminton, paddleboats, horseshoes, miniature golf, shuffleboard, Ping-Pong, sauna, and square dancing.

Cost: High-season summer, in cabin, adults $460 per week; kids eleven to twelve $390, eight to ten $300, three to seven $160. June through September, adults $410, children eleven to twelve $350, eight to ten $260, three to seven $140. All cabins have minimum charge of two adult rates. Little Britches Special in November and April: each child up to age twelve half price if accompanied by paid adult.

Five night stays: in ranch house, adults $350; kids eleven to twelve $300, eight to ten $220, three to seven $110. In cabin $400 for adults; children eleven to twelve $340, eight to ten $260, three to seven $130. Two-night stay: in cabin $199 for adults; kids eleven to twelve $170, eight to ten $130, three to seven $65. In ranch house $175 for adults; children eleven to twelve $150, eight to ten $110, three to seven $55.

Nearby: Nine-hole golf course.

HOBSON'S BLUFFDALE VACATION FARM

Address: Eldred, Illinois 62027 (fifty miles north of St. Louis). Telephone: 217–983–2854.

In operation for more than thirty years, Hobson's Bluffdale is a sprawling 320-acre working farm where kids can help with such daily chores as tending the animals, feeding the pigs, chickens, or geese, and collecting eggs; Hobson's is a classic among rural family resorts. An 1828 stone house has a dining room with a huge fireplace and cozy indoor activities. Horseback riding is available for all ages, and the farm also has a heated pool, playground, hayrides, a surrey with fringe on top, campfires, boat rides on the pond, fishing, and even a trip to a nearby water park for the kids. Young archaeologists can visit the site of an archaeological dig.

Season: Mid-March to mid-November.

Accommodations: Hobson's accommodates up to thirty-four guests; three different family rooms have a full-size bed and a set of bunks. The two-bedroom suites can sleep five to six. All are air-conditioned and have private baths.

Special Features: Horseback riding begins after breakfast every morning. Younger children ride in the corral, while kids over nine can take trail rides with the adults. Once a week guests are taken to a nearby lake for canoeing and swimming. Evening activities include a hayride, a cook-out, bonfires, an ice-cream social, and a square dance. A special excursion to Raging Rivers water park is always tops with the kids.

Cost: Sunday to Sunday, all meals included, adults $350; children nine to thirteen $250, three to eight $200, under three $130. Two-night minimum for weekends. Nightly rates $60 for adults; children nine to thirteen $40, three to eight $35, under three $23.

WOLF LAKE RANCH RESORT

Address: Route 2, Box 2514, Baldwin, Michigan 49304 (sixty-five miles north of Grand Rapids).
Telephone: 616–745–3890.

Riding lessons are offered for novices at this popular ranch resort on sparkling Wolf Lake. The lake's sandy beach slopes so gently that volleyball games are set up in the clear water. Little ones can splash and swim without worrying about going out too deep. Two rowboats and a canoe are available for guests to use, or bring your own boat and use their dock. Summer packages run for three, four, or seven nights, and weekend packages are available for spring and fall. All packages include all-you-can-cat meals, two rides each day, and use of the recreational facilities on the ranch.

Season: Late April to early November.

Accommodations: Eight two-room units have a double or king-size bed in the front room and bunk beds in the back room. The Frontier House can sleep eight to sixteen people in four rooms with double beds and two sets of bunk beds. There is a washroom between the rooms and a large living room with a fireplace. All units are heated and bed linens are furnished, but guests must bring their own towels.

Special Features: Horseback riding is conducted on trails; children under six ride in the corral. The ranch has volleyball, tennis, basketball, water volleyball in the lake, a rec room with Ping-Pong, video games, jukebox, stereo, and fireplace, and evening campfires, hayrides, and square dancing. A launderette is available for guests' use.

Cost: Children five and under always stay free. Saturday-to-Saturday stays June through August, adults $390, kids eleven to sixteen $290, six to ten $190. Three-day stays (Wednesday to Saturday) in summer, adults $190; kids eleven to sixteen $150, six to ten $110. Four-day summer rates slightly higher. Spring and fall weekends (Friday to Sunday), adults $109; kids eleven to sixteen $79, six to ten $59. Three-day weekends, adults $139; kids eleven to sixteen $99, six to ten $79. Includes meals, lodging, riding, use of all facilities, a campfire on Friday night, and a hayride on Saturday night.

THE SOUTH

SCOTT VALLEY RESORT AND GUEST RANCH

**Address: Route 2, Box 270B, Mountain Home, Arkansas 72653
(two hours south of Springfield, Missouri).
Telephone: 501–425–5136.**

Rated three times by *Family Circle* magazine as one of the best family ranches of the year, Scott Valley has a gorgeous setting in the middle of the Ozarks with lots of horseback riding and recreational fun. Experienced and novice riders take separate trail rides, and summer months feature fishing on a nearby lake and ferryboat dinner trips. Two canoeable rivers are within a ten-minute drive, and the ranch's van will take guests and their canoes up the river so they can paddle down at their own pace. Young childen are given pony rides; baby-sitting while parents ride can be arranged for an additional fee.

Season: Year-round.

Accommodations: Sixteen two-bedroom units and twelve one-bedroom units have air-conditioning, private baths, and housekeeping service. Two-bedroom family units have a double bed in one room, two twins in the other.

Special Features: Five to six horseback rides are offered daily, and children age seven and over can take their own horse on trail rides. Younger ones can either ride double with a parent or go on pony rides back at the ranch. Facilities include a swimming pool, petting zoo, playground, tennis, volleyball, shuffleboard, cookout, hayride, and complimentary launderette. The fishing and boating lake is a ten-minute drive away.

Cost: Rates include riding, use of fishing boats and canoes, meals, music shows, and all recreational and sporting activities. Three-day minimum stay. June 15 to August 15, daily price for adults $82.50; children seven to twelve $65, three to six $42. Seven-night stays in summer $495 per adult; children seven to twelve $390, three to six $215. The rest of the year adults $71.50 per day; children seven to twelve $55, three to six $34. Four people sharing one unit get a 10-percent discount; children under three always stay free. Airport pickups in Mountain Home free of charge.

Nearby: Ozark Folk Center (see pages 286–287), Silver Dollar City, Dog Patch U.S.A., Blanchard Springs Caverns. The ranch will arrange tours of the caverns for guests, and if enough guests are interested they can get a discount and private tour.

THE NORTHEAST

GOLDEN ACRES FARM AND RANCH

Address: Gilboa, New York 12076.
Telephone: 800-252-7787 (New York only); 800-847-2151 (NJ,
MA, CO, RI, PA, VT, NH only); 607-588-7329.

Golden Acres is known for family fun in the Catskills, with riding and a
variety of other things to do. If the weather turns bad, steer your horse
to the indoor riding arena to practice walking, trotting, and cantering.
There are plenty of farm animals to pet—cows, horses, goats, sheep, ducks,
chickens, rabbits, dogs, cats—and baby animals in the spring and summer.
Children can milk a cow, collect eggs, and help feed the animals. A children's program that runs during the summer months keeps four- to twelve-
year olds busy all day, and a nursery is provided for infants and toddlers
ages three months to three years.

Accommodations: Families can choose between individual family
rooms, two-room suites, or an apartment with a kitchen and two rooms.
Golden Acres has a guest capacity of four hundred, so activities can get
crowded on busy summer weekends.

Special Features: Children's day camp and nursery, horseback and pony
riding and instruction, indoor and outdoor pools, fishing, tennis, basketball,
Ping-Pong, hayrides, badminton, movies, softball, fossil hunting, arts and
crafts, berry picking, archery, boating.

Cost: "You-cook" vacation apartments are the best deal if you don't
mind doing your own cooking, but you must bring your own towels,
cookware, and dishes. One-room unit with kitchen and private bath, air-
conditioning, and heat, which sleeps up to four people, $660 per week
for four, $560 per week for three. Two-bedroom suite for four people
$770 per week or $320 for three days and two nights. All recreational
and camp facilities included. Price goes up for shorter stays and down for
longer stays.

The next lowest price includes meals and lodging and bath shared with
two other rooms—adults $330 per week; kids eleven to sixteen $225,
four to ten $160, one to three $80, under one year free. The farm also
has campgrounds.

Nearby: Golf, lake and stream fishing, antiquing.

PINE GROVE DUDE RANCH RESORT

Address: Kerhonkson, New York 12446.
Telephone: 800–346–4626.

Pine Grove is practically a three-ring circus when it comes to dude ranches, with six hundred acres of fun in the sun, snow, or rain. The ranch has one of the largest indoor facilities (choose from tennis, swimming, archery, volleyball, basketball, bocci ball, miniature golf, and more) as well as plenty to do in the great outdoors. Winner of *Family Circle*'s Family Resorts of the Year Award for best ranch, Pine Grove can accommodate hundreds of people. The Tarantino family breeds Arabian horses for guests to ride, and there's always some wobbly foal testing its legs. Daily riding, a supervised children's program, and reasonable prices make this ranch a favorite of many who don't want to make the trip out to the "real West."

Season: Year-round.

Accommodations: One hundred twenty rooms have private baths and climate control. Most rooms have either two double beds or two double beds and a two-person sofabed. Four villas on the perimeter of the property for larger families have living rooms and one to four bedrooms.

Special Features: A children's day camp, supervised by counselors, has sports, games, arts and crafts, riding, and a complete teen program. There are pony rides for little ones, boating, fishing, leather workshops, steer-roping practice, cattle drives, swimming, tennis, a baby animal farm, fishing and boating on the lake, horseshoes, a children's playground, and more. Adults can ride, golf, swim, fish, and use any of the ranch's recreational facilities. Evening entertainment is always available. The Indian Village includes tepees, campfires, totem poles, and local Iroquois Indians demonstrating dances and telling legends. Big eaters will love the all-you-can-eat meals plus free unlimited snack bar food. Winter activities include downhill skiing, ice-skating, and tubing.

Cost: Children under four stay free; children four to sixteen half price. Rates vary depending on type of accommodation selected. Rooms with two double beds $99 per night per adult, $489 for seven nights and eight days. Slightly larger rooms and rooms located nearest the pool or dining room $109 to $119 per night per adult, $519 to $559 per week. You can opt for a stay of any length; the longer you stay, the better the daily rate. Villas $149 per adult per day, $629 per week. Many package deals available throughout the year; Family of Three Special, $999, includes seven days and six nights for three people, $40 per day for each extra child.

ROCKING HORSE RANCH

Address: Highland, New York 12528 (seventy-five miles from New York City in the Hudson Valley).
Telephone: 800–647–2624; 914–691–2927.

Rocking Horse Ranch Resort has been applauded by *Family Circle* and *Better Homes and Gardens* magazines as one of the best family resorts around. The ranch offers an all-inclusive package of activities for parents and kids, such as daily horseback riding, supervised day and evening children's programs, waterskiing, sporting facilities, and evening entertainment for adults and children. You can stay for as long or short a time as you like; the prices drop the longer you stay.

Season: Year-round.

Accommodations: One hundred twenty rooms in the main lodge and "Oklahoma Building" all have private baths and are air-conditioned. Most rooms can accommodate four to six people in two double beds and a sofabed.

Special Features: The children's program runs daily from 9 A.M. to 4:30 P.M. and again in the evening from 8 to 10 P.M. Kids do everything the adults do, but the activities are supervised and tailored to their abilities. Indoor and outdoor opportunities for children and adults include waterskiing, target shooting, fishing, hiking, riding, playground, Ping-Pong, horseshoes, badminton, squash, tennis, hayrides, indoor heated pool, paddleboats, outdoor swimming pool, miniature golf, bocci courts, fitness gym, sauna, arts and crafts, talent shows, and such nightly entertainment as bingo tournaments, limbo contests, music, and dancing. Older kids get their own evening entertainment several times a week, which might include bonfires, disco parties, and sing-alongs. In winter add skiing and ice-skating to the long list of things to do.

Cost: Many package deals are available, especially during certain weeks of the fall and winter, when kids pay only for meals. During holidays, stays of three nights or more bring another price break for the kids, so be sure to ask. Children under four stay free. Regular prices, seven-night stays, adults $615, kids four to sixteen $280. A two-night, three-day package is $205 to $245 per adult, $110 per child. Rates include everything except lunches and the 15-percent service charge added to your bill.

SECTION II
Ranches where riding costs extra but meals are included

DRAKESBAD GUEST RANCH

Address: Chester, California 96020 (in Lassen Volcanic National
Park, seventeen miles from Chester; the last four miles are on
a dirt road).
Telephone: 916–529–1512.

Nature lovers return year after year to this secluded hundred-year-old
ranch surrounded by thousands of acres of forests crammed with lakes
and streams. A trout stream cuts right through the middle of the ranch
for fishing and splashing, and a large swimming pool is heated by natural
volcanic heat. Knotty pine lodge rooms are lit by kerosene lanterns; the
ranch's lack of electricity makes for skies packed with brightly glowing
stars. Saddle horses are rented by the hour and Lassen Volcanic National
Park is within driving or hiking distance.
   Season: June through September.
   Accommodations: Nineteen units can house a total of forty to fifty
people. Lodge or cabin bedrooms have a private sink-and-toilet half bath,
with shared shower facility nearby. Bungalows and annex units are one
large room with two double beds; duplex rooms have bathrooms with
showers and are reserved for parties of four or more.
   Special Features: Hiking trails, fishing, volleyball court, evening bonfires, western barbecues. Lunch is a buffet; table service at breakfast and
dinner. Special diets can be accommodated.
   Costs: Adults in lodge rooms and cabins $76 nightly, $500 weekly; each
additional adult (over age eleven) $66 per night, $435 per week. Children
two to eleven $54 per night, $355 per week. Adults in bungalow or annex
rooms $85 per night, $560 per week; each additional adult $70 per night,
$460 per week. Children two to eleven $50 per night. The duplex houses
a minimum of four people: adults $91 per night, $600 per week. Each
additional adult $70 nightly, $460 per week; children two to eleven $50
per night. Includes use of the pool, three meals a day, and housekeeping
service. Saddle horses $20 for the first hour, $12 each additional hour.
Book as early as possible; many return guests book a year in advance.
Summer reservations are easier to get in early June and September.

HARMEL'S RANCH RESORT

Address: PO Box 944, Gunnison, Colorado 81230 (four and a half hours from Denver and three and a half hours from Colorado Springs).
Telephone: 800–235–3402.

This family ranch, set in the middle of the Rocky Mountains, has a variety of options available for families that want to tailor a ranch vacation to their specific interests and abilities without having to pay for a total package. Prices do not include horseback riding, river rafting, or mountain bike rentals. From mid-May to mid-June you can rent housekeeping cottages; after that the ranch shifts to modified American plan that includes breakfast and dinner daily.

Season: Mid-May through September.

Accommodations: Individual cabins or duplexes have a living room, private bath, and one, two, or three bedrooms. Some units have kitchens and all have refrigerators and daily housekeeping service. Guests make their own lunches or buy box lunches from the resort. Total capacity is 150 people.

Special Features: Three trout streams have excellent fishing. Other facilities include a heated swimming pool, a playground, hiking, cookouts, a kids' program, square dancing, horseshoes, hayrides, and a children's menu.

Cost: Rates include breakfast and dinner, daily housekeeping service, all activities except rafting, horseback riding, mountain bike rentals, and trap shooting. In high season, modern family cottages $1,475 per week for four people. Lodge rooms and family cabins $1,375 per week for four people. Children's discount: for kids ages five to ten subtract $50 per week, for age four and under subtract $100 per week. Cabins rented from mid-May to mid-June and after Labor Day only, $650 per week for four.

Ninety-minute horseback rides $18, half-day rides $45. White water river rafting two-hour trips $22 to $27. Mountain bike rentals $22 for full day, $12 for half day.

Nearby: Old mining sites and ghost towns, and boating on Blue Mesa Reservoir, forty-five minutes away by car.

DEER FORKS GUEST RANCH

Address: 1200 Poison Lake Road, Douglas, Wyoming 82633
(seventy-five miles from Casper, Wyoming and twenty-five miles
southwest of Douglas).
Telephone: 307–358–2033.

Deer Forks Guest Ranch is a working cattle ranch with a herd of 320 cows
on 14,000 acres. The ranch takes two or three groups of families at a time
so that guests really can participate in ranch life. Cabins are furnished
with kitchens, but guests can choose a modified American plan package
that provides breakfast and dinner. Two trout streams are on the property,
so bring your fishing gear—or just wade, swim, and watch birds by the
water. A spring-fed pond on the lawn has a muskrat and provides hours
of entertainment for children. Kids also can help milk a cow and feed
orphan lambs from a bottle.

Season: June through mid-September.

Accommodations: Guest houses are equipped with kitchens, and those
not eating with the family need to bring their own food supplies. A trailer
hookup and two furnished cabins are available. One cabin sleeps nine, in
a sleeping loft, bedroom and sofabed; the other cabin sleeps seven, in two
bedrooms and a sofabed. Bedding and towels are provided.

Special Features: Horseshoes, volleyball, hiking; riding costs extra.

Costs: Cabin rental fees depend on number of people in a unit: adults
$25 per night, $150 per week. Children under sixteen $10 per night.
Modified American plan (two meals per day), adults $50 per day, $300
per week, kids under sixteen $25 per day, $150 per week. Rates include
all on-ranch activities except riding.

Morning horseback rides $20 per person, afternoon rides $5 per hour
per person; $20 per day minimum. Trailer hookup available (price in-
cludes sewer, water, and electricity): adults $6 per day, $30 per week;
children under sixteen $5 per day, $30 per week. Airport pickup in Casper
$50.

Nearby: The Wyoming State Fair and Pioneer Museum in Douglas, a
stop on the Oregon Trail, rodeos, historical sites.

EAGLE HURST RESORT AND DUDE RANCH

Address: HC 88, Box 8638, Huzzah, Missouri 65565 (two-hour drive
from St. Louis, sixteen miles east of Steelville).
Telephone: 314–786–2625.

If the kids have any energy left after horseback riding along wooded trails
and tubing down the clear Huzzah River, they can play lawn games, swim

in the spacious swimming pool, or amuse themselves on the play equipment placed throughout the resort. A supervised morning program in summer is available for three- to ten-year-olds so that parents can play in shuffleboard, horseshoe, and Ping-Pong tournaments. This American plan resort provides three delicious meals a day, but the children we interviewed liked the hot dog cookout best.

Season: Memorial Day through September.

Accommodations: Thirty cabins and duplexes accommodate families of different sizes in one, two, and four bedrooms. Most of the cabins have a combination of double and single beds and all have air-conditioning, daily housekeeping service, and small refrigerators for between-meal snacks.

Special Features: Swimming pool, tubing on the Huzzah River, shuffleboard, horseshoes, Ping-Pong, badminton, pony rides for kids under ten (kids must be tall enough to reach the stirrups in order to go on trail rides), bingo, hayrides, a song fest, a talent show, square dancing, tennis.

Cost: In one-bedroom cottages: weekly stays, adults $279 to $300, children three to ten $150. Stays of three to six nights, adults $50, children three to ten $27 per night. In two-bedroom cottages: weekly stays, adults $279 to $305, children three to ten $155. Stays of three to six nights, adults $57, children three to ten $26. Nightly rate $57 per adult, $30 per child. Children under three always stay free.

Memorial Day and Labor Day packages available; 10-percent discount for reservations between late May and mid-June and after the middle of August. Horseback rides $12 per hour and two breakfast rides $18 each.

SECTION III
Ranches with housekeeping cabins and riding rentals

SEA HORSE GUEST RANCH

Address: PO Box 277, 2660 Highway 1, Bodega Bay, California 94923 (sixty-five miles north of the Golden Gate Bridge).
Telephone: 707–875–2721.

Set back on a rise overlooking the Pacific Ocean, Sea Horse Guest Ranch has rooms with private baths. Its stable has horse rentals and guided trips into the dunes along the beach or into the hills above the scenic coastline of northern California. The Sea Horse is a working ranch with cows, sheep, goats, horses, rabbits, ponies, dogs, and cats and is an excellent weekend getaway for city families with kids who want to ride. Children under twelve stay free in parents' rooms, and there is a complimentary continental breakfast.

Season: Year-round.

Accommodations: The Bunk House is the best place for families to stay: it has two rooms, each with a queen-size and a double bed, private bath, and shared kitchen facility and living room. Guests may use the kitchen to prepare their own meals. The Ranch House has three rooms with private baths, one with a king-size bed and twin daybed, one with a queen-size bed and double sofabed, and one with a double bed only.

Cost: Bunk House rooms $70 to $75 per day; Ranch House rooms $70 to $80 per day. Guided horseback rides $20 per hour and $35 per two-hour ride; 10-percent discount for ranch guests.

Nearby: Beaches, the Russian River, giant redwoods, whale watching during the early part of the year.

PAHASKA TEPEE RESORT

Address: 183-R Yellowstone Highway, Cody, Wyoming 82414.
Telephone: 800–628–7791; 307–527–7701.

Put your own ranch vacation together, stage a family reunion, or just use this resort as headquarters on a visit to Yellowstone or the historic town of Cody. The original Pahaska Lodge was built by Buffalo Bill Cody himself and is listed on the National Register of Historic Places. A restaurant and tavern in the original lodge display some fascinating Buffalo Bill memorabilia, and the resort's convenient location is minutes from the entrance to Yellowstone and an hour from Cody. Guests can choose from hotel rooms in log cabins, a housekeeping cabin, or a family reunion lodge, and they can rent horses, play in the river, or book a river-rafting trip nearby.

Season: Year-round.

Accommodations: There are eighteen log buildings on the property, each divided into several "hotel" rooms with private entrances and private baths. Rooms in the main lodge and cabin rooms sleep from one to six people. One housekeeping cabin is available with a fully equipped kitchen and two queen-size beds. A family reunion lodge has seven bedrooms and eleven queen-size beds as well as a deluxe kitchen, Jacuzzi, and more.

Special Features: Fishing and swimming in the cold river, horse rentals, rafting a few miles down the road. Rafting ends in late June or early July. The resort also contains a restaurant and tavern, gas station, and grocery store and rents snowmobiles for touring Yellowstone in the winter.

Cost: Lodge and cabin rooms $55 to $85, depending on time of year. Simple housekeeping cabin $85 per night. Family reunion lodge $550 per night, $3,000 per week; it can sleep up to seven families, so is well priced if you have a big group. Make reservations for reunion lodge one year in advance. Horse rentals $12.50 per hour, half-day rides $40.

CHICO HOT SPRINGS

Address: PO Box 127, Pray, Montana 59065 (twenty-five miles from Livingstone and thirty miles from the north entrance to Yellowstone; the nearest airport is Bozeman, ninety minutes away). Telephone: 406–333–4933.

Miners used Chico Hot Springs as a laundry and bathtub when gold was discovered nearby in the late 1800s, and a hotel was built in 1902 so that guests visiting Yellowstone could "take the waters." Part of the hotel still stands, but today's guests stay in a more modern facility. Many families visit Chico on their way into or out of Yellowstone, but it is well worth visiting on its own merits. An Olympic-size pool is warmed by mineral water and a hot soaking pool right next to it soothes aching muscles after a long trail ride. Motel-like units are available, as are housekeeping condominiums and a log house. If you tire of lazing around the pool you can rent horses or mountain bikes, take white water rafting trips, or go hiking or fishing.

Accommodations: Lodge rooms have two double beds and either shared or private baths. A small condominium has a loft with three double beds plus a fully equipped kitchen, washer, dryer, and dry sauna. One larger condominium has a loft with three double beds and a private bedroom downstairs. The log house has a fully equipped kitchen and sleeps up to ten people in two private bedrooms with double beds, a sofabed, and rollaways.

Special Features: Horseback riding and mountain bike rental, Olympic-size hot springs–fed mineral water pool, and a smaller hot soaking pool next to it. Whitewater rafting and fishing trips are available for an extra fee. The excellent restaurant serves breakfast and dinner with dishes such as roast duckling Grand Marnier, smoked trout, escargots, buffalo steak, and wild game mixed grill. The prices match the high-quality menus, but it is worth the splurge for a special treat. A poolside grill serves simpler and less expensive fare. Guests can dance to live music on weekends and go cross-country skiing or dogsledding in winter.

Cost: Lodge rooms with two double beds and shared bath $49 per night for two people, $5 or $10 for each additional person over five. Children five and under stay free. Rooms with private baths $66. Small condominium or the log house $139 per night, large condominium $169. If you stay six nights you get the seventh night free. Horseback riding $10 per hour; river rafting $25 for adults, $15 for kids for four-hour ride; mountain bike rental $5 an hour, $15 per half day, $25 for all day; children's sizes available.

Nearby: Guests who like to fish can do so at Daley Lake.

WESTERN HILLS GUEST RANCH

Address: Box 509, Wagoner, Oklahoma 74477 (fifty minutes east of Tulsa).
Telephone: 918–772–2545.

Calling itself a "western theme destination," Western Hills Guest Ranch is run by the Oklahoma Parks Department. It offers lodging in a resort hotel or in individual cabins that accommodate two, four, or six people. Horseback riding is available by the hour and other recreational options are varied and plentiful. There is a free supervised children's program during the summer, boating, swimming, golf, tennis, hayrides, stagecoach rides, and more. Its location on a peninsula on Fort Gibson Lake in Sequoyah State Park offers breathtaking lake views.

Season: Year-round.

Accommodations: The resort hotel has rooms and suites that face the pool or the lake. Some rooms are doubles, some have two double beds, and others are set up for three people. There are twenty-four cabins for two people, fifteen cabins for four people, and four cabins for six people. Some cabins have kitchenettes, but guests bring their own dishes and utensils. All accommodations are air-conditioned and include bedding and towels. Also on the grounds are campsites and RV hookups.

Special Features: A free supervised children's recreation program operates during the summer months, with daily planned activities that include water games in the pool, a train ride through the park, arts and crafts, sports, games, and silly contests. There is an eighteen-hole golf course, a swimming pool, riding stables, tennis courts, boat rental, archery, badminton, a nature center, hiking, playgrounds, stagecoach rides, hayrides, and more. A Little Wrangler's Night for children five to twelve is offered regularly by the park recreation staff during the summer. Kids are taken on a two-hour outing where they roast hot dogs over a campfire and enjoy cowboy beans, s'mores, and a beverage and get a souvenir bandana ($5.95 for the outing).

Cost: Kids under eighteen stay free in parents' rooms. Resort hotel room rates vary depending on time of year, time of week, and location. Highest rates, in summer, $52 to $67 per night. Winter rates $40 to $60. Suites $99 to $175. Cabins with kitchens $55 to $95, depending on season and size; two-night minimum on summer weekends. If you check in Sunday or Monday and spend three nights, the fourth night is free. Stays of seven consecutive nights receive a 15-percent discount.

Horseback riding (ages nine and up) $8.50 per hour; bike rentals $2.50 per hour, $12 per day; golfing green fee $8; miniature golf $2.50; paddleboats $6 per hour for two people; hayrides $3.

The Cowboy Adventure Package includes two nights' lodging; all meals, beginning with dinner upon arrival and ending with breakfast on departure; snacks; instruction in horse care, riding, and roping; trail riding; a T-shirt; and all taxes and tips. Minimum age nine years. Adults double occupancy, $185 per person, single occupancy $235; children nine to eighteen sharing parents' rooms $110 each. Or you can participate for the day for $35 per person.

CIRCLE K RANCH

Address: 26525 Gay-Dreisbach Road, Circleville, Ohio 43113 (thirty miles south of Columbus).
Telephone: 614–474–3711.

Circle K has a large family cottage for rent by the week in the summer and on weekends in the spring and fall. Guests do their own cooking, but a one-hour morning horseback ride is included in the price of a week-long stay. The ranch has plenty of animals, and children can help feed the horses, ducks, chickens, goats, and rabbits. This peaceful two-hundred-acre farm has fifteen acres of woods, a fishing and boating pond, a creek running through it, and an above-ground pool. It's a family enterprise with the hosts' four adult children helping out during the summer.

Season: Open mid-May through mid-October. The cottage is rented by the week (Sunday to Saturday) only in June, July, and August and on weekends in spring and fall.

Accommodations: The six-room cottage sleeps six people comfortably but can sleep more; one family of nine has come for many years. Two upstairs bedrooms contain three double beds and a crib. Downstairs is a living room, dining room, kitchen, and bathroom; there is a daybed and chaise in the dining room. All linens are provided.

Special Features: Rides, offered daily during the summer, are included in the price. Children must be nine or ten (tall enough to reach the stirrups) to go on guided trail rides; younger ones stay behind and are led around on gentle ponies. There is a cookout on Sunday when people arrive and homemade ice cream on Friday night. Guests have unlimited use of the tennis court, above-ground pool, farm pond for boating or fishing, and hiking trails around the property.

Cost: Week-long stays in the summer are $300 for four people, $25 for each additional person, regardless of age. Weekend stays in spring and fall (from as early as you want on Friday and to as late as you want on Sunday) $25 per person (minimum $75). Horseback riding $8 per person for one-hour trail ride. Book early for summer.

Nearby: Columbus Zoo; outdoor theater in Tecumsa; many caves within an hour's drive.

NATIONAL PARKS

*O*ur country's national parks, although spectacular, do not have the automatic kid appeal of Disneyland. Their attractions can be as small as the rustle of a fast-moving snake or the deep purple of a spring-blooming violet. While a mirror-clear glacier lake might not dazzle your children, the parks have loads of thrilling outdoor activities, from trail rides to river float trips, that will inevitably win them over. An eagle-eyed twelve-year-old can hunt for arrowheads in Utah's Canyon Country, ride cowboy style in Wyoming's Grand Tetons, or take up the challenge of learning to climb rocks in the High Sierras.

If you are not entirely convinced, how about this: compared to other destinations, national parks have dirt-cheap lodgings, from rustic tent cabins and family hostels to midpriced historic lodges. It's actually a challenge to spend money in some. There aren't many fancy places to eat, so you can save your money for outdoor sports and activities.

Camping is obviously the least expensive way to experience national parks, as campsites cost only a few dollars per night. If your family thrives on spending time outdoors, nothing tops sleeping under an open sky. The sheer beauty of nature works wonders on alleviating the stress of everyday life. For a list of the campgrounds maintained by the National Parks Service, send $4 to the Superintendent of Documents, U.S. Government Printing Office, Washington, D.C. 20442 (202–512–0000), for the *National Park Camping Guide.* Another helpful and inexpensive resource is the *Complete Guide to America's National Parks,* with camping and hiking information, climate charts, and state and regional maps. Contact the

National Park Foundation at 1101 Seventeenth Street, Suite 1102, Washington, D.C. 20036 (202–785–4500).

Some recommended pretrip reading materials include *Sharing Nature with Children* and *Sharing the Joy of Nature,* with activities and games designed to get you and your children in touch with the out-of-doors, by Joseph Cornell (Dawn Publications, 1979; $6.95 each), and *The Young Naturalist,* by A. Mitchell (EDC Publishing, 1982; $6.95). These books and many others designed for children are available from the Glacier Natural History Association, Box 428, West Glacier, Montana 59936 or the Rocky Mountain Nature Association, Rocky Mountain National Park, Estes Park, Colorado 80517.

In this chapter we list cabins, motels, inexpensive lodges, and family hostels in or near national parks where families can enjoy a bit more comfort than camping in a tent provides. If you are planning a summer visit, be prepared: it is crowded out there. The biggest crush occurs in the middle of summer. To protect the quality of these treasured sites, development is closely controlled and there aren't enough rooms to meet demand. It is wise to make reservations nine to twelve months in advance for the least expensive and most desirable rooms or cabins.

WEST COAST

YOSEMITE NATIONAL PARK, CALIFORNIA

Renowned for its magnificence, Yosemite National Park is one of the few national parks with many organized activities designed specifically for children. Its towering granite domes and peaks, waterfalls, glacial lakes, and giant trees attract close to three million visitors annually, so advance reservations for all accommodations are essential.

During spring and summer, gentle ponies are available for rent by the hour at all four park stables for $10 an hour. Guided saddle rides for children age seven and up depart from the Yosemite Valley Stables (Easter to mid-October) and at Wawona, White Wolf, and Tuolumne Meadows (summer only). Rides range from two hours ($28) to half a day ($36) to all day ($55). Four- and six-day rides to the High Sierra Camps are available, too. Call 209–372–1248 for information.

Eight- through twelve-year-olds can join a national park ranger in search of "secret places" in Yosemite. For children five through seven, a special hour with a ranger is offered each day in summer. There are also ranger-led family discovery walks. Sign up for all of these at the Happy Isle Nature Center (shuttle stop no. 16).

The Indian Cultural Museum, next to the Yosemite Valley Visitor Center,

has an authentic recreated Ahwahnichi Indian village. The Pioneer Yosemite History Center at Wawona has historic park buildings from the
1800s and rangers and docents in period costume.

There are many tours of the park, including a two-hour tour in an open-
air tram and a full-day tour of Glacier Point, 3,214 feet above the valley
floor. Stop by a tour desk at any hotel or call 209–372–1240. Tour costs
range from $13.75 to $37.75; children twelve and under are half price,
and those under five are free. The Art Activity Center holds free art classes
next to the post office; the Yosemite Theater offers live performances and
movies.

The valley has miles of bike paths; bike rental $4 per hour or $14 per
day at Yosemite Lodge or Curry Village. River rafting on the Merced River
is available at Curry Village in early summer. The Merced has many sandy
beaches open mid- to late summer. You also can swim at the Curry Village
and Yosemite Lodge swimming pools.

The park is renowned for rock climbing, an excellent sport for building
teamwork. Children under fourteen participate in a group lesson; older
kids can enroll in a private class. Classes are offered daily from June
through September at the Yosemite Mountaineering School in Tuolumne
Meadows. From October through May classes are held at Curry Village.

A winter visit to the park is your chance to soak up its grandeur during
a more peaceful season. Take advantage of Yosemite's Midweek Ski Package: lift tickets and ski lessons at the Badger Pass resort, cross-country ski
lessons, bus transportation from one point to another, ice-skating, ski area
baby-sitting, and nature-history-wildlife ranger-led programs are available
at a fraction of the cost for similar services at other ski centers. Downhill
skiing at Badger Pass, a small resort with a gentle terrain, is great for
beginners. Many of the 350 miles of trails for cross-country skiing in the
park begin at Badger Pass. Trail passes are free. The park hotels have many
social events in the evenings, culminating in a delicious Thursday night
ski buffet at the magnificent Ahwahnee Hotel. The Midweek Ski Package
(minimum two-day stay between Sunday and Thursday) is $25 per day
for adults, $15 per day for children six to twelve, $20 per day for children
under six, plus lodging at the Yosemite Lodge (from $28.50 per night,
double occupancy; children stay free). Free baby-sitting services are offered as part of this package. Call 209–454–2000 for reservations.

The Curry Village Ice Rink is an outdoor rink where families can skate
in the shadow of Glacier Point with a spectacular view of Half Dome. An
open fire next to the rink is ideal for warming chilled little hands and wet
bottoms. Call 209–372–1441 for information. Open daily November
through March.

Winter is also time for ranger-led snowshoe walks and the "Discover
Yosemite" Daytime Naturalist Program, in which an instructor from the
Yosemite Institute leads families on a two-hour walk to identify trees and
spot animal tracks. Sign up at the tour desk at Yosemite Lodge.

Note: In addition to the lodgings listed below there is a family camp in the Sierra Nevadas near Yosemite run by San Jose Family Camps. See pages 139–140 in our chapter on family camps.

YOSEMITE LODGE

Address: Yosemite Park and Curry Company, Yosemite National Park, California 95389 (hotel is near the base of Yosemite Falls). Telephone: 209–252–4848.

Season: Year-round.
Accommodations: A large, modern hotel with 495 rooms ranging from deluxe to the more affordable standard rooms. There are also cabins with a private or central bath. Beds, blankets, and linens are provided in the cabins. They do not have kitchens.
Special Features: Swimming pool; wide range of dining facilities, including poolside fast food; bike rental; tour desk; amphitheater.
Cost: Standard rooms with private bath $52 to $75 per night, double occupancy, depending on season. Cabins with private bath $50 to $60 per night, double occupancy, depending on season; with central bath $27 to $46. Additional adult $6 to $7.50, depending on accommodation; additional child $3 to $3.75.
Nearby: Yosemite Falls and bike paths.

CURRY VILLAGE

Address: Yosemite Park and Curry Company, Yosemite National Park, California 95389 (hotel is beneath Glacier Point on the valley floor). Telephone: 209–252–4848.

Season: Year-round.
Accommodations: Among the 628 accommodations, inexpensive choices include standard hotel rooms, cabins with either private or central bath, and canvas tent cabins with a central bathhouse.
Special Features: Curry Village has a camp store, restaurants, the Yosemite Mountaineering School (open September to June), a swimming pool, bike rental, boat rental for river rafting, an ice rink, and cross-country ski rental.
Cost: Depending on season, standard rooms with private bath $52 to $75 per night, double occupancy. Cabins with private bath $50 to $60 per night, double occupancy; with central bath $27 to $45. Canvas tent cabins with central bath $26 to $32 per night, double occupancy. Addi-

tional adult $5 to $7.50, depending on accommodation; additional child $2.50 to $4.
Nearby: Mirror Lake, stables, trailheads to Vernal and Nevada falls, bike path.

HOTEL WAWONA

Address: Yosemite Park and Curry Company, Yosemite National Park, California 95389 (hotel is twenty-seven miles from Yosemite Valley on California 41).
Telephone: 209–252–4848.

Season: Easter week through Thanksgiving. Re-opens mid-December through January. During January, February, and March, only open Thursday through Sunday.
Accommodations: This Victorian-style hotel, surrounded by manicured lawns, is one of California's oldest mountain resort hotels. Established in 1879, it was designated as a national historic landmark in 1987. There are 104 rooms.
Special Features: The hotel has swimming, tennis, nearby snow skiing, golf (nine-hole course), horseback riding on the grounds, lawn barbecues, and a home-style dining room.
Cost: The least expensive accommodations are rooms with central bath, $63 per night double occupancy. Additional adult $10; additional child $5.
Nearby: Mariposa Grove of the Giant Sequoias (winter guests can snowshoe there), Pioneer Yosemite History Center, and Chilnualna Falls.

HOUSEKEEPING CAMP

Address: Yosemite Park and Curry Company, Yosemite National Park, California 95389 (on the south bank of the Merced River along Southside Drive).
Telephone: 209–252–4848.

Season: Mid-June through Labor Day.
Accommodations: Each unit sleeps six and has a covered patio, double bed, table with chairs, and a wood-burning stove. There are 282 units with a central restroom.
Special Features: A wide, sandy beach is ideal for swimming and grand views of Yosemite Falls and Half Dome.
Cost: Units $36 per night.
Nearby: Laundry facilities and a small grocery store.

TUOLUMNE MEADOWS LODGE

Address: Yosemite Park and Curry Company, Yosemite National Park, California 95389 (at an elevation of 8,575 feet, this lodge is situated in a large subalpine meadow).
Telephone: 209–252–4848.

Season: Mid-June to Labor Day.
Accommodations: There are sixty-nine canvas tent cabins with beds (all bedding is provided) and centrally located restrooms. This is a favorite base camp for people heading to the High Sierra Camps or for day hikes in the Tuolumne Meadows area.
Special Features: Breakfast and dinner are available in a central dining tent beside the river.
Cost: Cabins $37 per night, double occupancy. Additional adult $6; additional child $3.
Nearby: Mountaineering school, stables, gas station, post office, hamburger stand, grocery store.

WHITE WOLF LODGE

Address: Yosemite Park and Curry Company, Yosemite National Park, California 95389 (hotel is in the high country, just off Tioga Road).
Telephone: 209–252–4848.

Season: Mid-June to Labor Day.
Accommodations: There are twenty-four canvas tent cabins with beds (all bedding is included) and four cabins with private baths. This is a popular base for day hikes to Lukens and Harden lakes.
Special Features: Breakfast and dinner are available. Its stables offer horseback riding for an additional charge.
Cost: Cabins with private bath $57 per night, double occupancy. Canvas tent cabins $33 per night, double occupancy. Additional adult $6 to $7, depending on accommodation; additional child $3 to $3.50.
Nearby: Camp store, restaurant.

HIGH SIERRA CAMPS

Address: Yosemite Reservations, 5410 East Home, Fresno, California 93727. Merced Lake, Vogelsang, Glen Aulin, May Lake, and Sunrise Camps are all located roughly eight strenuous miles apart in spectacular mountain settings. Visitors can either hike or ride in on their own or participate in a seven-day guided hike or guided saddle trips of four or six days. **Telephone:** 209–454–2002. Note: these accommodations are in great demand, as they offer a truly spectacular outdoor experience. Reservations are accepted beginning the first Monday in December for the following summer. Due to space limitations, only 10 percent of those who apply are accepted.

Season: Late June to Labor Day, conditions permitting.

Accommodations: The camps have dorm-style tent cabins with guests segregated by sex. All camps have beds, linens, blankets, and central restrooms with hot showers (welcome at the end of a day on the trail).

Special Features: Hearty breakfast and dinner are served in a central dining tent.

Cost: Approximately $78 per night per person includes breakfast, dinner, and showers. Children stay at reduced rates. Seven-day guided hike $590 per person; four-day guided saddle ride $493 per person; six-day guided saddle ride $777 per person. Rates include all meals and accommodations.

Nearby: Glen Aulin Camp is four miles from magnificent Waterwheel Fall. May Lake Camp is on the shore of May Lake beneath the eastern wall of Mount Hoffman. Sunrise Camp is located on a long, narrow shelf forty feet above Long Meadow. Merced Lake Camp, at the lowest elevation, is on the Merced River. Vogelsang Camp is the highest and the most dramatic, situated above the treeline near many alpine lakes.

SEQUOIA AND KINGS CANYON NATIONAL PARKS, CALIFORNIA

Sequoia National Park is known as the "land of the giants" because its trees range in diameter from 15 to 35 feet and tower to heights of more than 250 feet. Adjacent to the north part of Sequoia is Kings Canyon National Park, which has one of the country's deepest canyons, crystal-clear lakes, waterfalls, and mountain meadows. Besides viewing the big trees, guests can camp, hike, ride horses, fish, and ski.

Visitors seeking a quiet vacation might find Sequoia and Kings Canyon attractive; they remain relatively obscure because the Yosemite Valley, one hundred miles to the north, has been a more popular tourist magnet for decades.

The parks have more than nine hundred miles of marked hiking trails. A good place to enjoy the beauty of the sequoias is the Congress Trail near the General Sherman Tree, which is two miles from Giant Forest Village. On this two-mile self-guided trail you will find a number of other giant trees, including the Chief Sequoia and the President McKinley. Campfire talks are held regularly. Horseback riding corrals are located at Wolverton, Grant Grove, and Cedar Grove (open mid-May through September). From mid-June through September, Wolverton Pack Station offers guided pack trips into the backcountry as well as fishing and photography expeditions to areas accessible only by trails. Contact Wolverton Pack Station, PO Box 315, Sequoia National Park, California 93262, 209–565–3445. Underground cave formations are located at Crystal Cave (209–565–3341) and Boyden Cave (209–736–2708) mid-May through September.

Cross-country skiing within the snow-blanketed forests at Giant Forest and Grant Grove is popular and a bargain. There are more than seventy-five miles of marked trails that weave among the giant sequoias. Snowshoes are available at both centers. Ski touring opens with the first snow of winter and extends through mid-April. The Wolverton Ski Bowl features instruction for beginner and intermediate downhill skiing plus sled and toboggan runs and equipment rentals. The Wolverton area is three miles north of Giant Forest. For information at Giant Forest call 209–565–3435; for Grant Grove call 209–335–2314.

Note: Montecito-Sequoia is a family camp located between the two parks. See pages 140–141 in our chapter on family camps for details.

GIANT FOREST LODGE

Address: Sequoia Guest Services, PO Box 789, Three Rivers, California 93271 (hotel is in Giant Forest Village in the heart of Sequoia).
Telephone: 209–561–3314.

Season: Year-round; rustic cabins are closed in winter.

Accommodations: The lodge has 245 rental units. Motel rooms and deluxe cabins have two double beds and a private bath with tub and shower; standard cabins have one double and one single bed and a private bath with tub or shower. Family cabins have two rooms, beds for six, and a private bath. Rustic cabins (with or without private bath) have wood heat, patios with wood-burning cook stoves (utensils not provided); some do not have electricity, but kerosene lamps are provided. Some have tent roofs. A variety of sleeping arrangements are available. Cabins with four beds sleep up to eight; cabins with three beds sleep five.

Special Features: A cafeteria is nearby, and the lodge has a dining room that is open May through mid-October.

Cost: Family cabins $79 per night; standard cabins $57 to $70 per night. Motel rooms $69 to $90 per night. Rustic cabins without bath $32 per night; with bath $39 per night. All rates are for high season, double occupancy; rates are lower off-season (mid-October to April). Children under twelve stay free in parents' rooms. Cots and cribs $7.50 per day.

Nearby: Wolverton Pack Station.

STONY CREEK LODGE

Address: Sequoia Guest Services, PO Box 789, Three Rivers, California 93271 (hotel is fifteen miles north of Giant Forest in Sequoia National Park).
Telephone: 209–561–3314.

Season: May to September.

Accommodations: This small lodge has eleven motel rooms with private baths.

Special Features: There's a launderette next to the main lodge, which also has a restaurant and a grocery store.

Cost: Rooms $80 per night, double occupancy. Children under twelve stay free in parents' rooms with available bed space. Cots and cribs $7.50 per day.

Nearby: Wolverton Pack Station.

BEARPAW MEADOW CAMP

Address: Sequoia Guest Services in Sequoia National Park, PO Box 789, Three Rivers, California 93271 (camp is accessible by an eleven-and-a-half-mile hike from Crescent Meadow in Sequoia National Park. Incredible views and ice-cold lemonade await arriving guests).
Telephone: 209–561–3314.

Season: Late June to early September. Book early; these accommodations are in great demand, as they offer a truly spectacular outdoor experience.

Accommodations: The camp has tent cabins with beds and hot showers. All bedding is provided. This camp is ideal for those who want to see the

more remote parts of the park without having to pack their own food and bedding or for those who want a degree of comfort at the end of the day.
Special Features: Guests are served a home-style dinner and breakfast.
Cost: Adults $98 per night, children under twelve $59 per night. Rates include lodging, dinner, breakfast, and sales tax. Box lunches available for $11.50.

GRANT GROVE

Address: Sequoia Guest Services, PO Box 789, Three Rivers, California 93271 (hotel is thirty miles north of Giant Forest in Kings Canyon National Park).
Telephone: 209–561–3314.

Season: Year-round. Rustic sleeping cabins closed in winter.
Accommodations: Fifty-two units, which include small cabins with two double beds and private bath with tub. Rustic "semihousekeeping cabins" and rustic "sleeping cabins," both with shared baths, have wood heat and patios with wood-burning cook stoves and picnic table (utensils are not provided). There is no electricity, but kerosene lamps are provided.
Special Features: Grant Grove has a coffee shop, grocery story, and service station.
Cost: Cabins with private bath $69 per night. Rustic semihousekeeping cabins $34 per night; sleeping cabins $32 per night. All rates are for high season, double occupancy; rates are lower off-season (mid-October through April). Children under twelve stay free in parents' rooms. Cots and cribs $7.50 per night.
Nearby: Pack and saddle horseback riding at Grant Grove's Stable.

CEDAR GROVE LODGE

Address: Sequoia Guest Services, PO Box 789, Three Rivers, California 93271 (hotel is in South Fork Canyon, along the banks of the Kings River in the heart of Kings Canyon Park; it is sixty miles from Giant Forest).
Telephone: 209–561–3314.

Season: Late May through September.
Accommodations: This is a small, eighteen-room lodge. Rooms have two queen-size beds, private showers, and air-conditioning.
Special Features: Snack bar, market, bike rental, and laundry facilities.
Cost: Rooms $78 per night, double occupancy. Children under twelve

stay free in parents' rooms with available bed space. Cots and cribs $7.50 per night.
Nearby: Pack and saddle horseback riding at Cedar Grove Pack Station.

OLYMPIC NATIONAL PARK, WASHINGTON

Olympic National Park is an unspoiled landscape of sandy beaches, serene lakes, glacier peaks, meadows, streams, and forests. Families enjoy clamming, hunting for beach glass, kiting, hiking, biking, and fishing for salmon and steelhead on the nearby Quinault and Hoh rivers. The half-hour ferry ride from Port Angeles to British Columbia, Canada, is a fun side trip.

The park service runs wonderful naturalist programs for children that include beach and tide pool walks, meadow explorations, and a program called Sub-Alpine Secrets. Children eight and older can earn junior ranger certificates. Check with the visitor center on arrival. A trip to this part of the Olympic Peninsula is not complete without a visit to one of its rain forests. Easiest to reach is the Hoh Rain Forest, eighteen miles up the Hoh River from U.S. 101. Its visitor center provides information about the trails as well as raft trips on the Hoh and Queets rivers.

A number of firms offer day-long or overnight guided fishing and river float trips. Richard J. Wojt Guide Service (206–385–0058) offers guided backpacking and fishing in remote areas from late June through August ($75 per person in groups of three to five). Llamas carry tents and supplies while hikers carry their personal gear. Wildwater River Tours (206–357–5214) has white water raft trips on the Hoh River and a special rain forest raft float trip for $45 per person, which includes lunch; group rates are available.

KALALOCH LODGE

Address: HC 80, PO Box 1100, Forks, Washington 98331 (on U.S. 101 in the park, seventy miles north of Aberdeen/Hoquiam and thirty-five miles south of Forks; the lodge is perched on a bluff overlooking the Pacific Ocean).
Telephone: 206–962–2271.

Season: Year-round.
Accommodations: This is a great base if you want a mix of the beach, mountains, and rain forest. The lodge was built in 1953 to resemble an oceanside fishing village. The least expensive accommodations are the eight guest rooms in the main lodge (some have ocean views) and the "bluff cabins." Be aware that some of the lodge rooms are reported to be

noisy. Many of the bluff cabins have ocean views and all have kitchen facilities (utensils not included) and full baths (towels and bedding included).

Special Features: The main lodge has a coffee shop, a dining room with many Northwest seafood dishes, and a reading room. There is a small grocery store on site. The resort overlooks the beach, and the trail down is easy to negotiate. Beachcombers can collect driftwood, shells, agates, glass, and fish nets that have washed in from distant places. Bring kites, as the beach has great offshore winds. In April the beach usually is hopping with clammers. In late March or April you might be able to spot a pod of gray whales migrating. The water is too cold and dangerous for young children to swim in, but a small lagoon right in front of the lodge is ideal for paddling.

Cost: Mid-April to mid-May, all rooms $51 per night, double occupancy. During other months, lodge rooms $51 to $105 per night, double occupancy, depending on view; each additional person $10. You can only reserve rooms without an ocean view. Bluff cabins $81 to $105 per night, double occupancy, depending on view; each additional person $10. Children under five stay free.

Nearby: Protected beach coves farther north are ideal for summer swimming. This is a good base for day trips to the Hoh Rain Forest, a spectacular moss-hung rain forest in the park, or a walk along the three-mile boardwalk from Lake Ozette to remote beaches. Other excursions include a visit to the Makah Indian village at Neah Bay, where artifacts are on display. Also within easy access are the secluded beaches of the Kalaloch area, with sea stacks and tidal pools for viewing anemones and starfish.

LAKE QUINAULT LODGE

Address: PO Box 7, Quinault, Washington 98575 (from Hoquiam go north on U.S. 101 for forty miles to milepost 125; turn right onto South Shore Road and go two miles. The lodge overlooks Lake Quinault in the midst of one of the few rain forests in North America, in the heart of the park).
Telephone: 800–562–6672; 206–288–2571.

Season: Year-round.

Accommodations: The setting of this lodge is one of the best in the Olympic Peninsula. Built in 1926, it has a main lodge, lakeside rooms, and rooms with a lake view and/or a fireplace. The least expensive rooms, located in the main lodge, either share a bathroom between two rooms or have facilities down the hall. Some of these rooms have views of the parking lot instead of the lake, so be sure to inquire ahead of time.

Special Features: The lodge is geared especially to families. Adjacent to the pool there is a game room with equipment for horseshoeing, volleyball, and Frisbee, as well as pinball, Ping-Pong, and video games. Guests can play badminton and croquet on the meticulously kept lawn overlooking the lake. Canoes and paddleboats are for rent in the summer. Fishing on the lake is highly rated. The lodge's playground has swings, a see-saw, a slide, and rings. The lodge has a full-service restaurant. The staff at the lodge's front desk can inform you about the park's nature programs and will provide additional games and puzzles for indoor play. They also will help arrange baby-sitting; they even have rubber sheets for bed wetters!

Cost: Least expensive rooms $84 per night, double occupancy; each additional person $10. Children under five stay free. Two-night minimum stay on weekends. The lodge offers lots of special deals, including midweek or off-season specials, so it pays to inquire.

Nearby: Hiking trails through the rain forest start at the lodge; maps are available at the front desk.

RAIN FOREST RESORT VILLAGE

Address: Route 1, PO Box 40, Lake Quinault, Washington 98575 (at the southern gateway to Olympic National Park on Lake Quinault). **Telephone:** 800–562–0948; 206–288–2535.

Season: Year-round.

Accommodations: The resort's "fireplace cabins" have views of the lake; most are equipped with full kitchens and all have private baths (some have whirlpools). All bedding and towels are provided, along with daily housekeeping service. Cooking utensils are not provided. Rooms in the Village Inn are single or adjoining and have televisions and private baths. The least expensive accommodations are the rustic cabins; they are available only in the summer and are just for walk-in guests.

Special Features: The lake is ideal for canoeing, fishing, paddleboating, kite flying, and feeding the ducks.

Cost: Fireplace cabins $82 to $115 per night, double occupancy; rates depend on views and amenities. Village Inn rooms $70 per night, double occupancy. Each additional person $10 per night in cabins or rooms. Rustic cabin rates are significantly lower but cannot be reserved.

Nearby: The resort has trailheads leading through the Quinault Valley to the interior of the park.

LOG CABIN RESORT

Address: 6540 East Beach Road, Port Angeles, Washington 98362 (on Lake Crescent in Olympic National Park, eighteen miles from Port Angeles).
Telephone: 206–928–3245.

Season: Year-round.

Accommodations: The resort has lodge rooms with lake and mountain views that sleep four; these rooms have two queen-size beds and private bathrooms. A chalet located along the shoreline with lake and mountain views sleeps six and includes a small kitchen (no cooking or eating utensils provided), an outdoor barbecue, and a picnic table. Other accommodations include rustic cabins with kitchens and bare-bones camping log cabins (bring or rent bedding) with outdoor picnic tables and campfires.

Special Features: Restaurant, grocery store, and gift shop. The complex's marina rents canoes, rowboats, paddleboats, kayaks, and motorboats. There is a swimming area at the lake but no lifeguard. Campfire programs are scheduled regularly.

Cost: Lodge and chalet rooms $73 per night, double occupancy. Cabins with kitchens $63 per night, double occupancy; rustic cabins $53 per night, double occupancy. Each additional person age six and above $10. Camping log cabins $32 per night, double occupancy; each additional person $5; children ten and under stay free.

Nearby: Hiking, rowboating, and fishing on Lake Crescent; many picnic areas are around the lake. The trail to Marymere Falls, a spectacular ninety-foot waterfall, is a flat three-quarter-mile walk. The Hoh Rain Forest and the Kalaloch Beach area, with tide pools and clamming, are nearby. Other local beaches are Salt Creek, Park, and Rialto. Nearby Port Angeles has bowling, a public indoor pool, and rollerskating.

LAKE CRESCENT LODGE

Address: HC 62, Box 11, Port Angeles, Washington 98362 (on the shores of Lake Crescent on U.S. 101 in the park, twenty miles west of Port Angeles).
Telephone: 206–928–3211.

Season: May to October.

Accommodations: The lodge is a historic turn-of-the-century resort situated among giant fir and hemlock trees on the shores of deep blue Lake Crescent. There are rooms in the lodge, cottages with fireplaces from the 1930s (built for Franklin Roosevelt), modern motel rooms, and lake-view cottages. Many of the guests are older, but families are welcome.

Special Features: There's a nice beach at the lodge and on very warm days, swimming in Lake Crescent's cold water can be exhilarating. Rowboats are for rent. The dining room, which serves local seafood dishes, has high chairs, moderate prices, and so-so-food.

Cost: The least expensive accommodations are rooms in the historic lodge with shared bathrooms $68 per night, double occupancy; each additional person $10. Cribs or rollaway beds $10 per night.

Nearby: For warmer swimming it's a half-hour drive to the hot springs at Sol Duc. The short hike to majestic Marymere Falls is fun, as are fishing, hiking, beachcombing, and visiting the rain forests.

SOL DUC HOT SPRINGS RESORT

Address: PO 2169, Port Angeles, Washington 98362 (in a valley of 150-foot evergreen trees on the Soleduck River, thirty miles west of Port Angeles, twelve miles off U.S. 101).
Telephone: 206–327–3583.

Season: Mid-May through September. The hot springs are open only on weekends in April and October.

Accommodations: The resort has furnished cabins; some have kitchens. Modern one-room cabins have a full bath, heat, and either two double beds or one double bed and a sofabed.

Special Features: Three hot springs pools, swimming pool, toddler pool with lifeguards. Massages are available. There is also a family dining room, coffee shop, and grocery store.

Cost: Cabins $74 per night, double occupancy. Additional people age four and above $10; children under four stay free. Rates include use of the pools.

Nearby: Hiking along the well-maintained Olympic National Park trails and fishing for wild coho salmon, steelhead, and native rainbow trout.

HAWAII VOLCANOES NATIONAL PARK, HAWAII

According to legend, this park in the south-central part of the big island of Hawaii is the home of Pele, the Hawaiian goddess of fire. The Hawaiian goddess of the sea chased her from island to island, destroying each dwelling that Pele created. She finally came to Halemaumau, in Kilauea Caldera, where she lives today. She is said to preside over the local volcanoes, from the 13,796-foot Mauna Kea to Kilauea Crater, and is considered responsible for the eruptions and lava outpourings over the centuries.

Oval-shaped Kilauea Caldera is two and a half miles wide and about four hundred feet deep. Within it is Halemaumau Crater, where you can smell sulfur and hear steam hissing out of fissures in the rock. When Kilauea is erupting you can see seething lakes of molten rock, curtains of fire, and fountains of red-hot lava. Being this close to one of the world's most active volcanoes is the experience of a lifetime. For an eruption update, call 808–967–7977. Temporary road signs will direct you to safe vantage points whenever eruptions occur.

From the Kilauea Visitor Center, you can hike through or drive around the edge of the caldera. Also within the park are desert and rain forests; there are few places in the world where these dramatic extremes coexist. Mauna Loa, the world's tallest active volcano, is thirty-three miles northwest of the park's headquarters.

VOLCANO HOUSE

Address: PO Box 53, Volcano National Park, Volcano, Hawaii 96718 (at the rim of the Kilauea Caldera at approximately four thousand feet elevation).
Telephone: Information: 808–967–7321. For an eruption update call 808–967–7977.

Season: Year-round.
Accommodations: First built in 1846 as a thatched structure, the hotel has undergone many restorations and incarnations. Its forty-two rooms are currently furnished in a modern style with rare koa wood furniture and Hawaiian quilts. In 1935 *Ripley's Believe It or Not* claimed that the fire in the hotel's fireplace had burned continuously for sixty-one years.
Special Features: The Volcano House complex includes an art center and restaurant.
Cost: The least expensive accommodations are in the Ohia Wing; they do not have a crater view. Rooms $82 per night, double occupancy; each additional third and fourth person $10. Children twelve and under stay free in parents' rooms.
Nearby: Kilauea Caldera, the Kilauea Visitor Center.

NAMAKANI PAIO CAMPING CABINS

Address: PO Box 53, Volcano National Park, Volcano, Hawaii 96718 (three miles beyond the Volcano House [see above] at approximately four thousand feet elevation).
Telephone: Information: 808–967–7321. For an eruption update call 808–967–7977.

Season: Year-round.
Accommodations: Each cabin sleeps four with a double bed and two single bunk beds. There are electric lights, an outdoor picnic table, and

a barbecue grill. Guests provide their own charcoal and cooking utensils. There is a central bath and shower facility.

Special Features: This is part of a complex that also includes an art center and restaurant.

Cost: Cabins $33 per night; includes linens, towels, soap, and a blanket. Guests encouraged to bring an extra blanket or sleeping bag, as the cabins are not heated.

Nearby: Kilauea Caldera, the Kilauea Visitor Center.

ROCKY MOUNTAINS AND SOUTHWEST

GLACIER NATIONAL PARK, MONTANA

With crystal clear lakes and fifty ancient glaciers, Glacier National Park, along with its Canadian counterpart, Waterton Lakes National Park, spreads across 1.4 million acres of wilderness. All accommodations have easy access to hiking trails, picnic areas, ranger-naturalist programs, and boating activities on the park's many lakes. With seven hundred miles of back-country trails, you can even hike over the border into Canada.

Glacier Raft Company has a full range of programs from May through September, including white water raft trips (half day: adults $28, children $17), evening supper rides, and reasonably priced overnight raft trips on the Flathead River or through the Great Bear Wilderness. The company also has teamed up with the Bear Creek Ranch for reasonably priced combined horseback ride and raft excursions. Year-round reservations can be made by calling 800–332–9995.

Glacier Park Boats provides inexpensive boat tours and boat rentals from mid-June through September at Two Medicine Lake, Swiftcurrent Lake, St. Mary Lake, and Lake McDonald (call 406–888–5727 for information). There are riding stables at Many Glacier Stable (406–732–5597) and Lake McDonald Lodge (406–888–5670).

GRANITE PARK AND SPERRY CHALETS

Address: Belton Chalets, Southside U.S. Highway 2 East, West Glacier, Montana 59936 (in the park, near the Continental Divide. Granite Park Chalets are accessible only by a seven-mile contour hike along the Garden Wall on the Highline Trail from Logan Pass. Anticipate a four-hour walk in; you'll see spectacular panoramic views of rock formations, wildflowers, and occasional glimpses of mountain goats, sheep, and deer. Sperry Chalets are accessible only by a challenging

seven-mile hike beginning at Lake McDonald Lodge; allow four and
a half hours for the hike in).
Telephone: 406-888-5511.

Season: July through Labor Day.
Accommodations: These comfortable mountain hotels, built in 1914
of native stone, are reached only by hiking trails. They are ideal for those
who want to see the more remote parts of Glacier National Park on foot
or horseback without having to pack their food and bedding or for those
who want a degree of comfort at the end of the day. Both are on the
National Register of Historic Places and have landmark status. Nothing is
modern except the kitchens and shared outdoor restrooms. There are no
phones or electricity. Rooms are private; bedding, towels, soap, and can-
dles are provided. There are no showers or bathtubs; hot water for washing
is available in the restrooms.
Special Features: Mountain goats are daily visitors to the Sperry Chalets.
Cost: $74 per person per night. Children under twelve $60 per night.
Rates include three meals daily.
Nearby: Side trips from Granite Park Chalets are to Grinnel Glacier
Overlook (one and a half miles), Swiftcurrent Lookout (two and a half
miles), Ahern Pass (five miles), and Fifty Mountain (eleven and a half
miles). Side trips from the Sperry Chalets are to Sperry Glacier (three and
a half miles), Lincoln Peak (one mile), Lake Ellen Wilson (three miles),
and Gunsight Pass (five miles).

MANY GLACIER HOTEL

Address: Glacier Park Inc., Greyhound Tower, Station 1210, Phoenix,
Arizona 85077 (winter); East Glacier, Montana 59434-0147 (summer)
(hotel is on the shore of Swiftwater Lake, at the foot of Grinnell
Glacier).
Telephone: Mid-September to mid-May, 602-207-6000; mid-May to
mid-September, 406-226-5551.

Season: June through September.
Accommodations: Built in 1914, this historic Swiss-style hotel is the
park's largest resort.
Special Features: Broadway musicals, concerts, and sing-alongs by recruited college drama and music students entertain guests. There is a full-
service restaurant and a snack bar.
Cost: The least expensive rooms at this resort are the Evergreen rooms,
which sleep up to four people with either two double beds or one double
bed and two twin beds. They have a private bathroom and mountain

views: $82 for two; each additional person $5; children under twelve stay free in parents' rooms. Rollaway beds $5 per night; cribs $3 per night.
Nearby: Lake cruises, horseback riding, hiking.

LAKE McDONALD LODGE

Address: Glacier Park Inc., Greyhound Tower, Station 1210, Phoenix, Arizona 85077 (winter); East Glacier, Montana 59434-0147 (summer) (hotel is on the west side of the park, along Going to the Sun Road). Telephone: Mid-September to mid-May, 602–207–6000; mid-May to mid-September, 406–226–5551.

Season: June through September.
Accommodations: This complex of one hundred rooms has cabins, motel, and main lodge accommodations. Built in 1913, it has an Old West look and mood.
Special Features: Broadway musicals, concerts, and sing-alongs by recruited college drama and music students entertain guests. There is a full-service restaurant and a snack bar.
Cost: The least expensive rooms at this lodge complex are the motel rooms which sleep up to four people with either two double beds or one double bed and two twin beds. They have a private bathroom: $66 per night for two; each additional person $4. Cabins $54 for two; each additional person $4. Children under twelve stay free in parents' rooms. Rollaway beds $5 per night; cribs $3 per night.
Nearby: White water raft trips, lake cruises, horseback riding, hiking.

GLACIER PARK LODGE

Address: Glacier Park Inc., Greyhound Tower, Station 1210, Phoenix, Arizona 85077 (winter); East Glacier, Montana 59434-0147 (summer) (hotel is two miles east of the park, at the foot of Squaw Peak Mountain). Telephone: Mid-September to mid-May, 602–207–6000; mid-May to mid-September, 406–226–5551.

Season: June through September.
Accommodations: Built in 1913, this historic lodge has 155 rooms and a full range of activities. It is a gorgeous structure, supported by sixty enormous timbers that were five hundred years old when originally cut and set in place.

Special Features: Outdoor heated pool, nine-hole golf course.
Cost: The least expensive rooms at this lodge are the Evergreen rooms: $83 for two; each additional person $5. Children under twelve occupying a room with an adult stay free. Rollaway beds $5 per night; cribs $3 per night.
Nearby: Lake cruises, horseback riding, hiking.

VILLAGE INN

Address: Glacier Park Inc., Greyhound Tower, Station 1210, Phoenix, Arizona 85077 (winter); East Glacier, Montana 59434-0147 (summer) (hotel is just inside the park's west entrance in Apgar).
Telephone: Mid-September to mid-May; 602–207–6000; mid-May to mid-September; 406–226–5551.

Season: June through September.
Accommodations: Many of the thirty-six rooms in this modern inn overlooking Lake McDonald have kitchen facilities.
Cost: One-bedroom unit with kitchen $87 per night; each additional person $5. Children under twelve stay free in parents' rooms. Rollaway beds $5 per night; cribs $3 per night.
Nearby: Lake cruises, horseback riding, hiking.

RISING SUN MOTOR INN

Address: Glacier Park Inc., Greyhound Tower, Station 1210, Phoenix, Arizona 85077 (winter); East Glacier, Montana 59434-0147 (summer) (hotel is near Many Glacier Hotel, page 101).
Telephone: Mid-September to mid-May, 602–207–6000; mid-May to mid-September, 406–226–5551.

Season: June through September.
Accommodations: The complex includes a seventy-four room motel and cabin facility as well as a campground area with views of St. Mary's Lake.
Special Features: Camp store, coffee shop.
Cost: Motel room for two $66 per night; each additional person $4. Cabins $53 for two; each additional person $5. Children under twelve stay free in parents' rooms. Rollaway beds $5 per night; cribs $3 per night.
Nearby: Lake cruises, horseback riding, hiking.

SWIFTCURRENT MOTOR INN

Address: Glacier Park Inc., Greyhound Tower, Station 1210, Phoenix, Arizona 85077 (winter); East Glacier, Montana 59434-0147 (summer) (in the center of the park, near Swiftcurrent Lake).
Telephone: Mid-September to mid-May, 602–207–6000; mid-May to mid-September, 406–226–5551.

Season: June through September.
Accommodations: Eighty-eight motel rooms and cabin units.
Special Features: Camp store, coffee shop.
Cost: Motel room for two $66 per night. Motel room for two at Timberline Motel $58 per night. Each additional person $4. Two-bedroom cabin without bathroom $32 for two; each additional person $3. Children under twelve stay free in parents' rooms. Rollaway beds $5 per night; cribs $3 per night.
Nearby: Lake cruises, horseback riding, hiking.

BROWNIE'S GROCERY AND HOSTEL

Address: 1020 Montana Highway 49, Box 229, East Glacier Park, Montana 59434.
Telephone: 406–226–4426. Reservations are essential July through August. Phone reservations are accepted with eight-hours notice; call 800–662–7625.

Season: May through October.
Accommodations: A pleasant, two-story log building near hiking and biking trails, this thirty-bed hostel has two family rooms.
Special Features: Kitchen, laundry facilities, baggage storage area, and on-site parking. Linens are provided. The hostel is above a small grocery store.
Cost: AYH members $10 per night for adults; nonmembers $13. Children five to ten half price; kids under four stay free.
Nearby: A wide variety of hiking rails, naturalist-guided hikes, boat tours, and horseback trips are available nearby, as are the national park's living glaciers, rushing streams, tumbling waterfalls, towering peaks, and abundant wildlife.

KALISPELL/WHITEFISH HOME HOSTEL

Address: Call prior to arriving; the managers will give you directions. Located between Kalispell and Whitefish, twenty-five miles from the west gate of Glacier National Park. **Telephone:** 406–756–1908. Reservations are essential.

Season: Year-round.

Accommodations: This home hostel on six acres of land in the beautiful Flathead Valley has two family rooms; each have three beds. The hostel accommodates twelve guests.

Special Features: Shared kitchen, linen rental, baggage storage area, and on-site parking. Guests can borrow bicycles.

Cost: AYH members $10 per night for adults; nonmembers $13. Children five to ten are half price; kids under four stay free.

Nearby: Alpine skiing is twenty minutes away at the Big Mountain ski area.

GRAND TETON NATIONAL PARK, WYOMING

For those who want a real western-style adventure, a vacation in the Grand Tetons will most certainly fit the bill. Amid these spectacular craggy, cloud-high peaks, which seem to rise out of nowhere into the wide Wyoming sky, are many opportunities to fish, hike, ride horses, visit rodeos, and see some of the wild animals that today's children usually know only from books, including elk, cow moose, bison, bald eagles, and white pelicans.

The Tetons offer spectacular hiking for all abilities. Trail rides lasting from one hour ($15) to half a day ($28) are available at Jackson Lake Lodge and Colter Bay Corrals. Hearty cowboy breakfast rides or evening campfire rides on horseback ($24) or by wagon ($13) are great fun for kids eight and older. Check with the activities desk at Jackson Lake Lodge. Bar-T Ranch (307–733–5386) in Jackson leads a chuck wagon ride to a cowboy cookout complete with "Indians" pursuing the wagons.

Narrated cruises on Jackson Lake (including breakfast or an evening steak fry) range from $5.50 to $20. Check with the activities desk at Jackson Lake Lodge. Motorboats ($13 per hour), rowboats, and canoes ($7 per hour) are available for rent at the Colter Bay Marina. Try Teton Boating Company at 307–733–2703 for boat rides on Jenny Lake. Fishing on the park's clear, cold lakes and streams draws countless aficionados.

The Grand Teton Lodge Company leads river float trips down the Snake River in rubber rafts—a scenic, not white water, expedition. Their ten-mile trips cost $12.50 for kids six to sixteen and $22.50 for adults. Ask for details at Jenny Lake Lodge or Colter Bay Village. More extended family float trips on the mild and flat waters of the Snake River and on Jackson Lake (for children over four) and white water rapid trips (suitable for older children) are offered June through September by Outdoor Adventure River Specialists (209–736–4677). Many other guides lead half-day white water rafting trips on the lower section of the Snake. The chamber of commerce (209–223–0350; PO Box E, Jackson, Wyoming 83001) can send you a list.

Summertime alpine slide toboggans, a thrill for older kids, run down the slopes of Snow King Resort (307–733–5200). Just outside the park, kids love taking the tram ride in Teton Village or poking around the town of Jackson. There's an afternoon "shoot-out" in the town square and a twice-weekly town rodeo in the summer.

The Jackson Hole Golf and Tennis facility near the park's southern boundary is open to day guests and is renowned for its scenic and challenging eighteen-hole championship golf course ($36 per person). There is also a swimming pool ($5 per person) and tennis courts ($12 per one and a half hours).

JACKSON LAKE LODGE

Address: Grand Teton Lodge Company, PO Box 240, Moran, Wyoming 83013 (located in the heart of the park, on a bluff overlooking the marshlands of Willow Flats, with gorgeous views across Jackson Lake to the glacial tips of the Teton Range. In spite of its name, the lodge is not located on the lake). Telephone: 307–543–2811.

Season: Late May through September.

Accommodations: This full-service large resort hotel has 42 guest rooms in the main lodge and 340 rooms located on either side of the main building.

Special Features: Guests can swim in a large heated pool or go on organized float trips. There's a corral with many different trail rides, and there are many dining options. Moose can be observed from the lodge in the marshy area of Willow Flats.

Cost: The least expensive rooms are those in the main lodge: $83 per night, double occupancy; each additional person over twelve $7.50. Children twelve and under stay free in parents' rooms. Rollaway beds $7.50; cribs free.

Nearby: All of the park's activities are within easy reach.

COLTER BAY LOG CABINS

Address: Grand Teton Lodge Company, PO Box 240, Moran, Wyoming 83013 (in Colter Bay Village, near the shores of Jackson Lake).
Telephone: 307–543–2811.

Season: Mid-May through early October.
Accommodations: This complex has 209 log cabins with bathrooms that sleep up to six.
Special Features: Along the lakeshore is a beach and a full-service marina. In the village is a restaurant, grill, laundry facilities, sports shop, corral, and fully stocked grocery store. The village is popular with families.
Cost: Depending on size, one-room cabin with private bath $50 to $72 per night, double occupancy. Two rooms with connecting bath for up to four people $73 to $97 per night, double occupancy, depending on size. Each additional person over twelve $7.50. Children under twelve stay free in parents' rooms. Rollaways $7.50 per night; cribs free.
Nearby: Registered cabin guests can use the pool at Jackson Lake Lodge (five miles away). Float trips, the Indian Arts Museum, trail rides at the Colter Bay Corrals, and guided fishing are all within easy reach. Nearby is the National Park Service amphitheater, with naturalist programs and guided nature hikes.

COLTER BAY TENT CABINS

Address: Grand Teton Lodge Company, PO Box 240, Moran, Wyoming 83013 (in Colter Bay Village).
Telephone: 307–543–2811.

Season: Early June to early September.
Accommodations: Constructed of canvas and logs, each tent cabin has an outdoor grill, wood stove, two double-decker bunks (without bedding), table, and benches. Sleeping bags, cooking utensils, and ice chests can be rented at a central facility, where there is also a shared restroom.
Special Features: Along the lakeshore is a beach and a full-service marina. In the village is a restaurant, grill, laundry facilities, sports shop, corral, and fully stocked grocery store. The village is popular with families.
Cost: Cabins $20 per night, double occupancy; each additional person over twelve $2.50. Cots $4 per night.
Nearby: Float trips, trail rides at the Colter Bay Corrals, the Indian Arts Museum, and guided fishing are all within easy reach. Also nearby is the

National Park Service amphitheater, with naturalist programs and guided nature hikes.

SIGNAL MOUNTAIN LODGE

Address: PO Box 50, Moran, Wyoming 83013 (on Jackson Lake). Telephone: 307–543–2831.

Season: Mother's Day through the first Sunday in October. Make reservations three to four months in advance.

Accommodations: Log cabins with one or two rooms or lodge-style rooms set in the trees are available. Lodge-style rooms sleep up to four with two queen-size beds and a small refrigerator. If you have a large group, family bungalows on the waterfront are a good value, as they accommodate up to ten people and have large decks, outdoor barbecues, living rooms, a bedroom, and a kitchen. Bedding is included.

Special Features: Staff will arrange for Snake River float trips (adults $22, children $15) and guided lake fishing ($35 per hour). The resort has its own marina and rents rowboats, canoes, and paddleboats for $5 per hour and motorboats for $60 per half day. There is also a restaurant and a convenience store.

Cost: The least expensive accommodations at this resort are the log cabins with one or two rooms. One-room cabin with one double and one twin bed $63 per night; with two double beds $72 per night. Lodge-style rooms $79 per night, double occupancy; each additional person $7.50. Family bungalows with kitchens on the waterfront for up to ten people $110 per night, double occupancy; each additional person $7.50.

Nearby: All the park's activities are within easy reach.

HOSTEL X

Address: 3600 McCollister Drive, Box 546, Teton Village, Wyoming 83025 (in Teton Village, eight miles from the national park). Telephone: 307–733–3415. Reservations are essential; you can reserve by phone or fax (307–739–1142) with a credit card.

Season: June through September.

Accommodations: This hostel operates as a ski lodge in winter and offers discount rates during the summer season. Family rooms available.

Special Features: Laundry facilities, baggage storage, on-site parking, game room, television room, and nightly movies.

Cost: AYH members $15 per night for adults; nonmembers $18. Children five to ten half price; kids under four stay free.

Nearby: The Snake River is great for rafting.

ELK REFUGE INN

Address: PO Box 2834, Jackson Hole, Wyoming 83001 (one mile
north of Jackson).
Telephone: 307–733–3582.

Season: Year-round.
Accommodations: A twenty-two unit motel with ten kitchen units. Each
room has a full bath, color television, phone, and private patio with valley
views.
Special Features: The inn is adjacent to the National Elk Refuge, which
attracts eight thousand elk in winter and a variety of birds year-round.
The inn also has horse corrals and a pasture, picnic tables, and barbecue
grills. The butte behind the inn is the winter home for mule deer, which
often roam the grounds.
Cost: Kitchen rooms $73 per night; motel rooms $68 to $78 per night
in summer, $39 to $54 per night in fall and winter. Children under twelve
stay free in their parents' room.
Nearby: Grand Teton and Yellowstone national parks, Snake River float
trips, horseback riding, sailboarding, two top-rated golf courses, tennis,
fishing, and biking. The inn is two miles from the Snow King ski area and
fourteen miles from the Jackson Hole ski area.

YELLOWSTONE NATIONAL PARK, WYOMING

Larger than the states of Rhode Island and Delaware combined, Yellowstone was the world's first national park. Get ready to hold your nose at
its steaming, sulphurous mud holes. Memorable features include Old Faithful, the world's most famous geyser, which sends thousands of gallons of
water thundering into the sky—and, unfortunately, the summer crowds.
To avoid the rush, try for a May, early June, or fall visit. Summer will not
be as much of a problem if you make reservations well in advance and
hit the popular sites early in the day.

Yellowstone has a variety of accommodations and activities to fit any
family's budget. The park's western-style activities include horseback riding, stagecoach rides, and dinner cookouts via covered wagon or horseback. Guided horseback rides for children age eight and older (one hour
$11, two hours $20) are available June through August at Mammoth,
Roosevelt, and Canyon. An Old West cookout and stagecoach rides are
available at Roosevelt (see Roosevelt Lodge, pages 113–114).

Yellowstone Lake has excellent fishing and a marina with boat rentals
(rowboats, outboards, and charters). One-hour sightseeing cruises June
through September on Yellowstone Lake cost $3.50 for children five
through eleven, $6.50 for adults. Rowboat rentals are $4 per hour,

outboards are $20 per hour; cabin cruisers can be chartered for $34 per hour (for one to six people).

Winter activities include cross-country skiing, snowmobiling, and guided tours in enclosed snow coaches. Call 307–344–7311 for information about all activities.

Note: In addition to the lodgings listed below, see pages 165–166 for a description of the Cliff Lake Lodge, a lakefront resort near Yellowstone featured in the chapter on lake and river vacations.

CANYON LODGE AND CABINS

Address: Yellowstone National Park, Wyoming 82190 (near the spectacular Grand Canyon of the Yellowstone, Hayden Valley, and Lower Falls, which are twice as tall as Niagara Falls). Telephone: 307–344–7311.

Season: Mid-June through early September.

Accommodations: All accommodations here are single-story units in clusters of four or more, with private bathrooms.

Special Features: The main lodge has a dining room and a cafeteria. Horseback rides (one and two hours) are available at its corrals from mid-June through August.

Cost: Cabins with private bathrooms $44 to $74 per night, double occupancy; additional person or bed $7 per night. Children eleven and under stay free.

GRANT VILLAGE

Address: Yellowstone National Park, Wyoming 82190 (situated on the shore of Yellowstone Lake). Telephone: 307–344–7311.

Season: Early June through late September.

Accommodations: This is the park's newest and southernmost facility, completed in 1984. All accommodations have private bathrooms with showers.

Special Features: Summer marina activities include scenic cruises and hourly outboard and rowboat rentals. Guided fishing boats are available for charter. A dining room overlooks the lake and a steak house is perched over the water's edge.

Cost: Hotel rooms $58 to $63 per night, double occupancy; additional person or bed $7 per night. Children eleven and under stay free.

LAKE YELLOWSTONE HOTEL AND CABINS

Address: Yellowstone National Park, Wyoming 82190 (situated near Bridge Bay Marina and the shores of Yellowstone Lake).
Telephone: 307–344–7311.

Season: Late May through late September.

Accommodations: A classic old hotel, the lodge was completed in 1891 and remodeled in 1903 with its current colonial look. Fifty-foot Ionic columns are its trademark. Accommodations at this deluxe hotel include moderately priced private cabins. All have their own baths. Cabins sleep up to five with two double beds and a rollaway bed.

Special Features: Summer marina activities include scenic cruises and hourly outboard and rowboat rentals. Guided fishing boats are available for charter. There is a lake-view dining room.

Cost: "Frontier" cabins with private bathrooms $53 per night, double occupancy. Additional person or bed $7 per night; children eleven and under stay free.

LAKE LODGE AND CABINS

Address: Yellowstone National Park, Wyoming 82190 (situated near Bridge Bay Marina and the shores of Yellowstone Lake, within walking distance of the Lake Yellowstone Hotel).
Telephone: 307–344–7311.

Season: May to March.

Accommodations: The rustic lodge is built of logs and nestled in the trees with a magnificent view of the lake and surrounding mountains. All accommodations are cabins. The "western" and "frontier" cabins have private bathrooms with showers.

Special Features: Summer marina activities include scenic cruises and hourly outboard and rowboat rentals. Guided fishing boats are available for charter. The central lodge has a cafeteria.

Cost: Western cabins $74 per night, double occupancy; frontier cabins $42 per night. Additional person or bed $7 per night; children eleven and under stay free.

MAMMOTH HOT SPRINGS HOTEL AND CABINS

Address: Yellowstone National Park, Wyoming 82190 (in the region of Mammoth Hot Springs, a thermal area where abundant hot springs have formed the tinted limestone terraces).
Telephone: 307–344–7311.

Season: Mid-December to February, late May to mid-September.
Accommodations: Built in 1937, the hotel has cottage-type cabins as well as regular hotel rooms. Four of the cabin units have private hot tubs. Frontier cabins sleep up to five with two double beds and a rollaway bed. Budget cabins sleep up to four and have a central, shared bathroom. Linens and towels are included.
Special Features: One- and two-hour guided horseback rides are available from late May to mid-September. The hotel's Map Room contains a large wooden map of the United States made of fifteen different woods from nine countries. There is also a full dining room.
Cost: Although the hotel is expensive, moderately priced hotel rooms are available for $35 to $55 per night, double occupancy. Cabins $27 to $53 per night, double occupancy. Rates vary depending on whether rooms have a private bathroom. Additional person or bed $7 per night; children eleven and under stay free.

OLD FAITHFUL INN

Address: Yellowstone National Park, Wyoming 82190 (in close proximity to Old Faithful).
Telephone: 307–344–7311.

Season: May through mid-October.
Accommodations: Built in 1903 of local logs and stone and recently designated as a national historic landmark, the original hotel with its atrium lobby and massive four-sided fireplace is the largest known log structure of its kind.
Special Features: Restaurant.
Cost: Although the hotel is expensive, moderately priced rooms with private baths are available for $57 to $73 per night, double occupancy. Rooms without private baths are $35 per night, double occupancy. Additional person or bed $7 per night; children eleven and under stay free.

OLD FAITHFUL LODGE AND CABINS

Address: Yellowstone National Park, Wyoming 82190 (in close proximity to Old Faithful).
Telephone: 307–344–7311.

Season: Late May through mid-September.
Accommodations: Rebuilt in 1927, these vintage cabins have private baths or shared bathrooms a short walk away. Frontier cabins will sleep up to five with two double beds and a rollaway bed. Family cabins also sleep up to five and have a toilet and sink in the room.
Special Features: The lodge's lobby has a giant fireplace and a spectacular view of Old Faithful.
Cost: Cabins $21 to $34 per night, double occupancy, depending on shared or private bathroom; additional person or bed $7 per night. Children eleven and under stay free.

OLD FAITHFUL SNOW LODGE CABINS

Address: Yellowstone National Park, Wyoming 82190 (near Old Faithful).
Telephone: 307–344–7311.

Season: Mid-December through mid-March; late May through late October.
Accommodations: This is an intimate facility with rooms and cabins.
Special Features: The main lodge has a dining room.
Cost: Hotel rooms with shared baths $35 per night, double occupancy. Cabins $53 to $73 per night, double occupancy, depending on shared or private bathroom. Additional person or bed $7 per night; children eleven and under stay free.

ROOSEVELT LODGE AND CABINS

Address: Yellowstone National Park, Wyoming 82190 (in the northeast region of the park).
Telephone: 307–344–7311.

Season: Early June through early September.
Accommodations: So named because it was a favorite campsite of President Teddy Roosevelt, this lodge retains the rustic charm of another era. There are a limited number of rustic cabins—most are "Rough Riders," with wood-burning stoves and no bathrooms, or rustic shelters, which

are the least expensive in the park. Rustic shelters have no bathrooms or running water. There is a central bathhouse. No linens or towels are provided. There is wood heat. Frontier cabins have electric heat and full baths. The main lodge has a giant fireplace at each end and a cozy atmosphere.

Special Features: Roosevelt Corral offers horseback riding (one- and two-hour rides) June to August. Summer stagecoach rides offer families a jaunt through rolling sagebrush-covered hills. The lodge also serves as the departure point for the Old West Cookout, a steak dinner cookout via wagons or horses through the mountains to historic Yancey's Hole, located two miles away (June through August); prices range from $16.50 to $36 per person, depending on mode of transportation and age of child. Children under five are free.

Cost: Cabins with private bath $53 per night, double occupancy; "family" cabins with toilet and sink $37 per night, double occupancy. Budget, or Rough Rider cabins with bath facilities nearby $21 per night, double occupancy; rustic shelters with bath facilities nearby $19 per night, double occupancy. Additional person or bed $7 per night; children eleven and under stay free.

ROCKY MOUNTAIN NATIONAL PARK, COLORADO

Rocky Mountain National Park is less than a two-hours' drive from Denver but it seems worlds away with three hundred miles of hiking trails plus wildlife, including mules, deer, elk, bighorn sheep, coyotes, black bears, mountain lions, and bobcats. Families can choose from a range of inexpensive accommodations and activities. To start, at the Park Village North (at the park's entrance on U.S. 34) young kids can ride a miniature train and climb the park's observation tower.

In Estes Park, just outside the national park, horseback and pony rides are available at the National Park Village Stables (303–586–5269), Sombrero Stables (303–586–4577), and Cowpoke Corner Corral (303–586–5890), and at Hi Country Stables in the park at Glacier Creek and Moraine Park (303–586–3244). River rafting is available through Rapid Transit Rafting (303–586–8852). At Estes Ride-A-Kart (303–586–6495) there are go-carts, bumper boats, and a miniature train. Golfing is available at Regulation 9 (303–586–8146) or at two public courses. In town there is an aerial tramway (303–586–3675). Dick's Rock Museum (303–586–4180) has rocks, geodes, and crystals.

The Estes Park Health Club (303–586–2223) has racquetball, Nautilus equipment, an indoor track, and a hot tub. The Estes Park Aquatic Center (303–586–2340) has an Olympic-size pool, kiddie pool, diving tank, and lap areas. Water Tube Express has three hundred wet and wild feet of loops and drops on its water slide (Moraine Avenue West and U.S. 36).

Putt through caves and under waterfalls at Tiny Town Miniature Golf (303–586–6333) or at the Cascade Creek Mini-Golf (303–586–6495). You can rent all the equipment you need for boating, fishing, or sailboarding at the Lake Estes Marina (303–586–2011).

A helpful book to order before you go is *A Family Guide to Rocky Mountain National Park* by Lisa Evan (Seattle: The Mountaineers, 1991; $12.95), which lists family hikes and activities. It is available from the Rocky Mountain Nature Association, Estes Park, Colorado 80517, 303–586–3565.

Note: in addition to the lodgings listed below, there are two family camps adjoining Rocky Mountain National Park in a magnificent alpine setting. Details about these accommodations, the YMCA of the Rockies at Estes Park Center and at Snow Mountain Ranch, are on pages 20–22 in the family camps chapter.

MACHIN'S COTTAGES IN THE PINES

Address: PO Box 2687, 2450 Eagle Cliff Road, Estes Park, Colorado 80517 (located within the park, three miles from downtown Estes Park).
Telephone: 303–586–4276.

Season: Mid-May to early October.

Accommodations: Seventeen secluded cottages are situated among tall pines on fourteen shaded acres. There are one-, two-, and three-bedroom units; each has a combination tub-shower, gas heat, a fully equipped kitchen, cable TV, a fireplace, and its own private picnic area with charcoal grill, table, and lawn chairs. Bedding is included; high chairs, cribs, and bed rails are available for a small fee.

Special Features: Guests can observe many forms of wildlife. There are many safe areas for kids to play, including a well-equipped playground. Shuffleboard and horseshoes are available for adults.

Cost: Six of the cottages cost under $577 per week. Cabin 7, which sleeps up to three people, $63 per night, $410 per week, double occupancy; each additional person $8 per night. Four cabins that sleep up to six people $88 per night, $572 per week for four; each additional person $8 per night. Babies under one year stay free. Extra beds or cribs $2 per day. Two-night minimum stay.

Nearby: The cottages are one-eighth of a mile from a small brook and a one-and-a-quarter-mile hiking trail that goes through Beaver Meadows to the spectacular mountain valley of Moraine Park. From there there are many other national park trails. Estes Park (ten minutes away) has shops, grocery stores, laundry facilities, a golf course, a swimming pool, and tennis courts (activities in Estes Park are described on pages 21–22). There are

several stables nearby, and trout fishing is available in the many lakes and
streams in the area.

MILES MOTEL AND COTTAGES

**Address: 1250 South St. Vrain Avenue, Long's Peak Route, Estes Park,
Colorado 80517 (in a residential area off State Biway 7).
Telephone: 303–586–3185.**

Season: Year-round.

Accommodations: Three acres of land amid tranquil mountains surround the motel's fully equipped housekeeping units, condominiums, and
motel units.

Special Features: Outdoor heated swimming pool (in season), playground, and picnic area under the trees. Rooms have color TV and daily
housekeeping service for all accommodations.

Cost: One-bedroom units $69 to $79 per night for four people, depending on season. Two-bedroom units, which sleep up to six, $70 to
$84 per night for four people, $78 to $91 per night for five, $85 to $99
per night for six, depending on season. Additional people $7 per night;
cribs or rollaways $4 per night.

Nearby: Two lakes, municipal swimming pool, horse show arena, country music theater, restaurants, shopping center, tennis courts, and bowling
alley are close by. There is a paved path from the motel to downtown
Estes Park. Rocky Mountain National Park, horseback riding, and skiing
are a short drive away.

TRAILS WEST ON THE RIVER

**Address: 1710 Fall River Road, Box 1631, Estes Park, Colorado 80517
(on U.S. 34 West, midway between the village of Estes Park and
Rocky Mountain National Park).
Telephone: 303–586–4629.**

Season: Year-round. Reservations are essential during holidays and the
peak season, May through October.

Accommodations: Cabins are located along the Fall River and have a
private balcony or a river-view patio. Each has a fireplace, color TV, and
refrigerator. Fully equipped kitchen units with outdoor barbecues also are
available.

Special Features: An outdoor hot tub overlooks the river.

Cost: Least expensive cabins $81 per night for three people and $88
per night for four; children under three stay free. Portacribs $2 per night.
Housekeeping service $10 per night.

Nearby: See the descriptions of Estes Park and Rocky Mountain National Park on pages 114–115.

VALHALLA RESORT

Address: PO Box 1439, Estes Park, Colorado 80517 (right on the edge of the park, off Highway 66).
Telephone: 303–586–3284.

Season: Year-round.
Accommodations: Each cabin has a living room with a fireplace, color TV with cable, a fully equipped kitchen, a bath with tub or shower, beds of various sizes and numbers, a private deck with barbecue grill, and outdoor furniture.
Special Features: Guests can hike into the national park right from their cabin door. There is a heated outdoor swimming pool and a hot tub, miniature golf, shuffleboard, Ping-Pong, and a launderette. A golf package is available at two local mountain courses, as is a ski package at the Eldora Mountain Resort.
Cost: In summer, cabins for four people $81 to $91 per night, $525 to $594 per week; additional person $12 per night. There is an $8 per night charge for cribs, but if you bring your own, babies stay free. Cabins that sleep as many as twelve are available. Continental breakfast included. Rates are lower from mid-October to Memorial Day. Five-night minimum stay in summer and from Christmas through New Year's.
Nearby: See the descriptions of Estes Park and Rocky Mountain National Park on pages 114–115.

H-BAR-G RANCH HOSTEL

Address: 3500 H-Bar-G Road, PO Box 1260, Estes Park, Colorado 80517 (adjacent to the park in the Roosevelt National Forest).
Telephone: 303–586–3688. Reservations are essential in July and August. Phone reservations are accepted with a credit card.

Season: June through mid-September.
Accommodations: A former dude ranch, this 130-bed hostel has family rooms available. At an altitude of eighty-two hundred feet it offers a stunning view of the park's entire front range. The history of the ranch, which dates back to 1892, is captured in a collection of photographs and other memorabilia displayed in the hostel's common room.
Special Features: Kitchen, linen rental; rental cars are available; tennis, volleyball, and hiking on the grounds. The hostel also provides visitors

with information about nearby attractions, including old mining towns and the Arapahoe-Roosevelt National Forest.

Cost: AYH members $7.50 per night for adults; nonmembers $10.50. Children five to ten half price; children four and under stay free.

Nearby: The hostel manager shuttles guests to and from town. In addition to the park's diverse hiking trails, bike trails are close by.

SHADOWCLIFF HOSTEL

Address: 405 Summerland Road, PO Box 658, Grand Lake, Colorado 80447 (adjacent to the park next to North Inlet Stream, overlooking Grand Lake Village and the Colorado Great Lakes area). Telephone: 303–627–9220. Reservations are recommended; phone reservations are accepted with a credit card.

Season: June through September.

Accommodations: This thirty-two bed hostel, perched on a cliff overlooking Grand Lake Village, has family rooms.

Special Features: Kitchen, linen rental, meal service, on-site parking.

Cost: AYH members $7.50 per night for adults; nonmembers $10.50. Children five to ten half price; children four and under stay free.

Nearby: The area's many lakes and streams provide great places for fishing, sailing, and canoeing. Grand Lake and Granby Reservoir are popular in the summer. Cycling, hiking in the national park, and golf courses are close by.

MOAB, ARCHES, AND CANYONLANDS NATIONAL PARKS, UTAH

Dinosaurs once roamed the rocks and prehistoric earthscapes of the southeastern corner of Utah, from Moab to the San Juan River, an area that now awaits adventure-seeking families. Arches and Canyonlands are down the road from each other; together they form a landscape in which the earth's crust reveals itself in layer upon layer of sedimentary rock, stacked and swirled into strange spires and pinnacles. Spring and fall are the best times to visit, as summer temperatures can top one hundred degrees. The city of Moab is the gateway to these parks.

Activities in Arches

Trails lead off from the eighteen-mile park road. One of the best for young children is the walk to Sand Dune Arch; it is short and flat but thrilling. At one point, you squeeze through a crevasse so narrow, your shoulders barely fit. Youngsters also enjoy the quick hike around Balanced Rock, a huge boulder (the size of sixteen hundred cars) that teeters atop an eroding stone pedestal.

Griffith River Expeditions (800–332–2439; from Colorado call 800–332–3200) provides one- to ten-day white water raft trips and river float trips for families and groups May through October. Lin Ottinger Tours (801–259–7312) leads guided tours of the park by jeep. Its shop at 600 North Main Street in Moab is a treasure chest for rock hounds and geology buffs. For under $10 kids can buy rare mastodon teeth or a chunk of petrified dinosaur bone. World Wide River Expeditions (801–566–2662) leads one- to six-day river-rafting and float trips from late May through August. Niskanen and Jones Tag-along Tours (801–259–8946) also leads river-rafting and float trips from mid-April through mid-October and year-round four-wheel-drive jeep trips. For trail rides, pack trips, and horseback riding call Horsehead Pack Trips (801–259–8575).

Activities in Canyonlands
Young science buffs will enjoy the short hike to Upheaval Dome; one theory asserts that the dome's giant crater was formed by the impact of an ancient meteorite. All of the businesses listed above in Arches also run trips in Canyonlands. Adrift Adventures in Canyonlands (801–485–5978) leads year-round float river-rafting trips, guided fishing expeditions, and trail rides. Colorado River and Trail Expeditions (801–261–1789) leads guided white water raft trips May through September.

We found the canoe treks offered by Tex's Riverways (PO Box 67, Moab, Utah 84532, 801–259–5101) to be an especially good deal. Tex's offers canoe treks on the Green and Colorado rivers through desert canyons, including the remote and wild parts of Stillwater Canyon in Canyonlands. Floats on the Green River last from four to ten days; the floating is safe and the water calm, especially in July and August. You are ferried up the river to your starting point either by ground shuttle or by jet boat. The Colorado River floats are shorter, lasting from a half day to three days, and a wide variety of trips take you through natural arches, Indian ruins, and scenic canyons. Deer, beaver, desert bighorn sheep, coyotes, and birds commonly are seen. The Labyrinth Canyon of the Green River trip (four to five days) costs $40 per person by ground shuttle and $15 per day for the canoe, paddles, and life vests. Stillwater Canyon trips through Canyonlands National Parks past Indian ruins and Anasazi Indian petroglyphs costs $105 per person by jetboat and ground shuttle and $15 per day for canoe, paddles, and vests.

Mountain Biking in Moab
Moab has long been a taking-off point for Arches and Canyonlands national parks, but in the past few years it has hit the map as the mountain bike center of North America. Not only is its slick-rock bike trail a demanding, technically thrilling route, but it also runs through magnificent high desert

country that includes canyons, unusual rock formations, and dramatic drop-offs. Its mountain bike competitions are world famous, and mountain bike enthusiasts from all over the world come to try this challenging trail. If your children love to ride but are not up to the demands of this particular trail, there are plenty of other great rides to try. The U.S. Bureau of Land Management's public lands have marked trails and dirt roads. Be sure to stay on roads, trails, slick rock, or sand, as the fragile desert environment takes a beating from bike tires; it can take several years to recover from damage. There are helpful mountain-biking maps and books available at local bike shops and bookshops in Moab. One helpful map published by Trails Illustrated color codes the trails according to degree of difficulty.

Spring and fall are the best times to ride in Moab, as this high desert location gets extremely hot in the summer. Bring plenty of water whenever you go. Several outfitters rent mountain bikes, or you can bring your own; shuttle services are available to take you to the top of a trailhead or pick you up at the bottom. Rent bikes at Poison Spider Bicycles (487 North Main Street, Moab, 800–635–1792 or 801–259–7882) for $22 to $26 per day; cost includes helmet, rear rack, two water bottle cages, and complimentary water bottle. The shop also repairs bikes and sells parts and accessories.

Arrowhead Shuttle Service (2831 Cactus Road, Moab, 801–259–7356) will drop you off at your beginning point and then drive your car to your final destination. The cost depends on how far you go. Day-long trips cost about $25, two-day trips $50. Shuttles are available for bikers, rafters, canoeists, hikers, and anyone else who needs a ride. Another shuttle service, called 259-TAXI, run by Hugh Glass (801–259–8294 or 801–259–7474) has raft, canoe, and mountain bike shuttle services. Prices vary, depending on the number of people shuttled and the distance traveled. The service can take up to twelve passengers and equipment to the starting point of your bike or boat trip so that you can ride or float back to your own car, or they can move your vehicle from the starting point of your trip to the ending point. Bike fees are $10 to $50; the more passengers you have, the lower the rates.

Activities in and near Moab

Slam on the brakes! Now back up, get out of the car, and pay to see the five-thousand-square-foot "tribute to Albert and Gladys Christenson" carved and sculpted out of the rocky cliff outside of Moab. This World Famous Hole 'N The Rock (fifteen miles south of Moab on La Sal Route on U.S. 191, 801–686–2250) was an intensive project of Albert's; he spent twelve years on these fourteen rooms, excavating fifty thousand cubic feet of sandstone.

In Moab is the Hollywood Stuntmen's Hall of Fame (801–259–6100), an organization devoted to preserving the history of the stunt professions; it features exhibits devoted to stunts from Indiana Jones and John Wayne films. A theater shows videos of outstanding action films and old-time serials.

About two hours from Moab, along U.S. 191 en route to Bluff, Newspaper Rock State Park on Utah 211 makes a fun side trip. Its face is covered with ancient petroglyphs and pictographs of deer, bison, hunters on horseback, lizards, and snakes. The Cedars Historical Monument in Blanding has excavated Anasazi dwellings that kids can climb through. The Anasazi Indians lived in the region from 1220 B.C. and disappeared mysteriously in the 1300s.

Hovenweek National Monument, which is a two-hour round-trip drive west from U.S. 191, has a self-guided hike through a canyon of stone towers where Anasazi Indians lived. Think twice if you have tired kids; the road is bumpy and dusty. The monument has a junior ranger program.

No bones about it: Vernal, a few hours' drive from Moab in the northeastern part of the state, is the dinosaur capital of the world. Dinosaur National Monument, twenty miles east of Vernal, has a fossil bone deposit in a sandbar of an ancient river. At the Dinosaur Quarry you can see the fossilized remains of more than two thousand bones in relief in the two-hundred-foot-long wall. Other exhibits and displays explain the life and times of the dinosaurs whose remains were preserved in the quarry. Tours are available.

The Dinosaur Gardens in Vernal have life-size replicas of such dinosaur superstars as Tyrannosaurus Rex, Brontosaurus, Stegasaurus, and "Dinah," a twelve-foot-tall orange dinosaur that wanders around the grounds posing for pictures with children. Adjoining the gardens is the Utah Field House of Natural History, which offers a walking tour through re-created prehistoric and geologic time with Indian artifacts, fossils, rocks, and minerals. Kids will enjoy re-created dinosaurs "Big Tooth," "Thunder Lizard," and "Run Faster." Don't miss the museum's gift shop, where for $1 a machine will crush a fresh penny into a copper medal bearing a likeness of T. Rex. If you visit in the evening the statues are lit with colored lights; at Christmas they are draped with tiny Christmas lights.

RECAPTURE LODGE AND PIONEER HOUSE

Address: Box 309, Bluff, Utah 84512 (close to the Four Corners, where the borders of Utah, Arizona, New Mexico, and Colorado meet. Bluff is about 85 miles south of Canyonlands and 115 miles south of Arches. Monument Valley is forty-eight miles away). Telephone: 801–672–2281. This is a jumping-off point for river rafters, llama trekkers, and bird watchers, so reserve well in advance.

Season: Year-round.
Accommodations: This motel has a friendly, homey, lodgelike ambience. Its Pioneer House is on the National Register of Historic Places.

There are twenty-eight rooms in the main lodge and six in Pioneer House. The lodge has motel rooms and one-bedroom kitchenette units that sleep four in a queen-size bed and a sleeper sofa. Pioneer House has an apartment that sleeps up to ten and six private rooms that sleep two to six people.

Special Features: The lodge offers a geology slide show and geologist-guided tours; overnight llama packing; an outdoor pool; a playground; vehicle shuttles for river runners, hikers, and bicyclists, and laundry facilities. Adventurous families can lease a llama to carry their gear for a day or an overnight backpacking trip. Your hosts will give you topographical maps and suggest places to go. Kids can lead llamas on lunchtime treks to ruins—a great motivator for kids who hate to hike! Mountain bike rentals also are available, as are four-wheel-drive tours of Monument Valley and the surrounding area.

Cost: One-bedroom motel units with kitchenettes and private rooms in the Pioneer House $46 to $50 per night for a family of four. Their Pioneer House apartment, which sleeps ten, $75 per night for four people; each additional person $6.

Bicycles are $15 for half day, $20 for full day. Llama treks $25 per llama per day. Overnight llama pack trips $125 per person per day; includes all meals. Interpretive tours of area $60 per day per person; shorter tours $40 per person. Four-wheel-drive tours $60 per person; includes lunch at a Navajo camp.

Nearby: You can hike to the Navajo Indian Reservation and Fourteen Window Ruin, a one-thousand-year-old Anasazi cliff dwelling, reached by a creaky suspension bridge over the San Juan River. The San Jaun River runs through town and borders one edge of the lodge. Kids can play in and around the river. Comb Ridge, an easy walk from the lodge, has a pioneer cemetery; Sand Island, four miles away, features petroglyphs and a good swimming area.

Wild River Expeditions (PO Box 118, Bluff, Utah 84512, 800–422–7654 or 801–672–2244) offers day-long white water raft trips down the San Juan River ($70 per adult, $54 per child) past Anasazi Indian rock art and ruins as well as unique geologic features. For more activities in this general area, see pages 118–121.

PACK CREEK RANCH

Address: Box 1270, Moab, Utah 84532 (ranch is in the foothills of the La Sal Mountains, about ten miles southeast of Moab; Moab is thirty-five miles from Canyonlands).
Telephone: 801–259–5505.

Season: Year-round. Special activities are organized for Thanksgiving and Christmas. The restaurant is closed in November and December, so guests cook for themselves.

Accommodations: The ranch has eleven rough-hewn log cabins on three hundred acres. Several are large enough to sleep a family of four; one can accommodate ten people. Cabins have stone fireplaces and books; most have kitchens. The cabin for four has sleeping alcoves where kids can bunk down under the rafters, with a separate room for parents.

Special Features: Swimming pool, Jacuzzi, sauna, and a massage room (massages cost extra), and twenty-two horses that guests can ride. The ranch specializes in three- to four-night guided pack trips through the Grand Gulch Primitive Area, known for its Anasazi Indian ruins. Kids six and under must ride with an adult.

Cost: In mid-March through October, the least expensive accommodations are in the Orchard House: $84 per night per adult, children one to twelve $63 per night, plus tax and gratuity (5 percent for rooms, 15 percent for meals). Rates include breakfast, lunch, dinner, and trail rides. One-time crib fee $10. Winter rates $58 to $79 per night for adults, depending on room; children $10 less.

Nearby: Hiking in the national parks, raft trips, jet boat tours, four-wheel-drive tour of Canyonlands, Lake Powell tours, guided cross-country ski tours at Pack Creek, mountain biking. See pages 118–121 for additional activities in this general area.

CANYON VIEW COTTAGE

Address: Navajo Heights, Moab, Utah 84532 (six miles south of Moab, above the new eighteen-hole golf course, in a parklike setting. Moab is thirty-five miles from Canyonlands).
Telephone: 801–259–7830.

Season: Year-round.

Accommodations: This single cabin has a luxurious sunken living room and a bedroom that opens on a veranda, with gorgeous views of the canyon and the snowcapped La Sal Mountains. It has a fully equipped kitchen, two queen-size beds, a dining room, and two telephones as well as a color television, butane barbecue on the deck, and sleeping bags should your kids want to sleep on the veranda. Linens are provided.

Special Features: The hosts, Mr. and Mrs. Weiable, are tour guides in Canyonlands and Arches national parks.

Cost: $79 per night for three people, $89 for four. Lower rates off season.

Nearby: Raft or jet boat trips on the Colorado River and jeep rides in Canyonlands are popular with guests. For more activities in Moab and this general area, see pages 118–121.

CEDAR BREAKS CONDOS

Address: Center and Fourth East, Moab, Utah 84532 (in a residential area within walking distance to Moab; Moab is thirty-five miles from Canyonlands).
Telephone: 801–259–7830.

Season: Year-round.

Accommodations: Three newly furnished suits have one or two bedrooms with king- or twin-size beds, full baths, and fully equipped kitchens.

Special Features: The living area has cable TV, a stereo, books, and maps of the area. The upstairs condos have views of the La Sal Mountains. Laundry facilities are available.

Cost: Two-bedroom suite $74 per night for three people, $84 per night for four; each additional person up to six people $10 per night. Includes full breakfast (ham, eggs, fruit, juice, and more) that you prepare in your own kitchen. Lower rates off-season.

Nearby: The condos are four blocks from Main Street and a short distance from the main shopping area, tennis courts, library, and municipal swimming pool. An eighteen-hole golf course is four miles away. Raft and jet boat trips on the Colorado River and jeep rides in Canyonlands are popular organized activities. For more activities in Moab and this general area, see pages 118–121.

BIG BEND NATIONAL PARK, TEXAS

Known as the last frontier of Texas, Big Bend National Park is in the center of the western part of the state. It is a land of dramatic contrasts—from the lush vegetation of the Rio Grande flood plain to the high country of the Chisos Mountains, which rise from the surrounding stark Chihuahuan Desert. A flavor of Old Mexico pervades, especially in the village of Boquillas, with its backdrop of the Sierra del Carmen and the Fronteriza mountain ranges.

Year-round horseback riding, from short trail rides to all-day trips and overnight pack trips, start at Basin Station. Call Chisos Remuda Saddle Horses (915–477–2374) for information. Raft trips down the Rio Grande, from a short ten-mile jaunt through Colorado Canyon to a seven-day camping expedition through the park's Lower Canyons, are available through Far Flung Adventures (800–359–4138). Specialty float trips for children and their parents, from half a day to ten days, are run by Big Bend River Tours in Lajitas (800–545–4240). Outback expeditions that combine float trips on the Rio Grande with backcountry hiking to old ghost towns, Indian camps, cavalry camps, canyons, and springs is run by Outback Expeditions (915–371–2490). On the east boundary of the park, the town Lajitas on the Rio Grande has many accommodations set in realistic reconstructed Old West buildings.

CHISOS MOUNTAINS LODGE

Address: Big Bend National Park, Texas 79834 (situated in the center of the Chisos Mountains).
Telephone: 915–477–2291.

Season: Year-round.
Accommodations: Seventy-two rooms of varying types and prices are available at the lodge. These include motel-style rooms, lodge rooms, and stone cottages that accommodate up to six people. All have mountain views.
Special Features: Dining facilities and a camp store are on the premises.
Cost: Rooms with two beds and private bath in the thirty-eight room Casa Grande Motor Lodge or motel $65 per night, double occupancy. "Lodge units" with one room, one double and one single bed, private bath, and covered porch $61 per night, double occupancy. The most requested park accommodations are the six stone cottages, which were constructed by the Civilian Conservation Corps and have stone or native adobe walls: $70 per night for three people. Each additional person in any accommodation $10.

CENTRAL UNITED STATES

ISLE ROYALE NATIONAL PARK, MICHIGAN

Set on an island in the northwestern section of Lake Superior, Isle Royale has no roads or cars. It is accessible by boat from Grand Portage, on Minnesota's North Shore, or from Houghton and Copper Harbor in the copper country of Michigan's Upper Peninsula. Summer water activities here include boating along six hundred square miles of waterways and swimming.

Superior Trips (612–788–4560) offers scuba-diving explorations of shipwrecks for $80 per day for a group of six, meals included. The island has wonderful hiking trails through moss-carpeted forests and ridges, with panoramas of Lake Superior and Canada along its shorelines. Kids enjoy the hike to the island's old copper mine. In the middle of the island are remote lakes to explore, moose roam at its southwestern end, the Windigo area. The trout fishing here is superb.

ROCK HARBOR LODGE

Address: PO Box 405, Houghton, Michigan 49931 (on the shores of Rock Harbor).
Telephone: May through September, 906–337–4993; October through April, 502–773–2191.

Season: June through September.
Accommodations: There are twenty housekeeping cottages which have one room with a kitchenette (utensils are supplied), one double bed, and two bunk beds.
Special Features: The island is known for blueberry picking (the dining room serves delicious pancakes). In August many people swim in the harbor, and there are motorboats and canoes for rent. Cottage guests can eat at the lodge dining room; a grocery store and laundry facilities are nearby.
Cost: Housekeeping cottages $51 per night, double occupancy; additional person $18.
Nearby: A marina with boat rental, guided fishing tours, and hiking trails.

BADLANDS, SOUTH DAKOTA

You will feel like you've made a trip to the moon when visiting this landscape of strange and eerie eroded buttes, ridges, and canyons. Bison, pronghorn, mule deer, prairie dogs, and coyotes drift across the old homesteads and hunting grounds of the Sioux Indians. The ranger-led childrens' programs and fossil trails are worth joining, as the park has preserved thirty-seven- to twenty-three-million-year-old fossils of extinct animals as well as sites important to Indian history.

CEDAR PASS LODGE, INTERIOR

**Address: Box 5, Interior, South Dakota 57750 (eight miles south off
I-90 at exit 131 on the South Dakota Loop 240).
Telephone: 605–433–5460.**

Season: May through mid-October.
Accommodations: These twenty-four air-conditioned knotty pine
cabins are operated by the Ogala Sioux tribe.
Special Features: The central dining room features Sioux Indian fry
bread, buffalo burgers, and Indian tacos made with buffalo meat. The lodge
shop sells authentic Indian crafts.
Cost: Cabin with two beds, shower, and air-conditioning $41 per night,
double occupancy; each additional person $4. Two connecting bedrooms
$56 per night for three people, $58 per night for four people.
Nearby: This is a convenient stopover for trips to the Black Hills and
Mount Rushmore (114 miles away) or Wind Cave National Park (161
miles away).

THE SOUTH

EVERGLADES NATIONAL PARK, FLORIDA

Only two hours south of Miami, the Everglades encompass 1.5 million
acres of watery subtropical wilderness. The park is made up of vast
sawgrass prairies, deep mangrove swamps, subtropical jungle, and the
warm waters of Florida Bay. Among its wildlife are three hundred species
of birds, the elusive Florida panther, which still stalks in the bush, croc-
odiles, woodstorks, otters, and alligators. The major tourist season is from
mid-December through mid-April, due to rainstorms and abundant insects
in summer.

The Anhinga Trail, like many other trails throughout the park, has a
boardwalk so that you can safely observe alligators, otters, snakes, turtles,
herons, anhingas, gallinules, and many other birds and animals. Bicycles
can be rented year-round at the Flamingo Marina store and the Shark
Valley Visitor Center. The best place to see birds are at ponds, such as
Eco Pond, and at Mrazek and Coot bays; go in the early morning or late
afternoon in the dry winter months.

Because more than one-third of the park is comprised of marine areas
and estuaries, boating is the best way to explore. Canoe trails are plentiful.
Almost every type of marine organism native to the Caribbean is found

in these waters. Throughout the park naturalists lead hikes, canoe trips, and tram tours. Backcountry cruises and sailing tours are available through TW Recreational Services; call the Flamingo Lodge (below) for details. Other privately operated sightseeing boat tours include Everglades National Park Boat Tours (813–695–2591), which leads boat trips through the mangrove wilderness and islands.

The Chekikia Recreation Area was recently added to the park. Here you'll find a swimming lagoon, campground, and nature trails. On Tamiami Trail, just west of Shark Valley in the park, don't miss the Miccosukee Indian Village (305–223–8380), which gives a realistic view of the traditional Miccosukees, who lived amidst thatched roof cypress huts. Its museum has artifacts and canoes carved from trees; you can watch Chekikia women weave baskets out of sawgrass. Visitors like to watch the alligators wrestle; alligators once were caught by the Indians for their hides and meat.

FLAMINGO LODGE MARINA AND OUTPOST RESORT

Address: PO Box 428, Flamingo, Florida 33090 (thirty-eight miles southwest of the park entrance on Florida Bay).
Telephone: 305–253–2241 (toll-free for Dade County residents); 813–695–3101.

Season: Year-round for cottages and the marina; November through April for other facilities. Winter is the peak season, when rainfall and mosquitos are at a minimum. The weather from June through November is very uncomfortable.

Accommodations: Sixteen spacious air-conditioned cottages each have a fully equipped kitchen, separate living room, and bedroom overlooking Florida Bay. The recently remodeled lodge has one hundred air-conditioned rooms with two double beds, television, and private bathroom.

Special Features: Guests can go on sightseeing cruises on Florida Bay, take a white water bay cruise, or a two-hour wilderness tram tour. Motorized skiffs rental $47 per half day, $65 full day; canoes $20 per half day, $25 full day. Bikes $7 per half day, $12 full day. There is a pool for lodge and cottage guests as well as a dining room and laundry facilities.

Cost: April and November through mid-December, lodge rooms $80 per night, double occupancy; cottages $93 per night, double occupancy. Mid-December through March, lodge rooms $95 per night, double occupancy; cottages $110 per night, double occupancy. Rates May through October approximately $60 per night for lodge rooms, $71 per night for cottages, double occupancy. Each additional person $11. Rates include tax. Children under twelve stay free if no extra bed is needed; cribs are free.

MAMMOTH CAVE NATIONAL PARK, KENTUCKY

The world's longest network of underground corridors extends for more than three hundred miles beneath Mammoth Cave National Park's picturesque hills and valleys. Guided tours will show you colorful stalactites and stalagmite formations, huge cavern rooms, and spectacular pits and domes. Families can dine in the gypsum-clustered Snowball Room, 267 feet underground. The cave's temperature is a steady fifty-four degrees. The park has many interpretive programs around a campfire. Horseback riding and bicycle trails range from easy to strenuous. Boating and canoeing on the Green and Nolin rivers are popular from April through October.

MAMMOTH CAVE HOTEL

Address: Mammoth Cave, Kentucky 42259 (right by the park's entrance, connected to the park's visitor center by an arched bridge).
Telephone: 502–758–2225.

Season: Year-round.
Accommodations: This nondescript brick hotel overlooks a ravine and has simple air-conditioned rooms with private baths.
Special Features: Rooms have televisions, private patios, and balconies. Tennis and shuffleboard courts are adjacent to the hotel.
Cost: Rates are $40 to $63 per night, double occupancy, depending on season; each additional person $6.

SUNSET POINT MOTOR LODGE, MAMMOTH CAVE

Address: Mammoth Cave, Kentucky, 42259 (located near the Mammoth Cave Hotel at the edge of the forest overlooking Sunset Point Bluffs).
Telephone: 502–758–2225.

Season: Year-round.
Accommodations: Each room has a bathroom with shower and tub, electric heat, air-conditioning, and television.
Cost: Three-person room $46 to $72 per night, four-person room $53

to $68 per night, depending on season; each additional person $6. Two parents and children under sixteen can stay in a one-room family unit. Rates range from $40 to $65 per night, depending on season.

WOODLAND COTTAGES, MAMMOTH CAVE

Address: Mammoth Cave, Kentucky 42259 (secluded cottages in the forest, a short distance from the Mammoth Cave Hotel). Telephone: 502–758–2225.

Season: May through October.

Accommodations: Forty individual cottages with either two, three, or four rooms; all have private bathrooms with showers.

Cost: Two-room cottage $45 per night for three people, $51 per night for four; each additional person $6. Two parents and children under sixteen can stay in a one-room family unit. The rate is $45 per night.

SHENANDOAH NATIONAL PARK, VIRGINIA

This park is a protected mountain wilderness with deer, bears, bobcats, and untouched forests. Hiking trails lead to numerous waterfalls and old homesites. The Stony Man and Whiteoak Canyon trails are easy and beautiful, and there are many naturalist programs for children.

Shenandoah River Outfitters (703–743–4159) have tube and canoe rentals for rides down the Shenandoah. The Mountain Heritage Festival Days, held the last Saturday and Sunday of July, feature dancing demonstrations, games for children, craft demonstrations, and exhibits. Hoover Days is a special festival held at the Big Meadows Lodge area the second weekend in August.

Near the park the Luray Caverns (703–743–6551), fifteen minutes from the junction of the park entrance and U.S. 211, feature the "Great Stalacpipe Organ"—it actually plays concert-quality music. The Skyline Caverns, known for flower formations called anthrodites, are a five-minute drive from the junction of the park entrance and U.S. 340 in Front Royal. Forty minutes from the junction of the park entrance and U.S. 211 is the New Market Battlefield Park (703–740–3101), a 240-acre park with a museum focusing on the history of the Civil War.

SKYLAND LODGE

Address: PO Box 727, Luray, Virginia 22835 (set at the highest point along Skyline Drive, with majestic views).
Telephone: Information, 703–999–2211; reservations, 800–999–4714.

Season: Late March through early December.
Accommodations: Founded in 1894 as a summer retreat, the lodge's least expensive accommodations are the quaint and rustic cabins and new lodge rooms. Cabins sleep four to eight people. Most have twin and double beds. Bed linens and towels are provided. Lodge rooms sleep four and have two double and two queen-size beds.
Special Features: Guided horseback riding ($16 per hour) for children taller than four feet ten inches from April through October; pony rides are $4 for thirty minutes. The playground has swings, bars, and seesaws; the restaurant is known for its blackberry ice-cream pie.
Cost: Cabins $42 to $77 per night, double occupancy; lodge units $75 to $86 per night, double occupancy. Each additional person $5. (The higher rates are for Friday and Saturday nights.) Rates are slightly higher during the peak fall foliage season in October. Special two-day weekend packages in late March through late May and November through early December can cost as little as $63 per night.
Nearby: Fishing with barbless hooks (the fish are returned to the stream).

BIG MEADOWS LODGE

Address: PO Box 727, Luray, Virginia 22835 (on a high plateau overlooking the Shenandoah Valley, in a grassy meadow).
Telephone: Information, 703–999–2211; reservations, 800–999–4714.

Season: Late March through early December.
Accommodations: Built in 1929, the least expensive accommodations are the rustic cabins and the rooms in the main lodge. Cabins sleep four to eight people. Most have twin and double beds. Linens and towels are provided. Lodge rooms sleep four with two double or queen-size beds.
Special Features: Horse-drawn wagon rides (children ten and under $3.50, adults $7), campfire programs, a playground, and a restaurant on the premises.
Cost: Cabins $65 to $70 per night, double occupancy; main lodge rooms $48 to $73 per night, double occupancy. (The higher rate is for Friday and Saturday nights.) Each additional person $5. Rates are slightly higher during the peak fall foliage season in October. Special two-day weekend

packages in late March through late May and November through early December can cost as little as $63.

Nearby: The cascading waterfall of Dark Hollow Falls is an easy hike. Fishing with barbless hooks (the fish are returned to the stream).

LEWIS MOUNTAIN

Address: PO Box 727, Luray, Virginia 22835 (milepost 57.6 in the park).
Telephone: Information, 703–999–2255; reservations, 800–999–4714.

Season: Early May through October.

Accommodations: These rustic heated and furnished cottages each sleep four and have two double beds, bathrooms, towels, bed linens, a cooking-and-living area with a concrete floor, a fireplace, and a picnic table with an outdoor grill. Families stay in two-room cabins that are connected by a private bathroom. Bathrooms have a sink, toilet, and shower.

Special Features: Camp store and laundry are on the premises.

Cost: Two room cabins $80 to $82 per night, double occupancy. (The higher rate is for Friday and Saturday nights.) Each additional person $5. Rates are slightly higher during peak fall foliage season in October.

POTOMAC APPALACHIAN TRAIL CLUB CABINS

Address: 118 Park Street SE, Vienna, Virginia 22180 (five locations in the park, ranging from a 0.2-mile hike to a three-mile hike in).
Telephone: 703–242–0315. Reservations advised. Cabins can be rented by nonclub members.

Season: Year-round.

Accommodations: These eleven primitive cabins are maintained by volunteers. They are accessible on foot only and sleep eight, ten, or twelve people and are equipped with bunks, mattresses, blankets, cooking utensils, cutlery, and dishes. Stoves are woodburning; each cabin has a saw and an axe for gathering wood. Most have either indoor or outdoor fireplaces. There is no electricity; bring your own lanterns. Guests bring in water from a stream or spring, and the toilet is a privy. A booklet with photos of all cabins is available for $3.

Cost: Thursday through Saturday nights, cabins $15 per night for the first four people; $4 per night for each additional person. On weeknights, $4 per person per night. There is a $2 processing fee.

THE NORTHEAST

ACADIA NATIONAL PARK, MOUNT DESERT ISLAND, MAINE

Acadia National Park is one of the most varied family destinations. In summer you can hike, swim, canoe, cycle, take carriage and hayrides, and ride horseback. Winter visitors can cross-country ski and snowshoe. The park encompasses more than thirty-eight thousand acres of Mount Desert Island, where lobster cookouts, wildlife-filled hikes, and miles of dramatic coastline are all within easy reach.

The park has miles of hiking trails as well as bicycle and bridle paths. Carriage and hay wagon rides can be arranged at Wildwood Stable (Park Loop Road, 207–276–3622). Lifeguards are on duty in the summer at Echo Lake (fresh water) and Sand Beach (salt water). Tide pooling is a special way to experience Acadia; check a local tide chart and plan your visit as close to low tide as possible. The Mount Desert Oceanarium on Clark Point Road in Southwest Harbor (207–244–7330) has touch tanks, a lobster room, a scallop tank, a whale exhibit, and more. Inexpensive scenic cruises, including a daily nature cruise to the Cranberry Islands to watch seals, leave from Northeast Harbor; call the Islesford Ferry Company at 207–276–3717.

In Bar Harbor the Abbe Museum features Maine Indian artifacts. Whale-watching tours depart from Bar Harbor; call 207–288–9794 or 207–288–9776. A trail of less than one mile leads to outstanding views from the summit of Cadillac Mountain, the highest peak on the East Coast. The park has a junior ranger program for kids eight and older; check with the visitor center. Half- and full-day canoeing trips are a quiet and invigorating way to experience Acadia; call National Park Canoe at 207–244–5854. Coastal Sea Kayaking Tours glide across the clear waters leading eastward to Frenchman Bay or westward to Bluehill Bay. Half-day and full-day excursions as well as island camping outings are available; call 800–526–8615 or 207–288–9605.

SEASIDE COTTAGES

Address: RFD 1, Box 2340, Bar Harbor, Maine 04609 (at the head of Clark's Cove).
Telephone: 207–288–3674.

Season: Year-round.
Accommodations: Seaside has eight one-, two-, and three-bedroom heated cottages with modern, fully equipped kitchens. All are separated

for privacy and set on nicely landscaped lawns on a secluded, private beach at Clark's Cove. Living rooms have color televisions and beautiful views of the water; some have fireplaces. Bedding is provided.

Special Features: The ocean water of Clark's Cove is warm enough for swimming in summer, a sand-and-pebble shore. Rowboats and canoes for fishing or seal watching are available to guests at no charge. At low tide, guests can gather mussels. Outdoor furniture and gas barbecue grills are provided.

Cost: In summer, cottages $700 per week for three people, $814 per week for four. In spring and fall, $84 per night, $578 per week for three people, $105 per night, $708 per week for four. Rates are lower in early spring, late fall, and winter.

Nearby: Less than eight miles away are Acadia National Park and downtown Bar Harbor.

HALL QUARRY ROAD HOUSE

Address: Somes Sound, Maine; c/o Robert and Janet Brinton, 10 Brinton Road, Bethany, Connecticut (mailing address). Telephone: 203–393–3608.

Season: April through October.

Accommodations: This house, which sleeps seven to eight people, has beautiful views of Somes Sound and the mountains of Acadia from its large deck. The owners frequently rent to more than one family at a time. The first floor has a large, modern eat-in kitchen, a full bath, a living room, and three bedrooms. The refurbished basement has a large bedroom and a family room with a wood stove. The house is heated and completely furnished with dishes, linens, microwave oven, washer and dryer, television, and telephone. There is also an outdoor grill and picnic table.

Cost: In April, $368 per week; May and October, $473 per week; June and September, $576 per week; July, $840 per week; August $893 per week. Rates are not affected if the house is shared with another family.

Nearby: The home's wooded, private acreage near Acadia National Park's hiking trails, a safe swimming beach at Echo Lake, the ocean, and the stores and restaurants of Southwest Harbor and Bar Harbor are all close by.

BEECH HILL ROAD HOUSE

Address: Acadia National Park, Maine; c/o Robert and Janet Brinton, 10 Brinton Road, Bethany, Connecticut (mailing address). **Telephone:** 203–393–3608.

Season: April through October.
Accommodations: This house, which sleeps five to seven people, is on a quiet dead-end road near the park. The first floor has a modern kitchen, full bath, dining room with balcony, and living room with fireplace. The second floor has three bedrooms and a half bath. The house is heated and completely furnished with dishes, bedding, television, telephone, stereo tape deck, washer and dryer, and microwave oven. Its private rear deck has an outdoor grill and a picnic table.
Special Features: Large private yard with a swing set.
Cost: In April $368 per week; May and October, $420 per week; June and September, $473 per week; July, $682 per week; August, $735 per week.
Nearby: The home is convenient to Acadia National Park's hiking trails, Beech Mountain, Somesville Landing, Somes Pond, Long Pond, a safe swimming beach at Echo Lake, and the stores and restaurants of Bar Harbor.

HARBOR WOODS LODGING

Address: Main Street, PO Box 1214, Southwest Harbor, Maine 04679 (across the street from the harbor). **Telephone:** 202–244–5388.

Season: Year-round.
Accommodations: These fully equipped housekeeping cottages have full kitchens and separate living and sleeping areas. A one-bedroom cottage for four has two double beds, galley kitchen, shower bath, deck or picnic area. A two-bedroom cottage for four has two double beds and two twins, living area with galley kitchen, and deck. A cottage for six has one bedroom with two double beds, shower bath, living area with double sofabed, galley kitchen, and large deck.
Special Features: Cottages have decks, porches, and picnic areas.
Cost: Cottages $42 to $105 per night, double occupancy, depending on season and type of cottage; additional person $5 per night.
Nearby: Within walking distance to lobster pounds, shops, museums, and restaurants. A short drive from the national park, Echo Lake, the Bass Harbor Head Light, and Swan's Island Ferry.

FAMILY
CAMPS

*C*all them resorts without the room service, turned-down sheets, or gourmet restaurants—family camps often offer the same range of recreational activities but without the fancy accommodations or the fancy price. Mom and Dad won't have to cook, as three meals a day are served in the dining hall. Many family camps also have supervised children's programs, which allow parents time to themselves and kids the chance to be with others their own age.

Growing numbers of traditional children's summer camps are adding family camp weekends or weeks throughout the summer. A few now devote their entire summer to family camping. Family camp sponsors range from YMCA and 4-H organizations to university alumni associations, city parks departments, and private owners. The degree of luxury and types of accommodations vary considerably. Most camps have simple cabins with a common bathhouse, but other range from modern two- or three-bedroom suites to shared bunkhouses and tent cabins. Many ask that guests bring their own bedding and towels.

Family camps, found throughout the entire country, typically are situated in areas of great natural beauty—on lakes, rivers, or seashores. Expect to find swimming, boating, arts and crafts, horseback riding, volleyball, softball, basketball, and evening campfires and sing-alongs. The high and low ropes challenge courses, a relatively new addition to summer camp fare, can be found in many of the family camps listed in this chapter. High ropes courses have such elements as tightropes, catwalks, Indiana Jones—

style hanging bridges, cargo nets, and vertical wall climbs thirty to forty feet in the air. Participants are secured with harnesses and pulleys so that if they fall, they are caught and safely lowered to the ground. Low ropes courses have many of the same elements but are only four or five feet off the ground. If the participants fall, there is a spotter to catch them. Ropes courses are exciting for children and adults and build agility, self-confidence, and trust.

Family camps are one of the most economical vacations around; once you pay, there are no surprises awaiting your checkbook at the end of the week. They provide an opportunity for families to spend time together in a beautiful wilderness setting while enjoying the company of other families.

WEST COAST

FAMILY VACATION CENTER

Address: UCSB Alumni Association, Santa Barbara, California 93106.
Telephone: 805–893–3123.

The beach is at your front door at the University of California at Santa Barbara's Family Vacation Center. When you need a break from the sea and sun, choose from golf, tennis, swimming, arts and crafts, and lectures. Children of all ages are entertained and cared for from 9 A.M. to 9 P.M. except at mealtimes, when families eat together. Well over half of the families return each year for the range and quality of adult diversions and the variety of planned activities for children. Returning guests get first priority for reservations, and the month of August fills quickly. New guests should try to book by February or March.

Season: Late June through August.

Accommodations: Each family stays in a furnished suite of rooms that includes a living room with a refrigerator, two to four bedrooms, and a private bath. Daily housekeeping service is supplied. Three meals a day are included in the price, and weeks run Saturday to Saturday.

Special Features: The children's programs include swimming, bicycling, archery, hiking, team sports, group games, and arts and crafts. Older kids enjoy tennis, golf, local excursions, and a teen overnight. Adults can enjoy pool and beach swimming, tennis and golf lessons, tournaments, mixers, day hikes, arts and crafts, fitness programs, and faculty seminars on such topics as ethical capitalism, human sexuality, or holograms. Kayaking and a ropes course are available for an extra fee.

Cost: Adults (twelve years and over) $565; children six to twelve $445, two to five $400, under two $260. Kayaking trips $30; rope course $10. You must be a member of a University of California alumni association to attend the family program, but you need not have attended the University of California; annual membership fee $30.

EMANDAL FARM

Address: Hearst Post Office Road, Willits, California 95490 (140 miles north of San Francisco).
Telephone: 707–459–5439.

Family fun on the farm is Emandal's specialty, and it includes three home-cooked meals a day. Kids can gather eggs, see a goat milked, feed the pigs, or play in the shallow waters and sandy beaches of the Eel River. The farm offers week-long family stays in August and is open for weekend visitors in May, September, and part of October. Children love helping to plant and harvest in the farm's extensive garden, pick berries, and cook in the kitchen. Parents enjoy swimming, reading, hiking, and resting.

Accommodations: Eighteen rustic redwood cabins each have a double bed and a set of bunk beds, a washbasin, and screened windows. Modern bathhouses are nearby. Meals include German apple pancakes for breakfast, fresh bread and farm-fresh salads for lunch and dinner, and a salmon feed along the river one evening.

Special Features: Activities on the farm revolve around farm chores for that time of year: baby animals need tending, seeds need planting, and sheep need shearing in May; berries need picking in August; crops need harvesting and cider needs making in September. Many families spend their days lounging around the river or hiking.

Cost: Week-long stays (Sunday to Sunday), adults $483 to $595. Costs for children vary according to age, from $325 for ages twelve to seventeen to $85 for age two. Children under two stay free. Seasonal weekends of two to four nights, adults $164 to $325, kids twelve to seventeen $100 to $195, kids two to eleven $27 to $170, depending on their specific ages and length of stay.

SKYLAKE YOSEMITE CAMP

Address: 37976 Road 222, #25G, Wishon, California 93669-9714.
Telephone: 209–642–3720.

Six hours of horseback riding are offered each day at Skylake Yosemite Camp, where families have spent vacations together for the past thirty-five years. Many families never leave the camp during their stay, while others make a fifteen-mile trip to Yosemite National Park's Wawona gate to explore the park (see pages 85–87). A busy waterfront area on Bass Lake has waterskiing, sailing, canoeing, and sailboarding, and the ropes challenge course is offered twice a week. Family camp runs for the two weeks before Labor Day of each year.

Accommodations: Each family has its own screen house set among the trees (no electricity) with centrally located shower houses. The camp can accommodate thirty-four families.

Special Features: Children seven and under ride their horses in the ring, while older children and adults ride on trails. Other recreational options include arts and crafts, archery, tennis, and team sports such as softball and volleyball. There is a social hour every night on a lakeside porch with hors d'oeuvres; adults bring their own beverages. Evenings close with a campfire.

Cost: Adults and teens $275; children seven to twelve $245; three to six $158; infants $80. Horseback riding $11 per hour; water skiing $5.50 for a fifteen-minute trip; mountain bikes $6 for two hours. Reservations are open in January, and the first week of camp fills first.

SAN JOSE FAMILY CAMP

Address: San Jose Department of Recreation, Parks and Community Services, 333 West Santa Clara Avenue, Suite 800, San Jose, California 95113-1716 (mailing address); San Jose Family Camp, Star Route Box 200, Groveland, California 95321 (camp address).
Telephone: 408–277–4666.

Residents of San Jose get a small price break at this camp near Yosemite National Park, but anyone is welcome. The park operates from mid-June through August. Families arrive throughout the week and stay for an average of four nights, participating at their own pace in any of the many activities available. Interpretive programs introduce children and adults to the natural history of the Sierra foothills, and a supervised program for three- to six-year-olds allows parents to pursue activities of their own choice.

Accommodations: Tent cabins have cots with mattresses, benches, a table, a bookshelf, and outdoor decks. Shared restrooms and showers are located nearby. Guests provide their own linens.

Special Features: Swimming hole in the Middle Fork of the Tuolumne River, nature-oriented crafts projects, guided tours of Yosemite, nature hikes, fishing, volleyball, Ping-Pong, and sports tournaments are among the daily and weekly choices. Evenings feature campfires, talent shows, skits, and socials.

Cost: Rates include accommodations, three meals a day, and all activities; San Jose residents get a 20-percent discount. Adults $45 per night; children ten to fifteen $35, six to nine $25, three to five $18.

Nearby: The gold country, horseback riding, hayrides, and a golf course are not far. Many families explore Yosemite National Park—the park entrance is eight miles away; see pages 85–87 for more information on the park.

MONTECITO-SEQUOIA LODGE

Address: For reservations, 1485 Redwood Drive, Los Altos, California 94024-7252.
Telephone: 800–227–9900; 415–967–8612.

Montecito-Sequoia runs programs throughout the year and has dozens of things to do; family members can stay busy together or enjoy time apart. Located between Sequoia and King's Canyon national forests, Montecito offers swimming, canoeing, and sailing on a lake, elaborate children's programs tailored to different ages, and plenty of sports and games. Distinguished painters and cartoonists have residencies each week of the summer and offer arts experience to both adults and children. Horseback riding and waterskiing cost extra.

In winter guests can cross-country ski or ice-skate on the lake. Ski rental and lessons are available on thirty-five miles of groomed trails; if conditions permit you can ski from the lodge door.

Season: Year-round.

Accommodations: Thirteen rustic cabins sleep up to eight people each in a king-size bed and three sets of bunks. Bathhouses are nearby. Guests bring their own sleeping bags and towels. Thirty-six lodge rooms with a king- or queen-size bed and bunk beds sleep up to four people; all have private baths.

Special Features: The children's program is divided by age: six months to two years go to a special safe play yard with a napping facility; counselors take preschoolers on nature hikes and frog hunts; six- and seven-year-olds might get taken to the pool; kids eight and up have a free-choice program that includes canoeing, sailing, archery, tennis, and riflery. There are two children's sessions in the morning and two in the afternoon, for a total of five to six hours each day. Families meet for lunch. Evening activities vary from week to week but might include campfires, sing-alongs, a luau, a masquerade party, a family variety show, or a casino night for all ages. The winter program is not as extensive as the summer program.

Cost: Rates include all meals and activities (except riding and waterskiing). In summer, cabins $475 per adult, $425 for children three to twelve. Lodge rooms with private bath for a family of four $525 per adult,

$475 for children three to twelve. Riding $12 per hour and a quarter; water skiing $10 per hour. In winter, two nights' lodging, six meals, trail pass, youth games, and skiers' orientation on Friday night $179 per adult, $118 per child seven to eleven, $38 per child three to six. Children under three stay free. Ski rental extra.

In fall and spring there are no organized activities, but the pool, tennis courts, and boathouse are open and prices are reduced.

LAIR OF THE GOLDEN BEAR

Address: Lair Reservations, Alumni House, Berkeley, California 94720.
Telephone: 510–642–0221.

Adults like to "play hard" when they come to the University of California at Berkeley's family camps in the Stanislaus National Forest. Two different camps, Camp Blue and Camp Gold, have active and restful things for parents to do and organized programs for children and teens. The children's programs combine organized peer activities with unscheduled free time, and each group meets several times each day. "Kub Korral," for two- to five-year-olds, has games, music, nature activities, and arts and crafts. Six- and seven-year olds have nature activities, pool games, hikes, arts and crafts, and the "Lair Olympics." Eight- and nine-year-olds have nature projects, fishing, games, paddleboating, and storytelling. Preteens have water games, paddleboating, hikes, softball games, movies, and arts and crafts. Teen groups have plenty of athletic and social activities. All kids are well supervised. Guests must belong to the University of California at Berkeley's Alumni Association (a $40 membership fee), but members need not be graduates of the university.

Accommodations: Rustic tent cabins have a wooden platform and sides with a canvas top, twin beds with mattresses (bring your own bedding), and electricity. Small cabins sleep two people, medium cabins sleep four, and large cabins sleep up to eight. Bathhouses are nearby. Meals are served in an open-air family-style dining hall.

Special Features: Each camp has its own lodge, swimming pool, and dining hall. Camp Gold is located near a meadow and has a softball field that both camps share; Camp Blue is more heavily forested. Both have tennis, volleyball, Ping-Pong, horseshoes, arts and crafts, hootenannys, family dancing, and bingo. Pinecrest Lake, a twenty-minute walk from both camps, has sailing, swimming, and boat rental. Camps are staffed by University of California at Berkeley students.

Cost: Adults $350 per week; kids thirteen to seventeen $300, six to twelve $215, two to five $140, under two $75.

Nearby: Boating, fishing, golf, and horseback-riding facilities.

ROCKY MOUNTAINS AND SOUTHWEST

THE TRAILS END RANCH FAMILY CAMP

Address: Inquiries, PO Box 6525, Denver, Colorado 80206; Camp, PO Box 1170, Estes Park, Colorado 80517.
Telephone: 303–377–3616.

Each family stays in its very own Conestoga wagon at this unique family camp on the edge of the Rocky Mountain National Park. Guided hikes, tailored to different ages and abilities (minimum age is four), lead campers into the park, where marmots, chipmunks, elk, bighorn sheep, and deer are often sighted. Campers age twelve and over can learn technical climbing at no extra charge. In addition there is western riding, a ropes course, a separate arts and crafts shop, barn, archery range, and rifle range.

Accommodations: Each of the Camp's fifteen wagons accommodates four people in comfortable beds. Bathhouses are nearby. A log lodge has a dining room and lodge room with fireplace.

Special Features: Western riding, hiking, archery, riflery, arts and crafts, and a ropes course. The program designed for four- to eight-year-olds has simpler rides and easier hikes. Families are expected to participate in most activities together. There's a campfire each evening, with sing-alongs, old camp movies, and skits.

Cost: Program runs Tuesday through Sunday. Ages nine and up $325 per person, ages four through eight $175 per person. Costs include meals and all activities. The camp begins taking reservations in October for previous participants, and on November first for the public; cancellations are often available.

CENTRAL UNITED STATES

SHAW-WAW-NAS-SEE 4-H CAMP

Address: Northern Illinois 4-H Camp Association, 6641 North 6000 W Road, Manteno, Illinois 60950.
Telephone: 815–933–3011.

Camp Shaw-waw-nas-see is primarily a youth camp, but also has weekend family camp opportunities and a "Grand Camp" weekend for grandparents and their grandchildren. The camp covers 120 acres of rolling pine and hardwood forests with hiking trails and open meadows. Crafts projects, including leather working, copper enameling, and basket weaving, are popular with the kids. The swimming pool and creek see a lot of splashing action, and supervised children's activities give parents or grandparents a break during part of the weekend. Camp runs from Friday night to Sunday at noon.

Accommodations: Twenty-four wooden cabins with concrete floors have five sets of bunk beds in each; small families can share one with another family. Modern bathhouses are located near each cabin.

Special Features: Swimming pool, creekside swimming, rock climbing, arts and crafts, archery, volleyball, and campfires with singing, skits, and marshmallows.

Cost: Per weekend, adults (thirteen and up) $65; children four to twelve $50, three and under free. Rates include all meals and activities.

EDWARDS YMCA CAMP ON LAKE BEULAH

Address: 1275 Army Lake Road, PO Box 16, East Troy, Wisconsin 53120.
Telephone: 414–642–7466.

Four summer weekends are set aside for family camp along the wooded shores of Lake Beulah in southeastern Wisconsin. All types of families— single parents, double parents, grandparents, aunts, and uncles—are welcome and encouraged to attend one of the two- or three-day sessions. In addition to the more customary camp activities, Edwards has a two-thousand-foot boardwalk extending over marshland between two lakes. The camp offers special nature walks and classes. Another favorite pastime at the camp is tubing behind a boat; similar to waterskiing, you hold on to the inner tube while the boat pulls you along. More traditional water sports include canoeing, sailing, waterskiing, swimming, and touring Lake Beulah on a pontoon. A special New Year's Family Camp features cross-country skiing, tubing, ice-skating, and indoor and outdoor games.

Accommodations: Three types of housing are available, each with different prices. The Runge Lodge has rooms that sleep four people in two sets of bunk beds and share a bathroom with an adjoining room. The Hoffer Lodge, the newest of the bunch, also has rooms that sleep four people in two sets of bunk beds and share a bath with an adjoining room. Log cabins sleep up to twelve people each and have restrooms nearby. Meals, served in the dining hall overlooking the lake, include fresh vegetable bars and delicious home-baked desserts.

Special Features: Archery, riflery, arts and crafts, volleyball, softball, basketball, soccer, an observatory, game room, tetherball, campfires, special adult canoe trips, and a ropes challenge course.

Cost: Total cost is a combination of accommodations (price depends on facility) and food service. Families sleeping in a cabin, $85 for two nights, $130 for three nights. In the Runge Lodge, families $125 for two nights, $175 for three nights. Families in the Hoffer Lodge $145 for two nights, $200 for three nights. Two-night stays include five meals for $35 per adult (age twelve and over); children six to eleven $28, two to five $12, under two free. Three-night stays include eight meals for $58 per adult; children six to twelve $45, two to five $19, under two free. All activities are included.

YMCA STORER CAMPS

**Address: 7260 South Stoney Lake Road, Jackson, Michigan 49201.
Telephone: 800–288–0527; 517–536–8607.**

Family camping has been a tradition at Storer Camps for more than thirty years. Summer offerings include long weekend camps, a special weekend for single-parent families, and a week-long family camp in August. Horseback riding is a big attraction; kids seven and older take trail rides while little ones ride in the corral. A special children's activity program keeps youngsters busy with storytelling, pony rides, arts and crafts, and more, while parents enjoy tennis, sailing, swimming, and archery. Instruction in various activities is available to adults and children alike. Evening programs keep the fun rolling with square dancing, campfires, talent shows, and barbecues. A three-day New Year's Eve Camp includes winter activities such as broomball, skating, and tobogganing, and old-fashioned fun including scavenger hunts, cookie-making, night hikes, and sing-alongs.

Accommodations: Families usually stay in the "South Stockade," in either log cabins with bunk beds or cabins with activity rooms downstairs and bunks upstairs. Bathhouses are centrally located to all cabins. Meals are all-you-can-eat and often follow themes, such as Hawaiian luau, western night, or Italian night.

Special Features: Swimming, sailing, canoeing, kayaking, horseback riding, volleyball, tennis, campfires, cookouts, square dancing, and more; cross-country skiing in winter.

Cost: For long weekends (two nights and three days), adults $70 to $80, teens $55 to $65, children two to twelve $50 to $55. For a full-week program (Sunday to Saturday), adults $175, teens $145, children $125.

AL-GON-QUIAN FUN AND FITNESS FAMILY CAMP

Address: Ann Arbor Y, 350 Fifth Avenue, Ann Arbor, Michigan 48104-2294 (reservation office) (camp is thirty miles south of the Straits of Mackinac on Burt Lake).
Telephone: 313–663–0536.

Al-Gon-Quian's family fitness camp is a health spa vacation on the cheap. Adults can trim down and relax with fitness, yoga, aerobics, and stress management classes; children's programs are all supervised, so Mom and Dad can work out with confidence and concentration. Use of the fitness facilities is not mandatory, however; parents can participate in activities with their children or just sit and read. Twenty families participate in each week-long session. The kids stay entertained with summer camp mainstays such as horseback riding, canoeing, archery, and arts and crafts. Set on the western shore of Burt Lake in 150 acres of white birch, maple, and pine forest, the camp offers child care for preschool children during the activity periods at no extra charge. Another family option, the Memorial Day and Labor Day "weekend getaways," include hiking, canoeing, campfires, and games for families and adults.

Accommodations: Each family is assigned a wood-frame cabin with screened windows, bunk beds, and electricity. Bathroom facilities are nearby; meals are served in a dining hall. Guests supply their own bedding.

Special Features: Horseback riding, riflery, archery, arts and crafts, tennis, sailing, canoeing, waterskiing, campfire sing-alongs, swimming, miniature golf, woodworking, volleyball, and baseball. After breakfast, children are divided into classes according to the activities they're interested in. Preschoolers have special supervised programs.

Cost: Fun and Fitness Family Camp runs for six days: adults $315, kids thirteen and under $110, with a maximum of $700 per family no matter what the size. For family weekend getaways, adults $55, kids $20. Members of the Ann Arbor Y get a discount.

DANEBOD FAMILY CAMP

Address: c/o Gerry Werth, 3924 46th Avenue South, Minneapolis, Minnesota 55406-3604 (camp is in Tyler, Minnesota).
Telephone: 612–823–1574; 612–823–3410; 408–246–7299.

The Danebod Danish folk school is where you go "to learn how to live, not to make a living," according to those who return year after year to enjoy the camaraderie, discussions, folk dancing, singing, and crafts activities offered in three week-long sessions during the summer. Danebod has offered these family camp weeks since 1949 in historic buildings listed on the National Register of Historic Places. Guests come from all over the United States. Mornings generally include discussions for adults as well as singing and dancing opportunities for children and adults alike. In the afternoon families can choose from a variety of different crafts, such as mask making, leather work, Danish paper hearts, hair ornaments, paper making, rocket building, and stained glass. Following the crafts period is time for swimming and short field trips. All campers are assigned housekeeping jobs upon their arrival, as Danebod is operated completely by its members. Evenings feature more folk dancing, campfires, and skits.

Accommodations: This historic campus has an old stone hall and prairie church. Dormitory-style accommodations with shared baths are on the second and third floors. Older children are put into dorm rooms with others their own age. Clean linens are provided. Bring a fan, because there is no air-conditioning. Tents and RVs are welcome, and hookups are available.

Cost: Adults (eighteen and up) approximately $230 per week; children eleven to seventeen $200, six to ten $175, one to five $120, under one free. Stays of less than a week often can be arranged for lower rates. Book by March or April.

CAMP LINCOLN/CAMP LAKE HUBERT FAMILY CAMP

Address: 5201 Eden Circle, Suite 202, Minneapolis, Minnesota 55436 (camp is three hours north of Minneapolis).
Telephone: 800–242–1909; 612–922–2545.

Founded in 1909, this camp offers a week-long family camp in middle or late August. Each morning after breakfast, families select their activities for the day; sailing, windsurfing, or motorboating on Lake Hubert; horseback riding, archery; riflery; a high and low ropes course; or arts and crafts. Activity directors assist children and adults. The challenging high and low ropes courses are a big hit: kids breeze through them and enjoy watching their parents struggling to complete them.

Accommodations: Three families share one two-story cabin. Each cabin has a large central room with a fireplace, a bathroom with a toilet and sink, and three separate bedrooms. A showerhouse is near all the cabins, and most of the cabins overlook one of the lakes.

Special Features: The swimming beach has a sandy bottom and a gradual slope. The boating dock is separate from the swimming area and offers instruction in sailing, motorboating, and windsurfing. The fishing is good at another little lake inside the camp. Arts and crafts activities take place in a pottery shop and two other craft shops, and there are athletic fields for soccer and tennis.

Cost: Adult $380; children under ten $350; children under two stay free. Enrollment begins in late September and begins to fill to capacity by late April to early May.

CAMP OJIKETA FAMILY CAMP

Address: Camp: 27500 Kirby, Chisago City, Minnesota 55013.
Corporate headquarters: St. Paul Council Camp Fire, 235 Roselawn Avenue East, St. Paul, Minnesota 55117 (camp is twenty-five minutes north of the Twin Cities).
Telephone: 612–642–2772; 612–257–0600.

With more than a mile of frontage on Green Lake, Camp Ojiketa has a wide selection of water activities: sailing, fishing, canoeing, swimming, or just splashing on the sunny beach. Families also can try their hand at archery, volleyball, basketball, or exploring the eight kilometers (about five miles) of hiking trails. In winter choices include snowshoeing, ice fishing, cross country skiing, and tobogoning. Special recreational activities are planned for children six months to twelve years to give parents free time. Trained staff supervise the kids and instruct them in the use of all equipment. Family camping and special programs for single-parent families are offered throughout the year. Parents can choose from a variety of lodging options.

Accommodations: Simple rustic cabins with nearby shower houses and bathroom facilities can each accommodate a family of four. Other cabins are more like small homes, with private baths, bedrooms, fireplaces, and screened porches; they can accommodate larger families.

Cost: Four nights and five days worth of meals, activities, and lodging for a family of four ranges from $275 to $600 depending on type and location of cabin. Additional person $90; one less person, deduct $70.

CLEVELAND AREA YMCA FAMILY CAMPS

Address: Camps Division, 8558 Crackel Road, Chagrin Falls, Ohio 44022.
Telephone: 216–543–8184.

Choose from two camps, Centerville Mills or the Rolling Y Ranch, for special holiday family camp weekends throughout the year: Memorial Day, Fourth of July, Labor Day, and several other weekends in the early spring.

Centerville Mills features horseback riding, canoeing, and fishing on the lake; swimming in an Olympic-size pool; basketball, archery, and an individual and group ropes challenge course. The ropes course is similar to an obstacle course, with a vertical bridge and wall to climb and ten different stations. Families stay in individual cabins with a central bath-house in the center.

Rolling Y Ranch is a working western horse ranch with eight hundred acres of riding trails. There are pigs, goats, a stubborn mule, chickens, roosters, miniature horses, sheep, rabbits, a turkey, and more than fifty horses. During the three-day family camp, rides are held four different times a day. Instruction is given to beginners. All rides are guided, and routes are determined by the skill level of the riders. Children under seven ride in a corral. Rolling Y accommodations consist of six heated multi-family cabins that sleep fifteen people each, with a central bath-house.

Cost: Three-day, two-night camps $50 for the first person, $45 for the second, $43 for the third, $41 for the fourth.

CAMP CHRISTOPHER FAMILY CAMP

Address: CYO Family Camp, 404 Elbon Avenue, Akron, Ohio 44306-1500.
Telephone: 800–CYO–CAMP; 216–773–0426.

Horseback riding, four different lakes, or an "awesome" ropes challenge course can each lead to a memorable family camping session, and Camp Christopher has all three at its wooded 160 acres in Bath, Ohio. Adults and children of any age can ride; the lakes are all within a short walk of the cabins; and the ropes challenge area has eight high and twenty low courses. Children from infants to teenagers can attend with their parents. Each morning, the young campers are grouped by age and enjoy different activities under the supervision of qualified camp counselors. Parents and children participate together in a camp program each afternoon. After-dinner activities include carnivals, campfires, hayrides, Indian nights, and haunted houses. Camp Christopher Family Camp has been in business for more than thirty-five years.

Accommodations: Cabins are heated and carpeted, and most have rest-room and shower facilities at a nearby bathhouse. Thirteen duplex cabins sleep six to ten people on each side. Small families (usually fewer than four people) can share a cabin with another small family.

Special Features: Activities include horseback riding, swimming, boat-ing, fishing, hiking, hayrides, crafts and games, sports, and the ropes chal-lenge course. Each age group has a different course, and harnesses are provided for the highest ones. The courses go through the woods and vary with the landscape.

Cost: Adults $145, children $125 for the week, with a maximum fee of $650 per family.

THE SOUTH

GREAT SMOKY MOUNTAINS INSTITUTE FAMILY CAMP

Address: Great Smoky Mountains National Park, Townsend, Tennessee 37882.
Telephone: 615–448–6709.

Located in the heart of the Great Smoky Mountains National Park, the Institute's family camp takes place over a four-day weekend and is designed for parents with children ages six to twelve. Activities include storytelling, Appalachian music, nature study, swimming, and arts and crafts. The camp has a crystal-clear stream that is perfect for tubing or searching for salamanders, and a waterfall is a one-mile hike away.

Accommodations: Family camp lodging is in dorms; each dorm is split into four sections, each accommodating fifteen people, with bunk beds, a bathroom, and showers. The Institute also has a dining hall, an activity center, an outdoor pavilion, and a campfire area.

Special Features: The camp has scavenger hunts, campfires, and a popular ropes game called Monkeying Around. Special sessions on Appalachian bluegrass music include banjos, jute harps, dulcimers, and guitars. Crafts projects in the past have included kudzu vine basket weaving, screen printing and tie-dying T-shirts, and pumpkin carving. There is no day care available for children under six.

Cost: Adults and children $80 each per session, including meals.

CAMP FRIENDSHIP

Address: PO Box 145, Palmyra, Virginia 22963.
Telephone: 800–823–3223; 804–589–8950.

Camp Friendship offers campers lake and river canoeing, lake and pool swimming (swing off a rope into the water), pond fishing, a ropes course, horseback riding, and special sports and activities for all ages. Families can stay for the entire week of family camp held the third week in August, or for as little as three nights. Special rock climbing and caving trips are offered throughout the week, and scheduled activities for children allow parents time to themselves.

Accommodations: Families stay in cabins of various sizes sleeping four to ten people; all families get their own cabins unless they request otherwise. A few cabins have private bathrooms, but most use centrally located shower houses. Cabins have built-in bunk beds and electricity; bring your own bedding or rent linens for a small fee. Meals feature lots of fresh fruits and vegetables and fresh baked breads, and families are expected to help clear tables. Families may bring their own tents or RVs if they make arrangements in advance.

Special Features: Tennis, basketball, soccer, volleyball, archery, riflery, pool and lake swimming, arts and crafts, river and lake canoeing. Baby-sitting is provided for infants and very young children, and supervised children's activities are scheduled several times each day. Evening activities include campfires, a talent show, cookouts, a movie night, a games night, a barn dance, and a scavenger hunt.

Costs: Family package for the full six nights: family of four or more $900, two adults and one child $700, one adult and two children $600. Daily rate, adults eighteen and over $45 per day; children three to seventeen $40 per day; under three free. Minimum stay is three nights. If you plan to bring people who are not immediate family, they are charged the daily rate. Rock climbing trip and caving trip $10 to $15 per person; transportation is provided. Horseback riding lessons and trail rides $12 per person per hour.

SEAFARER FAMILY CAMP

Address: Route 65, Box 3, Arapahoe, North Carolina 28510-9716. Telephone: 919–249–1212.

An extensive sailing and motor boating program on the expansive Meuse River makes this one of the most popular family camps around. A freshwater lake is used for swimming. Kids particularly love the giant airbag in the lake: one person scoots down to its end, and when a second person jumps onto the bag, the first person goes flying into the water. The camp has a nine-hole par-three golf course, a ropes course, and a special supervised program for children under six. Family camp is offered over a spring and fall weekend, and for a week in late August.

Accommodations: The camp can accommodate forty families. Each lives in a cabin with a private bath, and bunk beds with mattresses: guests supply their own linens.

Special Features: The boat fleet includes sunfish, laser, Hobie Cats, flying scots, sailboards, Boston whalers, ski boats, inboard motor boats, and a large cruising boat. The river is about four miles wide. Tennis, golf (an 18-hole golf course is nearby), water aerobics, a nature program, archery, riflery, arts and crafts, and softball also are available. A supervised "kiddie corner" with activities for children under six operates in the morning and afternoon. Evening programs include a sunset cruise for parents, a talent show, sock hop, carnival, bingo night, and movies.

Cost: Week-long stays: Adults $330; children seven to twelve $265; six

and under $210. Rates include everything except arts and crafts proj-
ects. Weekend camp, Friday dinner to Sunday lunch: Adults $80; six to
twelve $65; under five free. Reserve as far in advance as possible; the
week-long camp can fill a year in advance. The weekend camps are easier
to get into.

THE NORTHEAST

CAMP CHINGACHGOOK

Address: Capital District YMCA, 13 State Street, Schenectady, New
York 12305.
Telephone: 518–374–9136.

Families have private cabins on Camp Chingachgook's three-day family
camps over Memorial Day and Labor Day weekends. The camp, established
in 1913, sits on the east shore of Lake George in the Adirondack State
Park. Its thirteen hundred feet of shoreline, two docks, and fleet of canoes,
rowboats, sailboats, and sailboards are available to campers; you also can
play tennis, basketball, softball, soccer, and other games. Don't miss the
chance to try the high and low ropes challenge courses.

Accommodations: Thirty cabins sleep eight each in bunk beds; all have
electricity but no heat. Bathrooms with hot showers are near the cabins.
Meals are served family-style in the dining hall and there is at least one
barbecue during each family weekend.

Special Features: Kids are wild about the camp's ropes course, which
includes a rope spiderweb to climb, a 150-foot rappelling line, and ropes
that go through trees. Adults are encouraged to try it as well. All participants are attached to harnesses. Evening activities include campfires,
sing-alongs, and dances.

Cost: Three-day family camping weekends $85 per adult and $65 per
child.

DOROTHY P. FLINT NASSAU COUNTY 4-H CAMP

Address: 1425 Old Country Road, Building J, Plainview, New York
11803-5015 (business office).
Telephone: 516–454–0900.

There's a down-home farm flavor at this 140-acre 4-H camp, where kids
can help take care of pigs, cows, chickens, ducks, and sheep, all of which
are available for petting any time of the day. A vegetable garden helps

provide food for campers, and at the end of the season, when there is often a surplus, kids can help pick the vegetables and buy them at a nominal fee to take home. Parents and kids stay together and have the freedom to choose supervised or unsupervised activities. Many families enjoy alternate days at camp with days exploring the surrounding area on Long Island Sound, but the camp will keep any group active with horseback riding, swimming in the Sound, arts and crafts projects, campfires, hayrides, tennis, treasure hunts, and much more. Family camping takes place over five different weekends in late spring, summer, and early fall.

Accommodations: Families are assigned their own cabins or can opt to bring their own tent or trailer. Unheated cabins are screened and can accommodate up to nine people; bring your own bedding. Bathroom facilities are in two centrally located wash houses. Meals are served family-style in the dining hall.

Special Features: Farm animals, horseback riding lessons, trail rides, arts and crafts, swimming, campfires, movies, hayrides, tennis, basketball, volleyball, and horseshoes are all part of the program. There are planned and organized activities for the entire family, but parents are responsible for their children, as there is no formal baby-sitting service. Laundry facilities on site.

Cost: Four-night stays $110 per cabin (includes all activities) plus meal fee of $55 to $65 per person (over twelve) and $20 to $40 per child five to eleven. Kids under five eat free. Shorter stays are less expensive.

WEONA FAMILY CAMP

Address: 2564 Delaware Avenue, Buffalo, New York 14216. Telephone: 716-875-2485.

Camp Weona offers three-day family camps over Memorial Day and Labor Day weekends. The camp's one-thousand acres of fields, streams, forests, and lakes give families unlimited opportunities for hiking, swimming, and exploring at their own pace. Or they can participate in the camp's more organized recreational activities, such as canoeing, outdoor games, horseback riding and the high and low ropes adventure course. Home-cooked family-style meals are served in the dining hall.

Accommodations: Families stay in private cabins that can sleep up to ten in bunk beds with a shared centralized shower and bathroom facilities, or in the Weona Lodge, which has dorm rooms and indoor showers and bathrooms.

Special Features: Swimming in outdoor heated pool, hayrides, horseback riding, a variety of sports, fishing, campfires, skits, short plays, and sing-alongs.

Cost: Cabins $65 per person per weekend. Lodge accommodations $75 per person per weekend; children under five free. Fees include lodging meals, and all programs.

CAMP MERROWVISTA

Address: Ossipee, New Hampshire 03864 (program inquiries); American Youth Foundation, 1315 Ann Avenue, St. Louis, Missouri 63104 (camp registration).
Telephone: Camp, 603–539–6607; foundation, 314–772–8626.

Two five-day family camps offer parents and children the chance to spend time together in a beautiful wilderness setting. Flexible programs with a wide range of activities are planned for all ages. The waterfront is equipped with swimming docks, rowboats, canoes, sailboards, and small sailboats. Merrowvista's state-of-the-art high and low ropes challenge courses are exhilarating fun, but also emphasize working as a team and learning together. The camp's extensive acreage includes hardwood forests, the gentle peaks of the Ossipee Mountains, Dan Hole Pond, and idyllic meadows. In addition to the adventure-based activities, Merrowvista's Family Camp Program works on enriching families through discussion and problem solving.

Accommodations: Guests can stay in the six-room insulated lodge (like a hotel) with private or shared baths, or in screened cabins with electricity and shared bathhouses. Each family gets its own room or cabin. Meals are served in a dining hall.

Special Features: Hiking trails radiate out from the camp for private hikes. Group nature studies, fishing, self-guided nature trails, and arts and crafts activities are all part of each session.

Cost: Adults $125, children (up to age seventeen) $100 for the session.

LAKESHORE
AND RIVERSIDE
VACATIONS

*N*othing compares to the rejuvenating quality of cool, clear water. It cools you down on a hot day, soothes seething tempers, and provides endless entertainment for children. Kids seem most content splashing and swimming, digging in the sand, and running in the sun. Lake and river visits teach children to be silent and still as well, letting the cool water of a creek rush over their body or silently watching beavers, turtles, and frogs go about their business. There are canoes and rowboats to paddle, fish to be caught, water skis to master, and sailboats to sail. As long as there is water nearby, most parents find that all family members stay busy and content.

This chapter covers cottages, cabins, rooms, and houseboats on rivers and lakes throughout the country; you'll find even more in the chapter on resorts. Most of the places we list have self-contained kitchens, so families can either do their own cooking or head to a restaurant for a special treat. The type of water recreation offered can be as simple as a sandy beach and an inner tube or two or as elaborate as a full-service marina supplied with a variety of boats, fishing gear, and scuba-diving equipment. The places we have selected are either right on the water or a stone's throw away. Both privately owned and state-run facilities are listed, and all offer excellent values to vacationing families. Most of the state park accommodations described have boat rentals with extremely economical prices. There are many other excellent state-run lodgings available by the water, too numerous to mention; see the chapter on state park cabins and resorts for more details on them. American Youth Hostel (AYH) listings, scattered throughout this chapter, have rock-bottom prices and often offer the complimentary use of boats. The hostels we list have family rooms available so that parents and children can enjoy some privacy and time together. Remember that many hostels are closed during the day and that kitchen privileges often are included in the price; see pages 7–8 for more general information on hostels.

WEST COAST

CONVICT LAKE RESORT

Address: Route 1, Box 204, Mammoth Lakes, California 93546. Telephone: 619–934–3800.

Named for a group of notorious escaped convicts who holed up in the area many years ago, Convict Lake is now famous for its abundance of trophy trout. Anglers can rent fishing boats, rowboats, and canoes from the resort. More than twenty housekeeping cabins are within an easy walk of the lake, and guided horseback rides take young wranglers on a tour around it. Swimming is a bit chilly during most of the year, although many children splash around in July and August, when the water temperature hits fifty-five degrees. An Olympic-size heated pool is a ten-minute drive away. The resort's gourmet restaurant is open for dinner only. Proximity to Mammoth Mountain ski area for winter downhill skiing and summer mountain biking (see next entry) makes this resort an excellent choice for sports-minded families.

Season: Year-round.

Accommodations: Twenty-one cabins and one large house can hold two to sixteen people. Many are set up for families, with a combination of single and double beds. All have fully equipped kitchens, and linens are provided, just bring your own food and fishing gear.

Special Features: Guided horseback rides are available from mid-May to September; horseshoes and hiking trails are available anytime, weather permitting.

Cost: Cabins can be rented by the night or by the week. Week-long stays offer a good value: one-bedroom cabins sleeping four $500 per week, sleeping six $510 to $560. Nightly stays $65 to $80 per week night for one-bedroom unit, $95 per weekend night. Three-night minimum stay on holiday weekends. Fishing boat rentals $40 per day or $10 per hour, canoes and rowboats $20 per day or $5 per hour. Guided horseback rides (for age seven and up), lake ride $20; three- to four-hour meadow or canyon ride $40; all-day ride to Lake Mildred, including lunch, $60. Children under seven can be led on horseback around the resort by their parents or by a wrangler for $7.50.

Nearby: Bodie Ghost Town, Mono Lake, Mammoth Lakes Basin Hot Creek.

MAMMOTH MOUNTAIN BIKE ADVENTURES

Address: P.O. Box 24, Mammoth Lakes, California 93546.
Telephone: 619–934–2571.

From July to September, winter ski trails turn into summer mountain bike trails at Mammoth Mountain. You don't have to be an experienced or even a strong rider to enjoy these trails; they come in all degrees of difficulty. In fact, Mammoth's bike program is aimed at beginners and intermediates who want to be introduced to the sport of mountain biking. Bikes can be rented at the bottom of the mountain, or you can bring your own. The gondola is the easiest way up to the 11,053-foot summit; your bike rides up with you on an outside rack. Once at the top, choose from a fast downhill run, a run that provides a few steep uphill climbs, and a leisurely course through flatter terrain, or do a little of everything. Seasoned riders will want to try the Kamikaze, with its steep switchbacks, radical downhills, and wide-open straightaways. Beginners can stay on the easier tracks and roads. Stop for a picnic lunch and a rest at the Mid-Chalet partway down the mountain.

Cost: All-facilities pass to the park $15 per adult, and $7.50 for children twelve and under; includes unlimited access to gondola, entire trail system, slalom course, and BMX track. Trail access pass $10 per adult, $5 per child; includes everything but gondola. New Schwinn Paramount mountain bike rental $30 for eight hours, $20 for four hours. Helmets must be worn and can be rented for $5 per day. Children's bikes and helmets are available. Guests also can rent paddleboats or outboards to explore Mammoth, rent horses for an hour or all day, go Roller-blading, play golf or tennis, and arrange wagon rides.

Nearby: The Mammoth area has many other backcountry cycling trails, some with tour operators and some self-guided.

Long Valley AYH Hostel

Open May through September, this youth hostel has a family room and complete kitchen and can be booked by members and nonmembers of AYH. Member price per night, adults $8.50 per night, children $4.50. Non–AYH members add $3 per person. This hostel is closed from 10 A.M. to 4:30 P.M. Guests need sleeping bags or sheets and pillow cases; These can be rented for 50 cents or you bring your own. **Address:** U.S. 395 and Crowley Lake Drive, RR 1, Box 189 B, Mammoth Lakes, California 93546. **Telephone:** 619–935–4377.

Edelweiss Lodge

Four knotty-pine-paneled cabins and four suites in a large chalet are tucked into a secluded, forested part of town just a hundred yards from Mammoth Creek. Paths lead to the creek, where the water is chilly but the fishing is good. All units have fireplaces and fully equipped kitchens, and five have been designated as nonsmoking.

Accommodations: There are two one-bedroom cabins and two two-bedroom cabins, all with knotty pine interiors and beam ceilings. The chalet has four suites, two upstairs and two downstairs. Each chalet unit has a sofabed in the living room, private bath, and all linens are supplied.

Cost: Summer rates are lowest: one-bedroom suites $60 to $80 per night, one-bedroom cabins $70 to $90 per night (both sleep four). Two-bedroom cabins (each sleeps six) $90 to $110 per night. Two-night stays midweek receive a 10-percent discount; three nights, 15-percent discount; four nights, 20-percent discount; five nights, 25-percent discount. Two-night minimum stay on weekends. **Address:** PO Box 658, Mammoth Lakes, California 93546. **Telephone:** 619–934–2445.

PINECREST LAKE RESORT

Address: PO Box 1216, Pinecrest, California 95364 (several hours' drive east of the San Francisco Bay area, in the Stanislaus National Forest).
Telephone: 209–965–3411.

A large sandy beach and clear blue, warm waters make for great fishing, boating, and swimming at Pinecrest Lake Resort. Rent a paddleboat, play tennis, or watch movies under the stars in Pinecrest's outdoor amphitheater, and stay in a comfortable cabin, townhouse, or motel room. Some rooms have a lake view, and all are within walking distance of the lake. The forest service nearby has guided nature hikes, and there is a hiking trail around lake. In winter cross-country ski or head to Dodge Ridge (four miles away) for downhill skiing.

Season: Year-round.

Accommodations: Cabins and townhouses have complete kitchens. You must bring your own sheets and towels, or you can rent them for $3 a set. Fourteen two- and three-bedroom townhouses sleep six to eight people and have full kitchens, fireplaces, and barbecue areas on back decks. Seven two- and three-bedroom cabins sleep four to six people. The townhouse can sleep more, as it has a sofabed. Motel rooms have two queen-size beds.

Special Features: Sailboats, paddleboats, rowboats, and party boats can be rented at the marina. Other facilities include tennis courts and a restaurant and snack bar. Campgrounds are within walking distance.

Cost: Motel rooms for four people $425 per week in winter, $475 in summer; $65 to $80 per night. Two-bedroom cabins sleeping four $475 per week in winter, $525 in summer; $75 to $90 per night. Three-bedroom cabins sleeping six $550 per week in winter, $590 in summer; $85 to $100 per night. Two- and three-bedroom townhouses $595 to $850 per week, $95 to $150 per night. In July and August cabins and townhouses are rented by the week only.

Tennis courts $5 per hour. Motorboats $35 for half day, $50 all day; rowboats $22 half day, $35 all day; paddleboats $6.50 per hour, $22 half day, $35 all day; sailboats $35 half day, $50 all day; party boats $27 to $35 for two hours, $74 to $85 half day, $100 to $120 all day (rates vary according to size of party boat).

Nearby: Restaurant, grocery store, sports shop, and post office are within walking distance. Horseback rentals are three miles up the road.

BONANZA KING RESORT

Address: Route 2, Box 4790, Trinity Center, California 96091 (seventy-five miles from Redding).
Telephone: 916–266–3305.

Bonanza King sits right on Coffee Creek, and every summer an enormous swimming hole is created right in front of the resort by a rock dam. Kids spend hours swimming and splashing, taking canoe rides, or wading up and down the creek. The cabins, which rent by the week in the summer, sit on a large grassy meadow amid breathtaking scenery. Coffee Creek meets the Trinity River about a mile away, creating a natural swimming hole that is a popular side trip for visiting children. The tiny hamlet of Coffee Creek is about a half mile away. The Lethbridge family has operated Bonanza King for the past fourteen years, and many of their guests come back each year to enjoy their warm hospitality and majestic setting.

Season: Mid-April to mid-October, depending on the weather.

Accommodations: Six furnished cabins house three to eight people. Most have a combination living room and kitchen, one bedroom, and sleeping lofts with beds. All pots, pans, and utensils are provided, as are towels and linens. Most cabins are heated by wood stoves; firewood is free.

Special Features: Grassy areas for playing, horseshoe pit, swimming hole, duck pond, volleyball, children's swing and sandbox, campfire area, fishing, one-mile hike to Trinity River.

Cost: Cabins $70 per night for three people ($500 per week) to $100 per night for a larger cabin for eight people ($700 per week). Rates are calculated by specific cabin and number of people in it.

RIPPLE CREEK CABINS

Address: Route 2, Box 3899, Trinity Center, California 96091.
Telephone: 916–266–3505; 916–266–3608.

Ripple Creek's seven cabins are secluded among the pines and cedar trees along Ripple Creek, overlooking the Trinity River. Guests can enjoy the swimming hole in the Trinity River, hike in the Trinity Alps Wilderness Area next door, read, and relax in the fresh air. Children can swim, poke around the woods, and explore the spectacular natural setting. Bicycles, including children's sizes, are made available to guests.

Season: Year-round.

Accommodations: Cabins vary in size and shape and can sleep from two to six people; cribs and rollaways are available free of charge. One two-story cabin with four bedrooms is perfect for large groups. All have fully equipped kitchens, bedding, towels, electric wall heaters, and wood stoves.

Special Features: Children's playground, Ping-Pong, volleyball, badminton, horseshoes, fishing (catch-and-release fly fishing is popular nearby). Kids enjoy feeding and petting the horses on the property. Cross-country skiing is available in winter.

Cost: In summer, rates have a five-day minimum; book five months in advance. Cabins $70 for two people per night, $5 each additional child two to eighteen; $435 per week for two people, $35 each additional child. Group cabin $100 per night for up to four people, $10 each additional adult, $5 each additional child; weekly stays $630 for up to four people.

Reduced rates available October 1 to May 1, excluding holidays: $60 per day and $350 per week for two, additional children $5 per night. Group cabin $85 per night, $500 per week for four people, $10 per additional adult, $5 per additional child per night.

Nearby: Trinity Lake is twenty minutes away. Horseback riding is twenty minutes away and white water rafting on the Lower Trinity below the dam is about an hour away.

CEDAR STOCK RESORT AND MARINA

Address: Star Route Box 510, Lewiston, California (one hour's drive northwest of Redding).
Telephone: 916–286–2225.

Families that love to swim, fish, and laze in the sun can share a houseboat for a week on Trinity Lake in northern California for the cost of a cabin vacation. If you go off-season you can save even more. The houseboats are cozy and comfortable; boaters usually eat and sleep in the house portion of the boat and play on the large rooftop deck and the decks at either end. Families that have done this successfully recommend that you alternate boating, swimming, and sunning with dropping anchor and enjoying a few planned activities on land.

Accommodations: Houseboats make clever use of space; most have bunk beds and sofabeds. Don't expect a lot of privacy.

Cost: In peak season, boats sleeping up to eight people $995 to $1,200 per week. Guests pay for gas. Life jackets and deck chairs included.

Nearby: Horseback riding, white water rafting, panning for gold in the Trinity River.

ODELL LAKE LODGE

Address: PO Box 72, Crescent Lake, Oregon 97425 (in the Deschutes National Forest, seventy miles east of Eugene and sixty miles west of Bend).
Telephone: 503–433–2540.

Set on the wooded shores of the lake with its own marina, Odell Lake Lodge offers housekeeping cabins and lodge rooms and plenty of recreational activities. Families can rent fishing boats, rowboats, canoes, and waterskiing equipment or rent mountain bikes to explore the many trails in the area. A lakeside restaurant has views of the wild birds that inhabit the lake, including ospreys and an occasional bald eagle from a sanctuary next door. Fishing is excellent here, with salmon and rainbow and lake trout. In the evening guests gather around the fireplace in the lodge's Great Room. Families will be most comfortable in the housekeeping cabins tucked into the forest.

Season: Year-round. There is lakeside recreation in the summer and cross-country skiing on groomed trails in winter.

Accommodations: Thirteen housekeeping cabins include kitchens, private baths, linens, and firewood. Several of the four-person cabins do not have ovens. Seven bedrooms are located in the lodge; many are set up for four people.

Special Features: There are barbecue and picnic areas, games, a small playground, family movies, and a wading area and sundeck on the lake. The lake is glacier-fed, and most people don't swim until late July or August, when it warms up, but kids enjoy playing in Odell Creek, which runs next to the lodge. Boat, mountain bike, and ski equipment rentals are on the premises, and the lakeside restaurant serves home-style breakfast, lunch, dinner, and snacks.

Cost: Lodge room for four people, $38 to $50 in summer, $42 to $50 in winter. Housekeeping cabin $50 per night for four people (seven of the cabins accommodate four) to $175 per night for sixteen people. Winter rates slightly higher; 10-percent discount for stays of more than five days.

Motorboats $35 to $45, canoes $15 per day. Mountain bikes $10 per half day, $15 per full day. Summer reservations accepted from March 1, winter reservations from June 1.

WAYFARER RESORT

Address: Star Route, Vida, Oregon 97488 (twenty-five miles east of Eugene).
Telephone: 503–896–3613.

Cabins are nestled back among the trees near the McKenzie River at this secluded ten-acre resort. Children enjoy playing and splashing in Marten Creek along one side of the resort and fishing from the rocky riverbanks. White water raft trips down the river are popular; a number of reasonably priced outfitters are nearby. Deer and squirrels often are spotted on the lawn.

Season: Year-round.

Accommodations: Thirteen cabins on the banks of the McKenzie River and Marten Creek can house three to eight people. All have open-beam ceilings, decks, fireplaces, sofabeds in the living room, and fully equipped kitchens. Port-a-cribs and laundry facilities are available. A three-day minimum stay is required from late April to mid-September.

Special Features: Swimming, fishing, tennis, volleyball, rafting, and hiking.

Cost: Two-bedroom cabins for four people $95 per night, one-bedroom cabin $80 for two people; additional person $6 per night. Children under two stay free.

Nearby: Several reservoirs with excellent swimming and an eighteen-hole golf course are a short drive away.

BAKER LAKE RESORT

Address: PO Box 100, Concrete, Washington 98237 (two hours from Seattle).
Telephone: 206–853–8325.

Families that like to fish will enjoy dropping a line in Baker Lake, which is filled with rainbow, steelhead, Dolly Varden, and silver trout. When you tire of fishing, take a dip in the lake, rent a rowboat or canoe, or simply take in the views of the snow-topped northern Cascade Mountains. Most of the cabins are situated near the lake and are fully equipped. This is the only development on Baker Lake; campsites and RV hookups are offered as well.

Season: April through October.

Accommodations: Twelve simple studio and one-bedroom cabins are available. Half have private baths and fully equipped kitchens; the other half do not have kitchens and use bathhouse facilities nearby. Each cabin has an outdoor fire pit and picnic table. Guests supply their own bedding.

Special Features: Playground, swimming pool, café, small store, boat rental, hiking, laundry services.

Cost: Weekly rates $240 to $525, depending on cabin size and amenities. Daily rates $40 to $45 for four-person cabins with shared baths, $55 to $90 for fully equipped cabins. Rowboats and canoes $20 per day on weekends, $15 per day weekdays; paddleboats $5 per hour.

ROCKY MOUNTAINS AND SOUTHWEST

RED FISH LAKE LODGE

Address: PO Box 9, Stanley, Idaho 83278 (at the headwaters of the main fork of the Salmon River, sixty miles north of Sun Valley in the Sawtooth National Forest).
Telephone: 208–774–3536.

Deer wander through the grounds of this idyllic lakeside complex in the morning, owls patrol after dark, and a family of ospreys have a nest nearby. Guests can stay in cabins, a lodge, or motel rooms; the lodge has its own marina. Boating, swimming, and fishing take up most of the day at Red Fish, which is the only lodging available on the lake besides a campground. A vast wilderness area begins at its southern end, and a shuttle service is available to give hikers a head start on exploring its rugged beauty.

Season: Late May through September.

Accommodations: Each of the twelve log duplex cabins with fireplaces or wood stoves sleep five to six people and have a small sitting room, at least one separate bedroom, and a front porch with furniture. Larger cabins have a loft or upstairs bedroom. Thirteen lodge rooms have shared baths and sleep two to three people. Motel units have two double beds; five lake suites can sleep four people and have a living room, bathroom, master bedroom, and private deck. Only one unit has a kitchen; it sleeps eight people and is rented by the week. The main lodge has a dining room and bar. Bedding and towels are provided.

Special Features: Marina with boat rental, general store, gas station, public showers, launderette. Hiking and riding trails radiate from the lodge. Horses can be rented by the hour, half day, and day nearby.

Cost: Standard motel rooms with two double beds $75 per night. Lodge rooms with one double and one twin bed $50 per night. Duplex cabins $90 per night. Lakeside cabins sleeping up to eight $225 per night. Additional person $10 per night; children under three stay free. Off-season specials in late May, early June, and late September.

Small motorboats $10 per hour, canoes $5 per hour, paddleboats $5 per half hour.

Nearby: Picnic areas and grills are in the state park next door, and there are ghost towns in the area.

HILL'S RESORT

Address: Route 5, Priest Lake, Idaho 83856.
Telephone: 208–443–2251.

A comfortable resort set on the sandy shores of Priest Lake, Hill's has been owned and operated by the same family since 1946. Accommodations range from deluxe to basic, and a gourmet restaurant overlooking the lake has excellent food when you need a break from cooking. Water recreation is the big attraction here, with swimming, fishing, kayaking, and canoeing. The broad and gently sloping beach has both sunny and shady spots for reading and relaxing.

Season: Year-round.

Accommodations: Condominiums, chalets, duplexes, and cabins are available. Lakefront housekeeping units and deluxe lakefront units have fireplaces, dishwashers, and balconies or decks. Individual cabins, which sleep four to ten people, are the most economical.

Special Features: Mountain bike and cross-country ski trails, hiking and jogging trails, boat rental, tennis courts, gourmet restaurant, and nearby golf course.

Cost: Late June through Labor Day, individual cabins $550 to $1,100 per week, depending on size, other times $475 to $900 per week. Nightly stays available in fall, winter, and spring. Canoes and rowboats $15 per day, $75 per week; Hobie Cats $55 per day, $250 per week; mountain bikes $15 per day; tennis court use $6 singles, $8 doubles per hour.

S BAR S RANCH

Address: 44285 RCR 129 Steamboat Springs, Colorado 80487 (ranch is seven miles from Steamboat Springs).
Telephone: 303–879–0788.

Host Bill May is a widely known cowboy poet and storyteller, and he practices his repertoire on his young guests when ranch work is done. The ranch has a large cabin for rent along the Elk River, just outside Steamboat Springs. Its proximity to the ski area and its low price make it a popular spot for both summer and winter stays. Guests can tag along for haying in late July and August. The trout fishing in the river is excellent, although the river is a bit too cold and fast moving for swimming.

Season: Year-round.

Accommodations: One large housekeeping cabin accommodates two to twenty people. It can be used by one large group or separated into upstairs and downstairs units and used by two families. The downstairs, which includes a bedroom, fully equipped kitchen, and bath, can sleep six people in a double bed, two couches, and a double sofabed. The upstairs has five bedrooms, a private bath, and a minimal kitchen with hot plate and refrigerator but no sink. All linens and kitchen equipment are furnished.

Cost: Prices based on sliding scale—the longer the stay, the lower the price. In summer week-long stay for three people $30 per night, for four people $35. Four people for three nights, $39 per night. Prices higher during ski season: holidays $51 per night for four people staying three nights; remainder of ski season $47 per night for four people staying three nights.

Nearby: Steamboat Springs, a well-known ski area, has a large, naturally heated swimming pool, Steamboat Lake, a quarry, and a gondola that goes to ski mountain.

LAZY J RESORT AND RAFTING COMPANY

Address: PO Box 109, Coaldale, Colorado 81222 (between Canyon City and Salida).
Telephone: 800–678–4274.

Headquarter at the Lazy J in comfortable cabins with panoramic views of the Sangre de Cristo Mountains and the San Isabel National Forest and take advantage of the half- or full-day river raft trips on the Arkansas River. Both calm water and exhilarating white water float trips are offered and can be tailored for any age; the Lazy J has taken people as young as two and as old as ninety-four out on the river. Horseback riding also is available by the hour. Guests can swim in the river or a heated pool. The Lazy J is a recent winner of Colorado's hospitality award.

Season: May through Labor Day.

Accommodations: Log cabins with one or two bedrooms have fully equipped kitchens. Motel rooms can accommodate two or three people.

Special Features: A restaurant with a deck overlooking the river is open for breakfast and lunch. Raft trips that last from an hour to two days, guided horseback trips, volleyball, and a heated pool are all available on the premises.

Cost: Cabins $45 to $70 per night, depending on size and number of people. Motel rooms $30 to $35 per night. Half-day trips $30 to $50, full day trip $60 to $80, lunch included. Children under twelve get a 10-percent discount on raft trips. Riding $9 per hour, $16 for two hours.

CLIFF LAKE LODGE

Address: PO Box 573, Cameron, Montana 59720.
Telephone: 406–682–4982.

Popular as a family reunion site, Cliff Lake Lodge allows guests to put together their own vacation package, including fishing, boating, horseback riding, and river rafting. Children enjoy wading and fishing in the creek that runs next to the cabins. The lake is several hundred yards from the lodge and cabins, with the boat dock and swimming area about a quarter of a mile away. A national bird refuge sits right behind the lodge, and visitors can be assured of spotting golden eagles, bald eagles, osprey, cormorants, pelicans, and many other bird species. River otters and beavers inhabit the lake.

Season: Almost year-round; the lodge closes for part of the winter when snow makes it inaccessible.

Accommodations: Choose from bed-and-breakfast rooms and modern or rustic cabins. A modern three-bedroom guest cabin sleeps four to eight people, and two modern log cabins can sleep up to twelve people; these cabins have every convenience, including coffee makers. Three bed-and-breakfast rooms are available for those who do not wish to do their own cooking. Seven rustic cabins for two to four people have one or two bedrooms, a front room-kitchen, and a tiny porch. Cooking is done on a wood stove or outdoor barbecue, and the only running water is out front; a shared bathhouse is nearby. Guests must bring their own cooking gear and towels.

Special Features: Guests can rent fishing boats with motors and canoes (all with life jackets); guided horseback tours are on site, and white water raft trips can be arranged. Several blue ribbon fly fishing rivers are nearby, and hiking trails to mountain lakes abound. If cabin guests do not want to cook they can arrange to have breakfast and a packed lunch prepared. Cross-country skiing is popular in winter.

Cost: Rustic cabins $30 for one bedroom, $40 for two bedrooms. Modern three-bedroom cabins $70 per night for four people, $10 each additional person (eight maximum). Modern twelve-person cabin $100 per night base rate, with additional charge for extra people.

Boats with motors $25 per half day, $40 per day. Canoes (holding three people) $25 per day. Full-day horse tours with lunch $50 per person per day; hourly rate $12. Dinner rides, adults $35, children $30.

Nearby: Yellowstone National Park is thirty miles away. See pages 109–110 for more on Yellowstone.

HOLLAND LAKE LODGE

Address: SR Box 2083, Condon, Montana 59816 (halfway between Kalispell and Missoula).
Telephone: 800–648–8859; 406–754–2282.

A waterfall at one end of Holland Lake is about a mile-and-a-half hike from the lodge. It's just the right length for even young children to walk and far enough away to make it a perfect picnic outing. Two wilderness areas surround Holland Lake Lodge, nestled in a valley between two mountain ranges. You can rent all kinds of boats for exploring the lake; or explore the surrounding terrain on horseback or on foot. Lodge rooms and cabins are available with and without kitchens and the lodge has a dining room.

Season: Year-round.

Accommodations: Five cabins (four have kitchens) sleep four to eight people. Nine lodge rooms have two shared hall bathrooms. Several of the double rooms can accommodate a double rollaway bed.

Special Features: Swimming, fishing, volleyball, horseshoes, hiking, pool table, piano, sauna. Create your own recreation package by renting canoes, rowboats, and paddleboats. Horseback riding is available by the hour or by the day. Breakfast, lunch, and dinner can be purchased in the dining room, and there is an all-beverage bar. Seven miles of cross-country ski trails are maintained in winter, and there is ice fishing on the lake. Dog sled races take place near the lodge in January and February.

Cost: In summer, cabins without kitchens sleeping four people $55 per night; cabins with kitchens sleeping four $68 to $80 per night. Cabins with kitchens sleeping eight people $80 to $95; cabin with kitchen sleeping seven $80. Lodge rooms with shared bathroom $33 in winter, $39 in summer; double room with double rollaway bed $50.

Canoes $4 per hour, paddleboats $6 per hour. Horseback riding $10 per hour; all-day rides $65. Reservations for July and early August fill a year or more in advance. Cancellations occur in January, when guests must place a deposit for that year; call mid-January to inquire. Reservations for other times of year are much easier to get.

Nearby: Roadside stands throughout the region sell cherries in July.

SLIDE ROCK STATE PARK

Address: Seven miles north of Sedona, Arizona, on state highway 89. Telephone: 602–282–3034.

Slide Rock is a quarter mile stretch of Oak Creek with a slick rock bottom and natural water slides. The current carries swimmers through the grooves and into pools in the creek; little ones can stay occupied for hours in its wide natural wading pools, while its natural rock chutes offer older kids an exhilarating ride. Try to visit on weekdays in the summer; weekends can be crowded, and the number of visitors is limited to the number of spaces in the park's parking lot. Slide Rock originally was homesteaded in 1907, and visitors can tour the old homestead and original apple orchard areas. There are picnic areas and barbecue pits and a volleyball area.

Where to Stay
Located just one-half mile from the Slide Rock swim area, Pfeifer's Slide Rock Lodge offers clean and comfortable rooms. It has a private creek frontage area just across the road on Oak Creek for fishing, swimming, and sunning, plus a large picnic area with barbecue grills and tables, a complimentary continental breakfast, and horseshoe pits. Twenty knotted pine–paneled motel rooms with two or three double beds can accommodate two to six people each for $65 to $75 per night. There are also cabins for two people with kitchens and fireplaces. The nearest restaurants

are two miles away. Address: Star Route 3, Box 1141, Sedona, Arizona 86336. Telephone: 602–282–3531.

Splash all day in the many natural swimming holes in Oak Creek next to Don Hoel's Cabins or head to Slide Rock State Park, six miles away. There's a landscaped playground for the kids, spectacular hiking, fishing, horseshoes, and Ping-Pong. Eighteen log housekeeping cabins have fully equipped kitchens, porches, and barbecues and can sleep two to six people in one, two, or three double beds for $55 to $75 per night, double occupancy. Motel rooms with kitchens are available for $50 per night. Extra people are $5 each per night. Address: Oak Creek Star Route, Box 200, Flagstaff, Arizona 86001. Telephone: 602–282–3560.

Nearby: Sedona, Montezuma's Castle, Tuzigoot Indian ruins, the Grand Canyon (see page 110), horseback riding, tennis, and golf.

CORKINS LODGE

Address: PO Box 396, Chama, New Mexico 87520 (two hours north of Santa Fe and about ninety minutes from Taos).
Telephone: 800–548–7688; 505–588–7261.

Backed by the eleven-thousand-foot-high Brazos Peak with a magnificent waterfall, "El Chorro," cascading down, Corkins Lodge has sixteen housekeeping cabins, a heated swimming pool, and excellent fishing in the Brazos River and its privately stocked pond. Deer wander down to the lodge and among the cabins regularly in the evening, hoping for a snack; be sure to bring plenty of apples and a camera, as they are tame enough to be hand-fed.

Accommodations: Sixteen cabins have fully equipped kitchens, and all linens except beach towels are supplied. Cabins house four to ten people. The four-person cabins have one big room with two double beds (and space enough to add a twin bed if you need to), and kitchen, dining room table, and chairs. The six-person cabins have two rooms: a bedroom and a kitchen and dining area with a sofabed.

Special Features: Heated swimming pool, river fishing a quarter of a mile away, hiking and mountain climbing, game room with pool table, Ping-Pong and video games, tether ball, volleyball, fishing pond.

Cost: Cabins for four $700 per week, $100 per night. Six-person cabins $810 to $1,000 per week, $120 to $135 per night. Cabins for eight $875. Pond fish 25 cents an inch.

Nearby: The Cumbres and Toltec Scenic Railway goes into Colorado from Chama, fourteen miles from the lodge. It's a very popular attraction during the summer, so advance reservations are recommended (505–756–2151).

CENTRAL UNITED STATES

OSAGE HILLS STATE PARK

Address: Red Eagle Route, Box 84, Pawhuska, Oklahoma 74056.
Telephone: 918–336–4141.

With a large fishing lake and turkeys, deer, and squirrels roaming its wooded, rolling hills, this state park is a favorite for families that love water sports and hiking, fishing for catfish, sunfish, or bass. You can swim in the pool, play tennis, volleyball, or horseshoes, and rent rowboats for an invigorating tour of the lake.

Season: Year-round.

Accommodations: Eight one- and two-bedroom cabins made of native stone have fireplaces, full kitchens, all linens, heat, and air-conditioning. Campsites and RV hookups also are available.

Special Features: Tennis, hiking, swimming pool (no lake swimming), playground, boating, basketball, volleyball, horseshoes, fishing.

Cost: One-bedroom cabins sleeping four people $47 per night; two-bedroom cabins sleeping six, $58 per night. You can book cabins up to a year in advance or just a few days in advance, depending on availability. Rowboat rental $5 for six hours.

Nearby: Osage Tribal Museum in Pawhuska; Woolaroc (in Bartlesville) has a wildlife preserve with one of Oklahoma's largest buffalo herds, museums, a children's zoo, a nature trail, and a historic lodge.

EMINENCE CANOES, COTTAGES, AND CAMP

Address: PO Box 276, Eminence, Missouri 65466.
Telephone: 314–226–3642.

The Ozark National Riverway has several private canoe concessionaires that offer canoe, kayak, and tube rentals, car shuttles, and accommodations to floaters. Eminence is one of the most family-friendly, with special "Quality Time" packages for parents and kids. The camp is on private land about a block away from a long beach. The water is deep enough for diving off "Button Rock," a three-tiered natural diving platform. Guests can take float trips on either the Jack's Fork River or the Current River. Both of these spring-fed rivers are so clear that you can see the fish swimming on the bottom. Turtles abound in these waters; you also might see beaver, deer, turkey, or mink.

Season: March through November.

Accommodations: Eight informal cottages have fully equipped kitchens, living and dining areas, one or more bedrooms, porches, barbecues and picnic tables out front, all linens, air-conditioning, and heat. Twenty-five campsites and six RV sites have bathrooms nearby.

Special Features: Volleyball, badminton, horseshoes, and croquet equipment can be checked out free of charge. Horseback riding is available next door.

Cost: Cottages $50 for two adults, additional person $10 per night. Children twelve and under $10 per child per stay, whether it's one night or one week. Canoes $27 per day for a Saturday or holiday trip, slightly less during the week. Kayaks $20 per day; tubes $4 per day, or $8 per day for tube and transportation. Private vehicle shuttles $10 per hour when they drive your vehicle, 50 cents per mile when you ride in their van.

The Quality Time Family Package combines lodging with canoe and tube rentals. Six days and five nights of cottage accommodations, two days of canoeing, tubing anytime, and the use of facilities $278 for a family of four. Be sure to ask about this arrangement. Horseback riding $10 per hour.

Nearby: The National Park Interpretive Centers offer wildlife hikes, plant identification walks, demonstrations of a three-story grist mill, and cave tours.

WILDERNESS RIDGE RESORT

Address: Big Piney Route, Duke, Missouri 65461.
Telephone: 314–435–6767.

This quiet getaway prides itself on its tranquillity and abundance of wildlife, including deer, wild turkey, and songbirds. Surrounded by the Mark Twain National Forest, it offers canoeing, rafting, fishing, and tubing on the Big Piney River. A well-priced family plan for Sunday through Friday nights includes accommodations, float trips, and special weekday activities. Cabins share bath facilities. You can opt for canoe, raft, or tube trips of different lengths. Your hosts will shuttle you upriver and let you float at your leisure back to the resort, swimming and picnicking along the way.

Season: April through October.

Accommodations: Two primitive log cabins and three newer cabins have simple but fully equipped kitchens. Bedding is supplied, but guests bring their own towels. Restrooms and showers near the cabins. Most cabins have two double beds; cots are available for larger families.

Cost: One-night stays $40 per couple, two or more nights $32 per night. Additional adults $5; children six to sixteen $3 per night, under six free. Family plan includes cabin, seven-mile float trip, unlimited use of inner tubes, special weekday activities, and a second seven-mile float trip if you stay four or five nights (not available over holidays). Two nights and three days $75 per couple, three nights and four days $100 per couple, four nights $150 per couple, five nights $160 per couple. Additional person charges as above. Primitive camping $4.50 per night, and $3.50 per night if you plan to rent a canoe.

Nearby: Many caves are nearby, Meramec Caverns is about forty-five minutes away, and Lake of the Ozarks is about fifty miles away.

FLOAT TRIPS ON THE MERAMEC RIVER

Address: Blue Springs State Park, PO Box 540, Bourbon, Missouri 65441 (off Highway N); Meramec State Park, PO 57, Sullivan, Missouri 63080 (Highway 185 south).
Telephone: Blue Springs, 800–333–8007 or 314–732–5200; Meramec, 800–334–6946 or 314–468–6519.

Stay in a comfortable cabin in Blue Springs or Meramec state parks and get an early start on a tube, canoe, or raft float down the Meramec River. Both parks offer bus rides to your starting point; float back five or ten miles to your cabin at your own pace.

Season: Blue Springs is open year-round; Meramec is open from March 1 to October 31.

Accommodations: Both Meramec and Blue Springs state parks have housekeeping cabins with fully equipped kitchens, living rooms, and all linens. They range in size from one to five bedrooms. Less expensive "camper unit cabins" without living rooms or kitchens but all with private baths, air-conditioning, heat, coffeepots, cooking griddles, and outdoor barbecues are available at Blue Springs.

Special Features: Blue Springs offers horseback riding, hayrides, cave tours, and fishing in a natural trout stream. Meramec has marked hiking trails, cave tours, and a dining lodge.

Cost. Meramec State Park cabins $30 to $100 per night, depending on size and number of people. Most four-person cabins $55 to $60 per night. Blue Springs cabins $50 to $80 per night. Less expensive camper unit cabins $30 to $40 per night.

Canoe rental $24 per day, rafts $40 to $60 per day, inner tubes $3.50 per day. Transportation upstream for the five-mile float $7. Guided horseback rides $7 per half hour, $12 per hour. Hayrides, adults $3, children $2.

TIMBER BAY LODGE AND HOUSEBOATS

Address: Box 248, Babbit, Minnesota 55706 (May to October); 10040 Colorado Road, Bloomington, Minnesota 55438 (November to April). Telephone: 218–827–3682 (summer); 612–831–0043 (winter).

Just south of the Boundary Waters Canoe Area on the shores of Birch Lake in the Superior National Forest is this quiet resort with cabins and houseboats. A supervised children's program, free use of bicycles, canoes, and paddleboats, plus many other recreational activities make this cabin resort a particularly good choice for families. Houseboaters travel on the private and semiwild twenty-mile-long Birch Lake, towing a complimentary fishing boat behind. Families can opt for a three-, four-, or seven-day houseboat trip.
Season: Early May through October 1.

Cabin Resort

Accommodations: Twelve log-sided cabins with one to three bedrooms are spaced far enough apart from one another to give real privacy. All have fireplaces, fully equipped, modern kitchens, decks, heat, bedding (bring your own towels), deck furniture, and outdoor charcoal grills. They are rented by the week (Saturday to Saturday) from mid-June to mid-August and daily or weekly in the early or late season.

Special Features: Waterfront activities include swimming, waterskiing, canoeing, sailing, and fishing. A children's program for five- to twelve-year-olds run by a full-time children's activities director operates from early June through late August and offers nature activities, crafts, hikes, and picnics. A part-time naturalist program for adults and children includes wildlife talks, nature walks, star gazing, and day canoe trips. In addition guests can play volleyball, horseshoes, badminton, archery, shuffleboard, and Ping-Pong.

Cost: Rates are based on double occupancy; additional person $10 per night or $50 per week. Children under five stay free. Mid-June to late August, one-bedroom cabins $550 per week, larger cabins $650 to $850 per week. Early- and late-season discounts of 10 to 20 percent. Waterskiing $30 per hour plus gas; pontoons $35 per half day, $60 per day. Golf, available nearby at the Babbitt Country Club, $8 per day.

Houseboats

Houseboats sleep two to ten people, and all have rooftop patios, porches, hot and cold running water, propane gas stoves, ovens, refrigerators, gas heat, twelve-volt electric lights, pollution-free toilets, and showers. Each boat comes equipped with life preservers and aluminum fishing boats (you can rent a motor if you wish). Guests supply their own food, sheets, and towels. Birch Lake is twenty miles long, and maps of its beaches, reefs, and water depths are provided.

Cost: Summer rates mid-June through mid-August: A thirty-two-foot houseboat that sleeps three to four people, $895 per seven-night week, $595 for a four-night midweek cruise, $550 for a three-night weekend cruise. Ten-percent discount from late May to mid-June and in late August, 20-percent discount available September and early May.

SPIRIT OF THE LAND HOSTEL

Address: 940 Gunflint Trail, Grand Marais, Minnesota 55604
(sixty miles from Grand Marais).
Telephone: 218–388–2241.

Tranquillity, serenity, and miles of peaceful canoe routes, where you'll spot moose, deer, bears, bald eagles, river otters and beavers, are at your front door. This AYH member is on an island in Seagull Lake in the heart of the Boundary Waters Canoe Area, where glaciers have carved out canoe routes on interconnected lakes. It is operated by Wilderness Canoe Base, a nonprofit group that runs youth camps, canoe trips, island camps, elder camps, and retreats in summer and winter. Spirit of the Land has several cabins, and a family can get one all to itself. Guests can bring their own food and do their own cooking in the hostel's kitchen or they can purchase meals with advance notice. Families should be prepared for an invigorating wilderness experience; children must be over five years old.

Season: Year-round.

Accommodations: There are three main cabins—the men's and women's dorms sleep six each and the central commons cabin has the kitchen, dining, and lounge facilities. Additional hostelers can be accommodated in wilderness cabins nearby; families should be sure to request housing together. Bathrooms are clean, high-quality outhouses, and there are hot showers and a sauna.

Cost. Lodging only, $10 per person, $5 per child under twelve; lodging plus meals, $18 per person per day. A special Wilderness Package includes hostel room, outdoor skills instruction, equipment use, guided group trips for three or more people, evening programs, and boat transportation. Four-day weekend (Thursday through Sunday) packages $120 per person, including three nights' lodging with all meals and outdoor programs. Mainland-to-island transportation $3 per person.

FENCE LAKE LODGE

Address: 1219 Frying Pan Camp Lane, Lac du Flambeau,
Wisconsin 54538.
Telephone: 715–588–3255.

When the kids get tired of playing tennis and lawn games they can head
over to the children's play park for climbing, sliding, and swinging. Or
they can begin their day with a volleyball game in the water of Fence
Lake. The lake's shallow shoreline allows for safe swimming and water
games; you must go quite far to reach deep water. All eight cottages face
the lake and come with a complimentary fishing boat. Motel rooms, some
with kitchenettes, are available as well. The lodge has two dining areas,
one upstairs, open for dinner only, and one downstairs, with a restaurant–
snack bar and drinks bar.

Accommodations: Cottages with two to five bedrooms have bedding
and fully equipped kitchens; guests bring their own towels. Rental is by
the week in July and August, with a three-night minimum the rest of the
year. Four of the fourteen motel rooms have kitchenettes.

Special Features: A fourteen-foot boat is included with each vacation
home rental (extra for motel guests); if you bring your own boat, docking
is available at no extra charge. Picnic tables and grills are located throughout the resort. Other activities include volleyball, tennis, badminton, shuffleboard, hiking, and boat rental. The boat house has games for children
to check out on rainy days.

Cost: Cottages $55 to $135 per day, $330 to $800 per week, depending
on size. Off-season rates available; be sure to ask. Fourteen-foot boat $10
per day, $60 per week; motor $15 per day, $90 per week; pontoon $100
per day; sailboards $10 per hour, $25 per half day. Book as early as possible;
many guests book for the following summer before leaving.

Nearby: An Indian reservation with a museum has powwows two nights
a week during the summer.

LAONA AYH HOSTEL

Address: PO Box 325, 5397 Beech Street, Laona, Wisconsin 54541.
Telephone: 715–674–2615.

Hostel guests can fish and boat on Scattered Rice Lake, a stone's throw
away from the hostel. There are other lakes nearby, and many hiking trails
and biking trails surround them. A public beach on Silver Lake is one and
a half miles away. Several different-size family rooms are available, and if
AYH members stay two nights, the third is free. Families should be sure

to take a trip on one or both of the old trains running through the area—the Nicolet Scenic Railroad makes a sixty-mile journey in restored rail cars from the twenties and thirties, and the Lumberjack Special steam locomotive takes passengers to an old logging camp that has been converted into a museum.

Season: Year-round.

Accommodations: Several different family rooms are available—one with six bunks, one with four bunks, and one with two bunks. Bathrooms are shared and kitchen facilities are available. The hostel is closed from 10 A.M. to 6 P.M.

Cost: Members $9 per night, nonmembers $12, children under twelve half price.

Nearby: Horseback riding is four miles away.

SUNSET RESORT

Address: Washington Island, Wisconsin 54246.
Telephone: 414–847–2531.

Back-to-nature types will want to take advantage of Sunset Resort's idyllic and quiet setting on Washington Island at the tip of Door County. Families swim on the lovely sandy beach, hike, relax, and explore the surrounding island. Biking is a popular way to get around the island; if you don't bring your own, you can rent a bike near the car ferry dock on the south side of the island. The resort serves breakfast daily during the summer and specializes in Norwegian grilled toast and Icelandic pancakes. Eleven rooms are available; one is set up just for families.

Season: Mid-May to mid-October. Busiest times are in July and early August.

Accommodations: Room no. 10 is the best for families, with a double bed in one room and another connecting room with two single beds. Cribs are available. All guest rooms are designated nonsmoking.

Cost: Room no. 10 $68 per night, double occupancy; additional person $5 per night.

SLEEPING BEAR DUNES NATIONAL LAKESHORE

You'll huff and puff to the top of these steep and rugged sand dunes, but once at the top you'll be rewarded with a fast run down, and your kids will never forget it. At the bottom, walk the rest of the way to Lake Michigan for a picnic or swim, then brace yourself for the climb back up and down the exhilarating slope. The best places to stay are around Big

Glen Lake and Little Glen Lake, where the many cottages for rent have boating and swimming in the summer. The area has many magnificent hiking trails leading to scenic views or through more moderately rolling dunes, beech and maple forests, and wooded low dunes. Be sure to take a trip to Leelanau's Fish Town on the wharf and wander through its shops, stopping for a bite at one of the restaurants. Canoeing on the Platte River, Manitou Island, and the Manitou Underwater Reserve are all close by.

Where to Stay

Miller's Cabins has three charming log housekeeping cabins that sleep five to seven people. The cabins are right on Big Glen Lake at the end of a quiet cul de sac, and owner Jeanette Miller prefers families with children. Guests can see the Dunes from their cabins. $650 to $700 per week. Call late February for reservations during the peak summer months. Address: Rt. #2, Maple City, Michigan 49664. Telephone: 616–334–4929.

Maple Lane Motel and Resort has beautifully decorated motel rooms, some with kitchenettes, and two apartments in an old carriage house. The beach is a half-block away, and guests have use of canoes and rowboats. A park-like area behind the motel has barbecue grills and picnic tables, a volleyball and basketball court, horseshoe pit, and a firepit. A separate recreation room in the resort has a player piano, puppets for kids, a lounge and seating area, and a kitchen area for guests to use. Rooms accommodating four people with kitchenettes cost $75 per night, and the apartments in an old carriage house cost $85 per night; both are rented out by the week only during the summer, but by the night during the rest of the year. All include a continental breakfast. Address: Route #1, Empire, Michigan 49630. Telephone: 616–334–3414.

LAVALLEY'S LODGE AND CABINS

Address: PO Box 99, AuTrain, Michigan 49806.
Telephone: 906–892–8455.

Simple, rustic cabins on the edge of AuTrain Lake are available year-round. Boating, fishing, canoeing, and mountain biking are popular during the summer months, and the mountain bike trails turn into snowmobile and cross-country ski trails in the winter. Nearby is the AuTrain River, where guests can rent canoes to leisurely explore its waters.

Season: Year-round.

Accommodations: Two cabins and a two-bedroom lodge unit are available. The one-bedroom cabin sleeps up to four people in a double bed and sofabed. The four-bedroom cabin sleeps up to eight people in two double beds, two twin beds, and a sofabed. Both have lake views and fully equipped kitchens; bring your own towels.

Special Features: Cabins have fire rings outside, and firewood is provided. A paddleboat and rowboats are available to guests. Mountain bike rentals and canoe rentals are nearby.

Cost: One-bedroom cabin $245 per week; four-bedroom cabin $375 to $475 per week, depending on number of people.

Nearby: Fishing, scuba diving, and underwater reserves with boat wrecks are close by. Lake Superior's sandy beaches are two miles away. Hiawatha National Forest, Pictured Rocks National Lakeshore, Alger Underwater Preserve, and the Hiawatha Folk, Craft and Art Center also are a short drive away.

PYMATUNING STATE PARK CABINS

Address: PO Box 1000, Andover, Ohio 44003 (in the northeast corner of the state, next to the Pennsylvania border, sixty-five miles east of Cleveland).
Telephone: 216–293–6329.

Comfortable cabins are next to a special swimming beach and boat tie-up area reserved for cabin guests, and motorboats and pontoons can be rented by the week or by the day. A family of beavers has been active at this park, and their dams are accessible via a short trudge through the woods. Be sure to ask the park office for the latest information on their whereabouts to see them at work. Swimming, boating, and fishing are popular summer activities, and nature programs are conducted during the summer with movies, slide shows, campfires, and junior naturalist programs. A water spillway a short drive away has an area where ducks actually walk across the fish.

Season: Year-round.

Accommodations: Twenty-seven deluxe housekeeping cabins with two bedrooms, kitchen, bathroom, living room, and screened porch can sleep up to six people each. Cabins are heated and available year-round. Thirty-five simple housekeeping cabins are available May through mid-September. They have a living room–kitchen combination and private bath and sleep up to four people separated by a curtained divider.

Cost: Deluxe cabins $335 per week, $65 per night, $670 for two weeks. Standard cabins $235 per week, $52 per night, $465 for two weeks. Reservations accepted a year in advance; weekly reservations are given preference in summer. Summers fill up by about mid-March, so be sure to book early.

FISH AND FUN RESORT

Address: 106 North Front Street, Syracuse, Indiana 46567.
Telephone: 219–457–3442.

Fish and Fun, on the shore of spring-fed Syracuse Lake, the largest natural lake in Indiana, has cottages that sleep four to six people. Each cottage has its own fishing boat or dock space. The fishing is excellent for pike, bass, crappie, and bluegill. A large pier and sundeck extends into the lake for sunbathers, and a gently sloping swimming area is safe for children. Fish and Fun is well located for trips to Amish Acres, Berkholder's Dutch Village, and gigantic flea markets. Sixty-five percent of its business is returning guests, and its friendly atmosphere and reasonable prices make its popularity well deserved.

Season: Year-round.

Accommodations: Seven modern cabins sleep from four to six people. Cabins have fully equipped kitchens and each has a picnic table and its own deck. All but one are air-conditioned.

Cost: Cottages $390 to $500 per week, depending on size. Boats are provided; motors $25 per day, $125 per week. Three- and four-day packages available in fall, winter, and spring; be sure to ask.

CHAIN O' LAKES CANOE TRIPS

Address: 2355 East 75 South, Albion, Indiana 46701 (thirty miles northwest of Fort Wayne).
Telephone: 219–636–2654.

Row, row, row your boat through the eight connecting lakes that make up this four-mile-long state park. Rent a canoe for two to four people and paddle from lake to lake along connecting natural channels through the chain. Stop about halfway at Sand Lake's broad swimming beach to swim and sun for awhile, then resume your journey to the canoe camping area next to River Lake, where you'll sleep out under the stars in a canoers' campsite. The next day you can paddle back to your starting point at Long Lake. Simple housekeeping cabins are available for rent by the week during summer months and nightly during the rest of the year. The park also has rowboats, paddleboats, and lifejackets for rent, and fishing, hiking trails, swimming beaches, and picnic spots.

Accommodations: The state park has eighteen cabins housing up to six people. Each has two bedrooms, a private bathroom, a wood-burning stove with a supply of firewood, and a porch with a swing and a picnic table. You can book them up to a year in advance by the day from September through May or by the week through the summer. Bring your own dishes, cooking utensils, and linens. Canoe campsites are primitive and must be reserved in advance.

Cost: Cabins $55 to $60 per night, $385 to $400 per week. Canoe, $9 per day, can seat two to four people, depending on size. Canoe campsites $4 per night.

THE SOUTH

BUFFALO OUTDOOR CENTER

Address: Two locations: PO Box 1, Ponca, Arkansas 72670 (upper river—at the junction of state highways 43 and 74); Route 1, Box 56, St. Joe, Arkansas 72675 (middle of the river at Silver Hill—U.S. 65 South).
Telephone: Ponca, 501–861–5514; Silver Hill, 501–439–2244.

The Buffalo River travels through 132 miles of some of the most spectacular sections of the Arkansas Ozark highlands. Multicolored bluffs tower five hundred feet or more above the water along with lofty waterfalls, massive boulders, and hairpin turns. Float trips down the river can be combined with comfortable cabin accommodations nearby. The best time to canoe is in March, April, and May.

Season: March through June.

Accommodations: Log cabins are equipped with a full kitchen, rock fireplace, barbecue grill, loft bedrooms with two double beds, main floor bedroom, towels and all bedding, all cooking and eating utensils, air-conditioning, and front porch swings. The cabins have three double beds and are designed to accommodate up to six people.

Cost: Cabins $79 per night for two people; each additional person $12. For up to six people, four-night stay $330, one-week stay, $550. Children under twelve stay free. Canoes $25 per day, rafts $15 per day, guided jonboats for fishing $75 per person per day, mountain bikes $12.50 per half day. Shuttle service is available.

PETIT JEAN STATE PARK

Address: Mather Lodge, Route 3, Box 346, Morrilton, Arkansas 72110.
Telephone: 800–264–2462; 501–727–5431.

The dramatic ninety-five-foot Cedar Falls, a fishing and paddleboating lake, hiking trails through forests, canyons, streams, and meadows, and a log-and-stone lodge are the trademarks of the first state park in Arkansas. Many of the park's housekeeping cabins share a bluff with the lodge, overlooking an impressive canyon. A boat house by the lake offers a snack bar, boat rental, and fishing supplies during the summer. Cabin and lodge guests have free use of the swimming pool, playground, and tennis courts. Hiking trails to the falls and forests radiate out from the lodge. Petit Jean is home to the Museum of Automobiles, a showcase of antique and classic cars.

Season: Year-round.

Accommodations: Twenty-four rooms in Mather Lodge have two double beds and private baths. Nineteen one-bedroom cabins with linens and fully equipped kitchens sleep four to six people. Cabins without kitchens sleep four people in two double beds.

Special Features: An interpretive program from Memorial Day to Labor Day has such scheduled events as trail hikes, puppet shows, and arts and crafts. The park has a campground, restaurant, playgrounds, recreation hall, swimming pool, tennis courts, and snack bar.

Cost: Accommodations are priced for two people, but children under twelve stay free in their parents' room. Housekeeping cabins $65, rollaway beds $5 per night. Cabins without kitchens $45 per night. Lodge rooms with two double beds $45 per night. Fishing boat rentals $6 per day, paddleboats $3.25 per hour.

CUMBERLAND MOUNTAIN STATE PARK

Address: Route 8, Box 322, Crossville, Tennessee 38555.
Telephone: 615–484–6138.

This park spreads across the Cumberland Plateau and has housekeeping cabins in the woods or near the shores of Bird Lake. When you tire of doing your own cooking, head to the restaurant overlooking the sparkling blue lake. Recreational options include fishing, boating, and swimming. A supervised nature and recreation summer program includes free activities, nature hikes, sports, and craft programs for children.

Season: Year-round.

Accommodations: Thirty-six cabins with full kitchens accommodate four to sixteen people in one-, two-, and three-bedroom units. Most have fireplaces.

Special Features: Swimming and fishing are free to cabin guests. Paddleboats, canoes, rowboats, and motorboats are available for rent; private boats are not allowed. Other facilities include hiking trails, tennis courts, badminton, volleyball, horseshoes, shuffleboard, Ping-Pong, softball, and basketball.

Cost: Weekly prices $205 to $360, depending on size of unit. Nightly rates $35 to $75.

BIG RIDGE STATE PARK

**Address: 1015 Big Ridge Road, Maynardsville, Tennessee 37807.
Telephone: 615–992–5523.**

Set along the southern shore of Norris Lake, Big Ridge State Park has nineteen rustic cabins, camping, and lots of activity down by the water. Children of all ages enjoy the sandy beach, which has a special enclosed area for little ones and lifeguards on duty during swimming hours. For the older kids, there's a diving area with diving stands and canoe, paddleboat, and rowboat rentals.

Season: Cabins can be rented from April through October.

Accommodations: Each cabin accommodates up to six people in two double beds and one sofabed. All have fireplaces, screen porches, and full kitchens. Linens and towels are provided.

Special Features: Basketball, volleyball, badminton, horseshoes, tennis (bring your own racquet and balls), picnic areas, hiking trails, and daily activities for families during the summer months, such as arts and crafts, campfires, nature walks, and organized sports activities.

Cost: Cabins, rented by the week only from mid-June to mid-August, $260 for six nights. The rest of the year $40 per night Sunday through Thursday, $50 per night Friday and Saturday. Rowboats $2.25 per hour, canoe or paddleboat $2.75 per hour.

SHELTOWEE TRACE OUTFITTERS

**Address: PO Box 1060, Whitley, Kentucky 42653.
Telephone: 800–541–RAFT.**

This outfitter has family raft, tube, and canoe trips around the Cumberland Falls and Big South Fork areas. The shortest trip and the best for young ones is the Rainbow Mist Ride, a guided raft tour of the Cumberland Falls. The Cumberland Falls Raft Trip includes five to seven miles of class-three white water in guided rafts, with enough thrills to impress even the most jaded teenager. The trip includes several swimming stops and a short hike to Dog Slaughter Falls, a wilderness waterfall. The five-mile tubing trip down Bear Creek to Blue Heron Mine (minimum age six) has a class-three rapid with a narrow chute and tricky turns. Family canoe trips range from five to twenty five miles and last one to two days. All canoe trips have light rapids and gentle currents. Sheltowee also arranges wild water raft trips and white water canoe trips for families with teenagers.

Cost: Guided raft tour of the Cumberland Falls, adults $4, kids $3. Cumberland Falls raft trip, adults $40, kids twelve and under $30. Five-mile tubing trip down Bear Creek $15 per person. Family canoe trips $20 per person per day, $25 per person for two days.

Where to Stay
See Cumberland Falls Resort, pages 32–33.

STEPHEN FOSTER STATE PARK

Address: Stephen C. Foster State Historic Park, Fargo, Georgia 31631. Telephone: 912–637–5274.

Way down upon the headwaters of the Suwanee River, right in the middle of the Okefenokee Swamp, this state park and nature center provides air-conditioned cottages, boat tours, and boat rental. A half-mile nature trail and boardwalk leads into the swamp where deer, birds, and alligators live. Take the guided ninety-minute boat tour through the swamp to learn more about its history, wildlife, and plants, then head out in your own boat; trails are clearly marked and it's virtually impossible to get lost. On Thursday, Friday, and Saturday evenings naturalists give slide shows, videos, and nature talks. Sunday morning nature walks led by naturalists further inform visitors about the odd flora and fauna of the swamp. The best months to visit are March, April, early May, October, and November. People visit year-round, but summers are hot, humid, and full of mosquitoes.

Season: Year-round.

Accommodations: Nine two-bedroom cottages have living rooms, dining areas, kitchens, screened-in porches, all dishes and linens, and central heat and air-conditioning.

Special Features: Boardwalk and nature walk, boat tours, boat and bike rentals.

Cost: Cottages $51 per night Sunday through Thursday, $61 Friday and Saturday. Boat tours, adults $7, children under twelve $5, kids under six free. Canoes and jonboats $9 per half day, $13 per day. Boats with motors $16 per half day, $26 per day. Bicycles $5 per half day, $8 per day. Reservations for cottages can be made up to eleven months in advance; and reservations for boats can be made thirty days in advance.

HOMOSASSA SPRINGS STATE WILDLIFE PARK

Address: 9225 West Fishbowl Drive, Homosassa, Florida, 32646
(seventy-five miles north of Tampa).
Telephone: 904–628–2311; 904–628–5343.

Go face to face with a manatee in this rehabilitation center for Florida's
native wildlife and endangered species. The high point of the park is the
floating observatory with an underwater viewing area, where you can see
thousands of fish and the mild-mannered manatees (once thought by
sailors to be mermaids) swim by. Manatees that have been injured in the
wild, orphaned, or born in captivity are reacclimated here before being
returned to the wild. Educational programs focusing on the manatee,
alligator, crocodile, native Florida snakes, and other wildlife native to
Florida are presented three times daily. Boat tours of Pepper Creek allow
visitors to see deer, bears, bobcats, otters, and cougars in addition to
dozens of birds.

Cost: Adult $6.95, children three to twelve $3.95, under three free.

Where to Stay

MacRae's has motel rooms and apartment units on the Homosassa River,
one and a half miles from the springs. A fleet of rental fishing boats is
available for anyone who wants to drop a line; the staff will give you a
map and point you in the right direction. One-bedroom apartments have
fully equipped kitchens and sleep six in two double beds and a sofabed
for $75. After a day on the river, relax in the front porch rockers. All units
are air-conditioned. Address: 5300 South Cherokee Way, PO Box 318,
Homosassa, Florida 32646. Telephone: 904–628–2602 (day); 904–628–
1315 (night).

ADVENTURES UNLIMITED

Address: Route 6, Box 283, Milton, Florida 32570 (twelve miles
north of Milton).
Telephone: 904–623–6197; 904–626–1669.

Stay in an air-conditioned cabin on the grounds of Adventures Unlimited
and then select the adventure to suit your family. Choose from canoeing,
tubing, kayaking, and paddleboating during your visit. Canoe trips range
from two hours to three days on spring-fed rivers through pristine state
forest property. If you need to stop for a swim or a snack there are plenty
of white sandy beaches along the banks. You'll be transported to your
starting point and float at your leisure back to your cabin. The best months
for float trips are March to late September.

Season: Year-round.

Accommodations: Efficiency and one-bedroom cabins are air-conditioned and have fully equipped kitchens, all linens, and private baths. Large family cabins have a full kitchen, bath, and living room and sleep up to twenty-six. Two styles of rustic camping cabins sleep four people in a double bed and bunk bed. The rustic cabins are not air-conditioned; shared bathhouses are located nearby. You also can opt to camp at the waterfront tent sites or hook up an RV.

Special Features: Playground, swimming beach, wilderness store, horseshoes, nature trails, volleyball, and picnic areas. You also can rent paddleboats, inner tubes, kayaks, and river rafts.

Cost: Rustic camping cabins $35 for up to four persons, $5 each additional person. Efficiency and one-bedroom cabin $60 to $75 per night for up to four people. Family cabin $150 for up to fifteen people, $10 each additional person (maximum twenty-six).

Kids twelve and under canoe free with two paying adults. A one-day canoe trip is $12 per person, and canoes can hold two adults and two children under age eight. Tube trips $6, kayaks $16 per day, paddleboats $24 per day. Shuttle transportation included.

HUNGRY MOTHER STATE PARK

Address: Box 109, Marion, Virginia 24354 (one-hundred miles south of Roanoke, four miles from Marion).
Telephone: 703–783–3422 (park office); 804–490–3939 (reservations).

Hungry Mother, with its sparkling lake set in forested mountains, has been a family favorite for years. Like some of the grand old resorts of the Northeast, people who came here as children are now bringing their own children back every year. Comfortable cabins are at one end of the lake near a sandy swimming beach watched over by lifeguards throughout the summer. A summer program for children and families includes arts and crafts, nature hikes, environmental awareness, survival skills, animal studies, and evening activities. The fun continues with paddleboat rentals, guided horseback rides, and excellent fishing off a special fishing pier. When parents need a break from cooking, a restaurant serves lunch and dinner buffets.

Season: Early May through August.

Accommodations: Rustic log cabins with one and two bedrooms were built by the Civilian Conservation Corps in the 1930s. One-bedroom cabins contain a double bed and can hold a rollaway bed or two. Seventeen two-bedroom cabins have two double beds and can hold several rollaway beds to accommodate up to six people. All have fully equipped kitchens, private bathrooms, fireplaces, and all bedding and towels. Campsites also are available.

Special Features: Large sandy beach, horse rental and bridle trails, thirteen miles of hiking trails, rowboat and paddleboat rentals, fishing, a restaurant with lunch and dinner buffets, and a visitors center.

Cost: One-bedroom cabins $225 per week; two-bedroom cabins $285 per week. Rollaway beds, available at the park office, $21 per week. Paddleboats $4.50 per hour, rowboats $3.50 per hour; horses $5 per half hour, $8 per hour. Reservations can be made up to a year in advance, and summer cabins rentals fill quickly; some guests book for the following year before they leave.

BLACKWATER FALLS

Address: Drawer 490, Davis, West Virginia 26260.
Telephone: 800–CALLWVA (reservations); 304–259–5429.

Explore the park on one of the many hiking or riding trails during the summer months. Lakeside entertainment includes swimming, sunbathing, rowboating, and paddleboating. A recreation center has arts and crafts projects for kids, and outdoor playing fields have volleyball, horseshoes, and tennis. Guests stay in the lodge or in housekeeping cabins; cabins require reservations six to eight months in advance, but lodge rooms are easy to get, especially midweek.

Season: Year-round.

Accommodations: Twenty-five cabins of different sizes sleep two to eight people. Heated cabins have fireplaces, full kitchens with modern appliances, and all linens. A fifty-five-room lodge and a campground also accommodate guests.

Special Features: Swimming in the lake, paddleboat and rowboat rentals, horse rental, playground, tennis, volleyball, and other game courts, horseshoes, nature center, recreation building.

Cost: Summer cabins $350 (two people) to $600 (eight people) per week, $52 to $100 per night, depending on unit and time of week. Horse rental $15 per hour, boats $3 per half hour.

Nearby: A golf course is ten miles away and fishing is nearby.

THE NORTHEAST

MOUNTAIN SPRINGS LAKE RESORT

Address: PO Box 297, Mountain Springs Drive, Reeders, Pennsylvania 18352.
Telephone: 717–629–0251.

Set in 450 acres of rolling woodlands and open lawns, this resort on the shores of a spring-fed private lake sits in the middle of several ski areas in the Poconos. During the summer, families can swim and play on the gentle, sandy beaches, go boating, fish, ride horseback, or play tennis; there's also a golf course nearby. Year-round lakeside and woodside units and seasonal lodging are available; every accommodation includes a rowboat at no extra charge.

Season: Year-round.

Accommodations: Lake view accommodations overlook the seventy-six-acre Mountain Springs Lake, and woodside accommodations are set in laurel woods just minutes from the lake. Seasonal accommodations, available May through October, are simpler and less expensive than the others. All units are no more than a five-minute walk to the beach.

Special Features: The beach is perfect for children of all ages, and there are canoes, sailboats, fishing equipment, tennis courts, and toboggans for rent. A snack bar is open during the summer, and a restaurant is open on weekends for dinner in spring, summer, and fall.

Cost: Seasonal cottages offer a price break for longer stays. Four-person cottages and apartments $415 to $550 during July and August, $350 to $455 the rest of the season. Lake view and woodside cottages for four people $700 to $1,000, depending on time of year and specific cottage. All accommodations have sofabeds and can take one or two additional people for $20 per person per night, $75 per week. Canoe $15 per day, $45 per week; sailboat $35 per day, $95 per week; tennis courts $5 per hour; toboggan $15 per stay. Safety flotation device $2 per stay.

Nearby: Horseback-riding rental, outlet malls, golf, Pocono Raceway, and hiking are close by.

HERRINGTON MANOR AND SWALLOW FALLS
STATE PARKS

Address: Route 5, Box 122, Oakland, Maryland 21550.
Telephone: 301–334–9180.

Herrington Manor State Park is adjacent to Swallow Falls State Park; the two are three miles apart by road and five miles by a picturesque hiking trail. Herrington Manor has twenty log cabins near a lake, while Swallow Falls has campgrounds with fully equipped tents and Maryland's tallest waterfall (fifty-five feet). In winter guests can cross-country ski, ice-skate, or go sledding. In summer guests swim at the lakeside beach, fish, and go boating.

Accommodations: Twenty log cabins for two, four, or six people are available. All have complete kitchens and bathrooms, heat, and a wood-burning stove. Fully equipped campsites have tent, Coleman stove, lantern, and sleeping pads.

Special Features: Activities include lake swimming, hiking, stocked lake with canoes and boats for rent, tennis, snack bar, athletic field with softball, tennis, basketball, and horseshoes. Guests can use athletic equipment free of charge.

Cost: Cabins $60 to $85 per night, $420 to $595 per week. Weekly minimum during summer, two-night minimum during rest of season. Canoe, paddleboat, and rowboat rentals $4 per hour, $15 per day. Reservations accepted up to a year in advance. November, end of March, and April are slowest times. During the fall, winter, and spring, if you rent for two nights midweek you get a third night free.

LAKE TAGHKANIC STATE PARK

Address: RD 1, Box 74, Ancram, New York 12502-9731.
Telephone: 518–851–3631.

With fifteen hundred feet of gently sloping shoreline, rolling hills, hiking trails, and a choice of cabins in the woods or cottages along the lake, Lake Taghkanic is the perfect spot for a family beach vacation. Summer months have a nature center with such family-oriented programs as film nights, nature hikes, arts and crafts and puppet shows. Special weekend programs continue into the fall.

Accommodations: Choose from sixteen one- to four-bedroom cottages along the lake with full kitchens and private bathrooms, or fifteen rustic cabins in the woods with cold running water and shared bathhouses.

Special Features: Two beaches for swimming (with lifeguards), one with a concession stand that sells ice-cream cones and hot dogs. There is a ball-playing field, a playground, boat rental, and a fitness trail. The nature center has a frog pond with a waterfall, displays, literature, and an arts and crafts area. Programs for families include ecology studies and special boat rides. In winter you can ice fish, ice skate, cross-country ski, and snowmobile.

Cost: Cottages on the beach $38 to $65 per night, $154 to $260 per week. Reservations accepted up to ninety days in advance. Rowboat $4 per hour.

STAR LAKE CAMPUS AYH HOSTEL

Address: Route 1, Box 60, Star Lake, New York 13690.
Telephone: 315–848–3486.

A private, lifeguarded beach on Star Lake is just a short walk away from the cabins and dorms of this summer hostel. Guests have free use of equipment, including canoes, paddleboats, rowboats, mountain bikes, and a fitness center. The hostel is open all day.

Accommodations: Families will be most comfortable in four-person bunk rooms and cabins that sleep four, six, or eight people. One simple two-bedroom family cabin has a private bath and bunk rooms. Small cabins share a bath with another room. No kitchen facilities are available, but if more than twenty-five people are staying at the hostel, guests can buy a breakfast, lunch, and dinner plan.

Special Features: Canoes, rowboats, bikes, hot tub, sauna, exercise room, Ping-Pong, billiards, volleyball, badminton. Laundry facilities are available.

Cost: Families of up to six people $70 per night. Vacation cabin sleeping up to six $350 per week. Meal package, adults $18, children $9.

LAKESHORE TERRACE

Address: Box 18, Wolfeboro, New Hampshire 03894.
Telephone: 603–569–1701.

Two miles from the popular resort of Wolfeboro on the shores of Lake Wentworth, Lakeshore Terrace has serviceable family units at excellent prices in a secluded setting. The spacious fifteen-acre property has six cottages cooled by the shade of pine trees; it's just a few minutes from town but feels miles away. Two private swimming beaches are shallow and perfect for little ones; a third, large, sunning beach backed by a garden is for sun worshippers and more accomplished swimmers. Lake Wentworth is much quieter than nearby Lake Winnipesaukee. Guests can expect to see beavers, tame ducks, and Gertrude and Frank, the loons who return year after year. Many families headquarter here to explore the surrounding area.

Season: Memorial Day to Columbus Day weekend.

Accommodations: Six unpretentious cottages house two to five people; all have screened porches and full baths, and four have full kitchens. The largest cottage, called Sand Box, is right on the swimming beach and holds five people. Week-long rentals are preferred in July and August. Week-long guests bring their own linens.

Special features: Rowboats are free for guests. There is a rose garden and an outdoor cookout area.

Cost: Most cottages $65 (without kitchens) to $75 per night, $225 to $450 per week. Sand Box cabin $110 per night, $770 per week for four people; $125 per night, $875 per week for five people.

Nearby: Steamer trip on Lake Winnipesaukee, eighteen-hole golf, tennis, fishing, sailing, and horseback riding are all nearby. A number of marinas in Wolfeboro rent sailing boats and power boats. Mount Washington is within an easy drive.

ANCHORAGE

Address: RFD 1, Box 90, Laconia, New Hampshire 03246 (nineteen miles north of Concord).
Telephone: 603–524–3248.

Set along the wooded banks of Lake Winnisquam, the Anchorage has three beaches, playgrounds for children (and adults), rowboats, sailboats, canoes, and paddleboats for guests to use. The entire thirty-five acre property is situated between the main road and the lake, offering privacy and quiet. Hiking trails lead through forest, orchard, and berry bushes.

Season: Mid-May through mid-October.

Accommodations: Cottages range in size from one to eight rooms. All have fully equipped kitchens and views of the lake from a screened front porch. Extended families can stay in the Trapp House (which has its own dock and secluded beach), as it sleeps up to eighteen people.

Special Features: A gently sloped swimming beach is perfect for young ones, and the lawns are groomed for baseball or soccer. There's volleyball on the beach, horseshoes, shuffleboard, weekly campfires in summer, and cookout areas with grills.

Cost: The Anchorage has two sets of rates, for peak season, from July to early September, and off-season, from mid-May through June and mid-September through mid-October. One-bedroom cottages sleeping four people, $675 per week peak season, $410 per week off-season. Larger cottages sleeping five to eight people $750 to $1,200 peak season, $450 to $720 off-season.

HARVEY'S LAKE CABINS AND CAMPGROUND

**Address: RR 1, Box 26E, West Barnet, Vermont 05821 (eight miles
from St. Johnsbury, nine miles from Danville, exit 18 on I-91).
Telephone: 802–633–2213.**

New owners Marybeth and Michael Vereline recently added seven log
cabins to this private cabin and campground resort that combines the
quiet serenity of the woods with the pristine beauty of the lake in Vermont's Northeast Kingdom. With eight-hundred feet of shoreline on Lake
Harvey and another one-thousand feet of canoeable river access, families
that enjoy water sports can spend their days swimming in the lake, exploring the waterway in boats, or fishing for rainbow and lake trout, bass,
perch, and sunfish. There are two different beaches, a grassy play area
with a swing set, and picnic areas near the water. All cabin guests can use
the rowboats and canoes, and there is a bike rental on the property.

Season: May 15 to October 15.

Accommodations: Seven new log cabins with decks overlooking the
lake have living rooms, dining areas, fully equipped kitchens, and an upstairs loft with two twin beds or a double bed. Each can accommodate
four people using the upstairs and a queen-size sofabed downstairs. Guests
rent linens or supply their own. No smoking is allowed in the cabins. Fifty-
three campground sites also are available.

Special Features: Recreation hall with pool tables, Ping-Pong, and video
games; horseshoe pit and small basketball court outside.

Cost: Cabins, rented by the week only in July and August, $425 to $525
per week for two, each additional person $50 up to the cabin's maximum;
children under twelve $25 per week extra. Linen rental $10 per week.
Cabins rent nightly from May 15 to June 15 and from September 1 to
October 15, $75 per night, double occupancy; additional person $10;
children under twelve $7. Bike rental $4 per hour, $10 per half day, $20
per full day.

Nearby: Maple sugar houses and hiking trails are close by.

LAKE SALEM LODGE

**Address: Derby, Vermont: 25 Woodland Place, Scarsdale, New
York 10583 (booking address).
Telephone: 914–723–7742 (reservations).**

A single compact cottage right on the shore of Lake Salem is perfect for
one large family or several family groups. Many families use it for reunions;
the largest one has housed nineteen people. The cottage sits on a level
acre with a creek at one end and plenty of space for croquet, badminton,

and other lawn games. Its private sandy beach has safe swimming in the lake's warm waters, and the fishing is fine.

Season: May through November.

Accommodations: This small, two-story cottage can sleep up to ten people in beds, and more if the kids bring sleeping bags. A large screened porch extends along one side. There are four carpeted bedrooms upstairs, two sleeping areas downstairs, a small kitchen, two bathrooms, and a living room with a fireplace and dining area. Guests should bring their own sports equipment, towels, and sheets.

Special Features: Boat rental, which must be arranged in advance.

Cost: Cottage, rented by the week only in July and August, $675. Weekly stays during rest of season $425; shorter stays can be arranged. Boat rental $10 per day.

Nearby: Montreal is ninety minutes away, Newport less than five miles away.

SEBAGO LAKE LODGE AND COTTAGES

Address: White's Bridge Road, North Windham, Maine 04062.
Telephone: 207–892–2698.

Set on the shores of Maine's second-largest lake, Sebago Lake Lodge and Cottages offers cottages by the week and lodge rooms (some with kitchenettes) by the day. The cottages are on a hill that slopes down to the lake, scattered among pines and white birch trees. The White Mountains can be seen in the distance from the lodge rooms. Five hundred feet of lake frontage is yours for swimming or boating, and the use of canoes and rowboats is included with all cottage and room rentals. Lakeside picnic tables are a popular spot for lunch, and in the evenings families gather around the large outdoor fireplace to cook hot dogs, roast marshmallows, and pop popcorn.

Season: Year-round.

Accommodations: Cottages range in size from studios to two bedrooms. One-bedroom cottages sleep four on a double bed and sofabed in the living room. Most cottages have screened porches and wood stoves. Lodge rooms can accommodate two to four people, and many have kitchenettes.

Cost: Cottages $395 to $625 per week, double occupancy, with 25-percent discounts for off-season rentals. Each additional child $25 per week. Lodge rooms $48 to $110 per night. Each additional child under age ten $5 per night, over ten $10 per night. Waterskiing and fishing boats $25 to $185 per day.

Nearby: Within an hour's drive is L. L. Bean, New Hampshire's White Mountains, amusement parks, the Maine coast, the Douglas Mountains, and many hiking trails.

ATTEAN LAKE LODGE

Address: Jackman, Maine 04945.
Telephone: 207–668–3792 (summer); 207–668–7726 (winter).

Guests park their cars along the shore of six-mile-long Attean Lake and take a ten-minute boat ride to their own private island, where memories of busy work and school days fade. They swim, read, or hike a short distance to a stream or pond where canoes have been placed for their use. Another favorite hike for families leads to a pond where moose often are spotted. Hand-hewn log cabins are lit by kerosene and heated by wood stoves or fireplaces. All have full baths with hot and cold running water, and guests enjoy three hearty meals a day. The Holden family has operated this lodge since 1900.

Season: Memorial Day through September.

Accommodations: Eighteen log cabins with private porches overlooking the lake are set amid pine, spruce, and birch trees; all have magnificent views. Cabins are completely furnished and accommodate two to six guests. The main lodge has a large fireplace, library, games, desk, and public phone.

Special Features: A large sandy beach along the lake is perfect for children, and boats can be rented for use on the lakes. Beach cookouts take place on Wednesday and Thursday, lunches come in picnic baskets. Hiking trails lead through forests and past rivers.

Cost: Rates include three meals a day. Adults $550 each per week, double occupancy; third person over twelve $375. Children under twelve $375, under five $50. Canoe $10 per day, aluminum boat $8 per day, boat motor $12 per day.

Nearby: Most guests enjoy the serenity and quiet of the lake and never leave, but other nearby attractions include Quebec City, two hours away, and public tennis courts and a nine-hole golf course in Jackman.

KAWANHEE INN

Address: Route 142, Weld, Maine 04285 (summer); 7 Broadway, Farmington, Maine 04938 (winter).
Telephone: 207–585–2243 (summer); and 207–778–4306 (winter daytime); or 207–778–3809 (winter evenings).

A gradually sloping fine white sand beach leads to the waters of Lake Webb, one of Maine's most beautiful bodies of water. The swimming is perfect, with summertime afternoon lake temperatures seventy-two to seventy-eight degrees. Cabins and a lodge containing bedrooms and a restaurant line the shore, which is wooded with white birches, pines, and pointed firs. Old-fashioned wooden rocking chairs grace the porches. A discounted rate is possible for guests who wish to provide their own linens and maid service. For a special treat head to the restaurant for an elegant all-American meal.

Season: Early May through late October.

Accommodations: Ten cabins have one, two, or three bedrooms. All cabins have living rooms, stone fireplaces, private baths, and screened porches. All two-bedroom cabins have kitchens, and one one-bedroom cabin is equipped with a kitchen. Fourteen comfortable bedrooms on the second floor of the lodge have private or shared baths. Minimum stay during the peak summer season is two nights.

Special Features: Canoe and boat rentals; a restaurant, which serves breakfast and dinner in the main dining room or on screened-in porches; and the many hiking trails that radiate out from the lodge.

Cost: Cabins rented by the week only from June 15 to Labor Day. Two-bedroom cabins $440 to $470 per week; one-bedroom cabin with kitchen $400; three-bedroom cabins $495. Bedding, towels, and housekeeping service included, unless you opt for the "bare-bones" arrangement in which you supply all linens and housekeeping for a 15-percent discount. Nightly stays start at $85 for one-bedroom, $135 for two-bedroom cabin. Inn rooms $55 double occupancy, $65 for extra-large rooms. For a private bath add $5. Additional person in inn rooms $10 per night. Canoe rental $10 per day.

BEACH
VACATIONS

*Y*ou can't beat the beach for keeping children amused and content, and parents usually find keeping watch a little more relaxing with the sand and surf in the background. But can you afford the beach bum fantasy? A Cape Cod–style house overlooking the water, a linen closet brimming with thick white beach towels, salty air, sea gulls, fresh lobster, a clean and safe beach where your children can swim and build sand castles . . . sound pricey?

It need not be so. To make the most of your beach vacation dollars, think about selecting a stretch of less popular coastline. For example, vacations along the North and South Carolina coast are far less expensive and equally as delightful as their New England counterparts. If you can break away in late May, early June, or September you will find the weather at most beach locales still appealing, the beaches less crowded, and off-season rates generally in effect.

Beach house rental fees vary widely, but houses typically are cheaper than hotel stays and offer more value and privacy for the money. Unfortunately, there is no National Association of Beach House Rentals, so renting an inexpensive beach house takes some sleuthing and some haggling. But even a three-day beach house escape can feel like a week off elsewhere—and there seems to be a house for every budget. Additional savings are met by cooking your meals at home and sharing expenses with another family. If families double up, renting a large house certainly is cheaper than staying at a hotel for the week. Privacy is one of the big drawing cards for beach house renters, along with a feeling of homey comfort. Many "beach houses" today are actually condominiums.

It is best to book six months to one year in advance. During peak seasons, such as July, August, Thanksgiving, and Christmas, it might night not be as easy to talk landlords out of enforcing their standard one-week-minimum rule. In recessionary times it is worth trying to negotiate the list price, especially during the off-season. When selecting a house, ask if bedding, towels, and kitchen utensils are provided. Expect to pay a security deposit (ours was $200, $50 of which was deducted as a cleaning fee).

Here we highlight a selection of great family beach destinations and provide listings of homes and condos for rent, as well as inexpensive hotels with kitchens and/or family amenities, state park cabins, and family hostels. If the area you plan to visit is not mentioned, write to the local chamber of commerce. They often keep lists of homeowners, agents, or property management firms that handle vacation rentals. The "vacation rental" columns of the area newspaper's classified section can also be helpful.

WEST COAST

MAUI, HAWAII

A Hawaiian vacation need not cost a fortune, especially in Maui. In fact, if you budget it right, your biggest expense could be your air fare. Before you go and especially if you plan to visit the other islands, write to the Hawaii Visitors Bureau (see page 334 for address). The bureau has compiled a list of places to stay for less than $99 per night on all of the islands, as well as many free or inexpensive places to visit and a guide to the state's least expensive restaurants. Among the listings are ethnic (including Hawaiian) restaurants tucked away in communities and a variety of fast-food places.

When booking a room, be sure to inquire about discounts for longer stays (usually more than four to seven days). High season in Hawaii is generally mid-December through March. However, you'll find that the weather is tropical and great for beaching it during the off-season when lower rates apply.

Maui's western shore has a variety of accommodations and things to do. Adventurous types can choose from biplane adventures, seawater rafting, diving, mountain and crater biking, snorkeling, and horseback riding. A visit to touristy Lahaina is fun, as every block is crammed full of shops, galleries, eateries, and historic buildings. There are charters for fishing or visiting neighboring islands at Lahaina's harbor.

Maui's idyllic eastern coast, near tiny Hana, has some of Hawaii's most glorious scenery. The three-hour drive to Hana winds along the ocean past black sand beaches, old lava flows, dense jungle growth, and lush groves of mango and monkey pod trees.

Maui's most spectacular site is Mount Haleakala, a volcanic crater large enough to hold Manhattan. Horse and bike trails descend into the depths of the crater's sides and meander across its moonlike surface. Cruiser Bob's Downhill Bicycle Adventure (808–579–8444) and Maui Mountain Cruisers (808–572–0195) lead these bike tours into the crater, while Pony Express Tours (808–667–2200) offers trail rides on horseback into the crater and tours of Haleakala Range, Maui's largest working cattle ranch.

Snorkelers can rent gear at Aloha Destinations (808–879–6263) or Snorkel Bob's (808–879–7449). Maui's best snorkeling spots are at Kapalua Beach, Mokapu Beach, Wailea Beach, Polo Beach, and Ulua Beach in Wailea; Kaanapali Beach, fronting the Lahaina Resort and the Maui Eldorado; Lahaina Beach, Honokowai Beach Park, Alaeloa Beach, Keoneui Beach, Honokeana Beach, and Olowalu Beach in West Maui; and Papalaua State Wayside Park. Guided scuba and snorkeling excursions are lead by Molikini Divers (808–879–0555) in Kihei. Blue Water Rafting (808–879–RAFT) has excursions through grottoes that feature a wide variety of exotic marine life.

Maui's safest beaches for children are at Launiupoko State Wayside Park in West Maui, with its man-made pool for kids on the beach; Papalaua State Wayside Park and Honokowai Beach Park in West Maui; Kapalua Beach, Keawakapu Beach, Mokapu Beach, Polo Beach, Poolenalena Beach, and Wailea Beach in Wailea; Hana Beach Park; Puu Olai Beach in Makena; and Kahului Beach.

MAUIAN

Address: 5441 Honoapiilani Road, Lahaina, Maui, Hawaii 96761.
Telephone: 800–367–5034; 808–669–6205.

Napili Bay is an idyllic reef-protected inlet of sea and white sand. The hotel sits on on a half-mile-long crescent of sandy beach along the bay, where the water is calm and the bottom is sandy. Napili Bay is also great for snorkeling. Rising behind Napili Bay are the slopes of the West Maui Mountains and views of Molokai and Lanai.

Season: Year-round.

Accommodations: This simple hotel has forty-four furnished studio units, each with a private lanai and a complete kitchen with microwave oven. Units have a queen-size bed, two twin beds, and a ceiling fan.

Special Features: Swimming pool, shuffleboard, and barbecues in a garden setting. Daily housekeeping service, beach towels, beach chairs, and tables are provided.

Cost: The hotel has flexible rates, based on the percentage of occupancy at the time the reservation is made. For example, in low season (April 15 through December 14), if the occupancy rate is up to 5 percent the double occupancy rate is $69 per night; if occupancy rate is 6 to 30 percent the rate is $78 per night; if occupancy is 31 to 50 percent the rate is $89 per night. A third person $9, fourth person $6. Children under twelve stay free.

Nearby: A great snorkeling beach and another that is ideal for kids are a short drive from the hotel at Honolua Bay, north of Kapalua. Walk the jeep road through a rain forest to the beach and follow the right shoreline as you snorkel out to the point. The water never gets deeper than five to ten feet and is loaded with fish. There is also tennis and a championship golf course at Kapalua. Fifteen minutes south of the hotel is the busy tourist town of Lahaina. Several fine restaurants are within walking distance.

LIHI KAI COTTAGES

Address: 2121 Iliili Road, Kihei, Maui, Hawaii 96753.
Telephone: 808–879–2335 (in Hawaii); 800–LIHIKAI (other states).
November 1 through March is the busiest time, so book as far in advance as possible.

Lihi Kai's nine beach cottages are set in a tropical garden thirty-five yards from the ocean. Uncrowded Kamaole Beach, a safe and sandy beach for children, is a two-minute walk away. Summer draws many families here for swimming, surfing, snorkeling, skin-diving, fishing, beachcombing, playing tennis, picnicking, or just being lazy in the sun.

Season: Year-round.

Accommodations: Furnished cottages each sleep up to four people in one bedroom and have a living room, dinette-kitchen, bath, sheltered lanai, and carport.

Special Features: A self-service laundry is located on the grounds.

Cost: Cottages $385 per week, double occupancy; additional person $10. Children under thirteen stay free. Housekeeping service available for additional charge.

Nearby: Wailea and Makena golf courses are a short drive away. Guided scuba and snorkeling excursions are led by Molikini Divers (808–879–0555) in Kihei.

WAIANAPANAPA STATE PARK CABINS

Address: Department of Land and Natural Resources, Division of State Parks, 54 South High Street, Wiluku, Maui, Hawaii 96793 (reservations). Approximately fifty-one miles east of Kahului Airport, which is about three hours' drive from west Maui on a spectacularly scenic road.
Telephone: 808–243–5354.

Season: Year-round.
Accommodations: Each cabin sleeps up to six people and has a living room with two twin beds and a bedroom with two bunk beds. They are completely furnished with bedding, towels, cooking and eating utensils, electric lights, hot water, showers, and toilet facilities. Guests must clean the cabins before departing. Clean linens and towels are supplied every third day.
Special Features: The park is on an ancient lava flow with numerous submerged lava tubes, arches, and other interesting coastal features.
Cost: For three people in cabin, adults $6.50, children $3.25 per night. For four people, adults $6, children $3 per night. For six people, adults $5, children $2.50 per night. Five-night maximum stay.
Nearby: Hana Beach Park is a great beach for kids. The hotel Hana Ranch (808–248–8211, ext. 3) has horseback-riding tours through ranch pastures or along spectacular shorelines. The tours are popular, so reserve well in advance.

SAN DIEGO, CALIFORNIA

Seventy miles of beaches, dozens of public parks, and many museums with programs for children await families visiting San Diego. Always popular with kids is the famous and innovative San Diego Zoo (619–234–3153), home to nearly four thousand animals, many of which are in open-air cages. Its children's zoo has a petting zoo and a nursery where baby animals are cared for by their substitute mothers. The unique Tiger River ecosystem has paths that lead you to groups of animals and plants coexisting as they would in their natural habitat. Adjacent to the zoo's entrance is a carousel and miniature train.

Sea World (619–222–6363) has cavorting penguins, a petting pool with dolphins, wild water-skiing maneuvers in a Beach Blanket Ski Show, and a new exhibit, Shark Encounter, which houses the park's largest collection of sharks. At the San Diego Wild Animal Park (619–234–6541), a monorail tram takes you on a fifty-minute safari to view twenty-five hundred animals roaming freely in surroundings similar to their native homelands.

At most beaches you can rent boogie boards, surfboards, or bikes. There are many coastal bike routes; for a map, call 619–231–BIKE. Roller skates are the mode of transportation here. The best skating spot for the younger crowd is along Mission Bay, which also has several playgrounds and miles of grass for kite flying. The best water vehicle for kids age eleven and older is the jet ski, which is very easy to learn to maneuver. For about $30 an hour you can rent them at Jet Ski Rentals (619–276–9200).

Also situated along Mission Beach is Belmont Park, a shopping center with two restored landmarks: the Plunge and the Giant Dipper. The Plunge is the largest indoor swimming pool in southern California, while the Giant Dipper is a vintage wooden roller coaster with more than twenty-six hundred feet of tracks and thirteen hills.

Morley Field, an athletic complex adjacent to Balboa Park, has a Frisbee golf course. Balboa Park also is home to the Natural History Museum (619–232–3821), where kids can get a close-up view of desert life, including replicas of dinosaurs; the Hall of Champions (619–234–2544), with exhibits of San Diego's finest athletes; the Marie Hitchcock Puppet Theater (619–466–7128); and the San Diego Model Railroad Museum (619–696–0199).

Budding scientists will want to visit the Reuben H. Fleet Space Theater and Science Center (619–238–1168), which has more than fifty hands-on exhibits and movies in its multimedia planetary center, or the San Diego Aerospace Museum and International Aerospace Hall of Fame (619–234–8291 and 619–232–8322), with seventy aircraft including World War II fighter planes.

The shoreline of La Jolla is one of the area's loveliest. Its Children's Pool Beach, a sheltered sandy beach at the foot of Jenner Street, has lifeguards on duty and good conditions for scuba diving and skin-diving. Kids can snorkel at La Jolla Cove. The Children's Museum, located at 8057 Villa La Jolla Drive (619–950–0767), is nationally known for its innovative hands-on exhibits. The Mingei International Museum, at 4405 La Jolla Village Drive (619–453–5300), showcases toys from around the world, and the Scripps Aquarium-Museum at 8602 La Jolla Shores Drive (619–534–FISH) is also worth a visit. At La Jolla and Casa coves and Scripps Park below Prospect Street, gnarled, wind-bent trees invite kids to climb when they are not running the expansive stretch of grass or checking out the underwater caves. Scripps Park is a picnicker's haven, with little thatched beach huts jutting off the rocks.

BEACH AND BAYSIDE VACATIONS

Address: 2722 Mission Boulevard, Mission Beach, San Diego, California 92109
Telephone: 800–553–2284; 619–276–8827.

These waterfront apartments are on South Mission Beach in the heart of Mission Bay Aquatic Park. The green lawns, wide, paved walkways, playgrounds, and sandy beaches of the park encompass seven square miles of San Diego Bay. On the bay side is a nice family beach.

Season: Year-round.

Accommodations: Beach and Bayside represents a number of waterfront accommodations on South Mission Beach. Two small families can stay in the one-bedroom units and make use of sofabeds, rollaway beds, or futons.

Special Features: Units have cable television, microwave ovens, telephones, laundry facilities, barbecues, off-street parking, linens, cookware, beach bikes, beach chairs, beach towels, and boogie boards.

Cost: June 15 through Labor Day one bedroom units $400 to $630 per week and two-bedroom units start at $800 per week. Rates are lower off season.

Nearby: The apartments are near dozens of shops and sidewalk cafés as well as the Mission Beach Plunge in Belmont Park. Just south of Mission Beach is Bonita Cove, a nice spot for families, with calm waters, grassy knolls for picnicking, and fun playground equipment. The apartments are a five-minute drive from Sea World, fifteen minutes from downtown San Diego, and twenty minutes from the San Diego Zoo.

LUDLOW APARTMENTS

Address: Solmar Realty, 2445 Morena Boulevard, Suite 100, San Diego, California 92109.
Telephone: 619–488–4654.

These oceanfront apartments are on Mission Beach, a busy and fun-filled strip. Its boardwalks have skaters, bicyclists, joggers, and skateboarders; the beach has several playgrounds and miles of grass for kite flying. The apartments are a short drive from Sea World, fifteen minutes from downtown San Diego, and twenty minutes from the San Diego Zoo.

Season: Year-round.

Accommodations: Apartments sleep up to six people and have one bedroom with a double and a twin bed, a double sofabed, a fully equipped kitchen, and a telephone.

Special Features: Each unit has cable TV, a VCR, linen service, and a washer and dryer.

Cost: A first-floor oceanfront apartment for six people or a second-floor oceanfront apartment with a large deck for five people $600 to $630 per week. A first-floor apartment on the back side of this oceanfront building for six people $400 to $420 per week. Housekeeping available for $45 per visit.

Nearby: Belmont Park shopping center (see page 199). The apartments also are near the quiet beach community of Pacific Beach. Its popular boardwalk draws both locals and tourists; there are roller skates and surfboards for rent near its roller coaster.

ELLIOTT INTERNATIONAL HOSTEL

**Address: 3790 Udall Street, San Diego, California 92107.
Telephone: 619–223–4778. Reservations are essential April to September; mail one night's deposit two weeks in advance. Phone reservations accepted with credit card.**

This hostel is an airy two-story building with a spacious outdoor courtyard in the Point Loma neighborhood, right by the beach. It is a short drive from the San Diego Zoo in gigantic Balboa Park (see page 199).

Season: Year-round. The hostel is closed from 10:30 A.M. to 3:30 P.M. daily.

Accommodations: Family rooms are available in this sixty-bed hostel.

Special Features: Large courtyard, travel library, baggage storage, kitchen, and linen rental.

Cost: AYH members $12 per night, nonmembers $15 per night for adults; children five to ten half price.

Nearby: The beach, San Diego Zoo, and Balboa Park are all close by.

LOS ANGELES, CALIFORNIA

In the greater Los Angeles area you can swim and surf off miles of beaches, see movies being shot on the streets or made at major movie studios, visit museums specifically for children, and please your youngsters with visits to one of the countless theme parks.

The beach areas of Santa Monica and Marina Del Rey are the best places to set up a relatively inexpensive base within the city. They have many family accommodations, are in less smoggy areas, and have easy access by freeway to all of the city's major sites. Both are about an hour's drive from Disneyland, which is twenty-seven miles south of downtown Los

Angeles in Anaheim. If you want to be closer to Disneyland and by the beach, you may want to try Orange County's sun-drenched areas of Newport Beach or San Clemente. Their sandy beaches are ideal for swimming, surfing, sunbathing, and boating. In Newport and neighboring Balboa Island there are ecological reserves, harbors, and coves perfect for a family beach holiday.

Frequent Disneyland visitors recommend planning a visit on a Thursday or Friday, when it is normally less crowded, and working your way from back to front. Two-day passports, only slightly more expensive than one-day tickets, are $50 for adults, $41 for kids ages three to eleven. We list inexpensive accommodations next to Disneyland and further tips about the park on page 13. You may want to pick up a copy of the *Unofficial Guide to Disneyland* (Prentice-Hall, 1991; $7.95) to help you plan your visit.

The Los Angeles Children's Museum (213–687–8800) in downtown Los Angeles is an interactive museum where kids can sing and make a tape recording in a simulated recording studio, watch themselves on television, dress up, or do art projects. A newer museum for kids is Kidspace in Pasadena (818–449–9143), with creative art projects, a simulated beach area, a soft area for toddlers to roll and jump in, and dress-up areas. The California Museum of Science and Industry (213–744–7400) in Exposition Park is another lively museum with interactive exhibits. Don't miss its earthquake exhibit with a realistic simulation of a large-magnitude temblor.

Griffith Park, in the Hollywood Hills, is home to the Gene Autry Western Heritage Museum (213–667–2000) a planetarium theater, a hall of science, pony and train rides, a merry-go-round, Travel Town, with outdoor displays of trains and other vehicles, and a recreation center with tennis, swimming, and golf. Located within the park is the enormous Los Angeles Zoo (213–666–4650); it's a good idea to get a map there and select a few areas to explore.

Show business is a big draw in Los Angeles. Many studios conduct tours; kids might enjoy attending an audience-participation television show. Tickets for many network shows are available through Audiences Unlimited (818–506–0043), ABC-TV (213–557–4396), and CBS-TV (213–852–4002). Behind-the-scenes tours are available through Paramount Studios (213–468–5575), the Burbank Studios Tour (818–954–1744), and KCET-TV public television (213–667–9242). In May and November NBC-TV has a special tour for children in grades one through six (818–840–3555) in which kids can join a simulated television production. NBC also has general studio tours year-round and tickets for audience-participation shows (818–840–3537).

The largest and most popular tour is at Universal Studios (818–508–9600), which is a thrill for kids over four. If this is your first visit, seasoned visitors advise spending the entire day and bringing all that you will need to feel comfortable to do so (such as sunscreen, visors, jackets), as many of the exhibits are outdoors. Attractions include a guided tram tour of the studio's back lot, where you encounter the world's largest animated figure of a thirty-foot King Kong, a collapsing bridge from television's "Bionic Woman," and scenes from the movie *Jaws*. Young kids enjoy the Animal Actors Stage, where trainers show how they get animals to perform.

The best beaches in the Los Angeles area are in Malibu, which is north along Pacific Coast Highway from Santa Monica. Leo Carillo State Beach (818–706–1310) has great swimming, a nature trail, tide pools and sea caves, restrooms, and lifeguards. One mile east is a smaller beach, Nicolas Canyon County Beach (213–457–9891). Zuma Beach (213–457–9891) has a large sandy beach with play equipment, restrooms, and lifeguards. Southeast from Zuma, secluded, family-oriented Westward Beach (213–457–9891) is a long and narrow beach with great swimming, boogie boarding, and surfing. There are lifeguards and restrooms too.

SANTA MONICA INTERNATIONAL HOSTEL

Address: 1436 Second Street, Santa Monica, California 90401.
Telephone: 310–393–9913. Reservations are essential from May to October. Phone or fax (310–393–1769) reservations are accepted with a credit card.

This modern four-story hostel is just two blocks east of the beach and the Santa Monica Pier. Built around a spacious courtyard, the hostel was designed around the oldest standing structure in Santa Monica, the Rapp Saloon, which dates from 1875. The saloon has been restored and furnished in period style and now serves as a common room.

Season: Year-round. The hostel is open all day.

Accommodations: The hostel has five family rooms called "quad rooms" and thirty-seven dorm rooms, in addition to many common areas. For example, a family of four can have four twin beds in a shared room with restrooms down the hall.

Special Features: Breakfast is served daily, and on Wednesday and Sunday nights there is a fun and delicious barbecue. The hostel has bicycle storage, an open-air courtyard, a self-service kitchen, laundry facilities, a library, linen rental, baggage storage, a television lounge, and a full-service travel store.

Cost: Family rooms $18 per person per night for AYH members, $21 per person per night for nonmembers; children ages five to ten half price. Breakfast $2 per person, all-you-can-eat barbecue $5 per person.

Nearby: Santa Monica Pier has arcades, shops, restaurants, and kiddie rides. Fun Zone at the pier, a summer ride area for young children, has a gorgeous carousel. You can rent bikes and roller skates near the pier at

Sea Mist Skate and Bike Rental (310–395–7076). Perched on the bluffs overlooking the ocean is Palisades Park, a one-mile stretch of walkways and lawns; it's great for biking. Santa Monica State Beach is a three-mile stretch of sand below the bluffs of Palisades Park, with all the facilities (and crowds) of a tourist-oriented beach. For fewer crowds, drive farther north. South of the pier is gymnastics equipment and volleyball courts. Douglas Park, near Wilshire Boulevard and Twentieth Street in Santa Monica, has a duck pond, wading pool, wonderful play equipment, and picnic facilities. For more activities in the greater Los Angeles area, see the introduction on pages 201–203.

COMFORT INN

Address: 2815 Santa Monica Boulevard, Santa Monica, California 90404.
Telephone: 800–228–5150; 310–828–5517.

A ten-minute drive from the beach, this is an excellent value for the location; it's also just minutes from Westwood, Brentwood, and Santa Monica. The staff at the Comfort Inn are very family-friendly. The large swimming pool has a good-size shallow area for young children, and children can play on the spacious outdoor patios adjoining the first- and second-floor rooms.

Season: Year-round.

Accommodations: The inn has eighty-one large rooms with private baths, air-conditioning, radios, and cable TV. Rooms with two double beds have room for a crib.

Special Features: Swimming pool, tour desk.

Cost: Rooms with one queen-size bed $68 to $78 per night, double occupancy, depending on time of the year; rooms with two double beds $78 to $89 per night. Each additional adult $10; children under eighteen stay free. Cribs and rollaway beds $10 per night.

Nearby: See Santa Monica International Hostel, above. For more activities in the greater Los Angeles area, see the introduction on pages 201–203.

JAMAICA BAY INN

Address: 4175 Admiralty Way at Palawan, Marina del Rey, California 90292.
Telephone: 800–528–1234 (reservations); 310–823–5333.

This small, nondescript hotel with spacious rooms is right on the water, fronting the harbor and a palm-dotted beach. Although not really a "budget" hotel, it is very well priced for a waterfront hotel in this area. There is a heated swimming pool, a whirlpool spa, a patio area, and a beach hut that rents beach cruisers, mountain bikes, tandem bikes, children's bikes, baby carriers, and helmets.

Season: Year-round.

Accommodations: Rooms have color TV, air-conditioning, and a balcony or patio. Cribs are available at no charge. King deluxe rooms have a microwave oven and refrigerator.

Special Features: Laundry service and a beachfront coffee shop with high chairs and booster seats.

Cost: The least expensive rooms are those without a bay view. October to May $90 to $105 per night, double occupancy; June to September, $100 to $120 per night, double occupancy. Additional person $10 per night. Children twelve and under stay free.

Nearby: Boat rental, roller-skate rentals, fishing, and sailboarding are close by. A fun park is Admiralty Park, on Admiralty Way, near the bird sanctuary between Palawan and Bali Way. Burton Chace Park is a nine-acre waterfront park at the end of Mindanao Way with picnic areas and a fishing dock. Peninsula Beach, at the end of Washington Street, is an attractive and not-so-crowded beach, especially the portion south of the pier. For more activities in the greater Los Angeles area, see the introduction on pages 201–203.

VACATION BEACH HOUSE

Address: c/o Playa Realty, 108 McFadden Place, Newport Beach, California 92663.
Telephone: 714–673–1900.

This vacation rental is one house from the beach along the two-and-a-half-mile Newport Peninsula. The main attraction here is the wide, safe, sandy beach and the harbor, where boats are for rent.

Season: Year-round.

Accommodations: Playa Realty represents a number of waterfront homes, from modest to luxurious. The least expensive beach rental is a one-bedroom house that sleeps four to five people. It is fully furnished, but guests must bring their own linens and towels.

Cost: For the house described above, $500 to $525 per week.

Nearby: At the foot of Newport Beach's pier you can rent fishing equipment, beach cruisers, and children's bikes at Baldy's Tackle (714–673–4150). The Newport Bay Ecological Reserve, ideal for biking, is a seven-hundred-acre park with all kinds of wildlife. Newport Dunes Aquatic Park (714–644–0510) is a family beach and park located on a fifteen-acre lagoon. It is a great place to swim in calm waters, build sand castles, and rent paddleboats, sailboats, aqua cycles, and kayaks. There's a playground, water slides, and lifeguards; floating whales mark off the kids swimming areas.

Also close by is the summer resort of the Balboa Peninsula and Balboa Island, which is reminiscent of Cape Cod. At the end of Balboa Pier is a nice public beach with play equipment, showers, and restrooms. The boardwalk is wonderful for skating and biking. You can rent bikes (even ones with child carriers) and roller skates at Ocean Front Wheel Works (714–723–6510). The Fun Zone, a small area along the waterfront near the Balboa Pavilion that is designed specifically for kids, has a Ferris wheel and a merry-go-round.

SAN CLEMENTE BEACH HOSTEL

Address: 233 Avenida Granada, San Clemente, California 92672 Telephone: 714–492–2848. Reservations are essential June to September; mail one night's deposit as early as possible. Phone reservations are accepted with a credit card.

A former library, this beach hostel promises guests plenty of fun in the sun. The hostel is a five-minute walk from the beach. Located midway between Los Angeles and San Diego, a short drive from Disneyland, San Clemente claims to have the world's finest climate, with average winter temperatures near seventy degrees. Swimming, volleyball, and surfing are the main attractions.

Season: Year-round. The hostel is closed from 10:00 A.M. to 4:30 P.M. daily.

Accommodations: This forty-five bed hostel is near the beach. Its family rooms are available with advance booking.

Special Features: Patios, baggage storage, kitchen, laundry facilities, linen rental, and on-site parking.

Cost: AYH members, adults $9 per night; nonmembers $12 per night. Children five to ten half price.

Nearby: Fishermen can hop on a boat at nearby Dana Point. The Mission San Juan Capistrano, near San Clemente, is the summer nesting spot of thousands of migrating swallows.

MONTEREY PENINSULA, CALIFORNIA

Santa Cruz is a charming year-round vacation town situated along Monterey Bay, seventy miles south of San Francisco. It is best known for its beautiful redwood groves, good swimming beaches, spectacular coastal scenery, and old-fashioned boardwalk. The beachfront boardwalk (408–

423–5590) features the Giant Dipper roller coaster, a classic 1911 merry-go-round, and an enormous game-filled arcade. West of the boardwalk and its adjoining wharf is West Cliff Drive, where families can roller-skate and ride bicycles. Bikes can be rented at the Spokesman (408–429–6062).

A path along West Cliff Drive hugs the ocean and passes Lighthouse Point all the way to Natural Bridges State Beach, which has spacious picnic areas, safe swimming, and rocky tide pools to explore, as well as an annual winter population of monarch butterflies to observe as they blanket the park's eucalyptus forests.

Next to the state beach is the University of California's Long Marine Lab (408–459–2883), with dolphin and sea lion tanks and an eighty-five-foot whale skeleton on display. Free tours are available. Six miles north of Santa Cruz in Felton is a six-mile steam train excursion through some of the state's oldest and tallest redwoods. The Roaring Camp and the Big Trees Narrow-Gauge Railroad (408–335–4400) is billed as a way to relive the pioneer days of the 1800s. It is not recommended for very young children, as the novelty of being on a train wears off quickly and gorgeous scenery does not seem to impress young kids.

Forty-five minutes down the coast from Santa Cruz is the spectacular Monterey Bay Aquarium (408–648–4888), along Cannery Row in Monterey. If you want the place to yourself, go after 3 P.M. and avoid holiday weekends. Kids enjoy the overhead exhibit of full-size models of sea mammals; the three-story-high Kelp Forest; the Touch Pool, where they can touch a variety of starfish and other tide pool life; and the Bat Ray Pool, where they can try to pat the passing bat rays.

About twenty miles north of Santa Cruz, past the town of Davenport, Greyhound State Beach is one of the county's most magnificent, with majestic cliffs, colorful abalone shells along the shore, and miles of wide-open sand. It is a steep climb down to the beach. In Pescadero, a bit farther north, the Año Nuevo State Reserve (415–879–0595) is best known for its winter elephant seal migrations and tours. Reserve tickets well in advance.

VACATIONS BY THE SEA

Address: 215 Monterey Avenue, Capitola, California 95010 (agent).
Telephone: 408–479–9360.

These apartments, condominiums, and beach houses are either on Capitola Beach or a short distance away. Capitola, just south of Santa Cruz, is a quaint resort town full of beach and craft shops and ice-cream vendors. The Soquel Creek feeds into its main beach, which is perfect for wading. There's a lifeguard on duty and paddleboats for rent in the summer.
Season: Year-round.

Accommodations: The least expensive accommodations are the one-bedroom, one-bath apartment (for up to three people) two blocks from the beach; a two-bedroom, one-and-a-half-bath apartment (for up to five people) less than two blocks from the beach; and one-bedroom condominiums (for up to five people) across the street from the beach. All are equipped for housekeeping; guests must bring their own sheets and towels.

Cost: June 15 to September 15 one-bedroom, one-bath apartment $450 per week; two-bedroom, one-and-a-half-bath apartment $550 per week; one-bedroom condominium $600 to $650 per week. Rates are lower off season.

Nearby: Capitola is fifteen minutes from Santa Cruz and forty minutes from Monterey-Carmel. The Capitola Movie Theater hasn't changed its prices in a decade; head there in inclement weather.

BEACH VACATION RENTALS

Address: Cheshire-Rio Realty, 107 Aptos Beach Drive, Aptos, California (agent).
Telephone: 408–688–2041.

This company rents apartments, condominiums, and beach houses in Rio del Mar, Seascape Beach, La Selva Beach, and Sunset Beach, which are beautiful seaside communities south of the city of Santa Cruz. Rentals also are available in Santa Cruz and Capitola.

Season: Year-round.

Accommodations: Of particularly good value is the three-story house at 126 Venetian, one block from the beach in Capitola, which sleeps ten. It has a fireplace, dishwasher, barbecue, washer and dryer, and ocean views from its decks. Another good deal is the Seacliff Beach condominium at 313 Searidge, which sleeps five. It has a view of the ocean from the living room, a fireplace, color televisions and a VCR, dishwasher, barbecue, washer and dryer, and microwave oven.

Cost: In summer, Capitola rental for ten people $695 per week; off-season it can be rented by the night. Seacliff Beach condominium for five people $525 per week year-round.

Nearby: Capitola and Seacliff Beach are fifteen and twenty minutes, respectively, from Santa Cruz and about forty minutes to Monterey-Carmel.

PIGEON POINT LIGHTHOUSE HOSTEL

Address: Pigeon Point Road and California Highway 1, Pescadero, California 94060 (fifty miles south of San Francisco on the coast, twenty miles south of Half Moon Bay, and twenty-seven miles north of Santa Cruz).
Telephone: 415–879–0633. Reservations are essential from May to September and on weekends; mail one night's deposit as early as possible. Phone reservations are accepted with a credit card up to one week in advance.

Perched on a cliff overlooking the ocean on the central California coast, this 110-foot lighthouse is one of the tallest in America. Guiding mariners since 1872, it was restored recently as a hostel. There are several breathtaking beaches close by for beachcombing, surfing, jogging, horseback riding, and sailboarding. If you visit between November and April you may be lucky enough to see the annual gray whale migration from the boardwalk behind the lighthouse's fog signal building.

   Season: Year-round. The hostel is closed from 9:30 A.M. to 4:30 P.M. daily.

   Accommodations: The hostel has fifty-two beds, and family rooms are available.

   Special Features: Outdoor hot tub, baggage storage, kitchen, laundry facilities, linen rental, and on-site parking. The hostel offers programs in outdoor education to elementary and secondary school students, including music and puppet shows, an elephant seal tour, and visits to tide pools and marshes.

   Cost: AYH members, adults $9 per night; nonmembers $12 per night. Children five to ten half price.

   Nearby: One hundred yards north of Pigeon Point is a tide pool area that's fun to explore. Pescadero Marsh is the feeding and nesting place for more than 150 species of birds. A short drive south is the Año Nuevo State Reserve, the breeding site of northern elephant seals (see page 207 for more information).

THE NORTH COAST, CALIFORNIA

The coast from San Francisco to Oregon is known throughout the world for its unparalleled beauty. Curving roads hug cliffs that lead to steep drops and the raging ocean below. Although the ocean water here is rough and quite chilly, there are great spots to beachcomb, camp, hike, fish, clam, and whale watch.

POINT MONTARA LIGHTHOUSE HOSTEL

Address: Sixteenth Street at California Highway 1, PO Box 737, Montara, California 94037 (between Montara and Moss Beach). **Telephone:** 415–728–7177. Reservations essential from April to September and on weekends; mail one night's deposit as early as possible.

Overlooking the ocean on the rugged California coast twenty-five miles south of San Francisco is the Point Montara Fog Signal and Light Station. Established in 1875, these turn-of-the-century buildings have been preserved and restored to serve as a base for exploring this spectacular stretch of coastline and watching the annual migration of gray whales between November and April.

Season: Year-round. The hostel is closed from 9:30 A.M. to 4:30 P.M. daily.

Accommodations: The light tower, which sits atop seventy-foot cliffs, and its Victorian-style lightkeeper's quarters are now part of the hostel's forty-five bed facility. There are six family rooms.

Special Features: Outdoor hot tub, baggage storage, kitchen, laundry facilities, linen rental, and on-site parking. Staff members present special interpretive programs on the ecology of tide pool and intertidal zones of the San Mateo coast.

Cost: AYH members, adults $9 per night; nonmembers $12 per night. Children five to ten half price.

Nearby: The James Fitzgerald Marine Reserve, a four-mile stretch of tide pools filled with starfish, crabs, mussels, abalone, and sea anemones, is one-half mile north and accessible by a trail. There are also several breathtaking beaches for swimming (the water is cold), beachcombing, surfing, jogging, horseback riding, and sailboarding.

POINT REYES HOSTEL

Address: Box 247, Point Reyes Station, California 94956 (off Limantour Road). **Telephone:** 415–663–8811. Reservations are always advisable; mail one night's deposit as early as possible.

This hostel is two miles from the ocean in a secluded valley of the national seashore. Summer at the seashore, a sixty-five-thousand-acre wilderness area, features fresh air, blooming wildflowers, and marshes full of birds. The park is known for its migrating birds as well as abundant flora and fauna, including bobcats, foxes, deer, elk, harbor seals, and sea lions. Many trails in the park lead to wooded hills, rocky coves, and long, sandy beaches.

Season: Year-round.

Accommodations: Family rooms are available for parents with children under six. Other families stay in the dorm-style accommodations of this thirty-bed hostel.

Special Features: Kitchen, linen rental, patio with an outdoor barbecue, and on-site parking.

Cost: AYH members adults $9 per night; nonmembers $12 per night. Children five to ten half price.

Nearby: Limantour Beach, with its rolling sand dunes, is two miles from the hostel and easily accessible by car. It is ideal for summertime wading. At the end of the Limantour Spit you can watch for harbor seals. Drakes Beach (a forty-minute drive) is famous for the high, white cliffs backing its swimming strand, and is the only spot at the seashore with food service. Sculptured Beach is the best for tide pool exploring; check the tide table at the visitor centers. Point Reyes Lighthouse, twenty-five miles from the hostel, is the best place in the Bay Area for whale watching from January to April.

The park's Bear Valley Visitor Center has exhibits of the area's animals as well as lists of park activities. Visit the center's Miwok Village, which reconstructs the daily life of the Miwok Indians who first inhabited Point Reyes, and walk the Earthquake Trail along the San Andreas Fault to see remaining evidence of the 1906 San Francisco quake. Behind the visitor center is the Morgan Horse Ranch, where you can learn about the horses' history and see them grazing. Horses can be rented at two nearby stables (Bear Valley Stables, 415–688–1570 or Five Brooks Stables, 415–663–8287). Bikes can be rented at Point Reyes Bikes (415–663–1768) or Trailhead Rental (415–663–1958).

THE INN AT SCHOOLHOUSE CREEK

Address: 7051 North Highway 1, Little River, California 95456 (on the coast highway, three miles south of Mendocino).
Telephone: 707–937–5525.

Facing the Pacific Ocean, this cozy historic inn is located on ten acres of gardens, meadow, and forest. It was once part of a large coastal ranch. Mendocino, with its artisan shops and galleries, is three miles away. Also close by are many rivers, harbors, beaches (the water is cold but the beach is great for kite flying, running, and beachcombing), and spectacular state parks.

Season: Year-round.

Accommodations: The inn has separate cottages with kitchens and decks that were built at the turn of the century. Other accommodations include rooms from the 1930s and more contemporary rooms in small buildings. All rooms have ocean views, private baths, and fireplaces.

Special Features: The inn's "Ledford Home," built in 1862, has a comfortable lounge with a fireplace. Breakfast is available there.

Cost: Rooms dating from the 1930s start at $73 per night, double occupancy; cottages $58 to $110 per night, double occupancy; contemporary rooms $68 to $84 per night, double occupancy. Each additional person $10. Children seven and under can stay in the cottages only. Two-night minimum stay on weekends.

Nearby: Mendocino's visitor center, in the historic Ford House on Main Street, has a calendar of events that lists children's activities including an annual sand castle building contest on Labor Day, Easter egg hunts, and Fourth of July carnival. Three miles south of Mendocino is Van Damme State Park, which has a relatively safe beach, hiking trails, and the Pygmy Forest Discovery Trail, where you can see decades-old trees that are only a few feet tall. Mendocino Headlands State Park has surfing, sport diving, and fishing. Its Big River Beach has tide pools, rocks to climb, and lots of room to romp. Canoe rental is available for rides down the Big River from Catch a Canoe at the Big River Lodge (707–937–0273).

LOST WHALE BED AND BREAKFAST INN

Address: 3452 Patrick's Point Drive, Trinidad, California 95570 (one mile off U.S. 101, fifteen minutes from the Arcata-Eureka Airport). Telephone: 707–677–3425.

Unlike most bed-and-breakfast establishments, this Cape Cod–style inn overlooking the Pacific enthusiastically welcomes families. In fact, the owners have young children of their own. A private path leads to the beach, which has a secluded cove of jutting rocks, tide pools, and sea lions. On the inn's enclosed grounds children can pick berries or have fun in the playhouse and playground. There are bunnies and goats to feed and books, puzzles, and games to entertain kids at sundown.

Season: Year-round.

Accommodations: The inn has six suites, all of which have ocean views and private bathrooms. Two of the rooms have step-out balconies and sleeping lofts for children.

Special Features: Included in the price is a hearty breakfast of casseroles and quiches, home-baked muffins, fresh fruit, and locally smoked salmon. Cappuccino, sherry, and home-baked pastries are available at the end of the day. The hot tub has views of crashing waves. Bikes are available for guests to cruise the nearby quiet roads. Child care is available with advance notice, as are cribs, bassinets, and high chairs.

Cost: November to April rooms $90 to $120 per night double occupancy; May to October $100 to $130 double occupancy, depending on type of room. Additional adult $15; additional child ages three to sixteen $10; under three stay free. Rates include breakfast.

Nearby: Patrick's Point State Park is a short walk away. Also close by is Agate Beach, which has wonderful driftwood formations, agates, jade, and tide pools. Trinidad is a quaint fishing village with a marina for deep-sea charter boats, surf fishing, lagoons for summer swimming, sailing, and sailboarding. Hiking trails through the redwoods and Fern Canyon, with its thousands of ferns and beautiful waterfalls, are a twenty-minute drive north.

THE OREGON COAST

The Oregon coast is a scenic wonder with mountains, lakes, rivers, and easily accessible broad-sandy ocean beaches. Coastal towns offer a wide selection of indoor activities for rainy days. Every area has its unique attractions, such as Haystack Rock, the third-largest monolith in the world, south of Cannon Beach, and exceptional tide pools at low tide. Oregon's coast has many well-equipped state parks, municipal swimming pools, golf courses, tennis courts, and playgrounds.

EDGEWATER COTTAGES

Address: 3978 Southwest Pacific Coast Highway, Waldport, Oregon 97394 (fifteen miles south of Newport and two and a half miles south of Waldport, on the beach).
Telephone: 503–563–2240.

Edgewater, as it name implies, is situated on a wonderful expanse of very safe beach. The owners claim this to be "a good place for kids and dogs and well-behaved adults."

Season: Year-round.

Accommodations: Cabins have an ocean view, fireplace, fully equipped kitchen, sliding glass door, and sundeck. The largest unit, the "Beachcomber," accommodates up to fifteen people and it is rented to only one group at a time; it has three bedrooms, a kitchen, a television-game room, a solarium, a children's playroom, three bathrooms, and a two-person Jacuzzi.

Special Features: Lawn for Frisbee or soccer. Beach access via stairs. Cribs and baby-sitting are available with advance notice.

Cost: Cabin rates depend on size and number of people. Cabin for four $47 to $75 per night; cabin for six $88 per night. Beachcomber rates based on number of people and number of rooms used: $88 per night for four people using two bedrooms. Two-night minimum stay most of the year, four-night minimum stay from Memorial Day through the third week in October.

DRIFTWOOD SHORES

Address: 88416 First Avenue, Florence, Oregon 97439 (fifty-two miles south of Newport, sixty miles west of Eugene, on the beach). Telephone: 800–824–8774 (outside Oregon); 800–422–5091 (in Oregon); 503–997–8263.

This oceanfront resort of 135 units is relaxing and clean but not fancy. Decks overlook a sandy, expansive, driftwood-strewn beach. An indoor heated swimming pool and indoor spa are nice for rainy weather.

Season: Year-round.

Accommodations: Units include two- and three-bedroom suites. Some have fully equipped kitchens and fireplaces, and all have private balconies with an ocean view.

Special Features: Laundry facilities, moderately priced restaurant with high chairs.

Cost: Room with two double beds and full kitchen $94 per night Friday and Saturday, $73 per night the rest of the week. Children under thirteen stay free. Cribs available at no charge.

Nearby: North on U.S. 101 are the Sea Lion Caves and the Heceta Head Lighthouse, listed on the National Register of Historical Places. Also nearby is the Oregon Dune National Recreation Area, where you can take dune buggy tours. There are stables close by for horseback riding on the beach and dune trails.

LIGHTHOUSE BEACH VACATION HOME

Address: 19590 Cape Arago Highway (beach house); George Kaufer, 3405 NW Moro Place, Beaverton, Oregon 97006 (reservations). Telephone: 503–645–0727.

This vacation home for eight just north of Sunset Bay, a popular and scenic beach, has a private stairway that leads to a semiprivate beach with plenty of sand for children. The water is cold, but the beach is great for playing, tide pooling, clamming, crabbing, and birdwatching. At low tide you easily can harvest a supply of mussels for dinner.

Season: Year-round.
Accommodations: The house sleeps eight and has two bedrooms, two bathrooms, a fireplace, a dishwasher, and a washer and dryer. The living room has nearly twenty-eight feet of picture windows that face the ocean. The kitchen and master bedroom also have ocean views.
Special Features: Guests can use the crab nets in the garage to catch delicious Dungeness crabs, available year-round, at the piers in Charleston.
Cost: June to October $550 per week, November to May $450 per week. In winter, nightly rates are available with a two-night minimum stay.
Nearby: The house is two miles from Shore Acres State Park and the Botanical Gardens. There are tide pools at Sunset Bay and golf at the Sunset Golf Course or Coos Country Club. Party boats available in Charleston for rock fishing year-round and salmon fishing in season. The biscuits and gravy at the Harbor Cafe in the Charleston boat basin are said to be the best on the Oregon coast.

SEA STAR HOSTEL

Address: 375 Second Street, Bandon, Oregon 97411.
Telephone: 503–347–9632. **Reservations are recommended from June to September. Phone reservations are accepted with a credit card.**

Bandon, near Coos Bay, has some of Oregon's most scenic coastline, with dunes, cliffs, rock formations, and miles of expansive, sandy beaches. The hostel is in the town's historic Old Town Waterfront District and overlooks the harbor. Unlike many hostels, Sea Star is open all day and has an international bistro that serves breakfast, lunch, and dinner.
Season: Year-round.
Accommodations: This thirty-five bed hostel features family rooms, skylights, exposed wood beams, a cozy wood-burning stove, and a deck with a harbor view. Family rooms sleep three to six people and have a variety of double, twin, and bunk bed arrangements.
Special Features: Courtyard, kitchen, laundry facilities, linen rental, and baggage storage area.
Cost: AYH members, adults $8.50 per night; nonmembers $11. Children under twelve half price. Family rooms have an additional surcharge of $3 per room.
Nearby: Bandon has summer stock and community theater groups and numerous artisans' studios.

ISLANDS IN THE PUGET SOUND, WASHINGTON

This magnificent archipelago of islands off the coast of Washington has everything for a well-rounded family vacation of outdoor activities, comfortable lodgings, and delicious food. There are 172 islands in the San Juan Islands, many of which are a short ferry ride from either Seattle or Tacoma. Orcas Island, one of the largest, has quiet roads through rolling countryside dotted with small farms and many accessible beaches. It is not difficult to find your own quiet lagoon on a sandy beach with lots of driftwood. Moran State Park, on the island, has two freshwater lakes for swimming, boating, and fishing. Other popular island activities include biking and kayaking.

Whidbey Island, the second-largest island in the continental United States and not far from the Seattle area, is a long, narrow island with miles of beaches and six state parks. Also in the sound near Seattle is primitive Vashon Island, home to one of the American Youth Hostel's most unusual accommodations: authentic tepees. Both Vashon and Orcas are ideal for bicycle touring; in fact, once you leave the ferry landing you will see more bikes than cars.

BEACH HAVEN RESORT

Address: Route 1, Box 12, Eastsound, Orcas Island, Washington 98245 (sixty miles north of Seattle, accessible by ferry from Anacortes; west of Orcas lies Vancouver Island and Victoria, British Columbia).
Telephone: 206–376–2288.

This secluded island retreat with no phones or TVs is set on ten acres of gently sloping pebble beach on Orcas Island. The water reaches up to the decks of thirteen waterfront fifty-year-old log cabins, which are sheltered by a dense, old-growth forest. The cabins are rustic but clean and comfortable. You can walk from the cabins to more than fourteen hundred feet of beach.

Season: Year-round. There is a one-week minimum stay in summer.

Accommodations: All cabins have log walls, floors, electric heat, and wood stoves. Some have covered decks on the beach. Apartments with sliding glass doors to balconies over the beach also are available. All accommodations are designed for full housekeeping; linens and towels are provided.

Special Features: Swimming in the sound; books, popcorn, and games for evening fun.

Cost: Two-bedroom cabins or apartments that sleep up to four $76 per night, $535 per week. Three-bedroom cabins or apartments that sleep up to six $87 per night, $610 per week.

Nearby: Moran State Park has thirty miles of trails and five lakes with swimming, rowboats, paddleboats, and freshwater fishing. Oceanfront Obstruction Pass State Park has tide pools. Sea kayak tours are available for all levels; call 206–376–4041 or 206–376–4755. A unique way to explore the island is by moped; Key Mopeds (206–376–2474) has a large number of them for rent.

NORTH BEACH INN

Address: PO Box 80, Eastsound, Orcas Island, Washington 98245 (Orcas Islands, sixty miles north of Seattle, accessible by ferry from Anacortes; west of Orcas lies Vancouver Island and Victoria, British Columbia).
Telephone: 206–376–2660.

These twelve simple no-frills cottages are in a wooded setting facing a third of a mile of pebble beach on Orcas Island. Behind the cottages are ninety acres of woods and fields with views toward the Canadian San Juan Islands. Moran State Park, on the island, has two freshwater lakes for swimming, boating, and fishing. Biking and kayaking are also popular on Orcas Island. At night, families staying at the inn often build fires on the beach.

Season: Year-round.

Accommodations: Cottages are simple and clean. Each has a fireplace, electric heat, and a fully equipped kitchen. Linens and towels are provided.

Special Features: A dining room, open in summer, is well suited for children.

Cost: In summer, one-bedroom cottage for three $490 per week, two-bedroom cottage for four $610 per week; $100 more per week for five to six people. Daily rates also available. Fifteen-percent rate reduction from September 15 to May 15.

Nearby: See Beach Haven Resort, above.

MUTINY BAY RESORT MOTEL

Address: PO Box 249, Freeland, South Whidbey Island, Washington 98249.
Telephone: 206–321–4500.

This resort has chalets on the beach and less expensive cabins set among the trees a short distance away. The small beach in front of the resort is good for clamming and shell hunts; the owners lend pails and sand toys to children. In summer you can swim in the bay or fish from a long dock.

Season: Year-round.

Accommodations: Cabin no. 3 sleeps three; it has one bedroom, a living area with a sofabed, a fully equipped kitchen, a dining area, and a three-quarters bath, with a toilet and sink. Cabins have no showers or tubs; guests use the showers provided in the resort's camping area. Chalets on the sandy beach sleep seven. Each has two bedrooms, a fireplace, an additional loft bedroom, a color TV, and a fully equipped kitchen.

Special Features: Private dock for fishing and boats, crab pot and fishing pole rentals, small yard, and sport court with recreation equipment.

Cost: In summer, cabins $47 to $57 per night, chalets $105 per night (both rates for double occupancy). Additional person $5 per night. Guests receive one night free if they stay for one week. Rates are lower during the rest of the year.

Nearby: Deception Pass State Park, at the island's north end, has freshwater Cranberry Lake right next to a beautiful ocean beach. Whidbey is two and a half hours from Vancouver.

VASHON ISLAND HOTEL

Address: 12119 S.W. Cove Road, Vashon Island, Washington 98070 (a five-minute ferry ride from Tacoma, fifteen-minute ferry ride from West Seattle; also accessible by ferry from the Kitsap Peninsula or downtown Seattle).
Telephone: 206–463–2592. Reservations are essential June through August; phone reservations are accepted with a credit card.

This hostel's hand-hewn log cabins and five Sioux Indian tepees with family rooms, set on ten acres, provide an unforgettable getaway. Guests also can sleep in cozy covered wagons that surround a campfire. In pleasant weather Indian drumming is performed around the fire. Parents who want a special getaway while vacationing with their children can stay on the premises in an antique bed-and-breakfast room while their older children stay in the tepees. (Parents determine if their children are old enough for this). In the second week of July, Vashon has an annual strawberry festival with street dancing and colorful fanfare.

Season: May through October.

Accommodations: Family rooms in private tepees have three to four cots. The antique bed-and-breakfast room for adults is beautifully furnished.

Special Features: Outdoor kitchen with western facade, indoor kitchen, linen rental, baggage storage, and on-site parking. Pancakes made from an old family recipe are served each morning. Bikes available at no charge for touring the island. Free pickup by hostel managers at the ferry. A slide show describes the building of the log cabins.

Cost: AYH members, adults $8 per night; nonmembers $11 per night.

Children five to ten half price. Bed-and-breakfast room $50 per night.
    Nearby: Vashon Island, twelve and a half miles long and five and a half miles wide, is a paradise for cyclists. Guests can bike to the beach two and a half miles away.

THE WASHINGTON COAST

This area stretches from Neah Bay at the entrance to the Strait of Juan de Fuca south to Ilwaco, where the Columbia River spills into the Pacific. If you want a combined vacation of beaches, mountains, even a rain forest, your best base is the Kalaloch area near Neah Bay (see pages 94–98 in the national parks chapter). If endless beaches for beachcombing are more your style, head for the area south of Moclips to Ocean Shores, a stretch of about twenty miles with numerous beach turnoffs and small towns that are popular holiday and vacation spots for families. Razor clam digging is a popular sport here, as are kite flying, shell collecting, and driftwood gathering. The Ocean Shores area has golf, tennis, horseback riding, bowling, and ocean fishing.
    Farther south, the Long Beach Peninsula extending from Ledbetter Point to the Columbia River has more broad, sandy beaches. Beachcombers can hunt for old shipwrecks, glass fishnet balls, and shells. Long Beach and Seaview have amusement arcades and go-carts, many shops and galleries, and two nine-hole golf courses. Ledbetter Point State Park has pine forests, salt marshes, and sand dunes.

OCEAN CREST RESORT

Address: Sunset Beach, Moclips, Washington 98652 (one mile north of Pacific Beach).
Telephone: 206–276–4465.

This resort is in a natural forest setting with views of the Pacific and direct beach access. Although the water is too cold and rough for swimming, the beach is sandy and ideal for beachcombing and playing. Children will enjoy the resort's playground and indoor heated pool, which is handy in rainy weather.
    Season: Year-round.
    Accommodations: Lodgings consist of apartments or hotel rooms with fireplaces and cable TV.
    Special Features: Pool, spa, sauna, exercise room, sun decks, and lounge. Cribs are available for a $3 one-time charge.
    Cost: During high season (March 16 to September 30), apartments for up to six people and large studios for up to four people $72 to $108 per night, double occupancy, depending on number of bedrooms and view.

Additional adults $10 per day; children under fourteen $5 per night, under five free. Rates are much lower during the rest of the year.
Nearby: Ocean Shores, eighteen miles away, has mopeds for rent.

IRON SPRINGS OCEAN BEACH RESORT

Address: PO Box 207, Copalis Beach, Washington 98535 (three miles north of Copalis Beach, between Copalis and Pacific beaches on Washington 109).
Telephone: 206–276–4230.

This rambling hundred-acre oceanfront resort has secluded cabins and apartments among the trees on a low-lying bluff overlooking the ocean. There is a private, although steep, path to the beach. When the tide is high, the beach is accessible along the road as well. The main focus here is the beach; the water is too cold for swimming but wonderful for razor clam digging, crab and surf fishing, beachcombing, and setting campfires at night. A shallow creek that runs through to the ocean is especially appealing to small children.
Season: Year-round.
Accommodations: Each apartment and cottage has a fully equipped kitchen, electric heat, and a fireplace. Bedding is provided.
Special Features: Beach, heated pool, badminton net, playground for youngsters, coffee shop. Cribs are available. You can purchase cinnamon rolls and clam chowder that are home-cooked on the premises for $5.50 to take to your room. Bring your own TV or rent one here.
Cost: The least expensive accommodations are the apartments for four, $58 to $74 per night. One-bedroom cottages for four start at $74 per night. Additional adult $10 per night; additional child $6.

KLIPSAN BEACH COTTAGES

Address: Route 1, Box 359, Ocean Park, Washington 98640 (on Klipsan Beach, which is part of the Long Beach Peninsula).
Telephone: 206–665–4888.

The eight comfortable, cedar-shingled Klipsan Beach Cottages are very popular with families, and typically there are many children here in the summer. The beach is two hundred feet from the cottage decks. There is also a small rhododendron forest and a safe stretch of dunes between the cabins and the beach. Beachcombers can hunt for old shipwrecks, glass fishnet balls, and shells.
Season: Year-round.

Accommodations: Eight cottages have fireplaces and firewood, unobstructed ocean views, and fully equipped kitchens. Linens are available for an additional charge.

Cost: June through September, two-bedroom cabin for four $78 per night; A-frame for six $99 per night. October through May, cabins $50 per night, A-frame $86 per night.

Nearby: Long Beach and Seaview have amusement arcades and go-carts, many shops and galleries, and two nine-hole golf courses.

TEXAS

CORPUS CHRISTI, PORT ARANSAS, AND THE PADRE ISLAND NATIONAL SEASHORE

Endless beaches surround the Gulf Coast city of Corpus Christi, which is small enough not to overwhelm but large enough to have a full range of seaside pleasures. Less than thirty minutes south of downtown, you can choose between tame or wild shores. The Padre Island National Seashore is the longest remaining stretch of undeveloped ocean beach in the United States. With a vast landscape of wind-sculpted dunes, this sparkling preserve of white sand and shell beach stretches for some eighty miles all the way to the Mexican border. The beaches are ideal for swimming and sunbathing from April through December. Swimming is permitted all along the beach; lifeguards normally are on duty at Malaquite Beach (ranked Texas's number-one beach) in the summer. Surfing is popular along some parts of the beach, as are boating, waterskiing, and sailboarding in Laguna Madre. One of the most popular pastimes is surf fishing. Camping is available at Malaquite Beach Campground and various primitive sites, all near the beach. Various nature programs are offered on weekends during the off-season (September through May); in summer they are held daily and include beach walks, campfire programs, and such activities as making fish prints.

Just north of Padre Island is Mustang Island State Park, which also has an excellent swimming beach. Just down the road you can rent horses to ride on the beach. At the tip of Mustang Island is the island resort of Port Aransas, known for its miles of wide, white beaches and deep-sea fishing. Camping is available at City Beach, Mustang Island State Park, and the Padre Island National Seashore. Three beaches have lifeguards: Mustang State Park, on Corpus Christi's barrier island; Padre Bali County Park, just beyond the bridge on North Padre Island, and the day-use beach at the National Seashore.

Corpus Christi is home to the International Kite Museum (512–883–7456) and the Texas State Aquarium (512–881–1200), which focuses on marine life of the Gulf of Mexico and the Caribbean Sea; just down the road is the new theme park Pirate of the Gulf and Playland at the Beach (512–884–4774). Kids love to ride on the porpoise-feeding boat, the *Dolphin Connection,* which departs daily from downtown in March through October (512–882–4126). The ride includes opportunities to pet the dolphins.

EXECUTIVE KEYS FAMILY VACATION RENTALS

Address: Box 1087, Port Aransas, Texas 78373.
Telephone: 512–749–6272.

These vacation rentals are on a beach access road within walking distance of a nice Mustang Island beach. The water is warm enough for swimming in May through October. The resort complex has a freshwater swimming pool, volleyball court, game room, barbecue grills, and picnic area.

Season: Year-round.

Accommodations: Lodgings include large two-bedroom apartments with fully equipped kitchens, electric heat, air-conditioning, and cable TV.

Special Features: Laundry facilities, outside shower for removal of sand, fish-cleaning facilities, and housekeeping service.

Cost: During the summer, two-bedroom apartment for four $99 per night. Rates lower off-season.

Nearby: Swimming, fishing, shelling, and birdwatching are nearby. There are two eighteen-hole golf courses in the area and excellent municipal tennis courts that are illuminated for night playing.

PELICAN CONDOMINIUMS

Address: Box 1690, Port Aransas, Texas 78373.
Telephone: 800–888–4974; 512–749–6226.

Located on Mustang Island at the northern end of Padre Island, a private walkway across the dunes connects the Pelican's grounds to the beach. Most people come here to play on the beach and to fish. The ocean water is warm enough for swimming in May through October. All apartments have an ocean view and private balcony. The resort complex also has a playground, volleyball court, basketball hoop, and unheated swimming pool, all enclosed in a large fenced yard.

Season: Year-round.

Accommodations: Sixty-five two- and three-bedroom ocean-view apartments have fully equipped kitchens with microwave ovens, and comfortable living rooms with cable TV.

Special Features: Fish-cleaning and laundry facilities.

Cost: In summer, two-bedroom apartment for up to six people $605 to $630 per week, including tax; three-bedroom apartment for up to eight people $740 to $770 per week, including tax. Nightly rates also available. Rates lower off-season.

Nearby: Miniature golf, shell shops, and eateries are nearby. The Pelican is thirty minutes from either the Padre Island National Seashore or Corpus Christi and a ten-minute ferryboat ride from San Jose Island, an uninhabited island with a fishing jetty and miles of isolated shell-strewn beach.

THE SOUTH

CHINCOTEAGUE ISLAND, VIRGINIA

Famous for its expansive beaches, national seashore, and wildlife, Chincoteague Island is a favorite getaway for a quiet beach vacation. The island has many nature trails for hiking plus opportunities for fishing, clamming, crabbing, eating delicious salt oysters, boating, water-skiing, beachcombing, and bicycling.

Chincoteague Island is a gateway to the Chincoteague National Wildlife Refuge on the Virginia portion of the Assateague Island National Seashore, which also is famous for its wild ponies. You can see native ponies and miniature horses at the Chincoteague Miniature Pony Farm. Visitors can take narrated safaris through the back roads of the wildlife refuge and sunset cruises through the island's serene waters.

During the last two and half weeks in July Chincoteague has a carnival celebrating pony penning. The famous Pony Swim is held the last Wednesday in July; Thursday morning is the auction, and on Friday the remaining ponies return to Assateague. Other special events on the island include the Easter Decoy Festival and the October Oyster Festival.

Bikes can be rented at T and T Bike Rentals on Maddox Boulevard (804–336–6330). There is a miniature golf course at Surfside Golf on Beach Road. Many places rent small boats along Main Street and East Side Drive. Chincoteague Island is home to the only Oyster Museum in the United States.

The beaches on the Virginia portion of thirty-three-mile-long Assateague Island are clean; the water temperature ranges from fifty-five degrees in May to seventy-five degrees from August through November. There are no concessions on Assateague but you'll find many picnic areas. The information center on the island has a schedule of events that changes weekly. The island is fun for hiking, biking, and cruising the bay.

Nearby Wallops Island is home to NASA's Goddard Space Flight Center, which has a collection of spacecraft and flight articles as well as exhibits about America's Space Flight Program. During the summer there are tours of launch sites; NASA operates its experimental rocket program here.

Chincoteague Island Vacation Cottages, an agency, has a small listing of centrally located private homes either on the water or with a water view. The rates are either less expensive (especially if you have a large family) or comparable to island hotels. Most of the houses the agency represents are old-fashioned and quaint, with screened porches and sun decks, but they also are equipped with modern conveniences including dishwashers and air-conditioners. Ask for a booklet with descriptions and black-and-white photos of the listings. The agency recommends the following homes for families traveling on a budget.

CAPTAIN'S QUARTERS

Address: Church Street Extension; c/o Chincoteague Island Vacation Cottages, Route 1, Box 547, East Side Drive, Chincoteague, Virginia 23336.
Telephone: 804-336-3720.

Originally situated on Assateague Island next to the old fish factory, this attractive old house was moved to its present location in 1930. It is a short drive or bike ride over the bridge to Assateague Island, with its nice sandy beach (with bathhouses), exotic birds, sika deer, and Assateague shaggy wild ponies.

Season: Spring, summer, and fall.

Accommodations: This house sleeps eight adults and two children under thirteen. It has five bedrooms, two baths, a large eat-in kitchen, a living room with color television, and air-conditioning.

Cost: Spring and fall $370 per week; summer $520 per week. Miniweek and weekend rates available.

BIG PINE

Address: 3545 Willow Street; c/o Chincoteague Island Vacation Cottages, Route 1, Box 547, East Side Drive, Chincoteague, Virginia 23336.
Telephone: 804-336-3720.

This new home is three miles from Assateague Island's beaches and an easy walk to town and the carnival grounds, where the ponies are corralled during Pony Penning Week. It is also about five miles from Wallops Island.

Season: Year-round.

Accommodations: This house sleeps four adults and two children under thirteen. It has two bedrooms, one bathroom, a fully equipped eat-in kitchen with dishwasher and microwave oven, a living room with color television, a washer and dryer, and a small deck in back. There is central air-conditioning and heat.

Cost: Winter, spring, and fall $325 per week; summer $430 per week. Miniweek and weekend rates available.

ONE PINE ISLAND

Address: 7138 Piney Island Road; c/o Chincoteague Island Vacation Cottages, Route 1, Box 547, East Side Drive, Chincoteague, Virginia 23336.
Telephone: 804–336–3720.

This nicely remodeled house is on Little Piney Island, a short trip from the beach. There is a dock across its yard for crabbing, fishing, or mooring your own boat. It is close by car or bike to the Assateague National Wildlife Refuge, which is famous for its oyster beds, clam shoals, and wild ponies.

Season: April through November.

Accommodations: This house has two bedrooms, one bathroom, a fully equipped kitchen, a living room, air-conditioning, and a screened porch.

Cost: Spring and fall $325 per week; summer $430 per week. Miniweek and weekend rates available.

THE OUTER BANKS, NORTH CAROLINA

This region of North Carolina, best known for fishing, encompasses 120 miles of coastal beaches north of Oregon Inlet (Duck through Nags Head), Roanoke Island, Hatteras Island, and Ocracoke. Whatever the sport or activity—swimming, beachcombing, fishing, sailing, or sailboarding—sand and surf are within easy reach. The communities of Kitty Hawk, Kill Devil Hills, and Nags Head all have access to the beach, with bathhouses and lifeguards at many locations. Coquina Beach, south of Nags Head, and the public campgrounds along the Cape Hatteras National Seashore Park also offer protected beach areas.

The steady breezes that attracted the Wright Brothers to the Outer Banks in 1903 continue to attract kite flyers and hang gliders to the East Coast's highest dunes at Jockey's Ridge State Park in Nags Head. Be sure to visit the Wright Brothers National Memorial and the North Carolina

Aquarium, on the north end of Roanoke Island. The sound waters off Roanoke are warm and the sandy bottom is perfect for wading. The best swimming area is the "ole swimming hole" adjacent to the aquarium.

Berthed in Manteo is the *Elizabeth II,* a sixteenth-century English sailing vessel similar to those that brought colonists to the New World in 1584. During the summer this state historic site offers living history interpreters portraying roles of the mariners and colonists.

The Cape Hatteras National Seashore Park, a seventy-mile stretch of open beach that attracts surfers and sailboarders, begins south of Nags Head. A free forty-minute ferry ride from Hatteras takes you to historic Ocracoke Island. Descendants of the banker ponies, the island's first settlers, are cared for by the National Park Service.

SUN REALTY'S BEACH VACATION HOMES

Address: Sun Realty, PO Box 1630, Kill Devil Hills, North Carolina 27948 (agent).
Telephone: 800–843–2033.

Sun Realty represents a number of houses in various price ranges either on the beach or a short distance away. What makes these an especially good value is that many accommodate large groups, so families can double up. As an example, Holland House, on the ocean in Duck Ridge Shores, sleeps up to six people and has a large screened-in porch and roof-level deck with an ocean view. The four-bedroom Saint Bernard Villa, for up to ten people, is thirteen hundred feet from the beach on Duck's Bayberry Bluff. It, too, has a sundeck and a screened porch with picnic table and swing. Cartholina, for up to eight people, is one block from the beach in Kitty Hawk. It has a covered deck and sun deck with a partial ocean view and comes equipped with a playpen, stroller, and children's toys. Less expensive Beach-A-Houy, in Kitty Hawk, two short blocks from the beach, sleeps up to eight. It has an enclosed outdoor shower and a sun deck.

Season: Year-round.

Accommodations: Holland House has a kitchen, three bedrooms, and two bathrooms and sleeps up to six people. There is central air-conditioning and heat, color TV, VCR, phone, and microwave oven. St. Bernard Villa is a four-bedroom, two-bath house for up to ten people with a kitchen, central air-conditioning and heat, color TV, washer and dryer, phone, microwave oven, and ceiling fans. Cartholina has three bedrooms, and two bathrooms and sleeps up to eight people. It has a kitchen, central air-conditioning and heat, dishwasher, color TV, washer and dryer, phone, and microwave oven. Beach-A-Houy, which sleeps up to eight, has three bedrooms, two bathrooms, a kitchen, central air-conditioning and heat, color TV, microwave oven, and phone.

Special Features: Holland House has an enclosed outdoor shower, full-size crib, and high chair. St. Bernard Villa has a sundeck, enclosed outdoor shower, and a screened porch with picnic table and swing. Cartholina and Beach-A-Houy have decks and an enclosed outdoor shower.

Cost: Holland House and St. Bernard Villa $315 to $660 per week, depending on season; rates are highest in summer. Cartholina and Beach-A-Houy $285 to $630 per week, depending on season. Houses farther from the beach have summer rates as low as $470 per week.

Nearby: Kite flying and hang gliding on the high dunes at Jockey's Ridge State Park in Nags Head; Wright Brothers National Memorial; North Carolina Aquarium on Roanoke Island; Manteo's historical sites (for more activities in this area, see the introduction on pages 225–226).

COVE REALTY'S VACATION BEACH COTTAGES

Address: Cove Realty, PO Box 967, Nags Head, North Carolina 27959. Telephone: 800–635–7007; 919–441–6391.

Cove Realty represents many large beach properties along the shore in Nags Head in varying price ranges. As an example, four- to five-bedroom cottages in a cluster called the Nansemond Colony Cottages accommodate ten to twelve people. The home for twelve is the third house from the beach; the four-bedroom cottage is one hundred feet away. Less expensive is the two-bedroom cottage for six on Seabird Street, also one hundred feet from the beach. It has an ocean view from a screened porch and deck and an enclosed outdoor shower.

Season: Year-round.

Accommodations: The Nansemond cottage, with five bedrooms for twelve people, has a crib, three bathrooms, a kitchen, heat, telephone, dishwasher, color TV, outdoor shower, and garage. The Nansemond four-bedroom cottage for ten has two bathrooms, a kitchen, heat, ceiling fans in all bedrooms, TV, washer, and enclosed outdoor shower. The Seabird Street cottage for six has two bedrooms, full bath, a kitchen, air-conditioning, cable TV, and microwave oven.

Special Features: The Nansemond five-bedroom cottage has a picnic area, two balconies, and a large sundeck with an ocean view. The Nansemond four-bedroom cottage has a fish-cleaning table and screened and covered porches with ocean views. The Seabird Street cottage has a porch and deck with ocean views.

Cost: In summer, Nansemond cottage for twelve $695 per week; Nansemond cottage for ten $635 per week; Seabird Street cottage for six $490 per week. All are less expensive during mid- and off-season.

Nearby: Boardwalk and dunes. For more activities in the area, see Sun Realty, pages 226–227.

SEA WHISPER CONDOMINIUM COMPLEX

Address: Carolina Designs, Schrooner Plaza, 1211 Duck Road, Kitty Hawk, North Carolina 27949.
Telephone: 800–368–3825.

This modern complex is across the street from the beach. The beach is part of the undeveloped Cape Hatteras National Seashore Park, a seventy-mile stretch of open beach that attracts surfers and sailboarders. All units have uninterrupted views of the ocean and sound.

Season: Year-round.

Accommodations: Nine two-bedroom, two-bath units sleep six people, and nine one-bedroom, one-bath units sleep four people. All have private decks, kitchens, and cable TV. Some apartments have a phone, a microwave oven, and a whirlpool bath.

Special Features: The complex has picnic tables, grills, and fish-cleaning tables.

Cost: In summer, $460 to $595 per week, depending on size of apartment. Mid- and off-season rates lower.

Nearby: Pier, shopping, marinas, horse stables, and miniature golf. A free forty-minute ferry ride from Hatteras takes you to historic Ocracoke Island.

THE CRYSTAL COAST, NORTH CAROLINA

The wide, pristine shores of the Crystal Coast are ideal for swimming, surfing, and shelling. Beach rentals along this coast, especially in Atlantic Beach, are a bargain. From Portsmouth Island south to Core Banks, Shackleford Banks, and Bogue Banks are the barrier islands known as the Southern Outer Banks, which have secluded beaches accessible only by ferry as well as more developed beaches with many accommodations and activities.

Fun side trips include a visit to part of the Cape Lookout National Seashore, a fifty-five-mile stretch of undeveloped barrier islands that runs from Beaufort to Ocracoke Inlet, for fishing, shelling, clamming, hiking, and camping. Cedar Island's national wildlife refuge, northeast of Beaufort, has more than 270 species of birds as well as observation areas, a boat landing, a campground, and fishing areas. History buffs will enjoy visiting restored Old Fort Macon, which was built in 1834 and now houses a museum. Fort Macon State Park has nature trails, a modern bathhouse, beach access, protected swimming areas, surf fishing, and picnic facilities. Hammocks Beach State Park, four miles west of Swansboro, has a daily ferry in the summer to Bear Island, a nine-hundred-acre undeveloped barrier island with an undeveloped shoreline, sixty-foot sand dunes, channel and surf fishing, shelling, swimming, and ranger programs. Wild ponies are the only inhabitants of Shackleford Banks; they graze undisturbed by the swimmers and shellers along the shores of this coastal wilderness area. There are many waterfront boardwalks with live music, art shows, and fishermen and women preparing for the day's catch in the towns that hug the coast. Kids love Jungleland (919–247–2148), the largest theme park (with miniature golf) on the North Carolina coast, and the region's three aquariums, which have tour tanks for handling live sea creatures. There are numerous golf courses. Horseback riding is available at Acha's Stable (919–223–4478), Eterna Riverview Stables (919–726–8313), Whitesand Trail Rides (919–729–0911), and Zeigler Stables (919–223–5510).

August holds the Strange Seafood Exhibition at the Maritime Museum in Beaufort, while September heralds the Bald Headed Men of America Convention in Atlantic Beach. In October the Carolina Kite Fest takes place in Atlantic Beach, and Morehead City holds the North Carolina Seafood Festival.

ALAN SHELOR BEACH RENTALS

Address: Alan Shelor Rentals, PO Box 2290, Atlantic Beach, North Carolina 28512 (agent).
Telephone: 800–786–RENT; 919–240–RENT.

Atlantic Beach, located on the eastern end of Bogue Banks, has beautiful beaches, an amusement park, and many fishing piers. Alan Shelor Rentals handles a number of reasonably priced vacation rentals in Atlantic Beach, either on the beach or a short distance away. The Hires cottage, which sleeps eight, is in the second row of homes off the beach; it has a covered porch and an enclosed outdoor shower. The Abernathy townhouse, two blocks from the beach, sleeps six and has two decks with views of the ocean and sound. The less expensive Martin duplex for four people is also two blocks from the beach.

Season: Year-round.

Accommodations: The Hires cottage, for eight people, has three bedrooms, one and a half baths, and a large loft area on its top floor. It has air-conditioning, ceiling fans, microwave oven, TV, and phone. The Abernathy is a two-bedroom, one-and-a-half-bath townhouse with garage, microwave oven, two TVs, phone, washer and dryer, and central heat and air-conditioning. The Martin duplex has two bedrooms, one bath, microwave oven, TV, and central heat and air-conditioning.

Special Features: Linens, cribs, and high chairs available to rent.

Cost: Hires cottage $485 per week in summer, $360 per week off-season. Cleaning fee $40. Abernathy townhouse $465 per week in summer, $335 per week off-season. Martin duplex $385 per week in summer, $260 per week off-season.

Nearby: An amusement park is nearby. For other local activities, see the Crystal Coast introduction on pages 228–229.

A PLACE AT THE BEACH

Address: PO Box 1140, Fort Macon Road, Atlantic Beach, North Carolina 28512.
Telephone: 800–334–2667.

This condominium resort complex on Atlantic Beach has ocean view or oceanfront units. All apartments have private balconies. The complex has an indoor and outdoor pool with a giant waterslide as well as whirlpools and tennis courts. Golf, sailing, sailboarding, waterskiing, and scuba diving are all easily arranged, as are surf, pier, and deep-sea fishing.

Season: Year-round.

Accommodations: The one-bedroom, two-bath units have a convertible den area with sleeping arrangements for up to four people and a fully equipped kitchen. The two-bedroom, two-bath units have a wet bar, dishwasher, fully equipped kitchen, and sleeping arrangements for up to six people.

Special Features: Outdoor grills, washer and dryer, on-site restaurant, and lounges.

Cost: In summer, one bedroom for up to four $645 or $715 per week, depending on choice of ocean view or oceanfront apartment; two bedroom for up to six $725 or $825 per week. Rates lower off-season.

Nearby: Wild horses are ten miles away on the Barrier Islands. Also close by are numerous Civil War sites. For more nearby activities, see the Crystal Coast introduction on pages 228–229.

THE SOUTH CAROLINA COAST

Bargain hunters will be delighted by the many oceanfront state park vacation cabins along South Carolina's coast, an area also known for its isolated sea islands and miles of sandy beaches. Visitors arriving in the state from the north will find many resort amenities at Myrtle Beach and the nearby seaside communities along the fifty-five-mile Grand Strand. Myrtle Beach is popular in the summer for its many accommodations, shops, restaurants, carnival-type amusements, golfing, tennis, and water sports to keep every member of the family busy.

From Myrtle Beach south to Charleston along U.S. 17, Huntington Beach and State Park, adjacent to the lush Brookgreen Garden, has one of the best public beaches on the Grand Strand, with picnic facilities, a playground, safe ocean swimming, nature trails, ocean fishing, and interpretive programs. Kids will enjoy touring Charleston's eighteenth- and nineteenth-century historic district by horse-drawn carriage. Twelve miles from Charleston, the Isle of Palms is a quiet residential community. Spring, summer, and fall are warm and breezy. The island has a fine sandy beach for swimming, surfing, boating, and fishing.

South of Charleston the coast has many sea islands separated from the mainland by salt marshes. Islands such as Hilton Head are now upscale, contemporary resort communities with championship golf courses, tennis, and water sport facilities. You'll find twelve miles of expansive, pristine beach and a wonderful semitropical climate. Unlike Hilton Head Island, family-oriented Edisto Island still has remnants of the past, with old plantation houses, small fishing villages, abundant wildlife, and a shell-laden beach—although it, too, is slowly becoming more developed. Along with state park cabins, there are many cottages for rent at reasonable rates. The island has mild weather year-round, with daytime temperatures that average from the mid-eighties to nineties during the summer and mid-forties to low sixties in winter. Nearby Hunting Island is a large secluded barrier island with semitropical beauty and an abundance of wildlife near historic Beaufort. Its broad, sweeping beach with state park cabins is one of its main attractions as well as a great vacation bargain.

MYRTLE BEACH STATE PARK CABINS

Address: U.S. Highway 17, Myrtle Beach, South Carolina 29577. Telephone: 803-238-5325. Due to the popularity of these cabins, it is advisable to book by mail when reservations are first accepted on October 20.

This coastal park has five two-bedroom vacation cabins that sleep up to six people each and two apartments that sleep either three or eight. In addition to a great swimming beach you'll find picnic facilities, a playground, a pool, nature trails, ocean fishing, interpretive programs, and a nature center.

Season: Year-round.

Accommodations: All accommodations are furnished, heated, air-conditioned, supplied with linens, and equipped with all cookware and eating utensils.

Special Features: Laundry facilities.

Cost: Cabins $55 per night on weekend nights, $50 per night Monday through Thursday, $150 per weekend (Friday through Sunday), and $300 per week. Apartments $39 to $55 per night on weekend nights, $34 to $50 per night Monday through Thursday, $102 to $150 per weekend

(Friday through Sunday), and $204 to $300 per week. Rates lower November through March.

Nearby: See the South Carolina introduction on pages 230–231 for more area attractions.

EDISTO BEACH STATE PARK CABINS

Address: 8377 State Cabin Road, Edisto Island, South Carolina 29438 (on the ocean, fifty miles southeast of Charleston).
Telephone: 803–869–2156; 803–869–2756. Due to the popularity of these cabins, it is advisable to book by mail when reservations are first accepted on October 20.

This beachfront park is rich in Indian history and has some of the state's tallest palmetto trees. Its five vacation cabins are 1.8 miles from the beach. There is a salt marsh and a beach for swimming and beachcombing. Should you tire of the beach, there are also picnic areas, a playground, hiking trails, fishing, boat ramps, and seasonal interpretive programs.

Season: Year-round.

Accommodations: Cabins have two bedrooms and sleep up to six. All are furnished, heated, air-conditioned, supplied with linens, and equipped with all cookware and eating utensils.

Cost: Cabins $52 per night on weekend nights, $47 per night Monday through Thursday, $141 per weekend (Friday through Sunday), and $282 per week. Rates are lower November through March.

Nearby: See South Carolina's introduction on pages 230–231 for more of the general area's attractions.

VACATION BEACH RENTALS

Address: Edisto Sales and Rental Realty, 1405 Palmetto Boulevard, Edisto Beach, South Carolina 29438.
Telephone: 803–869–2527.

Family-oriented Edisto Island still has remnants of its southern past, with old plantation houses, small fishing villages, abundant wildlife, and a shell-laden beach. Edisto Sales and Rental Realty handles a number of reasonable vacation rentals either on Edisto Beach or a short distance away. For example, its Halekai I apartment sleeps four, is on the beach, and has an outdoor shower and a screened porch. Lelia B sleeps seven in the upstairs section of a house on the beach. It, too, has an outdoor shower and a large sundeck. Ravissant sleeps ten in the upstairs or downstairs section of a house on the beach.

Season: Year-round.

Accommodations: Halekai I has one bedroom, one bath, a kitchen, living area, and central heat and air-conditioning. Lelia B has three bedrooms, one bath, a kitchen, dining area, living area, ceiling fans, and electric heat. All linens, towels, and kitchen utensils are included. Ravissant has two bedrooms, one bath, a kitchen, dining area, living area, window air-conditioner, outdoor shower, ceiling fans, and gas heat.

Special Features: Beach chairs, beach towels, and floats are provided.

Cost: Halekai I $430 per week in summer, $325 per week off-season. Lelia B $460 per week in summer, $370 per week off-season. Ravissant $445 per week in summer, $360 per week off-season.

Nearby: Bike paths run from Sunset Street to Edisto Street. There's a golf course at Ocean Ridge. See South Carolina's introduction on pages 230–231 for more area attractions.

OCEAN RIDGE RESORT

Address: Edisto Sales and Rental Realty, 1405 Palmetto Boulevard, Edisto Beach, South Carolina 29438 (at the southeastern tip of the island).
Telephone: 803–869–2527.

This three-hundred-acre resort community includes an expansive beach and a variety of one-, two-, and three-bedroom villas that overlook a tennis complex, golf fairways, freshwater lagoons, or salt marshes. There is an eighteen-hole championship golf course, four tennis courts, swimming at the beach or in a pool, a kiddie pool, beach cabanas with decks and showers, miniature golf, bike rental, and a complete recreation center with an exercise room, VCR and movie rentals, tennis equipment rentals, video games, kites, and horseshoes.

Season: Year-round.

Accommodations: Among the least expensive accommodations are the cottages, which sleep from four to six, and the efficiency units that sleep four. More luxurious units that sleep from four to six have Jacuzzis and sundecks. All come fully equipped for housekeeping.

Special Features: Organized activities include "bike and hike," water aerobics, crabbing excursions, canoe and kayak trips, nature hikes, scenic river cruises, off-shore fishing, and tours to Charleston and Fort Sumter. The quiet family beach has lots of shells and shark's teeth and is popular for crabbing.

Cost: Cottage for four to six $485 to $535 per week in summer, $390 to $430 per week off-season, depending on the number of bedrooms. Efficiency unit for four $285 per week in summer, $230 per week off-season. More luxurious rental for four to six $435 to $650 per week in summer, $350 to $525 per week off-season, depending on number of bedrooms. Pass for use of the pool, recreational facilities, and all organized activities $4 per day, $12 per week.

Nearby: Bike paths run from Sunset Street to Edisto Street. There's a golf course at Ocean Ridge. See the South Carolina introduction on pages 230–231 for more area attractions.

HUNTING ISLAND STATE PARK CABINS

Address: 1775 Sea Island Parkway, St. Helena Island, South Carolina 29920.
Telephone: 803–838–2011. Due to the popularity of these cabins, it is advisable to book by mail when reservations are first accepted on October 20.

Hunting Island, near historic Beaufort, is a large, secluded barrier island with semitropical beauty and an abundance of wildlife. Its broad beach is excellent for swimming, and there are picnic areas, a playground, hiking trails, a boat ramp, a fishing pier, a boardwalk for nature observation, and seasonal interpretive programs. There are fifteen two- and three-bedroom vacation cabins that sleep six, eight, or ten people. Some of the cabins are oceanfront, others are a short walk from the beach.

Season: Year-round.
Accommodations: A few of the cabins have fireplaces. All are completely furnished, heated, air-conditioned, supplied with linens, and equipped with all cookware and eating utensils.
Cost: Cabins $65 to $80 per night on weekend nights, depending on type of cabin; $60 to $75 per night Monday through Thursday; $180 to $225 per weekend (Friday through Sunday); $360 to $450 per week.
Nearby: The park is sixteen miles east of historic Beaufort. See the South Carolina introduction on pages 230–231 for more area attractions.

OCEAN INN

Address: Box 323, 1100 Pavilion Boulevard, Isle of Palms, South Carolina 29451 (from Charleston follow U.S. 17 north across the Cooper River Bridge; follow South Carolina 703 through Sullivan's Island to the Isle of Palms).
Telephone: 803–886–4687.

The Isle of Palms is a quiet residential community with a sandy beach for swimming, surfing, boating, and fishing. Golf and tennis are available, and biking, volleyball, paddleball, sailing, and sailboarding are popular on the islands. The inn has one- and two-bedroom apartments just yards from a safe and wide sandy beach. The water is warm and shallow, with no steep dropoffs. Ocean Inn's main clientele are families.

Season: Spring through fall.

Accommodations: One-bedroom apartments sleep four; two-bedroom apartments sleep six. They are completely equipped for housekeeping, are air-conditioned, and have cable TV with HBO.

Cost: In summer one-bedroom apartment $375 to $395 per week, $70 per day; two-bedroom apartment $475 to $495 per week, $95 per day. In spring and fall, one bedroom $325 to $345 per week, $60 per day; two bedroom $425 to $445 per week, $85 per day.

Nearby: The apartments are within walking distance of a shopping center and restaurants and are twelve miles from Charleston. See the South Carolina introduction on pages 230–231 for more area attractions.

FOREST BEACH VACATION VILLAS

Address: Shoreline Rental Company, PO Box 6275, Hilton Head Island, South Carolina 29938 (agent).
Telephone: 800–334–5012.

We found the Hilton Head Beach Club Villas and Seascape Villas, both on Forest Beach and represented by Shoreline Rental Company, to be a bargain for the expensive resort community of Hilton Head Island. One of the island's main draws are its championship golf courses as well as its tennis and water sport facilities. The island has twelve miles of pristine beach and a wonderful semitropical climate. Hilton Head Beach Club villas are two-bedroom apartments on ground-floor level, just yards from a family-oriented beach. The Seascape villas have either two or three bedrooms; they are a short walk from another pleasant beach.

Season: Year-round.

Accommodations: With two bedrooms and one and a half bathrooms, the Hilton Head Beach Club apartments sleep four to six people. The Seascape villas sleep six to eight people in ground-floor units with either two or three bedrooms.

Special Features: The Hilton Head Beach Club has a swimming pool. Seascape Villas have a children's play yard and a pool. Both have free tennis passes for the Van der Meer Tennis Center.

Cost: In summer, Hilton Head Beach Club apartments $585 per week; in spring and fall $470 per week; in winter $355 per week. Seascape Villa's two- and three-bedroom units $565 and $695 per week in summer, $450 and $570 per week in spring and fall, and $340 and $430 per week in winter.

Nearby: Accommodations are close to shopping, restaurants, bike paths, and a water fun park. See the South Carolina introduction on pages 230–231 for more area attractions.

JEKYLL ISLAND, ST. MARYS, AND THE CUMBERLAND ISLAND NATIONAL SEASHORE, GEORGIA

In the late 1800s, beautiful Jekyll Island, off the southern Georgia coast, was the private getaway of the Vanderbilts, Morgans, and Rockefellers. The mansions of the old Wall Street families still exist (thirty-three have been restored for public viewing), but today the island is run by the state and is reasonably priced. It is great for bike riding; bike rental is available on North Beachview Drive (912–635–2648). Take a ride out to the island's northern tip, where there are small inlets great for catching crabs.

Golf is cheap here—for $19 you can play all day on three eighteen-hole courses. The island also has a tennis center that is illuminated for night playing. Fishing boats sail daily from the Jekyll Island marina to catch red snapper and black bass or to watch dolphins. There are covered picnic shelters along the beach and organized nature walks led by docents of the University of Georgia Marine Extension Service (912–635–2232).

The Jekyll Island Day Camp (912–635–2232) will keep your four- to twelve-year-olds busy with beach games, treasure hunts, swimming, and bike hikes ($8 per half day, $15 per day, $50 per week, includes lunch). There is also miniature golf, a fitness center with membership by the day (912–635–2232), cable water skiing (912–635–3802) on a twelve-acre lake without a boat, and an eleven-acre water park called "Splashtacular," with seven slides, an endless river, a huge wave pool, and a children's slide (912–635–2074).

Take a side trip to the magical and tranquil eighteen-mile Cumberland Island National Seashore, the southernmost barrier island in the Georgia Sea Islands, separated from the mainland by a salt marsh, the river, and the sound. On the ocean side of the island a vast beach stretches out of sight, speckled liberally with an abundance of shells at low tide. A barrier of high sand dunes protects the island. It is here among the sea oats that the female loggerhead turtles come ashore in summer to lay their eggs. Families with older children can help protect turtle nests and assist hatchlings on the way to the sea, see pages 290–291. The central part of the island is inhabited by armadillos, deer, raccoons, wild turkeys, and wild horses. The park is accessible by ferry from St. Marys. Summer temperatures range from the eighties to low nineties; during the summer it is best to visit the beach early and late in the day.

The Okefenokee Swamp Park (912–283–0583), eight miles south of Waycross on U.S. 1, is another wildlife sanctuary of astounding beauty with exhibits, trails, and boat tours on original Indian waterways. There is the Serpentarium and Wildlife Observatory, a "Swamp Creation Center," the "Living Swamp Center," and Pioneer Island's authentic swamp homestead, complete with rare artifacts. For more on the Okefenokee Swamp, see pages 182 and 291–292.

JEKYLL ISLAND COTTAGES

Address: Parker-Kaufman Realtors, PO Box 3126, Jekyll Island, Georgia 31527.
Telephone: 912–635–2512.

Jekyll Island has nine miles of beach with powdery sand sloping gently into the surf, making it an ideal beach getaway for families with young children. Behind the beach you'll often find deer grazing in the pine woods. Parker-Kaufman Realtors rents reasonably priced one- to six-bedroom cottages on the beach or a short distance away.

Season: Year-round.

Accommodations: All cottages have heat and air-conditioning, and each is furnished and equipped with full kitchen, pillows, and blankets; guests bring the remaining linens. Ask for a color catalog with pictures and descriptions of the available cottages.

Special Features: Cottages have washers and dryers, dishwashers, phones, cribs, and microwave ovens. Cable TVs with HBO and VCR are available for rent.

Cost: Among the listings are three-bedroom houses for eight within walking distance of the beach, $390 to $490 per week in summer.

Nearby: See the introduction to Jekyll Island on page 236 for specific activities on the island.

HOSTEL IN THE FOREST

Address: PO Box 1496, Brunswick, Georgia 31521 (located halfway between Savannah, Georgia, and Jacksonville, Florida, two miles west of I-95 on U.S. 82).
Telephone: 912–264–9738; 912–265–0220; 912–638–2623.
Reservations are not accepted.

This is one of America's unique and most-photographed hostels. Kids will not forget spending the night in its treehouses or geodesic domes. There is also a swimming pool and a fish pond. The hostel is ten miles from the beaches at Jekyll Island. The Cumberland Island National Seashore and the Okefenokee Swamp and National Wildlife Refuge are also nearby.

Season: Year-round.

Accommodations: Families can sleep together in the domes, tree-houses, or the small family rooms that are available with double beds in this forty-bed hostel.

Special Features: Baggage storage, kitchen, laundry facilities, linen rental, on-site parking, and shuttle service to downtown.

Cost: AYH members, adults $6 per night; nonmembers $2 more. Children under twelve half price.

Nearby: See the introduction on pages 236–237 for specific activities in this area.

CROOKED RIVER STATE PARK CABINS

Address: 3092 Spur 40, St. Marys, Georgia 31558 (ten miles north of the center of the town of St. Marys on the south bank of the Crooked River).

Telephone: 912–882–5256. Book eleven months in advance for any holiday stay (Christmas break, Easter); all other times of the year, reserve at least eight weeks in advance.

This five-hundred-acre state park just south of Cumberland Island and Jekyll Island has eleven reasonably priced vacation cottages as well as an Olympic-size pool, bathhouse, and picnic shelters. The cabins are located on the intercoastal waterway. Popular park activities include swimming, saltwater fishing, boating, and hiking. The park is forty-five miles from the nearest public access ocean beach at Georgia's Jekyll Island or at Florida's Fernandina Beach.

Season: Year-round.

Accommodations: Cottages have either two or three bedrooms and a living room, kitchen, screened porch, heat, and air-conditioning. The two-bedroom cottage sleeps eight; the three-bedroom sleeps up to twelve. There are two double beds in each of the bedrooms. All linens and cooking utensils are provided.

Cost: Two-bedroom cottages $50 per weeknight, $60 per weekend night. Three-bedroom cottages $10 more.

Nearby: Visit the nearby ruins of the McIntosh Sugar Works mill (built in 1825 and used as a starch factory during the Civil War). The ferry for the Cumberland Islands leaves from St. Marys. The park is less than an hour from Okefenokee Swamp. See the introduction to this region on pages 236–237 for more specific activities in this area.

ST. AUGUSTINE, FLORIDA

Founded in 1565, St. Augustine is the oldest permanent European settle-ment in the continental United States and is filled with reminders of its Spanish history. This blend of history and fine swimming beaches make it a popular family vacation destination. Oceanfront accommodations are primarily condominium resort complexes. Like many Florida beaches, cars are allowed on the beach here. If you are nervous about keeping track of young kids amid the vehicles, consider a quiet day by the pool at your condominium resort complex.

Guides in colonial dress will accompany you at no charge on a trip through the carefully restored Spanish Quarter for a glimpse of how this community of Spanish soldiers, settlers, craftspeople, and their families lived in the eighteenth century. History abounds in the country's oldest store, the oldest house, and the oldest wooden schoolhouse, as well as in the narrow cobblestone streets, colonial-style shops, and classic cathedral. There are many ways to explore the city—on foot, by tram, by horse-drawn carriage (boarded on the bayfront south of the fort), or even from a seventy-five-minute cruise along the bay.

Kids can get the feel of a real castle at Castillo de San Marcos (904–829–6505), built in 1672, with an impressive moat and drawbridge, huge cannons, and sentinel turret. Ranger tours that explain the fort's history, provided by the National Park Service, are easy for kids to understand. At the Fountain of Youth Archaeological Park (904–829–3168), where Ponce de Leon came ashore in 1513, there is a planetarium, Indian burial site, train station, and significant landmarks.

The Oldest House (Gonzalez-Alvarez House, 904–824–2872) has rem-nants that span hundreds of years. The kitchen and living areas have relics from as early as Florida's first settlement. Likewise, the Oldest Store Mu-seum (904–829–9729) shows how people shopped for such items as corsets and bicycles at the turn of the century. Students dressed in period costumes show how time was spent in school before the American Rev-olution at the Oldest Wooden Schoolhouse (904–824–0192). Visitors also can tour an authentic Old Jail (904–829–3800).

The city has its own Wax Museum (904–829–9056), where you can see Napoleon Bonaparte and many other historical figures. Ripley's Believe It or Not Collection (904–824–1606) is chock full of oddball displays, including a dummy of the world's fattest man. White Bird's Family Fun Resort has an eighteen-hole adventure golf course and arcade games. Zorayda Castle (904–824–3097), modeled after Spain's Alhambra in Gra-nada, has harem quarters, a mummy's foot, and mosaic tiles from an Egyp-tian mosque. East of the castle, the Museum of Weapons and Early American History (904–829–3727) has unique displays including items from the Civil War.

Reptile enthusiasts will want to visit the Alligator Farm (904–824–3337) south of the city, where you can watch them snapping away from an elevated walkway. Twelve miles south of the city is Marineland (904–471–1111), with one thousand species of marine animals and daily dolphin shows. St. Augustine is less than two hours from Disney World (see page 14) and Sea World and about two hours from the Kennedy Space Center.

South of Marineland, at Washington Oaks Gardens State Park on State Highway A1A, is Boulder Beach, a large, protected area of stone formations. The rocks are a bit tricky to navigate for children younger than seven. Its outcropping is a rocky mixture of shells, coral, and sand. A museum of natural and cultural history is on the grounds, as are tidal marshes, hiking trails, and a picnic area.

ST. AUGUSTINE HOSTEL

Address: 32 Treasury Street, St. Augustine, Florida 32804 (five blocks east off U.S. 1).
Telephone: 904–829–6163. Reservations are advisable January through March. Phone reservations are accepted.

The hostel, located in the city's old Spanish district, is three miles from the beach. It is within walking distance to the City Gates, restored houses, the Oldest Store Museum, the Oldest Schoolhouse, the Old Jail, and the Oldest House.

Season: Year-round.

Accommodations: Family rooms are available in this small four-room hostel. A family room has a double bed and bunk beds for children as well as its own private bathroom.

Special Features: Roof garden, baggage storage area, kitchen, linen rental, and on-site parking.

Cost: AYH members, adults $10 per night; third night half price. Nonmembers, adults $13 per night; third night $8. Children five to ten half price. Senior citizen discount available.

Nearby: See the introduction to St. Augustine on pages 239–240 for specific activities.

ST. AUGUSTINE OCEAN AND RACQUET RESORT

Address: 3300 Highway A1A South, St. Augustine, Florida 32084.
Telephone: 800–448–0066.

This resort complex has eight three-story buildings with fully equipped condominiums for up to six people each on the Anastasia Island beach. When you tire of the beach, there is freshwater swimming pool, outdoor Jacuzzi, and tennis and racquetball courts.

Season: Year-round.

Accommodations: Units sleep six and have two bedrooms, two bathrooms, living room, outdoor balcony, fully equipped kitchen, washer and dryer, phone, and cable TV.

Cost: March 15 to September 15, condos near the ocean $460 per week, on the ocean $560 per week. September 14 to March 14, condos near the ocean $310 to $360 per week, on the ocean $360 to $435 per week. Cleaning fee $35.

Nearby: The complex is a seven-minute drive to the downtown historical section and fifteen minutes from Marineland. Golf, fishing, and boating are nearby. See the introduction to St. Augustine on pages 239–240 for specific activities.

OCEAN GALLERY

Address: 4600 Highway A1A South, St. Augustine, Florida 32084.
Telephone: 800–940–6665.

This forty-acre oceanfront resort complex of four hundred condominiums on a quarter mile of St. Augustine Beach has fully equipped apartments, a game and weight room, two saunas, four tennis courts, two racquetball courts, four outdoor pools with Jacuzzis, one indoor heated pool, and two walkways to the beach.

Season: Year-round.

Accommodations: The condos are completely equipped for housekeeping and have washer and dryers. There are two- and three-bedroom units with two bathrooms on the ocean and less expensive two- and three-bedroom units a short walk from the beach. The two-bedrooms sleep up to six people, the three-bedrooms sleep up to eight.

Cost: March through August, oceanfront two-bedroom, two-bath unit $545 to $595 per week, depending on view. Three-bedroom, two-bath oceanfront unit $670 to $720 per week. Away from the beach, apartments $435 to $510 per week, depending on location and number of bedrooms. Off-season rates lower. Additional $10 security fee and $35 to $40 cleaning fee.

Nearby: The complex is a short drive from the downtown historical section and fifteen minutes from Marineland. Golf, fishing, and boating are nearby. See the introduction to St. Augustine on pages 239–240 for specific activities.

FORT MYERS, SANIBEL ISLAND, AND THE CAPTIVA ISLANDS, FLORIDA

Fort Myers Beach on Estero Island is regarded by many as the ideal family beach because there are no riptides or steep drops. You can walk the island's seven miles of sandy shores. Carl E. Johnson Country Park, on the island's southern tip, has outdoor showers, a pavilion, a concession stand, and canoe rentals. A tractor-driven train will take you along an old boardwalk over Oyster Bay and several mangrove islets to a public yet secluded beach called Lover's Key. In Fort Myers the Thomas Edison Home and Museum (813–334–3614) is worth a visit, especially for science buffs.

Sanibel Island and the Captiva Islands are the southernmost tropical islands in the chain of barrier islands stretching along Florida's Gulf Coast. With towering palms and pristine beaches, the islands are great for swimming, biking along landscaped bike paths, canoeing in bays and secluded bayous, fishing, golf, and tennis. Bike rentals are available at several places on the islands, and there are two golf courses as well as public tennis courts. The Sanibel-Captiva Recreation Complex has an Olympic-size swimming pool.

Sanibel's J. N. Ding Darling National Wildlife Refuge and the Sanibel-Captiva Conservation Foundation are known for birdwatching—the swooping antics of anhingas will hold even a young child's interest. Sanibel is famous for its shells; in fact, the "sand" here is composed of ground seashells. There are approximately 160 species of shells on its shores. You'll find pamphlets around the island to help you identify your findings.

ABACO BEACH VACATION VILLAS

Address: 131 Estero Boulevard, Fort Myers Beach, Florida 33931.
Telephone: 813–463–2611.

These four cottages are on a private section of Fort Myers Beach on the Gulf of Mexico. Each cottage has a veranda or patio overlooking the bay. Sailboats, beach chairs, and umbrellas are for rent on the beach outside your door, while tennis courts, bike rentals, and charter services are available next door. The complex also has a private ninety-foot fishing pier and marina.
Season: Year-round.

Accommodations: Cottages have either one or two bedrooms, one bathroom, complete kitchens with microwave ovens, towels and linens, and cable television. One-bedroom cottages sleep four, two-bedroom cottages sleep six to eight.

Special Features: Outdoor gas grills and laundry facilities.

Cost: One-bedroom cottage for four $545 per week; two-bedroom cottage for up to six people $530 to $590 per week; two-bedroom cottage for up to eight $760 per week.

Nearby: The cottages are close to Fort Myers Beach restaurants, shops, and golf courses. See page 242 for specific activities.

ANCHOR INN COTTAGES

Address: 285 Virginia Avenue, Fort Myers Beach, Florida 33931.
Telephone: 813–463–2630.

These ten waterfront cottages are in a lushly landscaped setting on the bay at the quiet end of Estero Island. Beautiful Fort Myers Beach is across the street. There is a heated pool with a hot tub as well as boat and fishing docks.

Season: Year-round.

Accommodations: The one-bedroom cottage sleeps up to four; the two-bedroom cottage sleeps up to six; the three-bedroom, two-bath cottage sleeps up to eight. All have fully equipped kitchens.

Cost: December 20 to April 20, one-bedroom cottage $500 per week or $75 per night, double occupancy; two-bedroom cottage $600 per week or $95 per night for four people; three-bedroom cottage $750 per week or $125 per night for six people. April 20 to December 20, one-bedroom $300 per week or $50 per night, double occupancy; two-bedroom $350 per week or $55 per night for four; three-bedroom $375 per week or $60 per night for six. Each additional person $5 per night. Daily housekeeping service $25 per day.

Nearby: The Gulf of Mexico is minutes away by car. See page 242 for specific activities.

GULF BREEZE COTTAGES

Address: 1081 Shell Basket Lane, Sanibel Island, Florida 33957.
Telephone: 800–388–2842; 813–472–1626.

Gulf Breeze is a small, friendly resort of thirteen individual cottages on its own Gulf of Mexico beach. Gulf Breeze is one of the few island resorts composed of individual cottages; most accommodations along Sanibel's shore are four-story condominiums. Located halfway between the lighthouse and the point on Shell Basket Lane, Gulf Breeze was built on a spot that reportedly has the most seashells on the island. Porpoises swim close to the shore, and you can watch them from your cottage porch.

Season: Year-round.

Accommodations: Units include large motel-room efficiencies with kitchens, one-bedroom cottages for up to four people, and two-bedroom cottages for up to six people. All units are furnished with cable television, air-conditioning, heat, linens, towels, and dishes.

Cost: May to mid-December, efficiency $420 per week, one-bedroom cottage $560 per week, two-bedroom cottage $630 and up per week. All rates are double occupancy; each additional person $7 per day. Rates are higher December 15 through April. Gulf Breeze reports that it keeps its prices the lowest on Sanibel.

Nearby: Fishing piers, marinas, boat rentals, golf courses, wildlife sanctuaries, shops, restaurants, and grocery stores are close by. See page 242 for specific activities.

GULF OF MEXICO (THE PANHANDLE), FLORIDA

Miles of white, sugar-fine sand beach stretch along the "panhandle" of the Gulf of Mexico in northwest Florida. May to September is the tourist season here, but the weather is pleasant year-round if you can break away during the less expensive off-season. Protected by the St. Joseph Peninsula, which extends into the Gulf like a barrier island, the beaches here are some of the safest in Florida. You can swim nearly year-round, although water temperatures in mid-winter might drop too low for all but the hardiest swimmers. Waterskiing, sailboarding, and boating are popular, as are snorkeling and diving among the reefs.

The Gulf Islands National Seashore has clear blue waters, gently sloping beaches, and coastal marshes. It stretches from West Ship Island in Mississippi to the far end of Santa Rosa Island in Florida. Fort Pickens on Santa Rosa Island, just west of Pensacola Beach, and Naval Live Oaks, one mile east of Gulf Breeze, are two areas with unspoiled beaches. Fort Pickens was constructed to secure the approaches to Pensacola Bay and the U.S. Navy Yard from foreign invasion in the early 1800s. Children can explore the fort and battery (904–932–9994); there is also a free museum with a sandbox, aquarium with native sea life (including reptile skins), and a small Indian exhibit. At Fort Pickens there are ranger-led classes for kids and various interpretive programs on topics from acid rain to eagles, as well as snorkeling classes and ghost stories around a campfire. A full-scale model of a section of the USS *Constitution,* built of the live oaks, is inside the Naval Oaks Visitor Center (904–934–2600).

THE SOUTH

ST. JOSEPH PENINSULA STATE PARK CABINS

Address: Star Route 1, Box 200, Port St. Joe, Florida 32456.
Telephone: 904–227–1327. These cabins are popular, so book at least one year in advance.

Eight rustic but modern cabins are on the Gulf of Mexico beach and St. Joseph's Bay. This 2,516-acre park is nearly surrounded by water. You'll find miles of unspoiled white sand beaches, many sand dunes, forests, freshwater ponds, and salt marshes. The park has nine miles of pristine white beach perfect for swimming, shelling, and fishing and eight miles of property on the bay with areas for snorkeling, fishing, and boating. There are three nature trails and an undeveloped wilderness area for hiking and camping.

Season: Year-round.

Accommodations: Each cabin sleeps seven people and is completely equipped for housekeeping, with all kitchen utensils and bedding provided.

Special Features: The park has a small store with basic supplies and snacks.

Cost: March through mid-September, cottages $70 per night for four persons; five-night minimum stay. September 16 through February, $55 per night for four persons; two-night minimum stay. Each additional person $5.

Nearby: See page 244 for other activities in this area.

WHISPERING PINES OF CAPE SAN BLAS

Address: Route 1, Box 533, Port St. Joe, Florida 32456.
Telephone: 904–227–7252.

Whispering Pines has reasonably priced bayside cottages nestled among pine, oak, and palm trees with views of St. Joe Bay from large screened porches. Swimming, boating, and fishing are all within walking distance. Cottages are a half mile walk from a nice swimming beach and a short drive from the beautiful beaches of St. Joseph Peninsula State Park. The cottages attract many families.

Season: Year-round.

Accommodations: Each cottage accommodates up to six people and has two bedrooms, one bathroom, fully equipped kitchen, central air-conditioning and heat, color TV, two double beds, one sofabed, and barbecue grill.

Cost: Spring and summer, $360 per week, $56 per day. Fall and winter, $260 per week, $42 per day.

Nearby: The cottages are within a mile's drive from many Gulf beaches. Also within easy driving distance are the Florida State Caverns, the wildlife preserves, and several other state parks. See page 244 for specific activities.

WATERFRONT COTTAGES

Address: Elizabeth Thompson Realty, Route 3, Box 167, Port St. Joe, Florida 32456.
Telephone: 904–648–5449.

Mexico Beach has sparkling water and white sand with no undertow. Elizabeth Thompson Realty handles fifteen reasonably priced, fully equipped waterfront cottages and houses across the highway from the beach that accommodate four to ten people.

Season: Year-round.

Accommodations: As an example, the cottage for eight on the beach has three bedrooms, two and a half bathrooms, dishwasher, washer and dryer, cable TV, central heat and air-conditioning, and fully equipped kitchen with microwave oven.

Special Features: The cottage for eight has a sun deck, barbecue grill, and screened porch.

Cost: Weekly rates $360 for four-person cottage to $760 for a cottage that sleeps ten. Cottage for eight (described above) $610 per week. Cottage across the highway from the beach that sleep four to eight $260 to $410 per week.

Nearby: Mexico Beach's City Park on 22nd Street has shuffleboard, horseshoes, tennis courts, and picnic tables. Canal Park on 43rd Street has a new walkway along Canal Bank for fishing, picnicking, and boating; there is also a lighted fishing pier on 37th Street. Charter boats are available for deep-sea fishing and scuba diving; call 904–648–8211. The St. Joseph Bay Country Club welcomes day guests for golf. Florida's oldest annual seafood festival is held the first weekend in November in Apalachicola, thirty-five miles east. See page 244 for other activities.

GULF COAST, MISSISSIPPI

The Mississippi district of the Gulf Islands National Seashore includes a sandy swimming beach with lifeguards in the summer on West Ship Island. The island has white sand beaches accessible by a seventy-minute ferry from both Gulfport and Biloxi. Ocean Springs has a visitor center with exhibits, numerous nature trails, a picnic area, and camping facilities.

GAYLE'S COTTAGES

**Address: 143-A Teagarden, PO Box 6081, Gulfport, Mississippi 39507
(located between Gulfport and Biloxi).
Telephone: 800–252–7161; 601–896–8266.**

Gayle's Cottages are duplexes two hundred yards from the beach, nestled under giant oaks and magnolias. There is a large deck patio with a barbecue grill, lounge chairs, and dozens of visiting squirrels and birds. The cottage's beach has swimming, jet ski and paddleboat rentals, and a new fishing pier. The owners will charter you in their new twenty-nine-foot twin-engine Cris-Craft boat for half-day excursions to Ship Island or for all-day fishing trips.

Accommodations: Furnished cottages have one or two bedrooms (each with a queen-size bed and a double bed), a living room with a sofabed, breakfast bar, cable TV with HBO, and a fully equipped kitchen with microwave oven. The one-bedroom sleeps four, the two-bedroom sleeps six.

Cost: One-bedroom cottage $52 per night, $285 per week (six nights). Two-bedroom cottage $78 per day, $395 per week.

Nearby: The cottages are ten minutes from several golf courses and coastal restaurants, forty minutes to Mobile, and one hour from New Orleans. A ferry leaves from town to the Gulf Islands National Seashore.

THE NORTHEAST

THE JERSEY SHORE, NEW JERSEY

Composed of a 127-mile continuous chain of barrier islands, the Jersey shore is noted for its sandy, rock-free beaches that extend from Sandy Hook in the north to Cape May in the south. In summer most beaches are packed with people, as the gentle ocean is warm. More than fifty towns dot the coast, each with its own personality. The most famous town of Atlantic City, eighty-five miles south of Sandy Hook, had its heyday in the early half of this century and was made famous by the Miss America Pageant and by its boardwalk. After a decline in the fifties and sixties, it has seen a resurgence since its gambling casinos reopened in 1978.

Most shore towns have lifeguards on duty at public beaches and a marina nearby for boat, jet ski, or sailboard rentals. Practically all have a boardwalk with ice cream, souvenirs, amusement parks, and saltwater taffy. Ocean City is considered the most family-oriented of the shore resorts. It is very clean and has a fun boardwalk with a giant Ferris wheel that rises 140 feet in the air. On the boardwalk is a water park with serpentine slides and shotgun falls.

Ocean City has an active arts center and a community center with an Olympic-size pool, racquetball courts, saunas, and exercise rooms. The playgrounds at 6th, 8th, 15th, 34th, and 52nd streets are centers for summer activities, including arts and crafts for youngsters and sports or field trips for older children. Bikes can be rented at many shore locations. In Ocean City try the Village Bike Shop (609–884–8500). Boat rentals also are numerous along the shore; in Ocean City, try the Blue Water Marina (609–398–9090). For jet ski rentals, call Yacht Charters of Ocean City (609–399–2169) or the Royal Flush Fleet in Wildwood Crest (609–522–1395). Surfing and sailboarding is popular; for rentals call Bayview Sailboats in Ocean City (609–398–3049). Water skiers can get set up at Speed and Ski in Ocean City (609–398–0424).

The Jersey shore has some unique special events. In late June the Ocean City Music Pier hosts the Baseball Card Show, with exhibits of cards and sports memorabilia. Late June through early July is the July Jubilee, with treasure hunts for kids, unusual contests, bike parades, and a giant display of Fourth of July fireworks preceded by a kite-flying contest. On the last Saturday in June more than a hundred boats are decorated for the Night in Venice on Great Egg Harbor. Early August welcomes the Miss Crustacean Pageant, a beauty pageant for hermit crabs, followed by hermit crab races. The next day is the oldest and largest Baby Parade on the Jersey coast, with more than four hundred participants. Weird Contest Week, held the third week of August in front of the Music Pier on the Ocean City boardwalk, includes an artistic pie-eating event, french fry sculpting, saltwater taffy sculpting, and animal or celebrity impersonating. For specific dates, contact the Ocean City Chamber of Commerce, PO Box 157, Ocean City, New Jersey 08226; 609–399–2629.

SANDY NOOK GUEST HOUSE AND APARTMENT

Address: 805 Fifth Street, Ocean City, New Jersey 08226.
Telephone: 609–391–1314.

Just one block from the beach and boardwalk, this family-run accommodation is a charming turn-of-the-century house with eight guest rooms and a first-floor apartment recommended for families. Guests can relax after a day on the beach on the large front porch overlooking the tennis courts. The premises also have an outdoor shower for sand removal and a patio area with a barbecue grill.

Season: Year-round.

Accommodations: The first-floor apartment sleeps six to eight people. It has two bedrooms, a living room, an eat-in kitchen, a washer and dryer, and a private parking area.

Special Features: Guests who stay three days or longer receive free beach tags. (Ocean City beaches charge $3 per day, $5.50 per week, $12 per season, for access tags.)

Cost: Apartment $560 per week prior to July 4, $610 per week through September 5, $510 per week for September and October.

Nearby: Sandy Nook is within walking distance to Main Street.

OSBORNE'S FAIRVIEW INN

Address: 601 East 15th Street, Ocean City, New Jersey 08226.
Telephone: In-season, 609–398–4319; off-season, 215–782–1326.

This family-run inn is less than one hundred yards from the beach and boardwalk. Accommodations include a separate cottage and a ground-floor apartment for six people or second-floor apartments for either four or eight people.

Season: May 23 to September 26.

Accommodations: A two-bedroom cottage separate from the main inn sleeps six people. The inn has a ground-floor apartment for six people with two bedrooms, a living room, a fully equipped kitchen, and a bathroom. On the inn's second floor there is a one-bedroom apartment for four with a living room, kitchen, and bathroom as well as a larger three-bedroom apartment for eight people with similar facilities.

Special Features: Beach tags and free parking provided.

Cost: Rates depend on time of summer. Second-floor apartment for four $185 per week in late May to $495 per week from late July through August. Cottage $210 to $530 per week; ground-floor apartment $210 to $530 per week; apartment for eight $245 to $950 per week.

Nearby: The inn is within walking distance to Main Street.

LONG ISLAND, NEW YORK

Like a huge fish, Long Island stretches 120 miles from nose to tail. At its eastern end the island forks into two peninsulas. The south fork, with its lovely dunes, has become a haven for the artistic and the very well-to-do, who congregate at summer parties in the Hamptons—America's answer to the French Riviera. Montauk, on the point, attracts fishing enthusiasts; its clear waters are brimming with swordfish and marlin. This part of Long Island generally is not a budget destination, but we were able to find two quite affordable destinations.

COLONIAL SHORES RESORT AND MARINA

Address: 83 West Tiana Road, Hampton Bays, New York 11946.
Telephone: 516–728–0011.

Hampton Bays is on the lower rung of the Hamptons' social ladder, but your kids won't care. They'll be too busy swimming at this resort's private bayfront beach or pool, learning to water ski, boating, and playing in its recreation room. The complex has individual cottages, efficiency apartments, and motel units facing either Tiana Bay or the pool. In addition to swimming, the beach is noted for clamming. Free rowboats are provided for guests.

Season: Year-round.

Accommodations: Efficiencies and motel units (standard rooms or one- and two-bedroom suites) accommodate two to eight people; they have full baths and electric kitchens. Individual cottages and apartments sleep three to four and have one or two bedrooms, a living room with cable TV, a full bath, and a full electric kitchen.

Special Features: Marina, swimming pool with diving board and slide for children, wooded and cool picnic area, indoor recreation room. Boat rentals are available for sailing and fishing (there is a tackle shop on the premises); water-ski instruction, boat rides, and tours.

Cost: In summer, motel rooms $495 to $595 per week, double occupancy, depending on amenities. One-bedroom suites $585 to $655 per week, double occupancy. Two-bedroom suites, apartments, or cottages $699 to $760 per week for three or four people. Each additional person in either arrangement $20 per night. Children under twelve stay free in their parents' room. Rowboats free; motorboats $55 per day.

Nearby: Shops and restaurants, golf, tennis, horseback riding, scuba diving, summer stock theaters, movies, historical sites, museums.

MAIDSTONE PARK COTTAGES

Address: 22 Bruce Lane, East Hampton, New York 11937 (off Three Mile Harbor Road).
Telephone: 516–324–2837; 718–347–4829.

We were surprised to find these affordable cottages set amid this legendary upscale resort town with magnificent beaches, magnificent mansions, and equally magnificent prices. The cottages have charming old-country surroundings, five miles northeast of East Hampton. Swimming and sunbathing at breathtaking Gardiner's Bay beach are just a short walk away. Ocean beaches are a short drive from the cottages, as is fishing from the jetty at Three Mile Harbor.

Season: May through Labor Day.

Accommodations: Shingled one- and two-bedroom cottages have full kitchen facilities, cable TV, brick patios, chaise lounges, and beach chairs. The one-bedroom cottage sleeps three, the two-bedroom sleeps up to five people.

Special Features: Beach passes are provided.

Cost: One-bedroom cottages $520 per week, two-bedroom cottages $630 per week. If you stay more than one week, successive weeks are discounted. Rates lower in May and June.

Nearby: It is a short walk to the bay and a short drive to the ocean, tennis, and golf. Sailboarding and water-skiing are easily arranged.

CAPE COD, MASSACHUSETTS

Cape Cod, a seventy-mile-long peninsula that juts straight out to sea from the southeastern corner of Massachusetts, has three hundred miles of shoreline, much of which is white sand. The Cape is known for its houses of gray cedar shingles, lobsterman's shacks, grassy dunes, sand castles, and wild berry ice cream from the dollhouse streets of commercial Provincetown. While summer is certainly the best time of year for swimming, fall is a popular and less expensive season on Cape Cod. The warmest ocean water and gentlest waves in Massachusetts are on the Cape's Atlantic side.

The Cape begins south of Plymouth, where the *Mayflower* landed in 1620. Stop there to see Plimoth Plantation, where costumed docents relive the day-to-day routine of America's first settlers amid thatched-roof cottages. Nearby is a replica of the *Mayflower;* children can visit below decks to see the hardships endured by the refugees. See page 303 for more on these attractions. On the way to the Cape, stop at the Edaville Railroad in Carver (508—866—4526) for a narrow-gauge train ride through working cranberry bogs.

The Cape Cod National Seashore, between Chatham and Provincetown, encompasses more than forty miles of protected beaches, trails, and dunelands. From late June through Labor Day the beaches charge a $5 user fee, and lifeguards are on duty at this time. The national seashore maintains miles of bicycle trails and self-guided nature trails that are open all year; pick up a map at the Salt Pond or Province Lands visitor centers. Ranger-guided activities held in spring, summer, and fall include sharing nature with children, shellfishing demonstrations, canoe discovery trips, tidal flats walks, and programs that lead to junior ranger certificates. Schedules are available at the park's two visitor centers or by writing Cape Cod National Seashore, Race Point Road, South Wellfleet, Massachusetts 02663.

Rates on the Cape are high in summer. We have selected inexpensive hostels, cottages, and resorts that offer a good value to larger families because of the low cost per person.

HYLAND HOSTEL

Address: 465 Falmouth Road, Hyannis, Massachusetts 02601.
Telephone: 508–771–1585; 508–775–2970 (after 5 p.m.). Reservations
are essential July through August. Phone reservations are accepted
with a credit card. Off-season, mail reservations to 75 Goody Hallet
Drive, Eastham, Massachusetts 02642, or call 508–255–2785.

This hostel, surrounded by acres of pines and evergreens, is a perfect base
for exploring the Cape, Nantucket, and Martha's Vineyard. Charter fishing
boats, whale-watching tours, and ferries for the islands leave from the
nearby town wharf. The beach, where you can swim, sailboard, or rent a
sailboat, is a few minutes away by car.

Season: March through November. Good times to visit are in the fall
or early spring, when the harbor towns are quiet.

Accommodations: This comfortable home-like hostel has fifty beds and
family rooms.

Special Features: Bikes for rent, kitchen, baggage storage area, linen
rental, and on-site parking. The staff will direct you to sailboarding and
sailboat rentals at the nearby Atlantic beaches.

Cost: AYH members, adults $10 per night; nonmembers $13. Children
five to ten half price.

Nearby: The town of Hyannis has a miniature golf course called Cape
Cod Storyland. The Cape Cod Railroad departs from the downtown Hyan-
nis Station at Main and Center streets for a tour of Historic Sandwich
Village and the Cape Cod Canal that lasts just under two hours. Kids also
enjoy watching (and sampling) potato chips being made at Cape Cod
Potato Chips on Breed's Hill Road in Independence Park, near the Cape
Cod Mall. For other activities on the Cape, see page 251.

BREAKWATERS

Address: Box 118, 432 Sea Street Beach, Hyannis,
Massachusetts 02601.
Telephone: 508–775–6831.

Just two hundred yards from the beach in a quiet residential area on
Nantucket Sound, these weathered gray housekeeping cottages are set
between a pool and the beach. Some units have private decks with views
of the sound. The heated pool has lifeguards, and swimming lessons are
offered every morning for children. The beach is safe and sandy, while
the grounds have barbecue grills, picnic tables, and lounge chairs.

Season: Year-round.

Accommodations: Cottages are fully equipped for housekeeping and have one to three bedrooms that sleep two to eight people. Units include cable TV, complete kitchens, and private phones.

Special Features: Housekeeping service is available in season at no extra charge.

Cost: The least expensive units are the one-bedroom cottages. Double occupancy rates $360 per week or $57 per night in winter, $465 per week in spring and fall, $560 per week in early summer (June 13 to June 27), and $860 per week in high summer. Additional adults $58 per week; additional children $32 per week. Babies in cribs stay free.

Nearby: Hyannis Center's shops and restaurants are one mile away. Boats leave from its wharf to Nantucket and Martha's Vineyard daily. For other activities in Hyannis, see the Hyannis Hostel entry above. For more things to do on the Cape, see page 251.

SEA BREEZE COTTAGES

Address: PO Box 553, Hyannis Port, Massachusetts 02647 (located on the beach at 397 Sea Street Beach, Hyannis).
Telephone: 508–775–4269.

These brand-new homes are in a secluded country setting with stone walls, pebble stone paths, and picturesque gardens nine hundred yards from Hyannis Port Harbor and a small family beach with lifeguards and picnic areas. The cottages are built with lots of glass and knotty pine wood; most have a large raised hearth, large skylights, and a sun deck or patio.

Season: Year-round.

Accommodations: Modern cottages and garden apartments have fully equipped kitchens with microwave ovens, bedrooms with double or queen-size beds and all linens, modern bathrooms, and living rooms with fireplace or skylight and color television.

Special Features: Cottages have private fenced yards with sun decks or patios, picnic tables, and barbecue grills.

Cost: In June and September, $660 per week for a family of four; $560 per week for a family of three. In July and August, $895 per week for a family of four; $795 per week for a family of three. Off-season, rates start at $72 per night, $415 per week.

Nearby: One mile from Hyannis Center's shops and restaurants and close to many other beaches, whale watching, golf, tennis, water slides, playgrounds, and arcades. For other activities in Hyannis, see the Hyland Hostel, page 252. For more things to do on the Cape, see page 251.

YARMOUTH SHORES COTTAGES

Address: 29 Lewis Bay Boulevard, West Yarmouth, Massachusetts 02673.
Telephone: 508-775-1944.

Yarmouth Shores is a small, family-oriented colony of thirteen cottages on two and a half acres of land with more than three hundred feet of gently sloping private beach. Many children stay here and enjoy the fun play area with swings on the premises. Many children's amusements are within four miles of the cottages, including the Aqua Circus, miniature golf, a wild animal farm, and horseback rides.

Season: Year-round.

Accommodations: Housekeeping cottages have a living room with fireplace, fully equipped modern kitchen, bedrooms with twin beds, bathroom with stall shower, electric heat, outside shower for sand removal, and picture windows with views of the bay.

Special Features: Guests can bring their own portable TV and bed linens. One blanket is provided for each bed. Rollaway beds free for one extra guest per unit; cribs are available for a small fee.

Cost: Two-bedroom cottages $455 per week in season, $240 to $275 per week off-season. Three-bedroom cottages $560 per week in season, $275 to $350 per week off-season. Four-bedroom cottages $695 per week in-season, $310 to $415 per week off-season.

Nearby: The Aqua Circus of Cape Cod on Route 28 in Yarmouth has daily sea lion and dolphin shows. The Hyannis Center, fishing, golfing, boating, movies, summer theater, restaurants, and churches are all minutes away by car. For other activities in Hyannis, see the Hyland Hostel, page 252. For more things to do on the Cape, see page 251.

PINES LAKEFRONT COTTAGES

Address: 51 Pond Street, West Dennis, Massachusetts 02670.
Telephone: 508-362-2509.

These cottages are spaciously situated among four acres of pines on beautiful Kelley's Pond and only one mile from the white sands and warm waters of mile-long West Dennis beach. You can fish, swim, or bring your own unmotorized boat to use on the pond should you want a day off from the sun-drenched beach. Cottages are simple but have all modern conveniences.

Season: May to November.

Accommodations: Each cottage sleeps four to five people and has two bedrooms (some with a double and some with two twin beds), full bath, outdoor shower, large living room, full kitchen, fireplace, and screened porch. All linens and cooking utensils are provided.

Special Features: Hookup for cable television (you can bring your own TV), charcoal grills, and picnic tables are provided.

Cost: In season, two-bedroom cottages $510 to $635 per week, depending on time of visit. Lower off-season rates available.

Nearby: Centrally located in the mid-Cape area, the cottages are convenient to a number of public golf courses, tennis courts, the Cape Playhouse theater, and swimming at many beaches or at Scargo Lake. The Cape Cod Rail Trail runs fourteen miles from Eastham to Dennis. Seaview Playland, an amusement center, is on Lower County Road in Dennis Port. Fans of the macabre may want to visit Curious Forms of Colonial Punishment in South Dennis with authentic pillories, stocks, and a whipping post. The free Jericho Historical Center on the corner of Trotting Park Road and Old Main Street in West Dennis has a barn museum and driftwood zoo. For more things to do on the Cape see the introduction on page 251.

OCEAN EDGE RESORT

Address: Great Vacations, PO Box 1748, Brewster, Cape Cod, Massachusetts 02631.
Telephone: 508–896–2090.

Ocean Edge Resort is a family vacation property located in the heart of the Cape. The resort includes four hundred acres of trees and ponds with houses and condominiums clustered in small villages. The accommodations are one-, two-, and three-bedroom houses. While this resort does not have "budget" rates, it is appealing to larger families because of the low cost per person. Included in the house rental is use of the resort's four swimming pools, its eighteen-hole golf course, tennis courts, and various family activities scheduled throughout the season.

Season: Mid-June through fall.

Accommodations: Houses and condominiums are clustered in small "villages." An example of the least expensive rental is a two-bedroom, two-bath house that sleeps six and includes a fully equipped kitchen with microwave oven, all linens and towels, washer and dryer, private telephone, cable television with HBO, dishwasher, and barbecue grill.

Special Features: Four swimming pools, including a children's wading pool; eighteen-hole golf course, tennis courts, driving range. The thirteen-mile paved Cape Cod Bike Trail runs through the property.

Cost: The two-bedroom, two-bath house for six described above $810 per week high season, $490 per week in June or September (the weather is still warm in these months).

Nearby: Miles of beaches, the national seashore, and Nickerson State Park all offer boating, swimming, and picnicking. The Museum of Natural History in Brewster has nature walks, family activities, and wonderful marine exhibits. Brewster also has an inexpensive petting zoo, puppet shows, an aquarium, and many historic sites of interest to children eight and up. For more things to do on the Cape, see page 251.

GIBSON COTTAGES

Address: PO Box 86, North Eastham, Massachusetts 02642.
Telephone: 508–255–0882.

These modest and inexpensive shingled cottages have a quiet, wooded setting on the private sandy beach of a beautiful, clean freshwater lake. Rowboats and sailboats are provided at no charge, and the lake is ideal for swimming and fishing. Should you tire of lakeside pursuits, the national seashore, ocean, and bay beaches are a short drive away.

Season: From Late June through Labor Day cabins are rented by the week. From April through June and September through November there is a two-night minimum stay.

Accommodations: Housekeeping cottages have one, two, or three bedrooms. Each cottage has a screened porch or deck, fully equipped kitchen, bathroom with shower, and baseboard heat. TVs are available for $25 per week.

Special Features: Many bicycle paths lead from the cottages.

Cost: In summer, one-bedroom cottage $510 per week, two bedroom $560 per week, three bedroom cottage $610 per week. Off-season (before the last week in June or after Labor Day), weekly rates $100 lower.

Nearby: Cottages are within walking distance of a general store and library. For more things to do on the Cape, see entry above and the introduction on page 251.

MID-CAPE HOSTEL

Address: 75 Goody Hallet Road, Eastham, Massachusetts 02642.
Telephone: 508–255–2785; 508–255–9762. Reservations are
essential July through August. Phone reservations are accepted with
a credit card.

This hostel's cozy cabins are surrounded by three acres of wooded land in a quiet rural area, just a fifteen-minute walk from Cape Cod Bay and four miles from the wide ocean beaches of the national seashore. Sailing instruction, Sunfish, and sailboard rentals are available to guests at the beach. The nearby Salt Pond National Seashore Visitors Center provides hiking and biking maps of the national seashore and has ranger-led tours.

Season: Late May through early September.

Accommodations: Two family cabins are part of this sixty-bed hostel.

Special Features: Bicycle rental, baggage storage area, kitchen, linen rental, and on-site parking.

Cost: AYH members, adults $10 per night; nonmembers $13. Children ages five to ten half price.

Nearby: For things to do in the area, see pages 251 and 259.

PINE TREE AND STARFISH COTTAGES

Address: c/o PO Box 5, Yarmouthport, Massachusetts 02675.
Telephone: 508–362–2509.

These simple and inexpensive cottages are set in a pine grove near the entrance to the Salt Pond National Seashore. They are a short drive to First Encounter Beach, Nauset Beach, Sunken Meadow Beach, Great Pond, and Provincetown. The grounds have a recreation room, a climbing structure with swings, and nets for badminton and volleyball.

Season: Mid-May through mid-October.

Accommodations: One- and two-bedroom cottages comfortably accommodate two to five people. Each cottage has a modern, fully equipped kitchen, bathroom with shower, hot water, and electric heat. Blankets and pillows are provided; guests bring their own sheets, towels, and pillowcases.

Special Features: Cable hookup if guests bring a TV, picnic table and charcoal grill.

Cost: In high season (July 4 through September 5), one-bedroom cottage for three to four people $360 to $395 per week; two-bedroom cottage for four to five people $535 per week. Lower off-season rates available.

Nearby: The nearby Salt Pond National Seashore Visitors Center provides hiking and biking maps of the Cape Cod National Seashore and has ranger-led tours. For more things to do in the area, see pages 251 and 259.

LITTLE AMERICA HOSTEL

Address: PO Box 402, North Parmet Road, Truro, Massachusetts 02666.
Telephone: 508–349–3889; 508–349–3726. Reservations are essential. Phone reservations are accepted with a credit card. Off-season, mail reservations to 75 Goody Hallet Drive, Eastham, Massachusetts 02642, or call 508–255–2785.

Originally a coast guard station, this hostel is the farthest out on the arm of the Cape. It is set atop a dune near the tip of the Cape Cod National Seashore, just a seven-minute walk from the beach. Large picture windows provide a spectacular view from the large kitchen and dining area. This makes a comfortable, inexpensive base for exploring the salt marshes, cranberry bogs, long beaches, and sand dunes of the seashore.

Season: Mid-June through early September.

Accommodations: There is one family cabin in this forty-eight-bed hostel.

Special Features: Kitchen, linen rental.

Cost: AYH members, adults $10 per night; nonmembers $13. Children five to ten half price.

Nearby: The National Audubon Bird Sanctuary is a few miles away. Provincetown is ten miles away and easily accessible by bike. On the way you can stop and climb the Pilgrim Monument, which commemorates the pilgrims' first landing in 1620. Whale-watching expeditions depart from MacMillan Wharf. For more things to do on the Cape, see page 251.

KALMAR VILLAGE

Address: Shore Road, Route 6A, North Truro, Massachusetts 02652.
Telephone: 508–487–0585.

Kalmar Village is a family resort of authentically styled Cape Cod cottages, efficiency units, and motel rooms on a private four-hundred-foot beach along the shore of Cape Cod Bay. The cottages are separated by green lawns with picnic tables, benches, and lounge chairs. There is a large freshwater swimming pool on the premises.

Season: May through October.

Accommodations: Cottages and efficiencies have fully equipped, modern kitchens, bedding, towels, electric heat, cable TV, and charcoal grills. Two-room cottages have a double bed and a twin bed in the bedroom and two double sofabeds in the living area. Deluxe two-room cottages have two double beds in the bedroom and two double sofabeds in the living area. Three-room cottages have one double bed and two twin beds in the bedrooms and a double sofabed in the living area.

Special Features: Laundry facilities, housekeeping service, and a list of available baby-sitters. Portacribs are available at no extra charge.

Cost: The most expensive time is July 18 through September 5; the least expensive time is May 23 through June 20 and September 12 through October 13. Nightly rates available off-season. Two-room cottage $410 to $710 per week; two-room deluxe cottage $445 to $785; three-room cottage $495 to $835 per week, depending on season. Rates are for four people; additional people $45 to $60 each per week.

Two-room efficiency $335 to $610 per week, $58 to $105 per night, double occupancy, depending on season. Motel room $40 to $68 per night, double occupancy, depending on season. Each additional person $45 to $60 per week, $5 to $10 per night.

NANTUCKET AND MARTHA'S VINEYARD, MASSACHUSETTS

The idyllic islands of Nantucket and Martha's Vineyard are generally not places to look for bargains, especially during high season. We have listed a few of the least expensive accommodations, however, because both islands provide an old-fashioned beach vacation with wide, pristine beaches, clean, salty air, historic towns, summer book fairs, and winding lanes with springtime blossoms of beach plum and blackberries. To save money, try a fall visit. The days usually are warm enough for swimming through September.

If the cottage or hotel you choose does not have access to a private beach, the best public beach on Martha's Vineyard for those with young children is State Beach, between Oak Bluffs and Edgarton. It has a long, flat shore and the water has a sandy bottom. Older kids will like the high waves at the public Katama Beach on the island's south shore, but it is generally quite crowded. Be sure to visit the Vineyard's breathtaking Clay Cliffs at Gay Head, Felix Neck Wildlife Sanctuary, and the Cape Pogue Wildlife Refuge.

Nantucket Island, with its clean beaches and open heath, is New England's historic whaling port, and you can still go whale watching aboard the *Yankee Clipper* from mid-May to mid-September (800–322–0013; 508–283–0313). The Nantucket Life Saving Museum near the town center recounts vivid rescues at sea. The town's Maria Mitchell Science Center has observatories, an aquarium, and natural science exhibits.

ROBERT B. JOHNSON MEMORIAL HOSTEL

Address: Surfside, Nantucket, Massachusetts 02575.
Telephone: 508–228–0433. Reservations are essential. Phone reservations are accepted with a credit card. Off-season, reservations: mail reservations to 75 Goody Hallet Drive, Eastham, Massachusetts 02642, or call 508–255–2785.

This hostel was built in 1873 as a lifesaving station and is listed on the National Register of Historic Places. Located three miles from the village of Nantucket, it is across the road from Surfside Beach. The island has beautiful sand beaches for swimming, sunning, sailing, and sailboarding. This hostel has no family rooms, so families stay in the dorm facilities and are segregated by sex. However, the hostel has allowed mothers to place a mattress on the floor by their bed for very young children.

Season: May through early October. The hostel is closed from 9:30 A.M. to 5 P.M. daily, except in inclement weather or if a guest is sick.

Accommodations: There are three rooms and sixty-four beds.

Special Features: Kitchen, linen rental.

Cost: AYH members, adults $10 per night; nonmembers $13. Children five to ten half price.

Nearby: The local Whaling Museum displays artifacts from the days when men hunted whales with hand-held harpoons from wooden boats.

CAUSEWAY HARBORVIEW

Address: Skiff Avenue, Box 450, Vineyard Haven, Martha's Vineyard, Massachusetts 02568.
Telephone: 800–253–8684; 508–693–1606.

Causeway Harborview has twenty-four apartments and cottages high on a hill, just a few minutes' walk from downtown Vineyard Haven. Facing the harbor and Nantucket Sound, its spacious landscaped property features a large pool, picnic sites with barbecues, and many views of the water. The apartments and cottages are a short drive to the vineyard's public beaches. Although more expensive than other listings in this book, these rates are "budget" for this extremely expensive island.

Season: Year-round.

Accommodations: Each of the apartments and cottages has color TV, a fully furnished kitchen, a full bath, homey furniture, and linens.

Cost: In summer (June 19 to September 7), two-bedroom apartment or cottage for four people $775 to $790 per week, three-bedroom apartment or cottage for six people $875 per week. Mid-season (April 16 to

June 18 and September 8 to November 14), two-bedroom apartment or cottage $455 to $465 per week, a three-bedroom apartment or cottage $480 per week. Off-season (November 15 to April 15), two-bedroom apartment or cottage $285 per week, three-bedroom apartment or cottage $320 per week. Each additional person $10 per day.

Nearby: The inn is within driving distance of golf, tennis, horseback riding, twenty miles of paved bicycle paths, world-famous fishing, and sailboarding. Swimming is available around the island at eight public beaches. For specifics, see page 259.

MANTER MEMORIAL HOSTEL

Address: Edgarton-West Tisbury Road, Box 158, West Tisbury, Martha's Vineyard, Massachusetts 02575.
Telephone: 508–693–2665. Reservations are essential. Phone reservations are accepted with a credit card. Off-season, mail reservations to 75 Goody Hallet Drive, Eastham, Massachusetts 02642, or call 508–255–2785.

This inexpensive hostel provides easy access to the beaches and traditional towns of this idyllic resort island. Rent bicycles and explore the island's network of trails that run through the towns, through wilderness areas, and along the coast.

Season: April through early November.

Accommodations: The hostel has six rooms with eighty-five beds. If a family of four or more stays they can have one of the smaller rooms to themselves. The hostel is in the process of creating one or two additional family rooms, which should be in place by 1993.

Special Features: Kitchen, baggage storage area, linen rental, and on-site parking.

Cost: AYH members, adults $10 per night; nonmembers $13. Children five to ten half price. Surcharge for a family room $5.

Nearby: Swimming is available around the island at eight public beaches. For specifics, see page 259.

BLOCK ISLAND, RHODE ISLAND

This summer beach resort is about ten miles south of mainland Rhode Island. Block Island is blessed with many sandy beaches, gently rolling hills dotted with wildflowers, open pastures, and hundreds of freshwater ponds. Because the island is a compact seven miles long by three miles wide, most people get around on foot or bicycle. You can bring your own

BEACH VACATIONS

bike or rent one at reasonable rates. Spectacular cliffs reminiscent of the white cliffs of Dover line the southern corner of the island. The island has excellent fishing; it is known especially for its striped bass, blues, and flounder. There are boats for rent and several charter boats for hire. Many of the restaurants here serve local lobsters and clams. Other island activities include swimming, tennis, scuba diving, sailboarding, snorkeling, sailing, and visiting the wildlife refuges. Ferries to the island depart from Point Judith and Newport, Rhode Island; Montauk Point, New York; and New London, Connecticut.

ISLAND MANOR RESORT

Address: Chapel Street, Box 400, Block Island, Rhode Island 02807. Telephone: 401–466–5567.

Just one block from town and the beaches, this establishment has efficiency units that sleep four people each. The host family has lived on the island for more than twenty-five years and eagerly shares its knowledge of the best spots for fresh- or saltwater fishing, snorkeling, swimming, surfing, cycling, and dining.

Season: Year-round.

Accommodations: Efficiency units sleep four with a queen-size sofabed and a double Murphy bed, private bath, equipped kitchenette, and cable TV.

Special Features: Portacribs are available at no extra charge.

Cost: In summer, efficiencies $685 per week, double occupancy; each additional person $15 per night. Children under twelve stay free. Significantly lower rates in spring, fall, and winter.

BARRINGTON INN

Address: PO Box 387, Block Island, Rhode Island 02807. Telephone: 401–466–5510.

This inn has two apartments in a separate barn adjacent to the main guest house. The main house is a century-old Victorian farmhouse situated on a knoll overlooking the new harbor area, with views of Trims Pond, the Great Salt Pond, and the mile of ocean beyond. The inn is a short walk to the beach and the town.

Season: April to November.

Accommodations: Each apartment accommodates up to five people and has a living room, fully equipped kitchen, two bedrooms, bathroom, and color TV. Both apartments have decks with beautiful water views. Linens and towels are not included.

Special Features: Barbecue grills and off-street parking. Cribs are available.

Cost: June through September $635 and $660 per week; September to November and April to May $460 and $485 per week.

Nearby: The apartments are less than a mile from the Old Harbor dock.

THE SOUTHERN MAINE COAST

Maine's southernmost coast may not have the rugged, windy, "down east" feel, but it offers sandy beaches and vacation amenities that vanish north of Portland. The summer colonies of York Beach, Ogunquit, and Wells have beaches of hard-packed sand and abundant beach cottages and motels. The water is clean (although chilly), the surf is gentle, and the crowds manageable, except for hot summer weekends. Ogunquit Beach is backed by the Ogunquit River, which is sheltered and waveless.

Kennebunkport has the picture-perfect Maine look, with white clapboard houses, manicured lawns, a rocky shoreline dotted with sandy beaches, beach cottages, and harbors bobbing with lobster boats. Consider a June or September visit; the rates will be lower and the weather usually is warm. You can pick strawberries in June, blueberries in July and August, apples in September, and pumpkins in October.

Area amusement attractions include Fun Town USA (207–284–7113) and Aquaboggin (207–282–3112) in Saco; Palace Playland (207–934–2001) on the beach at Old Orchard Beach and York's Wild Animal Kingdom (800–456–4911). Old Orchard Beach also has horseback riding at Long Horn Stables (207–934–9578) and miniature golf at Pirate's Island (207–934–5086). Wells has more miniature golf facilities. Deep-sea fishing and whale watching can be arranged from Kennebunkport, and there are golf courses at Kennebunk Beach, Arundel, and in Kennebunkport.

Kennebunk's Seashore Trolley Museum (207–967–2712) has a fun trolley ride, many examples of Victorian-era horse cars, and vintage streetcars from the 1960s. The Wells Auto Museum (207–646–9064) with its seventy vintage cars, is a must for motor fanatics. The Maine Aquarium (207–284–4511) in Saco has live sharks, seals, penguins, and a petting zoo.

Half an hour south from Kennebunk in Kittery are many factory outlets, including the Children's Place clothing outlet. Freeport, less than an hour away, has L. L. Bean, Coach, Patagonia, J. Crew, and Ralph Lauren outlets.

Note: We cover Maine's northern coastal area of Acadia, which includes Mount Desert Island and Bar Harbor, in the national parks chapter.

GARRISON HOUSE MOTEL AND COTTAGES

Address: RR 3, Box 510B, Wells, Maine 04090 (take exit 2 off I-95; turn left onto Route 109 to U.S. 1. The resort is on the ocean side, one mile south).
Telephone: 207–646–3497. July and August are peak season and require reservations. June and September have good weather and lower rates.

Situated on the coast between Ogunquit and Kennebunkport, Garrison House is a ten-acre resort overlooking the ocean, one mile from Wells Beach. It specializes in accommodating families. Fifteen motel units and seventeen cottages with views of the ocean and tidal inlet surround a large, heated swimming pool. Parents can relax while their children enjoy the swing set, play basketball, badminton, or baseball, fly kites, and swim.

Season: May to November.

Accommodations: Two-bedroom cottages sleep four to six people and have a full kitchen, linens, towels, and blankets. Motel efficiencies have two double beds, heat, air-conditioning, full baths, cable TV, and a compact kitchen. Motel rooms have two double beds, heat, air-conditioning, a small refrigerator, cable TV, and housekeeping service.

Cost: Two-bedroom cottage for four $260 per week off-season, $435 to $485 per week in July and August. Two-bedroom cottage for six $360 per week off-season, $585 per week in July and August. Nightly rates available off-season. Motel efficiency $48 per night, double occupancy, off-season; $58 to $82 per night, double occupancy, in July and August. Motel rooms $38 to $48 per night, double occupancy, off-season; $49 to $69 per night, double occupancy, in July and August. Each additional person $7 per night. Two-night minimum stay is required for motel rooms in July and August.

Nearby: The resort is on the trolley line and within walking distance from restaurants and tennis courts.

MAINE STAY INN AND COTTAGES

Address: 34 Maine Street, PO Box 500A, Kennebunkport, Maine 04046.
Telephone: 207–967–2117.

Although not a low-budget accommodation, the Maine Stay offers a good value to small families in this expensive area. This nineteenth-century bed-and-breakfast inn is a white clapboard Victorian house in a quiet residential area of Kennebunkport's historic district, a short drive from the beach.

Unlike most bed-and-breakfast establishments, the hosts welcome children; in fact, they have two young children of their own. The inn has a wraparound porch and beautiful grounds with lounge furniture, picnic tables, grills, croquet, and a climbing structure for children.

Season: Year-round.

Accommodations: The one- and two-bedroom fully equipped cottages with kitchens are best suited for families. Some have fireplaces and all have cable TV.

Special Features: Rates include a full breakfast (delivered to your cottage if you like) of fresh strawberries, yogurt, and homemade granola, blueberry blintzes, omelets, and French toast; afternoon tea; and daily housekeeping service. Parking permits for Kennebunkport beaches and Kennebunk Beach are free to guests. The hosts can arrange for babysitting. Cots ($10 one-time fee), cribs ($8 one-time fee), and high chairs are available. The parlor has a stack of children's books.

Cost: In summer, one-bedroom cottage $138 per night, double occupancy; mid-October to mid-June $78 to $88 per night, double occupancy. Each additional person $20 per night during peak season, $15 at other times of the year. Children under four stay free. Rates include breakfast, tea, and housekeeping service.

Nearby: The inn is convenient to the town and the beach. There are many bike paths, including an off-road trail from the Kennebunk beach area through marshlands and woods to town; bikes can be rented in Kennebunkport. Hiking along the Marginal Way in Ogunquit and through the Rachel Carson Wildlife Reserve are fun for older kids.

LEARNING
VACATIONS
AND DAY TRIPS

*L*earning vacations can take many forms. They can be as simple as a day trip to a living history village or cowboy poetry festival, or as involved as participating in a week-long archaeological dig for Indian relics. Teens and preteens, in particular, can benefit from a structured vacation with an educational dimension.

Many of our listings reflect the character of American culture, from its history and mythology to its icons, inventions, and cultural mix. We describe many of the unique attractions that children and adults can enjoy and learn from together—places that offer an excellent value, both educationally and financially. Many worthwhile organizations offer family learning vacations, but we have listed only those that fall into an affordable price range.

NATIONWIDE

SIERRA CLUB

Address: 730 Polk Street, San Francisco, California 94109.
Telephone: 415–776–2211.

The Sierra Club offers more than three hundred diverse and exciting outings throughout the United States and even more worldwide. It recently expanded its excellent and tremendously popular Family Outings Series. Parents with younger kids or those with minimal camping and nature study experience will most enjoy the trips designed with families in mind. Children twelve and older can participate in most of the other programs that the hundred-year-old institution offers.

The Family Outings are planned specifically to introduce parents and kids to the wonders of the outdoors and the pleasure of camping. Recent outings have included "Arches Adventures for Preschoolers" in Utah's Arches National Park, "Finger Lakes Toddler Tromp" in New York, and "Burros Invade Horse Heaven Family Trip" in the Inyo and Sierra forests of California. Some trips are planned for families with kids of all ages and others are for families with kids six to eight and older. Trips include opportunities to explore nature, hike, swim, and fish. Everyone shares in the camp chores, outdoor skills, and observation of plants, animals, and ecology. Single-parent families, grandparents, and other relatives are welcome.

Families also can participate in service outings, such as constructing nature trails, and enjoy recreational opportunities when off duty.

Accommodations: The style of camping varies. Sometimes pack animals transport food and equipment, sometimes campers stay in lodges, other times the group drives to the campsite and takes day hikes from there. Meals are usually included in the price and are prepared together.

Cost: Most trips last seven days and cost $295 to $565 per adult, $195 to $375 per child. Service outings $205 per adult, $140 per child.

NATIONAL WILDLIFE FEDERATION

Address: 1400 Sixteenth Street, Washington, DC 20036-2266.
Telephone: 800–822–9919; 703–790–4363.

The National Wildlife Federation offers "conservation summits" to teach people about natural history and ecology in some of the most beautiful areas in the United States. Its hands-on, experiential programs are structured so that every member of the family has a program geared to their abilities and interests. Preschoolers have touch-and-feel expeditions and nature crafts; five- to twelve-year-olds have games and wildlife investigations; teens are offered more physically challenging activities, such as orienteering and hiking. Adult activities include lectures, workshops, and day hikes. The word is out about the high quality and low cost of these programs, and more than half of the participants return from year to year, so book early.

Each year several different outdoor settings are selected to be the headquarters for the program—past choices have included Big Sky, Montana, and the Blue Ridge Mountains in North Carolina. Classes are led by naturalists and professors who are experts in their field. A Teen Adventure Program for ages thirteen to seventeen combines outdoor adventure, group interaction, and exploration; activities include orienteering, day hikes, outdoor skill sessions and field trips, and challenges to mental and physical abilities. The Junior Naturalist Program for ages five to twelve has activities including outdoor games, nature hikes, arts and crafts, wildlife investigations, stream studies, and bird walks. The morning preschool program for ages three and four has touch-and-feel expeditions, nature crafts, short hikes, and lots of hands-on activities. Many of the activities are created for families to enjoy together, such as sing-alongs, square dancing, and slide shows on natural history.

Accommodations: Housing ranges from first class to plain and simple. The federation's accommodations change from year to year, depending on where the programs take place. It uses the facilities of other organizations, such as college dormitories, resorts, and lodges. Meals are almost always included.

Cost: Fees are divided into two types. Program fees, which include all classes, field trips, special afternoon events, evening activities, transportation for all adult and youth field trips, and instructors, $200 to $225 per adult per week. Housing fees, which include lodging, meals, tax, meeting space, and recreational activities on the grounds, $175 to $650 per adult per week. Children usually pay one-third to one-half less. Each family must buy a membership in the National Wildlife Federation ($16 per year).

THE WEST

COWBOY POETRY FESTIVAL

**Address: PO Box 888, 501 Railroad Street, Elko, Nevada 89803.
Telephone: 800–748–4466; 702–738–7508.**

Cowboys and cowgirls bring the romance of the Old West to life at Elko's cowboy poetry festival, the granddaddy of all of the cowboy poetry festivals that have sprung up around the country. Well-told tales of true grit, lost loves, and life on the range (with plenty of humor thrown in) will enthrall even the most jaded of teenagers. The Western Folklife Center sponsors this five-day event in late January. Cowboy poets, musicians, and artists from seventeen western states and Canada take part in presentations, workshops, exhibits, dances, films, videos, and performances. Each year has a specific focus, such as family life on the ranch, bush poets from Australia, or the Spanish influence in the West. A "buckaroo breakfast" on Sunday morning ($3) is followed by a family matinee show. The Western

Folklife Center operates out of the old Pioneer Hotel, built in 1913; it has a retail store and interpretive center of folk life with a focus on cowboys. The center has a catalog of books, music, audiotapes, and videotapes of cowboy and cowgirl poets; stories about the American West for children and adults; and cowboy poetry memorabilia.

Cost: Daytime passes $10, concert tickets $15 per person. Special week-long and weekend passes available.

Where to Stay

Children stay free in their parents' room at Elko's Motel 6; rooms with two double beds are $40 per night. Rollaways are not available. Book early. Address: 3021 Idaho Street, I-80 East, Elko, Nevada 89803. Telephone: 702–738–4337.

ROCKY MOUNTAINS AND SOUTHWEST

YELLOWSTONE INSTITUTE

Address: PO Box 117, Yellowstone National Park, Wyoming 82190. Telephone: 307–344–7381, ext. 2384.

Families planning to visit Yellowstone would be wise to book one of the institute's family programs, in which they can discover what makes Yellowstone so distinctive. Rangers teach about the park's history, wildlife, ecology, plants, and geology through leisurely walks, hikes, and discussions. Free time is built into the program so that families can relax or explore on their own. Campfires and evening programs regularly take place after dinner. Seven to ten family classes are offered each summer, with five or six families accommodated in each. Most classes last three days. Many families take a class, then head out on their own to explore Yellowstone with their newfound knowledge. The classes usually are based at a group camp, but participants can opt for other accommodations nearby. The institute's pamphlet, *Field Courses and Nature Study Vacations,* describes all available classes. Family programs offered in the past have included "Family Days in Sunlight," "Three Days at Buffalo Ranch," and "Exploring the Park with a Ranger Family."

Accommodations: Most classes stay in campgrounds; if you do not wish to camp you can request accommodation information when you book. Participants are responsible for their own meals.

Cost: Three-day course $55 per person. Camping is extra, usually about

$5 per night. Courses that include food and lodging about $120 per person for three days. Discounts available to members of the Yellowstone Institute.

WYOMING TERRITORIAL PARK

Address: 975 Snowy Range Road, Laramie, Wyoming 82070.
Telephone: 307–745–3733.

"Evil-Doers of All Classes and Kinds" spent many a long and lonely year in the Wyoming Territorial Prison. Both men and women served time here. Built in 1872 by the federal government, it housed the likes of Butch Cassidy, Kinch McKinney, and other notorious outlaws. Today the prison is part of Western Territorial Park, a living history complex that blends history with entertainment to bring the legends of the Old West to life. The restored prison has sophisticated, state-of-the-art displays and interactive exhibits on frontier law and justice, the political role of women in Wyoming's past, and other aspects of western history. Outside the prison children and adults can try their hand at rope tying, branding, and other ranching skills. An archaeological dig shows visitors how the past is discovered.

The adjacent Wyoming Frontier Town has performances, crafts demonstrations, pony, horseback, and stagecoach rides, and plenty of opportunities to lighten your wallet with old-time portraits and souvenirs. Children particularly enjoy creating a personalized 1872 newspaper headline.

A permanent exhibit, "America's Star: U.S. Marshals 1789 to 1989," chronicles the two-hundred-year history of the nation's oldest law enforcement agency with artifacts and memorabilia of notorious outlaws and a fascinating series of displays. One display, "The Gunmen: Romance and Reality," deals with Hollywood's perception of the West and includes film clips of movies showing actors who played U.S. marshals, such as John Wayne, Clint Eastwood, and Ronald Reagan.

The park plans to add new features over the next few years. Look forward to a Plains Indians encampment, Mountain Man Rendezvous site, in-park steam train, cavalry outpost, and exhibits on mining and ranch life.

Try to plan your visit to include one of the park's special events. The Gem City Jamboree, usually held in late June, features cowboy and cowgirl poets and musicians. A Mountain Men Rendezvous in early July has frontier skill contests including black powder shoots and tomahawk throws.

A summer dinner theater, held nightly in the loft of the park's turn-of-the-century horse barn, features a musical review entitled *The Wild and Crazy West.*

Season: Late May through early September. Group tours can be arranged throughout the year.

Cost: Park admission, adults $6.95; children eight to twelve, $5.95, under eight free. Combination park entry and dinner theater: Sunday matinee (noon to 2:30), adults $14, children eight to twelve $12, children under eight $3; evening performance (6 to 8:30 P.M.), adults $22.50, children eight to twelve $19.95, children under eight $5.

Nearby: The Wyoming Colorado Scenic Railroad (307–742–9162) takes travelers on a day trip into the mountains west of Laramie. Lunch is served on the train and included in the price. Adults $26 to $38; children five to twelve $20, four and under free.

Where to Stay

Two Bars Seven Ranch, twenty-seven miles out of town, is described on pages 64–65.

Just thirty-five miles outside of Laramie, the Mountain Meadow Guest Ranch has housekeeping cabins available by the day in June and September and by the week in July and August. Cabins sleeping two to six people with fully equipped kitchens and private baths are $35 to $65 per night. Weekly stays start Saturday or Sunday and cost $210 to $390. Hiking trails and alpine fishing lakes a few miles away. Address: Box 203, Centennial, Wyoming 82055. Telephone: 307–742–6042.

In town try Annie Moore's Guest House. Once a boarding house operated by Mrs. Annie Moore, who settled in Laramie in 1922, it has been restored as a beautiful bed-and-breakfast inn best suited for adults and older children. Rooms cost $55 to $65; the largest room holds three people. Address: 819 University, Laramie, Wyoming 82070. Telephone: 307–721–4177.

BUFFALO BILL HISTORICAL CENTER AND THE CODY NITE RODEO

Named for Buffalo Bill Cody in 1896, Cody's current attractions are the Buffalo Bill Historical Center and the Cody Nite Rodeo. The Chicago, Burlington and Quincy Railroad began serving the town in 1901, filled with passengers bound for Yellowstone and big game hunting. Homesteaders were drawn to the area by Cody's name, and the growing city became the county seat in 1909. Tourism remains a big industry, as thousands of people still pass through Cody on their way to Yellowstone.

Buffalo Bill Historical Center

The Buffalo Bill Historical Center, with one of the nation's finest collections of western Americana, is made up of four museums. In addition to its permanent collections it has rotating exhibitions throughout the year, special events, and films.

The Buffalo Bill Museum has an enormous western collection, much of it relating to Buffalo Bill's career as a Pony Express rider, Civil War soldier, buffalo hunter, army scout, and, most of all, a showman. Visitors can see a stagecoach used in the Wild West Show, Annie Oakley's gloves and guns, and Wild Bill Hickok's handgun. Other items include posters and showbills, gifts to Buffalo Bill from foreign heads of state, photographs, playbills, and pocket watches. His boyhood home sits on the center's grounds.

The Plains Indian Museum's vast collection covers the twenty-seven Indian tribes inhabiting the area from the Mississippi River to the Rocky Mountains and from central Texas to central Canada. Examples of exquisitely beaded saddles, elaborate war bonnets, bows and arrows, carved leather bowls, and intricately painted body adornments show the viewer the importance of beauty and symbol in the lives of the Plains Indians. A large tepee hall exhibits numerous full-size tepees and a section of a tepee village.

Among the firearms in the Winchester Arms Museum are crossbows, hand cannons, and an 1860s rifle popular with frontiersmen. It documents the historical development of firearms in general but focuses on those manufactured by Winchester.

Western painter Frederic Remington's art studio has been reconstructed at the Whitney Gallery of Western Art. Paintings by Remington and other western greats, such as Charles M. Russell and George Catlin, give the viewer a glimpse of the romantic West. The collection begins with works by artists, such as Catlin, who accompanied explorers and recorded what they saw in drawings and paintings. It continues with works of landscape painters, such as Albert Bierstadt, who depict the striking natural beauty of the frontier world. The museum also includes paintings of Indians and the everyday life of settlers; outstanding collections of Remington and Russell contain more than one hundred works by each artist. Contemporary artists are represented as well.

Address: PO Box 1000, 720 Sheridan Avenue, Cody, Wyoming 82414.
Telephone: 307–587–4771.
Cost: Two-day tickets, adults $7; students thirteen and over $4; children six through twelve $2, five and under free. Open daily May through October; closed Monday in March, April, and November.

Cody Nite Rodeo
The Cody Nite Rodeo happens every night at 8:30 from June through August and features cowboys from all over the United States, Australia, and New Zealand. Try to get tickets for seats in the "Buzzard Roost" for great views of cowboys psyching up to straddle a two-thousand-pound bull and of animals exploding out of the chutes. These cost only $1 more than grandstand seats.

Address: Stampede Grounds, 421 West Yellowstone Avenue, Cody, Wyoming 82414 (on the western edge of town).

Telephone: 307–587–2992.

Cost: Regular grandstand tickets, adults $6, children seven to twelve, $3.50; Buzzard Roost seats $1 higher. Children six and under free.

Nearby: Visitors should plan a quick stop in the reconstructed frontier village Trail Town, with homestead cabins that date from 1880 to the early 1900s. The most popular cabin is "Hole in the Wall," where Butch Cassidy and the Sundance Kid holed up together (1831 Demaris Drive, Cody, Wyoming 82414; 307–587–5302; open 8 A.M. to 8 P.M.).

Where to Stay
Pahaska Tepee Resort (see page 80) has housekeeping units and lodge rooms that can be rented by the night. Rimrock Ranch (see pages 63–64) offers week-long packages.

The Lockhart Inn was the historical home of author Caroline Lockhart, who owned and edited Cody's weekly newspaper from 1919 to 1924. Families are most comfortable staying in the attached motel units or a fully equipped family cabin that sleeps up to five people for $75 per night, double occupancy, plus $10 for each additional person, including breakfast. The motel rooms, decorated in a western motif, have two double beds and private baths. Summer rates for two people are $65 per night, plus $10 for each additional person. Breakfast is included. Address: 109 West Yellowstone Avenue, Cody, Wyoming 82414 (near the rodeo, about two miles from the historical center). Telephone: 307–587–6074.

ANDERSON RANCH ARTS CENTER
Address: 5263 Owl Creek Road, PO Box 5598, Snowmass Village, Colorado 81615.
Telephone: 303–923–3181.

Anderson Ranch, near Aspen, offers a wide variety of workshops for parents and children age six and up. Kids can select classes such as outdoor clay sculpture, printmaking, or inventions, while parents can choose from ceramics, woodworking, photography, drawing, painting, or interdisciplinary studies taught by accomplished working artists. Children's workshops take place in a recently completed building. Kids' classes run Monday through Thursday or Friday and can be morning only, afternoon only, or all day. All children's class sizes are limited to fourteen. Adult workshops normally last one to two weeks.

Accommodations: The ranch is a mixture of renovated log cabins, barns, and new buildings. Students are housed in a campus dorm. The most economical arrangement is a shared room, with meals in the campus dining hall. Other options include renting or sharing nearby condominiums.

Special Features: Sunday and Tuesday night slide lectures by visiting faculty; exhibitions by current faculty. Some airline discounts can be arranged through the ranch's travel agency.

Cost: Children's workshops $65 to $125 for one week's instruction. One-week adult workshops $300 to $450. Nonrefundable registration fee of $30 for all students. Accommodations in nearby condominiums $535 per week for two-bedroom unit.

WHITE MOUNTAIN ARCHAEOLOGICAL CENTER

Address: HC 30, St. Johns, Arizona 85936 (four miles south of Lyman on route 180-666).
Telephone: 602–333–5857.

Can you dig it? Budding archaeologists should take note of this unusual opportunity: parents and kids age nine and over can work side by side with professional archaeologists to preserve and uncover a prehistoric pueblo occupied from A.D. 1000 to 1400. The Raven Site Ruin, inhabited by the Mogollon people to the south and the Anasazi people to the north, has a breathtaking setting that overlooks the Little Colorado River. The pueblo contains more than four hundred rooms and two kivas that are being excavated grid by grid and level by level. Many of the rooms will be restored to their original condition. Miles of petroglyph trails run throughout this area, and week-long participants help with the surveying.

The scientists who run this program have found children to be skilled and responsible team players, and all participants work beside the scientists, excavating the ruins, surveying petroglyph trails, working in the lab, and helping with restorations. A field laboratory and museum are on the dig site. Your visit can be as long or short as you like. The week-long program includes all aspects of fieldwork, while the daily program takes in just part of it. Most people arrange to stay at least three days. There is a campfire every night, and horseback riding is available, for recreation (extra fee) and as part of the fieldwork. A gift shop on the premises features educational materials, books, and the work of top-quality Native American silversmiths; on occasion the artists visit the ruin and demonstrate their crafts.

Season: May through September.

Accommodations: Families will be most comfortable in one of the four private family rooms. The center has beds for twenty-three people in family rooms and bunkhouses, but most groups are kept small, usually around twelve people. Shower rooms adjoin the bunkhouses. Tent camping is available.

Cost: Daily program, adults $35, kids nine through seventeen $18; fees include lunch. Overnight stays, adults $56, children $36; includes all meals, lodging, and archaeological activities. Weekly rates, adults $395, children $250. Horseback rides $18 for two hours.

NATIONAL COWBOY SYMPOSIUM

Address: Box 43201, Lubbock, Texas 79409-3201 (mailing address); Fourth Street and Indiana, Lubbock, Texas 79409 (street address). Telephone: 806–742–2498.

The Ranching Heritage Center stands on one corner of the Texas Tech campus in Lubbock, Texas, to preserve the cowboy history of the nation's ranching past. More than thirty historic ranch structures, from homes, barns, and ranch headquarters to corrals and windmills, have been restored and relocated to this center. Kids will particularly enjoy the one-room schoolhouse and the cowboy bunkhouse. Changing exhibitions held in the main building feature western saddles, branding irons, buggies, and western art. Special demonstrations on making lye soap, shoeing horses, shearing sheep, spinning, weaving, and quilt making take place periodically. Volunteers in authentic costume work on the grounds Sunday afternoons from late May to October.

Time your visit to coincide with the National Cowboy Symposium, held annually on the third weekend in May. The three-day event has four sessions running simultaneously each day, with a break for lunch. Daytime sessions include cowboys and cowgirls reciting tall tales and poetry, musicians singing old ballads and strumming original material, and lively panel discussions on western movie making, western clothes, and horses.

Music and poetry performances take place Friday, Saturday, and Sunday nights. Call ahead for tickets ($7 per plate) to the chuck wagon cook-off, when old-fashioned chuck wagons from all over Texas compete to create the best chicken-fried steak, potatoes and gravy, sourdough biscuits, and cobbler. Sundays begin with a chuck wagon breakfast ($5 per plate) and continue at the fairgrounds with competitions in team roping, horse contests, and team penning. Specialty sheepdog demonstrations, whip acts, and trick roping fill in between the main acts.

Cost: Tickets to the Friday and Saturday daytime symposia, adults $5, children $2.50, include admission to Thursday evening performance. Tickets to performances on Friday and Saturday evening, adults $5 per performance (there are two shows per evening), children $2.50. Sunday fairgrounds show, adults $5, children $2.50. Entry to the center grounds is free the rest of the year, although donations are welcome.

Where to Stay

The symposium arranges for local hotels to offer room discounts to ticket holders; contact the center for details.

TEXAS FOLKLIFE FESTIVAL

Address: PO Box 1226, Bowie Street at Durango Boulevard, San Antonio, Texas 78294 (in HemisFair Park in downtown San Antonio). Telephone: 512–226–7651.

Texas has attracted people from all over the world at different times and for different reasons. The state's varied and distinctive cultures are the focus of the four-day Texas Folklife Festival presented each August in San Antonio by the Institute of Texan Cultures. Food, crafts, music, and dance from thirty different ethnic and cultural groups create an explosion of sight, sound, and taste. This high-quality event has celebrated Texas's cultural diversity for more than two decades. Sample German bratwurst, Mexican burritos, Belgian waffles, Southern soul cooking, and cowboy chuck wagon fare while you listen to Texas blues, Tex-Mex and mariachi music, German and Czech polkas, cowboy ballads, and country and western bands.

Sunday is children's day. Kids get in free with an adult, and entertainment and activities—music, storytelling, dancing, puppet shows—are geared especially for them. Throughout the festival are many frontier activities for kids to try: roping a calf, making a hoecake, and grinding peanuts for peanut butter. The institute has a large "Back 40" with a tepee and one-room schoolhouse, where many of the children's activities take place.

The Institute of Texan Cultures also provides exhibitions, programs, and publications year-round. In the exhibition halls, kids are encouraged to touch the interactive displays, which focus on pioneer life and the contributions of various ethnic groups. The Gone to Texas Puppet Theater presents plays on a variety of Texas topics and music performances take place throughout the exhibition hall.

Both the festival and the institute are located in spacious HemisFair Park. Kids will want to wander by its fountains and take a quick trip to the top of the Tower of the Americas for a panoramic view of the area. An excellent children's playground is found in the park near the institute.

Season: The festival begins in the evening on the first Thursday in August and runs through Sunday afternoon. The institute is closed on Monday.

Cost: Admission to the institute is free. Tickets for the festival concerts and dance performances available at the door; adults $6, children six to twelve $2, children under six free. Tickets can be purchased in advance for $1 less.

Nearby: Don't miss the Alamo or the River walk, a section of river lined with shops, restaurants, and garden pathways, during a stay in San Antonio.

Where to Stay

The Silver Spur Guest Ranch (see pages 66–67) or the Mayan Guest Ranch (page 67), about an hour away, have reasonably priced rooms.

The Texas Guestel, about twenty minutes from town, has a pool, complimentary continental breakfast, and one-bedroom suites with kitchenettes for $75 per night. Address: 13101 East Loop 1604 North, San Antonio, Texas 78233. Telephone: 512–655–9491.

The Bullis House Inn, in a historic Texas mansion, has a number of affordable rooms that sleep three, four, or six people for $50 to $60 per night, double occupancy. Children under eighteen are $6 additional. Cribs are available at no charge for kids under three. Rates include continental breakfast, and guests have the use of a small kitchen, dining area, and picnic tables. A swimming pool is open mid-April to mid-October. Address: 621 Pierce Street, San Antonio, Texas 78208. Telephone: 512–223–9426.

Next door to the inn, the San Antonio International Hostel has double rooms for $30 to $50, each additional person $6. Guests bring or rent sleep sacks and towels. Special discounts are available for children, and guests have use of a reading room, small kitchen, dining area, picnic tables, and swimming pool. Both the inn and the hostel are located near Fort Sam Houston. Hostel address and phone number are the same as the inn, above.

CENTRAL UNITED STATES

RED EARTH FESTIVAL

Address: Red Earth, PO Box 25866, Oklahoma City, Oklahoma 73125. **Telephone:** 405–427–5228.

The largest, most authentic, and colorful of all Native American gatherings and festivals is Red Earth, held the second weekend in June in Oklahoma City's Myriad Gardens. It features dancing and traditional music presentations, musicians and singers talk about why they sing and play certain songs and the traditions from which they stem. Dance competitions and exhibitions are a mainstay of the festival and attract more than a thousand of the most accomplished Native American dancers from the United States and Canada. There are exhibitions of War, Jingle Dress, Grass, and Fancy Dress dances. Other events include a powwow and a juried Native American art show that features textiles, jewelry, pottery, clothing, cultural items, and contemporary paintings and sculptures. Speakers address the cultural traditions and heritage of Native American art and life.

Cost: Tickets to the dance competition free for children under twelve; adults $5. Evening dance performances, adults $10, children $5.

Nearby: Cowboy Hall of Fame. Address: 1700 North East 63rd Street, Oklahoma City, Oklahoma 73111. Telephone: 405–478–2250.

Where to Stay

Radisson Inn has large rooms with two double beds and extensive recreational facilities, including three outdoor swimming pools open during the summer; indoor pool open year-round; tennis; a jogging track; a health spa; and restaurants. Rates for two adults, two children $59–74 per night. Address: 401 South Meridian, Oklahoma City, OK 73108. Telephone: 800–333–3333; 405–947–7681.

INDIAN CITY U.S.A. AND AMERICAN INDIAN
EXPOSITION

Address: PO Box 695, Anadarko, Oklahoma 73005.
Telephone: 405–247–5661.

Anadarko is the place to be during the third week of August for the American Indian Exposition at the city fairgrounds. With parades, a war-dancing competition, all-Indian archery competitions, Indian rodeo, and nightly tribal dances, anyone fascinated with Native American culture will be deeply satisfied. When the activities at the fairgrounds slow down, visit Indian City U.S.A.'s outdoor displays of authentic Indian villages and indoor exhibits of artifacts, clothing, memorabilia, and photos. The reconstructed dwellings have been restored authentically under the supervision of the Department of Anthropology at the University of Oklahoma. If you reserve in advance you can stay in a cottage at Indian City's campground three miles to the south.

Season: Year-round.

Nearby: Also in Anadarko is the National Hall of Fame for Famous American Indians, the Delaware Tribal Museum, the Philomathic Pioneer Museum, and the Southern Plains Indian Museum and Crafts Center.

Where to Stay

Indian City U.S.A. has a few plain but serviceable cabins with private baths for rent at its RV park and campground south of Indian City. Cabins are small and house two to three people for $20 to $30 per night. There is a swimming pool and picnic grounds. Book accommodations early for the exposition. Address: Indian City Campground, Highway 8, Anadarko, Oklahoma 73005. Telephone: 405–247–5219.

Another option is Quartz Mountain Resort, one of Oklahoma's state resort parks (see pages 29–30).

MORE INDIAN ACTIVITIES IN OKLAHOMA

Oklahoma has the highest population of Native Americans of any state in the United States. Through the centuries some sixty-seven different Indian tribes have lived in Oklahoma, including Cherokee, Choctaw, Seminole, Creek, Cheyenne, Apache, Pawnee, and Chickasaw, and descendants from each of those tribes still reside in the state. The state travel and tourism office (Telephone: 800–652–6552 or 405–521–2409) publishes a list of the thirty-seven tribes that maintain council houses in Oklahoma, including dates of their powwows. A powwow is a gathering of many tribes for singing, dancing, feasting, and selling and trading arts and crafts. Visitors are welcome at many of them. During the summer there is a powwow somewhere in the state every weekend. Be sure to note the powwow etiquette tips included in the brochure before you head out.

LAURA INGALLS WILDER PAGEANT

Address: Laura Ingalls Wilder Memorial Society, 105 Olivet Avenue, De Smet, South Dakota 57231.
Telephone: 605–854–3383 (headquarters and gift shop); 605–854–3181 (society director).

If you're anywhere near De Smet, South Dakota, in late June and early July, visit this "Little Town on the Prairie" for the Laura Ingalls Wilder Pageant, held for three weeks near the original Ingalls homestead site. Wilder's popular books (made into a highly successful TV show) chronicle the life of a delightful pioneer family on the Great Plains. The outdoor pageant is based on the book *These Happy Golden Years* and is performed by an all-volunteer cast, including lots of children. The performance begins at sundown; plan to arrive early for children's horse-drawn wagon rides. The last several performances often have home-cooked meals for sale before the pageant at the Ingalls' Church in town. If you miss the pageant, the Laura Ingalls Wilder Society conducts tours of sites described in the books throughout the summer.

Six of Laura Ingalls Wilder's books are set in De Smet. The Ingalls family moved there in 1879 after unsuccessful attempts at homesteading in Kansas and Wisconsin. Their first winter the family lived in a surveyors' house, later moving to the house that "Pa" built in 1887; tours of both places are conducted year-round. The homes contain memorabilia and artifacts from the family; the five original cottonwoods that Pa planted still stand, and the surveyors' house contains the original chest of drawers that Pa built, where Laura accidentally discovered her Christmas present in *The Long Winter*.

The Laura Ingalls Wilder Society sponsors the pageant and owns the homes, and its gift shop next door to the surveyors' house is filled with wonderful books, posters, postcards, pictures, toys, and memorabilia relating to the Laura Ingalls Wilder books. Visitors also can tour sixteen other sites mentioned in the Little House books, including the schoolhouse where Laura and her sisters attended school and the cemetery where her parents are buried. The society will send you a catalog of its merchandise on request.

Cost: Tickets to the pageant, adults $4, children $3. Self-guided tours of the Laura Ingalls Wilder sites $3 per person. Visitors receive a map of all sites. The society is open 9 A.M. to 5 P.M. seven days a week from Memorial Day to September 15.

Nearby: The World's Only Corn Palace (604 North Main Street, Mitchell, South Dakota; 605–996–7311), an exotic Moorish-inspired structure decorated each year with murals composed of thousands of bushels of corn, grain, and grass grown by local farmers, is seventy-five miles away.

Where to Stay

The Cottage Inn Motel has large rooms with two double beds; nonsmoking rooms are available. Rates are $30 to $55; rollaways and cribs are $5 per night. Address: Highway 14, De Smet, South Dakota 57231. Telephone: 800–848–0215; 605–854–3396.

The Prairie House Manor Bed and Breakfast, two doors down from the Ingalls homestead, has rooms available for families of all sizes. All units have a private bath and TV, and a full breakfast is included in the price. Rates are $35 to $75 per night, depending on the size of your group and room. Address: 209 Poinsett Avenue, De Smet, South Dakota 57231. Telephone: 605–854–9131.

INTERNATIONAL MUSIC CAMP SUMMER SCHOOL OF
FINE ARTS

Address: 1725 Eleventh Street, SW, Minot, North Dakota 58701.
Telephone: 701–263–4211.

On the border between North Dakota and Manitoba in the International Peace Gardens of the Turtle Mountains, the International Music Camp Summer School of Fine Arts has week-long sessions for adults and children age ten and up. Select from intensive courses in band, chorus, piano, guitar, piping and drumming, baton twirling, dance, computers, art, creative writing, and much more. Sessions run Sunday to Saturday during June and July. A few classes are shorter (three days) or longer (two to four weeks). This is basically a study camp; classes range from beginning through advanced levels and are divided according to ability instead of age.

Recreational activities include record hops, movies, volleyball, softball, swimming, concerts, and arts and crafts. Student performances on Saturdays are free and open to the public. Friday night concerts are held in the International Peace Gardens. If you time your visit right you can catch the Old-Time Fiddlers Contest in early June. The International Peace Gardens have ten miles of paved roads that are great for biking; bring your own bike.

Season: Summer.

Accommodations: There are separate dorms for kids and grownups so that adults don't have to adhere to the lights-out policy for the youngsters. Dorms are large rooms with thirty to sixty beds in each and are chaperoned. Each dorm has its own set of bathrooms. Families that wish to stay together can use the camping facilities within walking distance of the school. There is a small additional fee for a campsite, but campers have full access to special recreational activities and cafeteria meals.

Cost: Approximately $200 per week per person for room, board, instruction, and recreational activities.

Nearby: Lake Metigoshe, twenty miles from the camp near Bottineau, has boating, fishing, cabins, and simple resorts. Don't miss the W'eel Turtle at Dunseith, a zany forty-foot-long, twenty-eight-foot-wide, and fifteen-foot-high turtle made of discarded automobile tires.

INDIANA UNIVERSITY, BLOOMINGTON MINI

UNIVERSITY

Address: Indiana Memorial Union, Suite 400, Bloomington, Indiana 47405.
Telephone: 812-855-5108.

Indiana University has a week-long program suitable for families. Adults can choose from an enormous list of classes and stimulating discussions in the arts, business, human growth and development, science, international affairs, health, fitness and leisure, or humanities. While the adults tune up their intellectual skills, kids four to sixteen enjoy themselves at Camp Shawnee Bluffs on Lake Monroe. They are taught and supervised by trained counselors; activities include swimming, boating, hiking, field games, archery, tennis, and more. Children ages one to four are cared for at a state-licensed nursery near campus.

Many activities are planned outside of the classroom, and guests have plenty of free time to pursue their own interests. Evening activities for adults always include arrangements for children's supervision.

Accommodations: On- and off-campus housing available. The Forest Quadrangle offers dormlike housing with shared baths; rooms have two twin beds, linens, and phone. Parents can bring cots for their kids and pay for just a food package if they wish. Hotel accommodations are available on and off campus.

Cost: Class registration, adults $90, children under eighteen $70 for the week. Dorm housing, including meals, $195 per adult, single occupancy, $165 double occupancy. Children eight and over, $135, children under eight $110. Children's meals-only rate $85, under eight $65.

CONNER PRAIRIE

Address: 13400 Allisonville Road, Noblesville, Indiana 46060 (northwest of Indianapolis).
Telephone: 317-776-6000.

Time has rolled back to 1836 at Conner Prairie with the sights, sounds, and smells of life in the small village of Prairietown, where village inhabitants go about their daily work. Wander about the village and chat with the "residents"; you'll hear the small-town chatter and conversation common to any prairie village of the 1830s. The more your children ask questions of the residents, the more they will get out of their visit. But beware: the costumed characters you'll be talking to know only of life in their own era. Talk to them about airplanes or automobiles and they'll think you a bit "touched in the head."

Three different historical sites make up Conner Prairie: the 1836 village, the William Conner home, and the Pioneer Adventure area. The village has thirty-nine buildings, including a store, schoolhouse, log cabins, and inn, all staffed with costumed interpreters who go about their business cooking, tending store, repairing rifles, and so on. William Conner was one of Indiana's first residents, and his house, which is original to the site, was recently restored.

Kids will want to headquarter in the Pioneer Adventure area, a hands-on activity center where they can try the different activities they've heard about while visiting the village and house. They can dip a candle, weave a basket, make soap, or create cornhusk dolls. There are many 1830 games available to play, such as stilts, a game similar to darts, and horseshoes. They also can practice washing clothes with a scrub board.

With advance reservations an entire family can spend a weekend on the grounds of Conner Prairie in a pioneer log cabin. Guests sleep on straw-stuffed tick mattresses and keep warm with a fireplace. Visitors bring their own food and blankets and cook on primitive cooking utensils over the fire. Restrooms and showers with twentieth-century plumbing are nearby. The cabin accommodates up to seven people.

Season: April to November.

Cost: Admission fees, adults $8, children six to twelve $5, children under five free. Log cabin $45 for one night, $75 for two nights.

Nearby: Take the time to explore the brick streets and restored buildings of Zionsville.

Where to Stay

If staying in the log cabin doesn't appeal to you, the Waterfront Inn in Cicero (about a twenty-minute drive) has rooms overlooking the water with kitchenettes for $50 to $80 per night. Children under twelve stay free in their parents' room; each additional person is $6 per night. Address: 409 West Jackson, Cicero, Indiana 46034. Telephone: 317–773–5115.

LINCOLN BOYHOOD NATIONAL MEMORIAL AND STATE PARK

Address: Box 216, Lincoln City, Indiana 47552 (state park); Box 1816, Lincoln City, Indiana 47552 (memorial).
Telephone: 812–937–4710 (state park); 812–937–4541 (memorial).
Theater reservations, 800–346–4665 within Indiana; 800–284–1816 outside Indiana.

Lincoln State Park and its neighbor, the Lincoln Boyhood National Memorial, combine the outdoors with history in a way that will interest even the most reticent young student. With well-staged historical musical dramas, a working pioneer farm, an interpretive center, and lots of outdoor activities, families can learn about the life and times of the sixteenth U.S. president while they enjoy numerous recreational diversions.

A fifteen-hundred-seat covered amphitheater in the state park stages repertory productions of *Young Abe Lincoln* and *Big River,* a musical about the life of Huckleberry Finn, nightly during the summer. The Lincoln Boyhood National Memorial, across the street, has an interpretive center with displays about Abraham Lincoln and a film describing the Lincoln family's time in Indiana. The Lincoln Living Historical Farm is a re-creation of an early-nineteenth-century farm; from April through September people dress in period attire and plant, plow, cook, harvest, spin, and quilt just as they did in Lincoln's time. Another trail takes visitors to the cemetery where Lincoln's mother is buried and to a memorial marking the site of one Lincoln family home. The self-guided Boyhood Nature Trail takes guests past species of trees that Lincoln's father, a master woodworker, might have used. A staff member explains what pioneers of the time might have made from that type of wood.

The state park, with its rolling hills and shady forest, is on Lake Lincoln and has a wonderful swimming beach, fishing, and boat rental. In summer a naturalist program sponsors free activities such as sand castle building contests and animal identification; choices are posted weekly.

Cost: Cost is $1 per person with $3 maximum family fee. Seniors and children sixteen and under free. Rowboats and canoes $1.75 per hour, $9 per day; paddleboats $4 per day, $2 per half hour; mandatory life jacket rental $1 per person.

Nearby: Holiday World Theme Park, the oldest theme park in the country, is nearby in Santa Claus, Indiana. Mega-maze in Dale is an enormous life-size maze with a miniature golf course in the middle.

Where to Stay

If possible, stay in one of the park's ten housekeeping cabins (they fill up quickly, so book early). Cabins rent by the week only in the summer ($210 to $250 per week) and by the night in April, May, and September through November ($30 per night). The park also has Rent-A-Tent sites for $15 per night in the campground, or regular campsites. The Rent-A-Tent sites supply a canvas tent mounted on a wooden platform, camp stove, lantern, cooler, cots and foam pads, picnic table, and fire ring. There are pit toilets and no showers.

The closest private accommodations are at the simple Stone's Motel in Dale (812–937–4448), four miles from the park.

HENRY FORD MUSEUM AND GREENFIELD VILLAGE

Address: PO Box 1970, 20900 Oakwood Boulevard, Dearborn, Michigan 48121-1970.
Telephone: 800-343-1929; 313-271-1620.

Instead of focusing on a single time period and location or on chronological exhibits, this collection spans 350 years of American history. Henry Ford founded the twelve-acre museum in 1929 to honor inventions, inventors, and the stuff of everyday life. Both the museum and the village reflect the quirks of their eccentric founder. Not only can you see the actual Menlo Park lab buildings where Thomas Edison produced more than four hundred inventions, but you'll also "see" his last breath, captured in a test tube. The automobile is well represented here, with dozens of cars of all sizes and shapes and an exhibit that explains how the automobile has been the single greatest force in shaping everyday life of the twentieth century.

Children appreciate the numerous hands-on activities; they can pedal a high-wheel bike, work on an actual assembly line to build a wooden car, operate a nineteenth-century printing press, play nineteenth-century children's games, or attend a class in an 1870s schoolhouse (if they're late they may have to sit in a corner and wear a dunce cap). At Innovation Station kids seven and older use teamwork to solve problems on a giant interactive learning game.

In addition to Edsels, old race cars, and a 1936 Stout Scarab, billed as a "living room on wheels," exhibits include period kitchens, the largest coal-burning locomotive ever built, and some old-fashioned American gore, such as the 1961 Lincoln Continental that JFK died in and Abraham Lincoln's blood-stained theater seat.

The Greenfield Village part of the complex contains eighty historic structures, including the bike shop where the Wright Brothers designed and built their first airplane and the place where Noah Webster wrote the first American dictionary. Other sites include operating sawmills, a pottery shop, glass-making plant, working farm with farm animals, and more. In summer visitors can take rides on a Suwanee Steamboat, a steam train, a carousel, and a 1931 bus.

The new "Made in America" exhibit explains how various products are made and describes the people who make them. Sixteen hands-on activities keep children engaged, while an overhead conveyer belt hums above throughout the exhibition.

Cost: Daily price, adults $11.50, children five to twelve $5.75, under five free. Separate fees charged for the museum, village, and rides. Your best bet is a combined ticket for the museum and village, which can be used over a two-day period: adults $20, kids five to twelve $10. Hour-long narrated tour of village on 1931 bus $3 per person; carousel ride 75 cents, steamboat ride $1, train ride $2.

Where to Stay

The Holiday Inn in Dearborn has an indoor pool, two outdoor pools, whirlpool and sauna, restaurant, and café. They often have special promotions; ask for the very lowest rate when calling. Double rooms are $75 per night, rollaway beds are $5. Kids under eighteen stay free. Address: 22900 Michigan Avenue, Dearborn, Michigan 48124. Telephone 800–465–4329.

The Best Western Greenfield Inn has an indoor pool and restaurant; a room with two double beds is about $75 per night. Address: I-94 and Oakwood Boulevard, Dearborn, Michigan 48101. Telephone: 800–528–1234.

THE SOUTH

OZARK FOLK CENTER

Address: PO Box 500, Mountain View, Arkansas 72560.
Telephone: 501–269–3851.

Celebrating the way of life in the Ozark Mountains pre-1920, the Ozark Folk Center is dedicated to preserving and perpetuating traditional Ozark Mountain crafts and music. Craft demonstrations (more than twenty) and music shows are a staple on the grounds of the folk center, and workshops and performances take place throughout the year for kids and adults.

The Young Pioneer Program gives visiting children the chance to do the kinds of things the kids of the Ozarks used to do: pottery making, corn shucking, rope and paint making, spelling bees, making and using feather pens, and Ozark games. It takes place five days a week, three times a day in June, July, and August. If you visit in September, October, April, or May, try to stay over on a Saturday; this is the only day the Young Pioneers Program operates during those months.

"Youth Weeks," which take place twice throughout the summer, usually in June and August, provide a hands-on tour of the folk center crafts area for young people seven to sixteen. Kids get to make and take home a candle, a pinch pot, a printed card, and other projects. The two-and-a-half-to three-hour tour is conducted daily and is included in the price of a child's admission ticket to the crafts area. At the end of the tour kids receive a special "Certificate from Yesteryear."

Special music and crafts programs for the entire family are planned throughout the year, but summers are the most active. If you time it right you can catch "Songs of the American West," a stringband jamboree, mountain dulcimer workshops, buckdancers, cloggers, odd instrument concerts, or old-time fiddling championships. The Ozark Mountain Center's house band is reputed to be one of the best around.

Overnight guests can stay on the grounds in the comfortable lodge. Don't miss some of the great Ozark food served on the grounds of the folk center, especially the hot fried pies and barbecue.

Cost: Crafts area and evening music show tickets can be purchased separately or as a package. There are many package deals, depending on the number of days you stay. Daily craft tickets, adults $5.50, children six to twelve $3.25; family tickets $16.25. Music tickets, adults $6, kids six to twelve $4; family tickets $16.25. Combination tickets, adults $10.25, children six to twelve $5.75; family tickets $29.95. Weekend and two-day passes are available, as are season passes, which save you money if you stay four or more days. If you stay in the Ozark Folk Center Lodge you can get further discounts on tickets.

Where to Stay
The Ozark Folk Center Lodge 800–264–3655; 501–269–3871), located on the folk center grounds (address above), has comfortable rooms with two double beds; windows and doors open onto the Ozark National Forest. Lodge guests have use of the swimming pool and game room, and the restaurant features home-style southern cooking. Rooms for four $40 to $55 per night, depending on season; summer rates are highest.

Jack's Motel and Fishing Resort on White River, six miles from the folk center, has motel rooms with kitchenettes. A unit with two double beds is $50 to $55 per night for a family of four. There is rafting, canoeing, and fishing at the resort, and horseback riding is about a mile away. Address: HC 72, Box 185, Mountain View, Arkansas 72560. Telephone: 501–585–2211.

Camping: The folk center is on the edge of the Ozark National Forest, and many families camp in the forest's recreation areas. Call 501–757–2213 for information.

CRATER OF DIAMONDS STATE PARK

Address: Route 1, Box 364, Murfreesboro, Arkansas 71958.
Telephone: 501–285–3113.

Hunt for gemstones at the Crater of Diamonds State Park, the only mine open to the public in North America where you can pocket what you find. Spend a few hours or a week searching a thirty-five-acre field for diamonds; more than seventy thousand already have been found. Although diamonds are the main attraction, other semiprecious gemstones you might come across include amethyst, garnet, jasper, agate, and quartz. Digging tools can be rented, and free gem identification and certification are provided by the park staff. The field is plowed monthly to turn up new specimens. Historical structures, old mining equipment, washing pavilions, and restrooms are located at the mine.

A short walk away from the mine area is a shady trail leading to the Little Missouri River, providing a cool break from the sunny mine. You can fish for bass, catfish, and bream along the bank, but you'll need a fishing license (available in Murfreesboro, two miles away). Special programs and slide shows are presented daily throughout the summer. The park has campgrounds, a restaurant, a visitor information center, a gift shop, laundry facilities, and a playground.

Cost: Admission to the mine area, adults $3.50, children six to twelve $1.25. Children under six free if accompanied by an adult. Screens, shovels, buckets, knee pads, and cultivator forks available for rent Memorial Day through Labor Day for $1 to $2 each per day.

Where to Stay

If you're not going to camp in the park, consider the Swaha Lodge, open May through October, which has cabins about three-hundred feet from Lake Greeson, near a swimming beach and a marina. Eleven units have kitchenettes, two double beds, and air-conditioning for $40 per night. A two-bedroom cabin sleeps up to eight people for $60 per night. Address: PO Box 226, Murfreesboro, Arkansas 71958. Telephone: 501–285–2272.

The Riverside Motel has cabins along the Missouri River with two double beds, fully equipped kitchenettes, air-conditioning, and heat for $45, double occupancy; each additional person $6. Bed linens and bath towels are supplied; but bring your own beach towels. You can swim in the chilly river, but most people head to Lake Greeson, less than a mile away. Route 1, Box 48, Murfreesboro, Arkansas 71958. Telephone: 501–285–2255.

NATCHITOCHES FOLK FESTIVAL

Address: Louisiana Folklife Center, Box 3663, Northwestern State University, Natchitoches, Louisiana 71497.
Telephone: 318–357–4332; or call the Natchitoches Tourist Commission, 800–259–1714; 318–352–8072.

Dance the Cajun waltz, stuff yourself on Creole gumbo, and turn the kids loose at the children's tent during the third weekend in July, when more than thirty Cajun, country blues, bluegrass, and zydeco bands take over the historic town of Natchitoches (pronounced *nak*-a-tish). Held in the air-conditioned coliseum of Northwestern State University, the festival features music, dancing, crafts, food, and a children's festival. Events on four different stages run throughout the day; headliner acts fill a main stage area that can hold an audience of forty-five hundred. Talks and demonstrations take place nearby.

The town of Natchitoches is a like a small version of New Orleans and a microcosm of Louisiana, blending the influence of six different ethnic groups—African-American, French, Spanish, Indian, Anglo-Irish, and French-African Creole—into its rich culture. The festival attempts to present folk traditions through storytelling, music, food, and crafts.

A parallel children's festival in a large outdoor tent includes elements from the larger festival but with a youthful twist. Kids can hear seasoned storytellers spinning folk tales; make wooden toys, pottery, Indian toys, and blow guns; and try arrowhead chipping. Craftspeople demonstrate their arts for the children, African stilt walkers perform and naturalists conduct a safety program. Other activities include a teddy bear clinic and face painting.

More than fifty traditional artists and craftspeople are invited to the festival to demonstrate and sell their work, selected for its authenticity and quality (no macrame plant hangers and crudely tooled leather belts here). Some of the more unusual crafts on view are nail art, in which nails of different sizes pounded into wood create patterns and pictures; flint knapping; and Mississippi mud art, in which mud gathered from the Mississippi River is sculpted into dolls' heads and other objects.

And the food! Indulge in crawfish, roast pig, meat pies, Creole gumbo, and pralines—then dance it all off. There are dance areas with lessons in both Cajun and country dancing; band after band plays everything from the latest zydeco to the oldest Cajun waltz and hottest Texas two-step.

Natchitoches, the oldest permanently inhabited area in the Louisiana Purchase territory, still has many eighteenth-century buildings, as the town was not burned during the Civil War. Walk through the historic district of the town and admire the structures; many have elaborate grillwork. Fort Saint Jean Baptiste, located on the banks of the Cane River between downtown and the university, has been reconstructed to its original 1732 architectural design. The fort originally was built as an outpost to prevent Spaniards from advancing into French Louisiana. Cane River Boat tours and City Belle Trolley tours are great fun for families.

Cost: Adults $5 per show, children under twelve $3 per show. All-show booklets $16 per adult, $10 per child. Twenty-percent discount for pre-festival ticket purchases up to Thursday at noon.

Where to Stay

Natchitoches does not have many budget overnight accommodations. Its historic downtown is filled with beautiful bed-and-breakfast establishments, most of which do not accept children; we list a child-friendly one below. A Super 8 Motel at the edge of town has rooms for four people at $40 per night. Address: 801 Highway 3110 Bypass, Natchitoches, Louisiana 71457. Telephone: 318–352–1700.

The Holiday Inn charges $50 per night for rooms with two double beds; rollaways are $6 per night. Kids under eighteen stay free in their parents' room. Book by the end of May for the folk festival. Address: Highway 1 South Bypass, Natchitoches, Louisiana 71457. Telephone: 318–357– 8281.

The Breazeale House Bed and Breakfast is a splurge. Its third-floor area has two bedrooms, a den, and a bath. Rollaway beds can be added to accommodate larger families. One family can have the entire area for $120 per night, which includes a hearty breakfast and use of the swimming pool. The house is within walking distance of the historic downtown area and about a five-minute drive from the university. The host, a grandmother, enjoys having children stay with her in this magnificent historic home, which was featured in the movie *Steel Magnolias*. Book early. Address: 926 Washington, Natchitoches, Louisiana 71457. Telephone: 318–352– 5630.

Visitors who are unable to find a room in Natchitoches often stay in Shreveport or Alexandria, both about an hour away.

CARETTA (LOGGERHEAD SEA TURTLE) RESEARCH
PROJECT, WASSAW NATIONAL WILDLIFE REFUGE

Address: Savannah Science Museum, 4405 Paulsen Street, Savannah, Georgia 31405.
Telephone: 912–355–6705.

Teenagers fifteen and over and their parents can participate in a hands-on research and conservation program involving the threatened loggerhead sea turtle on the beaches of Wassaw National Wildlife Refuge near Savannah, Georgia. Watch these giant turtles lay their eggs on the wild beaches of Wassaw Island or assist hundreds of tiny hatchlings as they scramble frantically from nest to surf.

The Savannah Science Museum, in cooperation with the U.S. Fish and Wildlife Service, runs these week-long programs to learn more about the nesting habits of the loggerheads and to enhance their chances for survival. Volunteers during the first half of the season patrol Wassaw Island's six miles of beaches looking for female loggerheads as they crawl out of the sea to nest. They tag the turtles, measure their size and path, and help protect the nests as needed. During the hatching season (usually late July into September), volunteers help escort hatchlings down the beach and into the water and record data on any unhatched eggs remaining in the

nests. Off duty, there are opportunities to hike, birdwatch, read, or just relax on the pristine beaches of this sea island, kept in its near-original state.
Season: Mid-May through mid-September.
Requirements: Participants must be at least fifteen and in good health, since the program involves walking two to three miles each night. Most important is a good mental attitude, as you'll be experiencing heat, humidity, occasional insects, and perhaps a rainstorm or two. No more than nine people are on a team each week.
Accommodations: Two small dorm-style cabins in the center of the island have limited electricity and shared housekeeping duties. Dinner is prepared by team members and eaten together; other meals are prepared on your own in the kitchen/dining area.
Cost: One week $400 per person for teams working the first half of the summer, $355 for teams working the second half of the summer. Rates include food, housing, training, and transportation to and from the island (you leave from the Savannah Science Museum).

OKEFENOKEE SWAMP EXPLORATION

Address: 711 Sandtown Road, Savannah, Georgia 31410-1019.
Telephone: 912–897–5108.

The Okefenokee National Wildlife Refuge's vast watery wilderness is teeming with wildlife and vegetation. Three- and four-day educational tours of the swamp are operated by Wilderness Southeast, a nonprofit "school of the outdoors." The Okefenokee Cabin/Canoe Program, suited to children age eight and up, allows families to explore the swamp by canoe and return each evening to a cozy cabin with air-conditioning, showers, and full kitchens. During the day observe basking alligators, wading birds, musk turtles, songbirds, life under the lily pad, and a once-thriving logging town on a small island. A packed lunch is eaten along the way. After a dinner break back at the cabins, an evening program might involve a short hike into the swamp with flashlights to search for wolf spiders, whose eyes flash brilliant green when light hits them. The program runs in the spring and fall. Wilderness Southeast offers other high-quality programs for families and adults.
Accommodations: Cabins at Stephen Foster State Park (for more information about the park, see page 182). Food is ample, healthy, and delicious and is prepared by the staff with help from participants. Meals are taken together. Small families might share a cabin; families of four or more usually have their own cabins.
Cost: Four-day programs, including meals, instruction, equipment, and accommodations, adults $375. Three-day programs, adults $325. Fifteen-

percent discount for children accompanied by one parent, 25-percent discount if accompanied by two parents. Participants can meet the naturalist guides at the park or leave with the staff from Savannah.

JOHN C. CAMPBELL FOLK SCHOOL

Address: Route 1, Box 14-A, Brasstown, North Carolina (seven miles east of Murphy).
Telephone: 800–562–2440; 704–837–2775.

The Little Middle Folk School of this excellent school of traditional crafts, music, dance, and folklore is offered just one week each summer, usually the last week of June. Children six to sixteen can take up to four classes, which are divided by age group. Many participants are from the Brasstown area, but a number of others come with parents who take courses that same week or who explore the area while the kids are occupied. Classes offered in the past have included mask making, pottery, watercolor, woodcarving, folk dance, folk tales, and outdoor adventure. Hundreds of classes for parents are offered throughout the summer, including papermaking, quilting, wood carving, basketry, Appalachian music, ceramics, and Navajo weaving. A Labor Day Family Music and Dance Weekend features programs that include traditional American squares, contras, circles, playparty games, and workshops for the whole family. Performances and dances take place throughout the week.

The 365-acre campus, in a beautiful mountain setting, has fully equipped studios, a hardwood dance floor, a nature trail, a crafts shop, and rustic lodgings. It is modeled after the Danish folk school concept of learning through the "living word," or personal exposure to the teacher, instead of through books, lectures, examinations, or grades.

Accommodations: Some housing is in dormitories and some in old residences on campus. One of the most beautiful is a native fieldstone house from the 1920s that has been renovated and modernized inside. Older rooms and rooms with shared baths are least expensive, and some of the rooms can accommodate three, four, or five people. All linens are provided. Meals are taken together in a dining hall; when the bell rings, it's chow time. The food is traditional farm-style. A campground with full hookups and hot showers is available.

Cost: Little Middle Folk School tuition $85 plus $6 materials fee; less for residents of the surrounding counties. Cost for adult classes averages $200 per week. Little Middle Folk School children's classes fill especially quickly, so register early. Extra materials fees for some classes.

Dorm room with four to five twin beds $175 per person for five nights, room and board. Campground prices do not include meals and are for two persons per site: $40 per five nights, meal packages $90 per five-day week.

AUGUSTA HERITAGE CENTER

**Address: Davis and Elkins College, 100 Sycamore Street, Elkins, West Virginia 26241-3996.
Telephone: 304–636–1903.**

A week at Augusta involves almost all of the senses: the sounds of old-time fiddle tunes, voices raised in four-part harmony, feet dancing an Irish jig or an Appalachian flatfoot on a wooden dance floor; the sight of African masks, traditional paper-cut silhouettes, and sparks flying from a blacksmith's anvil; and the smells and tastes of herbs collected in West Virginia's woods and waters, fresh mountain air, and spicy Cajun cooking. The center is well respected for its exceptional adult summer workshop program, dedicated to passing on the values and crafts of the early Appalachian settlers. A Folk Arts for Kids Program offers a five-week series of classes in traditional music, folklore, dance, and crafts.

The children's program offers classes for boys and girls ages eight to thirteen, and students have opportunities to learn from leading musicians, dancers, storytellers, and craftspeople. Classes meet for six hours each day, with children joining their parents for meals, concerts, dances, and other evening events. Some special events for the children involve the parents as well. The subject matter varies by week. One week focuses on southern old-time music taught on a fiddle and other instruments. Those with no fiddle experience build a xylophone and learn to play tunes on it. Several other weeks introduce children to a number of Appalachian folk arts, including lively games and traditional play parties, storytelling, songs, clogging, and crafts. Another emphasizes cooking, crafts, outdoor games, riddles, ballads, Appalachian singing games, and African stories.

Workshops for adults are offered on all levels and truly provide something for everyone with ninety week-long classes in music, dance, crafts, and folklore. Pick from flat-pick guitar, zydeco accordion, gospel piano, hammered dulcimer, Appalachian literature, storytelling, log house construction, basketry, Mexican folk dance, or clogging, to name just a few. The center also sponsors a spring dulcimer week and an "Old Time Week" in Appalachian music.

Public concerts and spontaneous jam sessions fill the halls, fields, and parks with blues, bluegrass, swing, Cajun, Irish, Scottish, and old-time music. There's so much spontaneous music that one dormitory is a designated quiet zone; jam sessions often go on elsewhere all night long.

The center also produces recordings by traditional West Virginia musicians and has a successful statewide West Virginia Folk Arts Apprenticeship Program that pairs students with master artists in a one-on-one study of a traditional or ethnic folk art or craft.

Accommodations: Families with all members enrolled in a workshop or class stay in college residence halls that have two beds and a shared bath. Children can bring a sleeping bag and share a dorm room with two adults. Sheets and pillows are provided, but students must bring their own blankets and towels. Meals are served in the cafeteria and provide a wide choice of entrées, including meatless dishes and a salad bar at every meal. Three campgrounds are located within ten miles of the campus and there are several private motels nearby.

Cost: Children's and adult workshop tuition $230 to $250 per week. Room-and-board package $175 per person for a six-night week.

SHAKER VILLAGE

Address: 3500 Lexington Road, Harrodsburg, Kentucky 40330 (twenty-five miles southwest of Lexington).
Telephone: 606–734–5411.

Known for their spare, elegant furniture, the Shakers were a religious sect that settled in the United States in the early part of the nineteenth century. They were named for their writhing, shaking dance motions in their rituals, and they invented a surprising number of household items, including the flat broom, the circular saw, and the washing machine. Shaker Village, their westernmost settlement, was an experimental agricultural station first occupied in 1804. By the last half of the century the Shakers had faded away, but modern interest in their buildings and way of life has revived their heritage. Thirty buildings have been painstakingly restored in accurate historical detail, and visitors can walk at their own pace through the village to observe broom makers, spinners, weavers, quilters, and coopers hard at work. The rooms are filled with the simple and elegant Shaker furniture coveted by today's antique dealers.

On a tour of the village, guides in nineteenth-century dress will acquaint you with the Shaker beliefs and way of life. Demonstrations of broom making and other activities, such as sheep shearing, spinning, and weaving, help children make a connection between past and present. If you visit in April through November you also can watch daily demonstrations of Shaker domestic life, including candle dipping, butter churning, open-hearth cooking, and natural dyeing.

A dining room is open for breakfast, lunch, and dinner throughout the year; advance reservations are a good idea, especially for dinner. From Memorial Day through October a summer kitchen is open for lunch. A children's menu for kids under twelve is available in both places, and the food is delicious Kentucky country fare.

During late spring through early fall the Shaker Village sternwheeler runs daily excursions on the Kentucky River. One-hour boat rides are led by an interpreter playing the role of a nineteenth-century Kentucky River traveler, who talks about life on the river, the Civil War, and the Shakers.

Accommodations: Overnight lodging is available year-round in fifteen restored Shaker buildings. Furniture is spare and simple and there are no closets, only pegs along the walls of the rooms to hold clothes and other possessions. Candle sconces have been wired for electricity; otherwise the walls are completely bare. Rooms have air-conditioning, heat, and private indoor bathrooms. For spring, summer, and fall visits reserve accommodations at least two weeks in advance.

Cost: Entrance fees to the village, adults $8; children twelve to seventeen $4, six to eleven $2, under six free when accompanied by parent. Consider a combination ticket, which includes the boat ride: adults $11; kids twelve to seventeen $6, eleven and under $3. Horse and wagon rides offered throughout the day on weekends for 50 cents.

Room rates, double occupancy, $55 to $95 per night; children under seventeen stay free in their parents' room. Rollaway beds provided at no charge. No tipping allowed for services at Pleasant Hill.

Nearby: Hiking trails extend from the village, which is seven miles from Kentucky's oldest city, Harrodsburg. Fort Harrod State Park has an outdoor drama called the *Legend of Daniel Boone* in the summer. Kentucky Horse Park in Lexington is thirty miles away.

COLONIAL WILLIAMSBURG

Address: PO Box B, Williamsburg, Virginia 23187.
Telephone: 800–HISTORY.

Colonial Williamsburg is one of the oldest living history museums in the United States. Many Americans who once visited it as children return with their own children to tour its historic district and special exhibits that bring eighteenth-century Colonial America to life. Horse-drawn carriages clip-clop through the streets, militia drills and fife and drum corps march about, master artisans demonstrate their art, and costumed characters reflect upon the social, economic, and political climate. Five hundred buildings range from dank jail quarters and simple homes, shops, and taverns to elegant government buildings. After dark Colonial Williamsburg has candlelight concerts, eighteenth-century plays, games, and "gambols," an old form of entertainment.

Special children's activities are offered at various times throughout the year. You might happen upon fife and drum presentations, oxcart rides, or magic shows, or take a children's tour in which a child in period dress tells about becoming an apprentice to one of the master tradesmen in the village. Ticket holders receive a copy of the *Visitor's Companion*, listing weekly outdoor events and the midday cannon firing. Study a copy to plan your day effectively.

Be sure to take one of the hands-on tours, such as the "Young Colonials Tour" for kids nine to thirteen or the "Once Upon a Town" tour for ages three to eight. Kids get a special tour of the city, with stories, lunch, and many hands-on activities. Children participate in colonial crafts and play games such as shuffleboard, miniature golf, lawn bowling, and croquet. Tours operate June through early September, weather permitting, from 9 A.M. to 1 P.M. and 2 to 6 P.M.

The Young Apprentice Program for ten- to twelve-year-olds allows kids to become apprentices for a short time in carpentry, bricklaying, boot and shoe making, cooperage, or silversmithing.

Cost: The best value is the Patriots Pass, which is good for a year and includes admission to all major exhibits: adults $28, kids six to twelve $17, kids under six free. General admission tickets are good for two days but do not get visitors into all of the sights: adults $23, kids six to twelve $14. Evening concerts and dramas $8 to $10 for children and adults. All admission tickets include the use of the Colonial Williamsburg transportation system, a copy of the *Visitor's Companion*, and admission to the introductory film *Williamsburg, the Story of a Patriot*. Special children's tours, $10 per child; parents free when accompanied by a child.

Where to Stay

Colonial Williamsburg has a number of "official" hotels, the most economical of which is the Governor's Inn, three blocks from the restored area. Its room rates vary depending on season and how full the hotel happens to be when you call for the dates you want. Rooms with two double beds are $50 to $70 per night. Rollaways are available at no charge. Rates include a continental breakfast, use of the outdoor pool, and a shuttle to the restored area. Address: 506 North Henry Street, Williamsburg, Virginia 23185. Telephone: 804–229–1000.

Other options are two Econo Lodges, where children under eighteen stay free in their parents' room. Both are about a mile away from the historic area, and prices for double rooms range from $50 to $70 per night, depending on the season. Rollaways are $5, cribs are $3. The King George Econo Lodge has an exercise room, indoor and outdoor pool, restaurant, whirlpool, and hot tub. Address: 706 Bypass Road, Williamsburg, Virginia 23185. Telephone: 800–553–2666; 804–229–9230. The Mid-town Econo Lodge has an outdoor pool, playground, sauna, and exercise room. Address: 1408 Richmond Road, Williamsburg, Virginia 23185. Telephone: 800–553–2666; 804–229–2981.

A nearby Motel 6 has an outdoor pool and rooms with two double beds for $32 to $40 per night. Address: 3030 Richmond Road, Williamsburg, Virginia 23185. Telephone: 804–565–3433.

THE NORTHEAST

PENN STATE ALUMNI COLLEGE

Address: 409 Kellor Conference Center, Pennsylvania State University, University Park, Pennsylvania 16802-1304.
Telephone: 814–863–6106 (information on registration and children's programs); 814–863–1744 (program information).

You don't have to be a graduate of Penn State to attend this three-day academic, recreational, and social program. Adults choose from a variety of lectures, discussions, and hands-on activities, while children of all ages are entertained and educated in either a day camp, a sailing day camp, a sports camp, or a day-care center, depending on their age. Families stay in air-conditioned dorms or in a nearby hotel. Registration fee includes instructional costs, materials, several meals, and snacks.

Children under six are cared for in an off-campus day-care center. Six- to thirteen-year-olds can participate in Penn State's Stone Valley Recreational Day Camp. Children eight to sixteen can join a sailing day camp with van transportation and bag lunches provided. Teenagers can attend a sports camp with softball, ice hockey, diving, girls' lacrosse, tennis, boys' volleyball, and cheerleading.

Adult instruction is offered by university staff of the liberal arts and agriculture departments. Past sessions have included workshops on landscape architecture, demonstrations of sheep shearing and colt training, discussions on how to get your book published, and much more. Each day is divided into a morning and afternoon session, with several choices for each. In the evening families are free to explore the town or campus or join the group on a hay ride or in ice-cream making. Families arrive the afternoon before instruction begins for a dinner and leave after noon the day following the end of classes.

Season: The program usually takes place in mid-July.

Accommodations: Select from air-conditioned suites with two bedrooms and a bath or a hotel nearby. Accommodations fee includes breakfast and lunch.

Cost: Tuition $195 for Penn State alumni, $220 for nonmembers (which covers alumni association membership costs). Day care is $20 per day. Day camp is $81 per session, plus a $30 registration fee. Full-day sports camps are $375 per week. Dorm accommodations $15 per night for a double room plus meal ticket. Meal tickets, adults $35 (three breakfasts, three lunches, one brunch); children eleven and over $25, six to ten $19 (three breakfasts, three bag lunches); children two to five $6 (three breakfasts, lunch provided by day care program).

Special Features: Programs in the past have included hayrides, field trips to museums, discussion groups, clogging demonstrations, and moonlight canoe trips. In addition students can opt for extra recreational and educational activities (usually for a small extra fee) such as mountain bike tours and paper-cutting and climbing courses.

CHAUTAUQUA INSTITUTION SUMMER SCHOOL

Address: Schools Office, Box 1098, Chautauqua, New York 14722 (between Buffalo, New York, and Erie, Pennsylvania). Telephone: Late June through late August, 716–357–6234. Preseason and postseason, 716–357–6255.

This charming Victorian village offers stimulating instruction in fine and performing arts, education, recreation, and religion. Set on the shore of Chautauqua Lake in western New York State, the area is a national historic district and offers a broad selection of courses, a lecture series, Children's School, Boys' and Girls' Club, and a Youth Activities Center. More than 175 courses are offered for adults and children in subjects including amateur astronomy, storytelling, humor writing, tap dance, foreign language, and magicianship. Most classes last one week and range in length from one to three hours, so you can take more than one class if you wish. There is a children's school for two-and-a-half- to six-year-olds, and a boys' and girls' club that acts as a day camp with a full program of recreational interests for six- to fifteen-year-olds. Activities include swimming, sailing, canoeing, arts and crafts, drama, music, and games. There are special youth classes, such as the Youth Artists Program. The back of each catalog lists classes best suited for kids. After class, head to the beach or take a swim in Chautauqua Lake.

Season: Nine weeks in summer.

Special Features: Special scholarship for families with demonstrated need.

Cost: Families attending the Chautauqua Institution have three different costs: the Gate (grounds admission) pass, tuition, and lodging. Everyone must buy a Gate ticket for admission into the institution. It allows access to all recreational facilities, beaches, concerts, lectures, and programs (separate tickets must be purchased for opera and theater performances). One-week gate ticket, adults $130; children ages thirteen to seventeen $52, twelve and under free. You also can buy admission to the grounds by the day or evening for concerts by such artists as Smokey Robinson and the Chautauqua Symphony Orchestra staged in an open-air amphitheater. Recreational facilities at your disposal include four beaches, a sports club with boat rental, softball fields, shuffleboard, badminton, horseshoes, volleyball, and more.

Course fees vary considerably. Five-day course, one to three hours per day, $40 to $60. Children's School $65 per week, less for a second child. Boys' and Girls' Club $85 per week, less for second child. Youth Activities Center participation fee $7 per week.

Where to Stay

Participants arrange their own accommodations. Choose from a wide variety of hotels, inns, guests houses, rooms, condominium rentals, houses, and apartments to rent. Ask the summer school office to send you an accommodations directory, which lists all suitable accommodations located at or near the institution. The Chautauqua Family Campground and Cabins has campsites and cabins near the lake within walking distance of the institute. Families can save on accommodations by camping, but the cabins are not substantially less expensive than some apartment rentals.

Accommodation costs vary, and can cost anywhere from $550 per week for a family of four to over $2000. Apartments are generally the best deal for a single family staying a week (for information, call 716–753–2212) and house rentals the best arrangement for two families that want to stay together. Some of the accommodations in Chautauqua have vacation packages that combine overnight lodging and Gate tickets. These can provide a savings for those staying just a few days; ask for information about vacation packages.

NATIONAL BASEBALL HALL OF FAME AND MUSEUM

Address: PO Box 590, Cooperstown, New York 13326.
Telephone: 607–547–9988.

Starting with the entrance turnstile, the green carpet of artificial turf, and the life-size carved wooden statues of Babe Ruth and Ted Williams at the door, this four-floor museum of baseball memorabilia has a distinct ballpark flavor. The displays and exhibits pay tribute to the greatest heroes of America's most beloved sport. For sheer atmosphere and nostalgia, top prize goes to the Ballparks Room, with actual dugout benches, grandstand seats, and turnstiles from such places as Forbes Field, Crosley Field, and the Polo Grounds, and the lockers that once belonged to Joe Dimaggio, Mickey Mantle, Lou Gehrig, and Hank Aaron.

Rare old photos and displays of artifacts trace the origin of the game, and an exhibit called Baseball Today showcases the highlights and heroes of the last five years to give young baseball fans a frame of reference. The stark Hall of Fame Gallery is filled with simple bronze plaques honoring the players who have been selected for their talent and dedication to the sport.

Statistics nuts can spend hours playing with the computers in the IBM Hall of Fame Sports Gallery. A complete statistical and audiovisual history of each inductee is available via touch-screen technology.

Other highlights include a two-hundred-seat movie theater, television monitors featuring continuous showings of Abbott and Costello's classic parody, "Who's on First?," a display of historic baseball cards, and The Great Moments exhibit, with a carefully selected montage of the most memorable events in the game's history.

Cost: Adults $6; children seven to fifteen $2.50, under seven free. Combination tickets for the Farmers Museum and the James Fenimore Cooper House (see below) are available.

Nearby: The lovely village of Cooperstown, named for American novelist James Fenimore Cooper, is at the foot of Otsego Lake, with beautifully preserved historic houses lining the streets. Two other museums are worthy of a visit: the James Fenimore Cooper House contains an excellent collection of American folk art. The Farmers Museum and Village has displays on rural life in America and a working village full of old-time blacksmiths, weavers, and printers. Three-way tickets can be purchased for the Hall of Fame, the Farmers Museum, and the James Fenimore Cooper House. Boat rides on the lake leave from a dock about two blocks from the Hall of Fame. The U.S. Soccer Hall of Fame is thirty minutes away, in Oneonta.

Where to Stay
Fieldstone Farm (see page 41).

MYSTIC SEAPORT MUSEUM

Address: 50 Greenmanville Avenue, Mystic, Connecticut 06355-0990. Telephone: 203-572-0711.

When wooden shipbuilding was at its peak in the mid-nineteenth century, Mystic produced some of the fastest clipper ships around. Today Mystic is a seventeen-acre indoor and outdoor museum of U.S. maritime history. Kids can climb aboard its historic vessels, including the *Charles W. Morgan,* the last wooden whaling ship in America; a full-rigged training ship built in 1882; and the wooden steamboat *Sabino.* They can interact with friendly interpreters in period dress and working craftsmen who forge iron, carve figureheads, and make barrels. Chantey singers, cooking on a fireplace hearth, and on-site boat building add to the atmosphere.

Families should make sure to stop at the Children's Museum, where kids can play with an extensive collection of nineteenth-century replica toys and games. At the boat-building area kids can build and launch their own boats, and a special area set aside for children under seven contains replicas of nineteenth-century clothes for dress-up play.

The busy seaport village gives visitors an impression of a historic sea-faring community. Kids also will particularly enjoy the Buckingham House, which features demonstrations of fireplace cooking, the Shipsmith iron-working demonstration, the Mystic Press printing demonstration, and the Shipcarver's Shop, with woodcarving demonstrations.

From mid-May through mid-October, the 1908 *Sabino* takes passengers on short Mystic River cruises for an extra fee. Passengers learn about the history of the boat and the Mystic River from costumed crew members.

If your kids start to get whiney, take them to the blubbering room on whaleship *Morgan*'s lower deck. They'll be amazed at the tiny berths and confining quarters where up to twenty-two sailors lived with very little light or ventilation.

An enticing array of high-quality annual events await visitors throughout the year. Best for kids are the Presidents' Birthday Party in February, with scavenger hunts, crafts, and family programs that focus on U.S. presidents and their families; the Horse and Carriage weekend in July; and the week after Christmas, when special activities, games, crafts, and entertainment are arranged for families.

Season: Year-round.

Cost: Adults $14.50, children six to fifteen $8.75, kids under six free.

Where to Stay

Many motels and inns are within walking distance of Mystic, most with rates of over $75 for a double room. Howard Johnson's has rooms with two double beds for $73 per night, and kids under eighteen stay free in their parents' room. Address: 179 Greenmanvillle Avenue, Mystic, Connecticut 06355. Telephone: 800–654–2000; 203–536–2654.

Winterbrook Farm, described on page 302, is about 90 minutes away from Mystic.

OLD STURBRIDGE VILLAGE

Address: 1 Sturbridge Village Road, Sturbridge, Massachusetts 01566-0200.
Telephone: 508–347–3362.

Massachusetts's Old Sturbridge Village is a re-creation of an 1830s New England rural community. About an hour west of Boston, it features more than forty historic buildings, a working farm, sawmill, covered bridge, and special programs. A staff of working artisans explain how everyday life was lived—shoemakers stitch shoes, tinsmiths decorate ornate lanterns, and blacksmiths form farm implements. Children can play historic games on the common, such as graces, hoops, and cup and ball. Daily during the summer and at scheduled times throughout the year, children can participate in apple cider pressing, stenciling, block printing, and other activities at no extra charge. An old-fashioned schoolhouse is complete with schoolmaster who is known to ask visiting students to read or recite.

Many events of special interest to families are scheduled during the summer. A family weekend the third week in June kicks off the summer with entertainment, a toy hot-air balloon flight, musket firing, music with dancing dolls, singing, and dancing. The Fourth of July is a lively affair with people in period dress, a parade, a reading of the Declaration of Independence, picnicking on the common, and live music. There is a haying contest in July, a summer garden day in early August, and other special programs designed for children.

The price of admission includes a second consecutive day free, so families can take their time and participate in all of the activities that interest them.

Season: Year-round.

Cost: Adults $15, children six to fourteen $7, kids under six free.

Where to Stay

Winterbrook Farm is a bed and breakfast that welcomes children. Youngsters can tag along while their hosts feed the sheep, pigs, goat, and chickens. Three-person rooms are $55 per night; additional cot $5. Double rooms are $40 per night. Rates include a full breakfast. In addition to raising sheep, the farm has a pick-your-own blueberry business in summer and a maple syrup business in March. Mystic Seaport (see pages 300–301) is about ninety minutes away. Address: 116 Beffa Road, Stafford Springs, Connecticut 06076. Telephone: 203–684–2124.

Deer Meadow Farm Bed and Breakfast, ten minutes away from Old Sturbridge Village, was built in 1780 and has since been restored and modernized. Double rooms are $45, with rollaway beds $10 additional. Children under five are not accepted. The farm specializes in blueberries and raspberries and is open to guests from May to October. Address: RFD 1, Bragg Road, West Brookfield, Massachusetts 01585. Telephone: 413–436–7129.

The family-oriented Green Acres Motel sits back from the road about a mile and a quarter from Old Sturbridge Village on six wooded acres. Four units have fully equipped kitchenettes. Other features include a swimming pool, basketball, horseshoes, volleyball, and a playground. Double rooms are $65 per night; rooms with kitchenettes are $75 per night. Rollaway beds are $10 per night; children under twelve stay free in their parents' room. Address: 2 Shepherd Road, Sturbridge, Massachusetts 01566 (street address); PO Box 153, Sturbridge, Massachusetts 01566 (mailing address). Telephone 508–347–3402.

PLIMOTH PLANTATION

Address: Plimoth Plantation, PO Box 1620, Plymouth, Massachusetts 02362.
Telephone: 508–746–1622.

Children will get a blank stare if they ask a costumed interpreter at Plimoth Plantation about anything having to do with modern life, or for that matter, of life past 1726. Interpreters speak in seventeenth-century dialects. This living museum of seventeenth-century New England harkens back to the time of the Colonists who settled in New England and of the Native Americans they encountered. Buildings in a recreated pilgrim village, where people assume the roles of the town's residents, contain accurate historical reproductions of household objects, and visitors are encouraged to touch just about anything they want. The town militia practices its drills twice each day around the village, women cook over an open-hearth fire, farmers milk cows, and there are baby animals to tend in the spring.

Next to the village is a Wampanoag Indian homesite, where interpreters in Indian period dress go about their business. Children can ask them questions about their lives; in fact, the more the children ask, the more they will get out of their visit.

A replica of the *Mayflower* on the Plymouth waterfront near Plymouth Rock, about two miles away, is also part of the museum. A trolley runs back and forth between them. The ship is set up as it might have been in 1621, just a few days before it set sail for its return voyage to England.

Children's activities are scheduled throughout the year, with a heavier concentration during the summer months. Hour-long nature walks for children in July and August explore the flora and fauna of the area with a staff naturalist. Children might discover where the deer run, listen for swans, and search for the burrow of a woodchuck. Other activities might include writing with quill and ink, dressing like a pilgrim in doublets and breeches, and learning to play Native American games. Older kids will like the games-making workshop, archaeological programs, and navigational and map-making workshops. Before you go, request a calendar of events so you can plan to visit when there are special programs for your kids.

The grounds house a cafeteria, picnic area, bake shop, gift shops, and a crafts center with artisans at work. The gift shops sell some reproductions of seventeenth-century children's games, such as one called "The Voyage of the Mayflower," and other children's books and toys.

Season: April through November.

Cost: Adult admission $18.50; children under twelve $11, under four free. Trolley $3.50 per person for all-day ticket. If you call in advance and become a member (family membership $60) you'll get free family admission, various discounts, and publications. Note that you cannot buy the family membership at door; the membership card will be mailed to you when you join.

Accommodations: Plimoth Plantation is twenty minutes from Cape Cod; see page 251 for accommodation ideas on the Cape.

COUNTRY DANCE AND SONG SOCIETY'S FAMILY WEEK

Address: 17 New South Street, Northampton, Massachusetts 01060.
Telephone: 413–584–9913.

The Country Dance and Song Society is a nationwide association of people who enjoy traditional, historical, and contemporary American and English folk dance, song, and instrumental music. Families at two camps—one in Massachusetts, one in West Virginia—enjoy dancing, traditional crafts, singing, swimming, storytelling, and more during week-long family programs.

Pinewoods Camp, in the woodlands near Plymouth, Massachusetts, has cozy cabins nestled under the pines near lakes. The largest lake is a mile long, and its clear blue water is suitable for swimming and canoeing. Four dance pavilions are set in the pine forest. Pinewoods sets aside two weeks of the year especially for families.

Buffalo Gap Camp, near Capon Bridge, West Virginia, is located on two hundred acres of a forested mountainside, part of which has been cleared for the camp's buildings. The property has a two-acre lake with swimming, a slide, and a diving board, swimming pool, and enormous dance pavilions. Housing is in bunk rooms, each of which holds about twelve people.

The programs at both camps follow the same format, combining music, dance, crafts, songs, and storytelling for children only as well as for families together. Two classes per day are arranged by age group and another class is arranged by interest. Children age four and up enjoy singing games and circle dances. For older children, the program includes more sword dance, contras, and English country dance. Crafts classes for kids offer wood carving, quilting, making marble mazes, and other activities.

Accommodations: Small bunk rooms or cabins have private baths or bathrooms nearby. Two families can be housed together in one bunk room. Families with very young children are housed in one building with double rooms. Meals are served in a dining hall and everyone pitches in with the work for perhaps a half hour each day.

Special Features: Kids three to twelve have daily classes of their own, while teenagers and adults can choose among classes in English country dance, square dance, clogging, carving, dance band, storytelling, and more. Twice a day the entire group gathers for singing, stories, and dancing.

Cost: Adults $415 to $455 per week; children thirteen to seventeen $383, seven to twelve $305, four to six $239, two and three $152, under two $20. Rates include lodging, food, tuition, and all activities. A special campers' week, in which the participants develop the program, costs less: adults $290; children thirteen to seventeen $255, seven to twelve $203, four to six $160, two and three $103, under two $20.

APPALACHIAN MOUNTAIN CLUB'S FAMILY EDUCATION PROGRAMS

Address: 5 Joy Street, Boston, Massachusetts 02108 (programs take place in New Hampshire and the Catskill Mountains). Telephone: 617–523–0636.

The Appalachian Mountain Club conducts top-quality workshops for adults and excellent family education programs for parents and children and grandparents and grandchildren. Sessions over a full weekend include family backpacking trips and workshops such as "Discovering the Natural World with Children." Shorter weekend morning programs are for families with children age six and up and include such topics as life in a stream and pond, the world of insects, and wildflowers, wild animals, and the wilderness. Children also are welcome on any of the club's easier guided hikes, a series that takes beginning and experienced hikers on a guided introduction to the flora, fauna, geology, and history of the White Mountains in New Hampshire.

Accommodations: Some of the weekend workshops are based at Valley View Lodge in the heart of the Catskills' high peaks region. The lodge has double rooms, shared baths, and dining and living rooms. Rates include all-you-can-eat meals.

Cost: Weekend sessions include lodging, meals, and instruction: Adults $92 to $150, kids twelve and under $41 to $75. Morning programs $5 or $7 per program. Discounts for club members (family membership $65 per year).

APPALACHIAN MOUNTAIN CLUB'S HUT-TO-HUT HIKES

Address: 5 Joy Street, Boston, Massachusetts 02108 (hikes take place in New Hampshire). Telephone: 617–523–0636 (AMC main number); 603–466–2727 (reservations).

The Appalachian Mountain Club operates eight alpine huts in New Hampshire, each a day's hike apart along the Appalachian Trail. Hikes to three of the huts—Zealand Falls, Lonesome Lake, and Carter Notch—are well within the ability of beginning hikers. The hut-to-hut hikes open the overnight hiking experience to families that otherwise would need to pack a tent, stove, cooking gear, and food. The huts provide comfortable shelter and fresh, hot dinner and breakfast. Hikers bring sheets or a sleeping bag, lunch, snacks, and other personal gear.

Lonesome Lake Hut, which stands in a birch and balsam forest, has lake swimming and a nearby beaver colony. Lonesome is the most popular family hiking destination because the hike is short (1.7 miles) and it has a refreshing lake. Individual bunk rooms for four, six, or eight people can be reserved for a family group.

Zealand Falls Hut is at the eastern edge of the Pemigewasset Wilderness along Whitewall Brook. The cascading waters and crystal-clear pools are popular swimming spots for families. Most hikers begin at a trailhead 2.7 miles away for an easy hike in. The hut accommodates a total of thirty-six people in twin bunk rooms.

Carter Notch Hut is a slightly longer hike, but it's popular with families whose kids can handle 3.8 miles up a gentle, steady grade. The hut is on a rise between two swimmable ponds. Separate twin bunkhouses with rooms for four or six each accommodate forty people.

Season: June through August.

Cost: Overnight lodging, breakfast, and dinner, adults $50, children $24 per night. The price is lower if you reserve midweek in June and is discounted further for club members. Rates for lodging and breakfast only, or lodging and dinner only, are available. Family membership in the Appalachian Mountain Club, $65 per year, entitles you to discounts for all AMC lodges, huts, and education programs. The huts are most popular on weekends and in July and August. Lower rates available in June, when fewer people are on the trails.

NATURE PROGRAMS AT PINKHAM NOTCH

Address: Box 298, Gorham, New Hampshire 03581.
Telephone: 603–466–2721.

Also run by the Appalachian Mountain Club, the Pinkham Notch nature programs for families vary in length from a few hours to all day. Topics change according to season but might include animal tracking, maple sugaring, birds and flowers, how nature prepares for winter, and off-trail navigation. The club will send you a listing of current programs on request. Make reservations to stay overnight at Pinkham Notch when you book the nature program.

Season: Year-round.

Accommodations: Pinkham Notch Lodge can accommodate one hundred overnight guests in two, three, and four-bunk rooms. Hearty meals are served for breakfast and dinner, and trail lunches can be purchased.

Cost: Program fees $5 to $7 for adults, free for kids under twelve. Accommodation fees include breakfast and dinner. Members, adults $38, children twelve and under $20; nonmembers, adults $44, children twelve and under $26.

FLETCHER FARM SCHOOL FOR THE ARTS AND CRAFTS

Address: RR 1, Box 1041, Ludlow, Vermont 05149.
Telephone: 802–228–8770 (summer), 802–247–3847 (winter).

"Don't forget your sneakers and a smile" are the words of advice to youngsters taking the arts, crafts, and dance classes at the Fletcher Farm School. Teachers strive to keep their young students comfortable and happy as they work on drawing, painting, wood carving, or dancing skills. Adults also can take week-long classes, on basketry, early American decoration, stained glass, paper cutting, carousel carving, or rug hooking, to name a few. Children ages six to sixteen are in class from 10 A.M. to 2 P.M. Parents who don't want to take a class can enjoy the area's great beauty, golf courses, nearby lakes, and quaint villages. The school is operated by the Society of Vermont Craftsmen, a nonprofit organization whose facility is on the site of a two-hundred-year-old farm in the Green Mountains of Vermont.

Cost: Tuition for five-day programs $80 to $100 for children's classes, $80 to $160 for adult classes. Some classes also charge a materials and lab fee.

Where to Stay

Adults taking classes can stay on the grounds of the farm school, but there are no accommodations available on the grounds for families. Camping is two miles down the road at the Hideaway Campgrounds (802–228–7871). Another option is to rent a vacation home or condominium on Lake Rescue or Echo Lake. Contact Vermont Rentals (800–628–0558; 802–259–2196) for a catalog of listings.

The Inn Towne Motel, in the center of the village of Ludlow, offers discounts to farm school students and has excellent prices and a pool but little character. Some units have kitchenettes. Address: 112 Main Street (Route 103), Ludlow, Vermont 05149. Telephone: 800–458–2059; 802–228–8884.

The Trojan Horse AYH Hostel has several inexpensive family rooms with three bunks; other rooms are dorm-style. It's open twenty-four hours, and guests have kitchen privileges. Across the street is a park with stream swimming, basketball, tennis, and playground. Canoes can be rented from the hostel for $15 per day, and bikes can be rented in town. AYH members pay $11 per night, and kids under age fourteen get a discount. Reserve several months in advance. Address: 44 Andover Street, Ludlow, Vermont 05419. Telephone: 802–228–5244.

STATE PARK CABINS AND RESORTS

*O*ne of the best-kept vacation secrets is that state parks have some of the lowest-priced resorts and cabins in the United States. Established in areas of great natural beauty, state parks range from areas with towering mountain peaks and crystalline lakes to soft, rolling green hills, vast prairies, harsh desert landscapes, and sites of historical significance. Every state in the union has parks that are open to the public and more than half offer remarkably low-priced cabin accommodations and resort facilities.

While private resorts might have several hundred scenic acres, most state parks are located on thousands of acres of unspoiled wilderness, usually selected for their breathtaking scenery. Many are located on lakes, rivers, and seashores, offering a wide selection of reasonably priced recreational activities. At the very least you can expect to find swimming, boating, or excellent hiking trails. And at the most state park resorts feature tennis, golf, boating, lawn games, nature centers, and horseback riding, among other activities.

Many of the first state parks were developed in the 1930s through the efforts of the Civilian Conservation Corps (CCC), one of Franklin Delano Roosevelt's most successful New Deal programs. Stone and log lodges and cabins contain the legacy of a conservation program that did much to preserve the natural and historical treasures of many states in the nation. Other, newer parks have since been developed, with up-to-date lodging and modern amenities.

All states will provide you with information on their state park accommodations, either through their tourist office or the state park office. Generally the parks are busiest on summer weekends and holidays and throughout the months of July and August. Some parks start taking reservations as early as a year in advance, others accept reservations no more than three months in advance. Because state park cabins and resorts are such a bargain, they are popular and fill up quickly. Cancellations occur, however, so there's always a chance of getting in. Do your homework and make sure you know the reservation system required by each state.

ALABAMA

Address: Alabama Department of Conservation and Natural Resources, Division of State Parks, 64 North Union Street, Montgomery, Alabama 36130.

Telephone: 800–ALA–PARK (reservations); 205–242–3333.

Stay in lakeview cottages, ridge-top chalets, beachside resorts, and tasteful lodges throughout the Alabama state park system. Eleven of the parks have family cottages and six have hotel units or resort lodges. All hotel and cabin guests have free lake fishing, boat launching, use of the swimming pool and beach areas, and tennis courts. Six of the parks have golf courses, two have full-service marinas, and most have hiking, nature trails, tennis and basketball courts, and playgrounds.

Gulf State Park, set between the Gulf of Mexico and the shores of Lake Shelby, is profiled on pages 34–35.

Accommodations: Older, rustic cabins have simple furnishings, fully equipped kitchens, heat, air-conditioning, and linens. Modern cabins are more comfortably furnished and have linens, air-conditioning, and more elaborately equipped kitchens. A few have fireplaces. Certain parks require a one-week minimum stay during the summer.

Cost: Rate ranges have seasonal adjustments, and the lowest and highest rates quoted here may vary, but not by much. Be sure to inquire about special getaway and golf vacation packages that are offered from time to time. Rates also vary from park to park. Rustic cabins $40 to $80 per night. Modern cabins $50 to $92 per night, depending on number of people and time of year.

ARKANSAS

Address: Division of State Parks, Arkansas Department of Parks and Tourism, One Capitol Mall, Little Rock, Arkansas 72201.
Telephone: 501–682–1191.
Nine state parks have cabins and four have lodges where children under age twelve stay free with an adult. Most parks present special guided hikes, lake tours, and historic demonstrations during the summer. The state's premier resort park is Degray Lake Resort State Park, on the north shore of a 13,800-acre fishing and water sports lake. Its full-service marina, golf course, pool, tennis courts, bike rentals, and many special events make it a popular destination. Families can stay in comfortable lodge rooms or in houseboats along the lake. Another family favorite, Lake Ouachita State Park, is situated at Lake Ouachita's eastern tip. Historic A-frame cabins overlook the lake, which offers swimming, water-skiing, scuba diving, boating, and fishing for bream, crappie, catfish, and trout. Arkansas's first state park, Petit Jean, is described in detail on pages 179–180, and an Ozark Folk Center listing is on pages 286–287.
Accommodations: Many of the one-, two-, and three-bedroom cabins have fireplaces, and nearly all have fully equipped kitchens. A few parks have "Rent-A-Camps" outfitted with tents, coolers, lanterns, and other camping gear, perfect for those who want an outdoor experience without having to bring all the equipment with them.
Cost: Cabins $45 to $70 per night. Each additional person (over twelve years) $5 per night in lodge rooms and cabins. Rent-A-Camps $21 per night. Advance reservations necessary; call or write the individual park. Reservations for April through October accepted beginning January 1 of the same year. Winter lodgings $10 lower than regular rates, except for special events periods.

FLORIDA

Address: Department of Natural Resources, 3900 Commonwealth Boulevard, Mail Station 500, Tallahassee, Florida 32399-3000.
Telephone: For a free state parks guide, 904–488–9872; Department of Natural Resources, 904–488–7326.
Eight of Florida's state parks have cabins, ranging from primitive to deluxe. Most offer swimming, hiking, and naturalist programs such as guided walks or campfire talks. Blue Springs State Park, near the St. Johns River, has a spring-fed water system for wonderful swimming and can-

oeing, and is one of the few natural manatee habitats in the United States. We profile another park, Port St. Joe, on page 245.

Accommodations: Primitive cabins have electricity, bunk beds, and a shared bathhouse. Other cabins all have linens and kitchens and range from basic to very modern and comfortably appointed.

Cost: Primitive cabins $20 to $25 per night, other prices vary by park. Most have cabins that cost $50 per night; several also have cabins for $55 to $110 per night, depending on degree of luxury and size.

GEORGIA

Address: Georgia State Parks Office, 205 Butler Street, Atlanta, Georgia 30334.

Telephone: 404–656–3530.

Twenty-four of Georgia's parks have cottages and lodges, all situated to provide scenic views of the lakes, mountains, valleys, and other spectacular natural riches in the state's park system. All cottages have fully equipped kitchens and many have porches and decks overlooking these vistas. For example, Cloudland Canyon State Park straddles a deep canyon cut into the mountains. At the bottom of the canyon are waterfalls accessible by hiking trails and a swimming pool and tennis courts for guests. Red Top Mountain State Park is about forty minutes from Atlanta on a two-thousand-acre peninsula in the middle of Lake Allatoona. Cottages border the lake; there is also a swimming beach, tennis courts, lodge and restaurant, seven-mile nature trail, and marina with boat rentals, including houseboats.

Detailed descriptions of Crooked River State Park Cabins in St. Marys and Roosevelt State Park on pages 238 and 31–32.

Accommodations: One-, two-, and three-bedroom cabins have complete kitchens and linens. All cottages have heat, and most have air-conditioning. Lodge rooms are available in five state parks.

Cost: Cottages $40 to $75 per night, depending on size and time of week. During summer months, reservations accepted by the week only. Maximum stay fourteen days. Reservations can be made up to eleven months in advance, but often there are last-minute cancellations.

HAWAII

Address: Division of State Parks, 75 Aupuni Street, PO Box 936, Hilo, Hawaii 96721.
Telephone: 808–882–1095.
With warm tropical waters, lush vegetation, and breathtaking scenery, Hawaii is a favorite vacation spot year-round. Several types of state-run accommodations on the islands of Hawaii and Maui offer the best-priced lodging anywhere in the island chain. Permits are granted for a maximum visit of five days. See page 198 for a description of the cabins in Hana, Maui.

On the big island of Hawaii, Mauna Kea State Recreation Area has seven housekeeping cabins for families. Each duplex cabin can accommodate up to six people, and all household equipment and bedding is provided.

Cost: Kids under twelve half the adult rate. Six people $5 per person per day, four people $6 per person per day. Two other sites, Pohakuloa and Kalopa, have cabins that accommodate up to eight people each. Rates vary depending on the number of people in the group: one person $8 per night; eight people $3.50 per person per night, $2.50 per person per night from the third night on. Hapuna Beach has six primitive camping shelters with bunks (guests bring their own air mattresses and sleeping bags) that accommodate up to four, cooking facilities, and central bathhouse. A flat rate of $7 per shelter is charged.

ILLINOIS

Address: Department of Conservation, Division of Land Management, 524 South Second Street, Springfield, Illinois 62701-1787.
Telephone: 217–782–7454; 217–782–6752.
Eight state parks have resorts with historic lodges, many of which were built in the 1930s and feature hand-hewn beams and rock fireplaces. All have been carefully restored. A number of the resorts have cabins on the grounds, and all have enough recreational opportunities to keep any family busy.

Once a popular pirate roost and now a popular state park, Cave-in Rock State Park Resort is near a bluff overlooking the Ohio River in the Shawnee National Forest. Cabin guests can enjoy the panoramic views that the pirates used. It has four duplex guest houses with eight suites, each with a private deck overlooking the river. A family-style restaurant serves breakfast, lunch, and dinner, featuring such specialties as southern fried catfish and homemade desserts. Extensive hiking trails, playgrounds, boating, and fishing are out the front door. Another family favorite, Starved Rock Park, has a historic lodge, canoe rentals, and other water sports on the Illinois River, and two types of cabins to rent. A spectacular waterfall within hiking distance of the lodge is especially dramatic when it freezes in winter.

Accommodations: Lodge rooms usually have one or two double or king-size beds and sofabeds. Cabins vary in size and do not always have kitchens. Deluxe cabins have fireplaces. Rollaway beds and cribs are available at most parks.

Cost: Summer rates (March through November) are higher: double rooms $50 to $65 per night, each additional person $5 per night. In winter, $44 to $55 per night. Children twelve and under stay free in their parents' room.

INDIANA

Address: Indiana Division of State Parks, Indiana Department of Natural Resources, 402 West Washington Street, Room 298, Indianapolis, Indiana 46204.

Telephone: 800–622–4931; 317–232–4124.

Indiana's eight state parks with inexpensive housekeeping cabins can be found along lakes, creeks, reservoirs, and hillsides. Most offer boating, swimming, fishing, hiking, and naturalist programs. Several have horseback riding rental, bike trails, and cross-country skiing. They begin taking reservations exactly one year in advance. Weekly reservations are required in June, July, and August.

See descriptions of Pokagon Resort Park on Lake James and Lincoln State Park on pages 26–27, and 283–284, respectively.

Accommodations: Cabins offer bedrooms, living areas, kitchens, and modern bathroom facilities. Extras vary from park to park; some provide linens and have fully equipped kitchens, while others do not.

Cost: Weekly rates $210 to $525; nightly rates $22 to $80, depending on size, location, and season. Most of the cabins cost about $400 per week.

IOWA

Address: Iowa Department of Natural Resources, Wallace Building, Des Moines, Iowa 50319-0034.

Telephone: 515–281–5145.

The most popular of Iowa's eight state parks with cabins is Backbone,

named for a unique limestone geological formation that sticks up out of
the middle of a river like the backbone of an enormous dragon or dinosaur.
Backbone has sixteen original cabins built in the 1930s by the CCC as
well as four newer two-bedroom cabins. People come to fish, swim, and
picnic in summer, cross-country ski and ice fish in winter. Iowa's state
parks boast excellent playgrounds that have undergone extensive reno-
vations and expansions in recent years.

Accommodations: Primitive cabins have a central bathhouse and do
not have kitchens. Older cabins have kitchens but lack air-conditioning
and heat and are open only in the summer. Modern cabins have kitchens
and private baths.

Cost: Primitive cabins $15 per night, $80 per week; older cabins $25
per night, $150 week; modern cabins $40 per night, $225 per week.

KENTUCKY

Address: Kentucky Department of Parks, 500 Mero Street, 11th floor,
Frankfort, Kentucky 40601-1974.

Telephone: 800–225–PARK; 502–564–2172.

Kentucky's impressive state lodgings include fifteen state resort parks
with lodges and fourteen resort parks with fully equipped housekeeping
cottages. Many have boating, miniature golf, fishing, horseback riding,
planned children's activities, and swimming pools. Cumberland Falls State
Resort Park, profiled on pages 32–33, has even more things to do. In
addition, many of the state parks have historic sites, outdoor museums,
dramas, reenactments, and special events. When requesting information,
ask for the brochure and listing of special events at the different parks.

Accommodations: All cottages have fully equipped kitchens, air-conditioning, and linens. Nine different cottage types range from efficiencies
to deluxe three-bedroom units. The newest and most deluxe are called
executive cabins, each with modern appliances such as a dishwasher and
microwave oven, stylish appointments, a fireplace, and two bathrooms;
they sleep eight to twelve people. A typical cabin for four would be a
two-bedroom with a living room, bath, fully equipped kitchen, and all
linens. Many cabins are duplexes. Most lodge rooms have two double
beds, and suites are available.

Cost: Two-bedroom cottages $70 to $140, lodge rooms $45 to $65,
depending on season and location. Children sixteen and under stay free.
Reservations accepted up to thirteen months in advance.

LOUISIANA

Address: Louisiana Office of State Parks, PO Box 44426, Baton Rouge, Louisiana 70804.
Telephone: 504–342–8111.
Seven of Louisiana's state parks have cabins and two of the parks have lodges suitable for a large family group or several families. Many have beautiful locations on lakes, bayous, or reservoirs. One of the most popular is Bayou Segnette State Park on the west bank of New Orleans, overlooking a bay. Cabins have screened porches or decks and their own private boat docks. The park boasts a wave pool, swimming pool, playgrounds, picnic sites, and nature trails.

Another favorite, Chico State Park, has several different types of cabins and is on a lake with water sports and excellent fishing. Its rustic lodge, built in the 1940s, sleeps twelve people in two double beds and four bunk beds. It's fully equipped with a kitchen, dining area, living room, air-conditioning, and heat.

People looking for a family reunion site would be wise to look into Louisiana's six different group camps, which have dorm-style accommodations, private swimming pools, and large kitchens. They sleep 50 to 150 people and cost $50 to $150 per night, depending on the size and facilities.

Accommodations: Four types of cabins are available throughout the state park system: cabin type no. 1 sleeps up to eight people and is brand new; cabin type no. 2, a bit older, also sleeps up to eight people; cabin type no. 3 sleeps up to six people; and cabin type no. 4, more rustic still, sleeps up to four to six people. All cabins feature fully equipped kitchens, heat, and air conditioning, and some have fireplaces. All bed linens are provided, but guests bring their own towels. Fully equipped lodges sleep ten to twelve people.

Cost: Cabin type no. 1 $50 per night, no. 2 $45 per night, no. 3 $40 per night, no. 4 $35 per night. Lodges $75 per night. Reservations for April 1 to September 30 accepted beginning January 2; reservations for October 1 through March 31 accepted beginning August 1. People reserve by phone for the first twenty-four hours and mail in reservation requests after that.

MARYLAND

Address: Maryland Forest, Park and Wildlife Service, Trawes State Office Building, 580 Taylor Avenue, Annapolis, Maryland 21401.

Telephone: 301–974–3771.

Rental cabins are available at five state parks in Maryland, most with swimming, boating, nature programs, and hiking. Herrington Manor and New Germany state parks have lake swimming, boat rentals, hiking, and fishing in summer and cross-country skiing in winter. Elk Neck State Park has swimming and boating along a river, and Jane's Island State Park has boating and fishing along the bay.

Accommodations: Most cabins are equipped for housekeeping with complete kitchens. Different sizes sleep four, six, or eight people. All park cabins have private baths except those at Elk Neck, which use a centrally located washhouse.

Cost: Four-person cabins $70 per night, $350 per week; six-person cabins $450 per week; eight-person cabins $450 per week. Reservations can be made up to one year in advance. Contact the park you are interested in directly by phone (the office above can provide phone numbers). Weekly reservations only for Memorial Day through Labor Day.

MASSACHUSETTS

Address: Division of Parks and Forests, 100 Cambridge Street, Boston, Massachusetts 02202.

Telephone: Mohawk Trails State Forest, 413–339–5504; Savoie Mountain, 413–663–8469.

Only two of Massachusetts's state parks have cabins: Mohawk Trails State Forest in the Connecticut River Valley and Savoie Mountain State Park in the Berkshires. Both have fishing, swimming, kayaking, canoeing, hiking, and mountain biking (bring your own bikes). In winter cabins often are accessible only on foot or cross-country skis.

Accommodations: Cabins have one to three rooms and are rather primitive. Larger cabins have cold running water and an indoor sink; all cabins have a fireplace and grill out front and bunk beds, table and chairs, and a wood stove inside.

Cost: Cabins $16 to $25 per night. Reservations accepted up to six months in advance and are by the week only in July and August, with a two-night minimum stay the rest of the year.

MICHIGAN

Address: Department of Natural Resources, State Parks Division, Box 30026, Lansing, Michigan 48909.
Telephone: 517–373–1270.
Eighteen of Michigan's state parks have primitive cabins as well as tents and authentic Native American replica tepees. Many cabins overlook lakes, rivers, or streams, and swimming, boating, and fishing are popular pastimes. In addition you can find horseback riding, biking, cross-country skiing, sailboarding, and even field dog training at some of Michigan's parks.

Accommodations: Smaller cabins are perfect for one family and the larger cabins are good for several families or a larger group. All have twin beds or bunks, table and chairs, and wood stoves for heat. Guests bring bedding, cookstove, cookware, and lanterns. There are outside pumps for water, and pit toilets. Tepees are twelve feet in diameter and fifteen feet high; most are on wooden platforms and sleep six people. Rent-A-Tent sites have lanterns, propane stoves, and coolers available for a fee.

Cost: Cabin fees, based on capacity and location, $20 to $50 per night. Tepees $18 per night, Rent-A-Tents $18 to $20 per night.

MINNESOTA

Address: Minnesota Department of Natural Resources, DNR Information Center, 500 Lafayette Road, St. Paul, Minnesota 55155-4040.
Telephone: MISTIX reservations, 800–765–CAMP; state park office, 612–296–4776.
The land of ten thousand lakes has several state parks with cabins and one with a historic lodge and inn. Children under twelve stay free, and cabins vary by park. Some are very large, such as the two-story, six-bedroom cabin at Saint Croix that rents for an unbelievably low $100 per night. Itasca, established in 1891, is the oldest Minnesota state park and has the widest selection of lodgings. It is here that the mighty Mississippi River begins its 2,552-mile journey to the Gulf of Mexico. Accommodations are in the historic Douglas Lodge complex built by the CCC, featuring cabins, an inn, and a lodge. Cabins at Scenic State Park come with their own private boat or canoe. Reservations are made through the MISTIX Corporation, a private reservation company.

Accommodations: Primitive two-bedroom cabins have kitchens, living rooms, dining room, and bathhouses. More modern cabins have fully equipped kitchens, fireplaces, and full baths.

Cost: Primitive two-bedroom cabins $50 per night, more modern cabins $50 to $85 per night.

MISSISSIPPI

Address: Department of Wildlife, Fisheries and Parks, PO Box 451, Jackson, Mississippi 39205.
Telephone: 601–364–2120.
Most of Mississippi's twenty-two parks with cabins are built around water. You'll find cabins along small creeks, immense lakes, and the sandy beaches of the Gulf of Mexico. Water sports are plentiful, and canoeing, swimming, boating, and water-skiing can keep you cool when the temperatures rise. One of the favorites and also one of the largest is Percy Quinn, with twenty cabins, a lake, swimming pool, canoes, paddleboats, fishing boats, miniature golf, a group camp, campgrounds, snack bar, nature trails, and a golf course under construction. Each cabin has its own fishing pier.
Accommodations: All cabins have air-conditioning and heaters and are furnished with linens and fully equipped kitchens. Cabins are classified by their architectural styles: "deluxe" are the most modern, "standard" were constructed in the fifties and sixties, and "rustic" were constructed by the CCC in the thirties with stone or rough-hewn wood. Cabins accommodate two to twelve people, with the majority holding four to six guests.
Cost: Cabins for two $35 per night, for four or six $35 to $55 per night, for twelve $65 per night.

MISSOURI

Address: Missouri Department of Natural Resources, Division of Parks, Recreation and Historic Preservation, PO Box 176, Jefferson City, Missouri 65102.
Telephone: 800–334–6946.
Eleven of Missouri's many state parks have housekeeping cabins, sleeping cabins, or simple motel rooms. All are on the edge of sparkling lakes, fast-running rivers, or more leisurely winding streams, perfect for canoeing. Recreational opportunities abound—you'll find excellent fishing, swimming, and boating, plus hiking trails, swimming pools, caves, and even forests with Indian petroglyphs. One of the state's oldest and most

popular parks is Bennet Springs, where nearly one hundred million gallons of water gush daily. The bubbling pool feeds a stream with excellent fishing for rainbow trout. Canoeing is popular on the nearby Niangua River, and there are cabins, a swimming pool, dining lodge, and visitors center.

Accommodations: Housekeeping cabins have linens and fully equipped kitchens. Sleeping cabins and motel rooms have linens. All cabins and rooms are air-conditioned. Most are open April 15 through October 31, although a few are open longer.

Special Features: Many of the parks have sailing, canoeing, fishing, swimming, and hiking.

Cost: Prices vary according to number of persons and number of bedrooms. Housekeeping cabins $40 to $105 per night, motel rooms $35 to $55, sleeping cabins $30 to $65. To reserve call or write the individual park of your choice; the Division of Parks will send you the list. Two-day minimum stay for summer reservations.

NEBRASKA

Address: Nebraska State Parks Commission, PO Box 30370, Lincoln, Nebraska 68503.

Telephone: 402–471–0641.

Nebraska, with its endless ranch lands, fertile farmland, and rolling hills, has accommodations in seven state parks. Many of the parks have horse rentals, fishing, swimming, and boating. Platte River State Park features unusual tepee accommodations along with inexpensive camper cabins. This former children's summer camp, now operated by the state, offers horseback riding, a swimming pool, and boating on a small lake. Another family favorite, Eugene Mahoney State Park, has a lodge, swimming pool and water slide, horseback riding, paddleboat rental, a driving range, and miniature golf. Western-style Fort Robinson State Park has cabins, lodge rooms, several larger houses to rent, horse rentals, a chuck wagon cookout, swimming, stagecoach rides, train tours, and a trail ride breakfast.

Accommodations: Fully equipped cabins have two to five bedrooms. Camper cabins are sleeping accommodations only. Canvas tepees are decorated with Indian artwork and set on a carpeted wooden platform; they sleep six to eight people and have grills and picnic tables out front.

Cost: Simple two-bedroom cabins $40 to $50 per night, tepees $10 per night, camper cabins $20 to $30 per night.

NEW JERSEY

Address: Division of Parks and Forestry, CN 404, Trenton, New Jersey 08625.

Telephone: 609–292–2797.

Six of New Jersey's parks have family cabins, one park has group cabins, and most have boating, fishing, swimming, children's playgrounds, and nature trails. One favorite, Stokes State Forest, has two lakes, Ocquittunk and Stoney. Rustic housekeeping cabins are next to Lake Ocquittunk, and lake swimming under the watchful eye of a lifeguard is possible seven miles away at Stoney Lake. Boaters can bring their own craft and use Lake Ocquittunk. Hiking trails abound, with sixteen miles of the Appalachian Trail running along the park's ridge.

Accommodations: Most cabins accommodate four to six people and several parks have cabins that sleep eight to twelve people. All cabins have toilets (but not necessarily showers or bathtubs), kitchen facilities, living rooms, and sleeping quarters. Some require guests to bring their own linens and cookware. Primitive camp shelters have four bunks. Enclosed lean-tos also are available.

Cost: Four-bunk cabins $28 per night, $196 per week. Six-bunk cabins $50 per night, $294 per week. Eight-bunk cabins $56 per night, $392 per week. Twelve-bunk cabins (at one park only) $70 per night, $490 per week. Reservation fees $7; firewood can be purchased at each park. Lean-tos $15 per night, camp shelters $20 per night. Cabin reservations are by lottery.

NEW YORK

Address: New York State Parks, Empire State Plaza, Agency Building 1, Albany, New York 12238.

Telephone: 518–474–0456.

Some of New York's state parks have dozens of cabins spread throughout forests and along lakes. One of the most beautiful is Letchworth State Park, sometimes referred to as the Grand Canyon of the East. Its eighty-four cabins are within hiking distance of three magnificent waterfalls. Grounds include swimming pool, hiking trails, an Indian museum, and an inn with a restaurant. Several types and sizes of cabins are available, from rustic one-room affairs to fully equipped two- and three-bedroom units. Allegany State Park near Jamestown has more than four hundred cabins spread over sixty-four thousand acres. The park is so large it is divided into two sides;

the most popular with families is the Red House Side, which has boating, swimming, miniature golf, bike rental, and horseback riding. Both sides have man-made lakes and naturalists take visitors on beaver colony tours and star-gazing expeditions. Cabins in these facilities are simple, with shared bathhouses.

Accommodations: Cabins must be reserved by the week during the summer, by the day the rest of the year. Modern two-bedroom cabins have kitchens and bathrooms; guests bring their own kitchenware and linens. More primitive cabins have cots, kitchens, and shared bathhouses.

Cost: Fully equipped cabins $65 per night and $205 to $250 per week; primitive cabins $35 per night, $100 to $126 per week.

OHIO

Address: Department of Natural Resources, Fountain Square, Building C-1, Columbus, Ohio 43224.

Telephone: 800–BUCKEYE (information); 800–282–7275 (lodge reservations).

Ohio's eight resort parks offer a wide range of scenic beauty with full-service accommodations and conference facilities. The natural settings for the lodges have been chosen to reflect the focal point of each particular park. Maumee Bay, at the edge of Lake Erie, has incomparable water views, a beach area, bike trails, tennis, and an eighteen-hole Scottish-style golf course, among other highlights. Mohican Lodge is set on the Clear Fork Branch of the Mohican River and has an indoor and outdoor pool, tennis, ball courts, and more. All of the lodges have restaurants, swimming pools, tennis courts, conference facilities, and playground equipment. Many also have exercise facilities, golf courses, bike trails, sports, and games.

Sixteen of Ohio's state parks have cabins on lakes and rivers or in woods and mountains; twenty-three of the parks have Rent-A-Camp programs, where guests are provided with a tent set up with cots, sleeping pads, cooler, propane stove, and lantern. Naturalist programs with slide presentations, movies, nature hikes, and animal talks operate at most of the parks.

Pymatuning State Park is profiled on page 177.

Accommodations: "Housekeeping" cabins usually sleep six people in two bedrooms and a sofabed in the living room. Most have screened porches, private baths, fully equipped kitchens, and linens. More rustic "standard" cabins are less elaborately equipped and vary from park to park. "Sleeper" cabins do not have kitchens or linens. Rent-A-Tents have a tent and camping gear. Lodge rooms vary by park; most are double rooms, some are rooms with lofts.

Cost: Housekeeping cabins $80 per night, $400 to $455 per week. Rustic cabins approximately $65 per night, $350 to $375 per week. Sleeping cabins $50 to $70 per night, $225 to $340 per week. Rent-A-Camp sites $12 to $15 per night. Lodge rooms $70 to $95 per night. Parks accept reservations one year in advance.

OKLAHOMA

Address: 500 Will Rogers Building, Oklahoma City, Oklahoma 73105-4492.

Telephone: 800–654–8240; 405–521–2464.

Oklahoma's five state resort parks each capture the scenic, cultural, and historical highlights of their location. All five offer swimming pools, golf, tennis, playgrounds, restaurants, fishing, boating, nature trails, camping, and year-round recreation programs. Guests stay in a lodge or inn, cabins, or campsites. Lake Murray Resort and State Park has turn-of-the-century decor in a country inn on the lake. Family fun includes a three-mile shoreline hike, swimming beach and pool, boating, water-skiing, horseback riding, miniature golf, and an eighteen-hole golf course. Lake Texoma Park has record-setting fish, golf, more water sports, and an indoor fitness center. Western Hills Guest Ranch features southwestern hospitality—see pages 82–83.

Nine state parks with such names as Tenkiller, Robbers Cave, Roman Nose, and Boiling Springs feature cabins for up to six people. Choose from timber or native stone, lakeside and river-view cabins. Many of the parks offer junior naturalist programs for children that feature hands-on interpretive lessons under the guidance of a naturalist.

Accommodations: All cabins are air-conditioned with fully equipped kitchens, private baths, sofabeds, and linens; most have one or two bedrooms. Resort cabins have TVs and phones; park cabins do not. Lodges are similar to motel rooms.

Cost: One-bedroom park cabins $40 per night; at the other end of the scale, cabins sleeping ten to fourteen people on Lake Murray $195 per night. Most cabins are about $55 per night. Children eighteen and under stay free in their parents' room.

PENNSYLVANIA

Address: Bureau of State Parks, 2150 Herr Street, Harrisburg, Pennsylvania 17105.

Telephone: 800–63–PARKS.

Pennsylvania has 275 cabins in twenty-six different state parks, all available at rock-bottom prices. Most have swimming, boating, fishing, and hiking in summer; many have ice-skating, sledding, cross-country skiing, and ice fishing in winter. Other special features include nature programs, exercise trails, and historical trails.

Accommodations: "Modern" cabins were built in recent years and have furnished bedrooms, living room–dining room areas, bathrooms with shower, and electric heat. "Rustic" cabins were built in the 1930s out of logs, stone, or boards, and are closed from mid-December to early April. Cottages, usually former residences that have been renovated, have an average of three bedrooms, plus modern kitchens, full baths, and large living rooms. Most sleep six to ten people.

Cost: Modern cabins sleeping six $55 to $65 per night, $235 to $260 per week. Rustic cabins $20 to $60 per night, $74 to $225 per week. Cottages $50 to $60 per night, $200 to $260 per week. Reservations by lottery system.

SOUTH CAROLINA

Address: South Carolina State Parks, 1205 Pendleton Street, Columbia, South Carolina 29201.

Telephone: 803–734–0156.

Thirteen state parks have cabins amid Blue Ridge Mountain scenery, beside sparkling inland lakes, and along sunny Atlantic beaches. Poinsett, on the edge of Wateree Swamp, combines rolling mountainous terrain with the moss-draped trees of the swamp. Santee, known for its excellent fishing, has cabins perched on piers over the water, and Oconee Station State Park has the oldest structure in the South Carolina upcountry, once used as an Indian trading post. We profile several parks on the ocean or a short distance away: see Hunting Island State Park Cabins, page 234; Myrtle Beach State Park Cabins, page 231; and Edisto Beach State Park cabins, page 232.

Accommodations: Most cabins are completely furnished, heated, air-conditioned, and supplied with linens and cooking equipment. Sizes vary, accommodating four to twelve people. Cabins must be rented by the week from April 1 through October 31 and by the weekend or for three consecutive nights the rest of the year. Shorter stays can be arranged if there are vacancies.

Cost: Rates vary considerably from park to park. Average price for cabin sleeping six people $350 per week; rates range from $180 to $475 per week. Reservations required; ask for the brochure that describes this simple process.

SOUTH DAKOTA

Address: South Dakota Game Fish and Parks, Division of Parks and Recreation, 523 East Capital, Pierre, South Dakota 57501-3182.

Telephone: 605—773—3391.

Six of South Dakota's state parks have rustic log camping cabins along rivers, in the prairies or in woodland areas. Two state parks, Custer and Lewis and Clark, have housekeeping cabins, lodge, and motel units.

The enormous Custer State Park in South Dakota's Black Hills near Mount Rushmore has several lodges and resorts with housekeeping cabins, motel units, and sleeping cabins. Buffalo roam freely through most of the park. The park contains three large streams for fishing and four lakes. Three of the lakes have sandy beaches for swimming, and the fourth is for waterskiing. A fun-filled junior naturalist program for children seven to twelve is available. For lodging information, call 800—658—3530.

Lewis and Clark is a water lover's paradise, with a full-service marina offering boating, sailing, and water-skiing. Hiking, biking, and horse trails run through the park. Lodgings include camper cabins, housekeeping cabins, and motel rooms; for Lewis and Clark lodging information, call 605—665—2680.

Accommodations: Camping cabins have one large room with a set of bunks and a double bed, a small table, and benches. All have electricity and nearby bathhouses, and the newer units have heat and air-conditioning. Each cabin is equipped with an outdoor picnic table and a fire ring. Custer and Lewis and Clark accommodations vary widely; contact each park for details.

Cost: Camping cabins $22 per night per cabin; reservations are accepted starting January 1. Other cabins at Custer and Lewis and Clark $60 to $100 per night; lodge rooms $75 to $100 per night.

TENNESSEE

Address: Tennessee Department of Conservation, Division of Parks and Recreation, 701 Broadway, Nashville, Tennessee 37243-0446.
Telephone: 800–421–6683; 615–742–6667.
Seventeen state parks have comfortable cabins and seven have gracious inns. Several of the parks have unusual recreational facilities, such as Frisbee golf courses (Meeman-Shelby, Forest, and Cedars of Lebanon) or skeet and trap ranges (Henry Horton). One of the most elaborately equipped is Fall Creek Falls State Park, with the highest waterfall east of the Rocky Mountains. Its eighteen-hole golf course, horseback riding, fishing, boat rental, hiking trails, restaurant, cabins, and inn make it a deservedly popular vacation destination. Another refreshing getaway, Real Foot Lake State Park, was formed by a series of earthquakes in 1799 that caused the Mississippi to alter its course, creating a cypress swamp with lily pads and water flowers. The motel-inn is right over the water (double rooms $55, children under seventeen stay free in their parents' room).

Accommodations: Cabins have kitchens, fireplaces, and all linens. Deluxe cabins have fully equipped kitchens, air-conditioning, wood stoves with complimentary firewood, rollaway beds, phones, and TVs. Smaller, rustic cabins do not have air-conditioning, phones, or TVs.

Cost: Prices differ from park to park. Larger, deluxe cabins sleeping six to eight $80 per night on weekends, $60 per night the rest of the week. Smaller, more rustic cabins $35 per night on weekends, $30 the rest of the week. Lodge rooms $50 to $75 per double room. Children stay free in their parents' room, no charge for rollaway beds. Parks accept reservations a year in advance.

TEXAS

Address: Texas Parks and Wildlife Department, 4200 Smith School Road, Austin, Texas 78744.
Telephone: 512–389–4890.
Six state parks have cabins that accommodate one to six people, and four parks have lodges. One architecturally notable lodge is pueblo-style adobe Indian Lodge, built by the CCC, with a restaurant and handmade cedar furniture. It has a swimming pool, hiking trails, scenic overlook, and horse rentals nearby. Balmorhea also has adobe units, plus a large swimming area warmed by hot springs. Bastrop State Park's many rustic stone and timber cabins were built by the CCC; its cabins are thought to

be some of the finest of that era. Its swimming pool, nine-hole golf course, playground, and small fishing lake make it a perennial family favorite.

Accommodations: Guests can stay up to fourteen days, and cabins vary considerably from park to park. All linens are provided.

Cost: Cabins for two people $35 per night, four people $45, five people $50 per night, six people $55 per night. Reservations accepted three months in advance at the desired park headquarters. Inn and lodge reservations accepted twelve months in advance.

VIRGINIA

Address: Virginia State Parks, 203 Governor Street, Suite 306, Richmond, Virginia 23219.

Telephone: 804–786–1712 (general information); 804–490–3939 (reservations).

Eight of Virginia's state parks have simple housekeeping cabins with either a lake or swimming pool and a wide selection of other recreational opportunities. The most visited park, Seashore State Park and Natural Area, offers the opportunity to explore a habitat that includes lagoons, large cypress trees, and rare plants. Seventeen miles of hiking trails wind through the natural area, and the visitor center explains about this coast environment. The park also has a bike trail and boat rentals. Fairy Stone State Park, home of the lucky "fairy stones," near the Blue Ridge Parkway, has a lake and reservoir for swimming and boating and a gospel music festival in May. We profile family favorite Hungry Mother State Park on pages 184–185.

Accommodations: One-bedroom cabins sleep two to four people; two-bedroom cabins sleep four to six people. All have combination living-dining rooms with kitchens and private baths.

Cost: One-bedroom cabins $200 to $220, two-bedroom cabins $285 to $425, depending on the park. Extra beds $21 per week.

WEST VIRGINIA

Address: West Virginia Division of Tourism and Parks, 1900 Kanawha Boulevard East, Charleston, West Virginia 25305.

Telephone: 800–CALLWVA will connect you with any park.

West Virginia has eighteen top-notch resort and cabin facilities. Four parks with lodges have golf courses; the off-season package deals are an especially good buy. Other parks have horseback riding, boating, fishing, scenic chairlifts, picnicking, and hiking. Many have nature programs with free activities and events just for kids.

One unusual choice, Cass Scenic Railroad State Park, has thirteen two-story guest cabins that once housed loggers who worked for the lumber industry. The railroad that once transported logs now operates as a tourist train; two different rides run during the summer. A hiking and biking trail begins at Cass; it runs seventy-six miles to North Cladwell with spectacular scenery and quaint little towns along the way.

We profile the resort park at Cacapon on pages 38–39.

Accommodations: Cabins fall into four categories: "modern" cottages and cabins have fireplaces, complete kitchens, private baths, and heat and sleep two to eight people. "Standard" log cabins have modern kitchens, private baths but no heat, and accommodate two to six people. "Economy" cabins are one big room with a small bath, kitchen area, built-in bunks, and a loft; most hold four people. "Rustic" cabins have gas lamps, a wood-burning kitchen stove, and gas refrigerator, with water and bath facilities outside. Most hold four to six people.

Cost: Cabins rent by the week only June 1 through Labor Day; nightly rentals available the rest of the year. Prices vary; per week, modern cabins $375 to $625, standard cabins $290 to $470, economy $242 per week, rustic $165 to $315. Make reservations up to one year in advance at individual parks.

APPENDIX I: BUDGET MOTELS

*M*any cost-conscious families stretch their vacation dollars by using no-frills budget motels when they need lodging en route to a vacation destination or in popular tourist areas where they won't be spending much time in their rooms. The following motels offer all of the basic amenities, including air-conditioning, private baths, and televisions; quite a few have such extras as swimming pools and restaurants. The typical double room in a budget motel costs $30 to $50 per night, double occupancy, and children under seventeen often stay free in their parents' room. Since many hotels and motels have rooms with two double beds, this option can work well for families with one child; larger families can add a rollaway bed for a small additional fee.

Most budget motels have a toll-free reservation line and will send you a directory of their locations, amenities, and prices. Another helpful publication for those who want detailed information is the *National Directory of Budget Motels* by Raymond Carlson (Pilot Books, 1992; $5.95). It contains a city-by-city listing for budget motels in each state.

Consumer Reports gives the highest marks to the following budget motels: Budgetel, Drury Inn, Hampton Inn, La Quinta, Red Roof, Shoney's, and Super 8.

BUDGET MOTEL CHAINS

Allstar Inns
805–687–3383

Arborgate Inns
800–722–7220; 614–755–6230
Children under eighteen stay free when accompanied by two adults in the same room.

Best Inns of America
800–237–8466; 618–997–5454
Children under eighteen stay free in their parents' room.

Best Western
800–528–1234; 602–957–4200
Children under twelve stay free in their parents' room.

Budget Host Inns
800–283–4678; 817–626–7064

Budgetel
800–428–3438; 414–272–8484
Children eighteen and under stay free in their parents' room.

Choice Hotels
800–424–4777; 301–593–5600
Children under eighteen stay free in their parents' room at most locations.

Clarion
800–221–2222; 301–593–5600
Children under eighteen stay free in their parents' room at most locations.

Comfort Inn
800–228–5150; 301–593–5600
Children under eighteen stay free in their parents' room.

Cross Country Inns
800–621–1429; 614–766–0037
Children under eighteen stay free in their parents' room.

Days Inn, Days Hotel, Days Suite, and Days Stops
800–375–2525; 404–329–7466
The Kids Stay and Eat Free Program offers free meals to children under twelve who are accompanied by their parents. Discounts are given when rooms are booked more than twenty-nine days in advance.

Drury Inns
800–325–8300; 314–429–2255
Children eighteen and under stay free in their parents' room.

Econo Lodge
800–553–2666; 301–593–5600
Children under eighteen stay free in their parents' room at most locations.

Economy Inns
800–826–0778; 619–438–6661

Exel Inns
800–356–8013; 608–241–5271
Children eighteen and under stay free in their parents' room.

EZ 8 Motels
619–291–4824

Friendship Inns
800–453–4511; 301–593–5600
Children under eighteen stay free in their parents' room at most locations.

Hampton Inns
800–426–7866; 901–758–3100
Children eighteen and under stay free in their parents' room.

Independent Motels of America
800–341–8000; 605–842–3418
This organization represents individual budget motels. Call for a directory.

Knight's Inn
800–722–7220; 614–755–6230
Children under eighteen stay free when accompanied by both parents.

La Quinta Motor Inn
800–531–5900; 512–366–6000
Children eighteen and under stay free in their parents' room.

McIntosh Motor Inns
215–279–6000

Master Host Inns
800–251–1962; 404–873–5924
Children under twelve stay free in their parents' room at most locations.

Microtel
800–365–6835; 716–436–6000

Motel 6
505–891–6161
Children under eighteen stay free in their parents' room.

Quality Inns
800–228–5151; 301–593–5600
Children under eighteen stay free in their parents' room at most locations.

Red Carpet Inns
800–247–4677; 404–873–5924
Children under twelve stay free in their parents' room at most locations.

Red Roof Inns
800–843–7663; 614–876–3200
Children under eighteen stay free in their parents' room.

Rodeway Inns
800–221–2222

Scottish Inns
800–251–1962; 404–873–5924
Children under twelve stay free in their parents' room at most locations.

Shoney's Inns
800–222–2222

Sleep Inn
800–627–5227; 301–593–5600

Super 8 Motels
800–800–8000; 605–225–2272
Children twelve and under stay free in their parents' room at most locations.

Susse Chalet
800–572–1880 (in New Hampshire); 800–258–1980 (outside New Hampshire)

Travelodge
800–255–3050; 619–448–1884
Children under seventeen stay free in their parents' room.

APPENDIX II:
U.S. TOURIST OFFICES

Alabama Bureau of Tourism and
Travel
401 Adams Avenue
Montgomery, Alabama 36103
800–252–2262; 205–242–4169

Alaska Division of Tourism
PO Box 110810
Juneau, Alaska 99811-0801
907–465–2010

Arizona Office of Tourism
1100 West Washington Street
Phoenix, Arizona 85007
602–542–8687

Arkansas Department of Parks and
Tourism
One Capitol Mall
Little Rock, Arkansas 72201
800–828–8974; 501–682–7777

California Department of
Commerce and Office of Tourism
PO Box 9278
Van Nuys, California 91409
800–862–2543; 916–322–2881

Colorado Department of Tourism
1625 Broadway, Suite 1700
Denver, Colorado 80202
800–255–5550; 303–592–5510

Connecticut Department of
Economic Development
Department of Tourism
865 Brook Street
Rocky Hill, Connecticut 06067
800–282–6863

Delaware Tourism Office
99 Kings Highway
PO Box 1401
Dover, Delaware 19903
800–441–8846; 302–739–4271

Florida Division of Tourism
126 West Van Buren Street
Tallahassee, Florida 32399–2000
904–487–1462

Georgia Tourist Division
285 Peachtree Center
Avenue NE, Suite 1000
Atlanta, Georgia 30303
800–847–4842; 404–656–3590

Hawaii Visitors Bureau
Waikiki Business Plaza, Suite 801
2270 Kalakaua Avenue
Honolulu, Hawaii 96815
808–923–1811

Idaho Travel Council
Hall of Mirrors
700 West State Street, 2d floor
Boise, Idaho 83720
800–635–7820; 208–334–2470

Illinois Office of Tourism
310 South Michigan Avenue, Suite
108
McCormick Place on the Lake
Chicago, Illinois 60616
800–545–7300; 312–567–8500

Indiana Department of Commerce
One North Capitol, Suite 700
Indianapolis, Indiana 46204
800–289–6646; 317–232–8860

Iowa Tourism Office
200 East Grand Avenue
Des Moines, Iowa 50309
515–242–4705

Kansas Department of Economic
Development
Travel and Tourism Division
4005 West Eighth Street, 5th
Floor
Topeka, Kansas 66603
800–252–6727; 913–296–2009

Kentucky Department of Travel
and Development
Capitol Plaza Tower, 22nd Floor
500 Mero Street
Frankfort, Kentucky 40601–1968
800–225–8747; 502–564–4930

Louisiana Office of Tourism
PO Box 94291
Baton Rouge, Louisiana 70804-
9291
800–334–8626; 504–342–8119

Maine Publicity Bureau
PO Box 23000
Hallowell, Maine 04347
800–533–9595; 207–582–9300

Maryland Office of Tourism
217 East Redwood Street
Baltimore, Maryland 21202
800–543–1036; 410–333–6611

Massachusetts Division of Tourism
100 Cambridge Street, 13th Floor
Boston, Massachusetts 02202
800–447–MASS, ext. 500; 617–
727–3201

Michigan Travel Bureau
Department of Commerce
PO Box 30226
Lansing, Michigan 48909
800–543–2–YES; 517–373–1700

Minnesota Tourist Information
Center
375 Jackson Street
Farm Credit Service Building
St. Paul, Minnesota 55101
800–657–3700; 612–296–5029

Mississippi Division of Tourism
PO Box 22825
Jackson, Mississippi 39205-2825
800–647–2825; 601–359–3297

Missouri Division of Tourism
PO Box 1055
Jefferson City, Missouri 65102
800–877–1234; 314–751–4133

Montana Promotion Division
1424 Ninth Avenue
Helena, Montana 59620
800–548–3390; 406–444–2654

Nebraska Division of Travel and
Tourism
PO Box 94666
Lincoln, Nebraska 68509
800–228–4307; 402–471–3796

Nevada Commission on Tourism
5151 South Carson Street
Carson City, Nevada 89710
800–237–0774; 702–885–4322

New Hampshire Office of Vacation
Travel
PO Box 856
Concord, New Hampshire 03312–
0586
800–258–3608; 603–271–2343;
603–271–2666

New Jersey Division of Travel and
Tourism
CN 826
Trenton, New Jersey 08625
800–JERSEY–7; 609–292–2470

New Mexico Travel Division
PO Box 20003
Santa Fe, New Mexico 87503
507–827–7400

New York State Division of
Tourism
One Commerce Plaza
Albany, New York 12245
800–225–5697; 518–474–4116

North Carolina Travel and
Tourism Division
430 North Salisbury Street
Raleigh, North Carolina 27611
800–VISITNC; 919–733–4171

North Dakota Tourism Promotion
604 E Boulevard
Bismarck, North Dakota 58505
800–435–5663; 701–224–2525

Ohio Office of Tourism
600 West Spring Street
Columbus, Ohio 43215
800–BUCKEYE; 614–466–8444

Oklahoma Division of Tourism
PO Box 6078
Oklahoma City, Oklahoma 73146
800–652–6552; 405–521–2409

Oregon Economic Development
Tourism Division
775 Summer Street NE
Salem, Oregon 97310-1351
800–547–7842; 503–378–3451

Pennsylvania Bureau of Travel
Development
Department of Commerce
216 Finance Building
Harrisburg, Pennsylvania 17120
800–847–4872; 717–787–5453

Rhode Island Department of
Economic Development
Tourism and Promotion Division
Seven Jackson Walkway
Providence, Rhode Island 02903
800–556–2484; 401–277–2601

South Carolina Division of
Tourism
1205 Pendleton Street
Columbia, South Carolina 29201
803–734–0122

South Dakota Division of Tourism
Capital Lake Plaza
711 Wells Avenue
Pierre, South Dakota 57501-3369
800–952–2217; 605–773–3301

Tennessee Tourist Development
PO Box 23170
Nashville, Tennessee 37202
615–741–7994

Texas Tourist Development
PO Box 5064
Capitol Station
Austin, Texas 78711
800–888–8839; 512–426–9191

Utah Travel Council
300 North State Street
Salt Lake City, Utah 84114
801–538–1030

Vermont Travel Division
134 State Street
Montpelier, Vermont 05602
802–828–3236

Virginia Division of Tourism
1021 East Cary Street, 14th Floor
Richmond, Virginia 232319
800–847–4882; 804–786–4484

Washington Development of
Trade and Economic
Development
Tourism Division
101 General Administration
Building, AX-13
Olympia, Washington 98504
800–544–1800; 206–586–2088

Washington, D.C., Convention and
Visitors Association
1212 New York Avenue NW, 6th
Floor
Washington, D.C. 20005
202–789–7000

Travel West Virginia
West Virginia Department of
Commerce
1900 East Kanawha Boulevard
Building 6, Room B-564
State Capitol
Charleston, West Virginia 25305
800–CALLWVA; 304–348–2766

Wisconsin Division of Tourism
PO Box 7606
Madison, Wisconsin 53707
800–372–2737; 800–432–8747;
608–266–2161

Wyoming Travel Commission
1-25 and College Drive
Cheyenne, Wyoming 82002
800–225–5996; 307–777–7777

INDEX

342

INDEX

GENERAL INDEX (cont.)

Outer Banks, North Carolina, 225–228
Ozark Folk Center Lodge, Arkansas, 287
Ozark Mountains, Arkansas, 30–31, 72, 179
Ozark National Forest, 287
Ozark National Riverway, Missouri, 169–170

Padre Island National Seashore, Texas, 221–222
Percy Quinn State Park, Mississippi, 318
Petit Jean State Park, Arkansas, 179–180, 310
Pinewoods Camp, Massachusetts, 304–305
Planning, early, 2–3
Platte River State Park, Nebraska, 319
Plymouth, Massachusetts, 251, 303–305
Pokagon State Park, Indiana, 26–27
Port Aransas, Texas, 221–223
Port St. Joe, Florida, 245–246
Prairie House Manor Bed and Breakfast, South Dakota, 280
Priest Lake, Idaho, 163–164
Provincetown, Massachusetts, 251
Puget Sound Islands, Washington, 216–219

Radisson Inn, Oklahoma City, 278
Rail, traveling by, 11
Ranching Heritage Center, Texas, 275–276
Real Foot Lake State Park, Tennessee, 325
Red Top Mountain State Park, Georgia, 311
Resorts, 15–51
Riverside and lakeshore vacations, 154–193
Riverside Motel, Murfreesboro, Arkansas, 288
Roanoke Island, North Carolina, 225–226
Rocky Mountain National Park, Colorado, 20–22, 114–118, 142
Rolling Y Ranch, Ohio, 147–148
Roosevelt National Forest, Colorado, 117–118

St. Augustine, Florida, 239–242
Salmon River, Idaho, 162–163
Salt Pond National Seashore, Massachusetts, 257
San Antonio International Hostel, Texas, 277
San Diego, California, 198–201
Sangre de Cristo Mountains, Colorado, 165
Sanibel Island, Florida, 242–244
San Isabel National Forest, Colorado, 165
San Juan Islands, Washington, 216
Savannah, Georgia, 290–292
Savoie Mountain State Park, Massachusetts, 317
Seascape Villas, South Carolina, 235–236
Seashore State Park and Natural Area, Virginia, 326
Sequoia National Park, California, 90–94, 140–141
Sequoyah State Park, Oklahoma, 82
Sharing the Joy of Nature, 85

Sharing Nature with Children, 85
Shawnee National Forest, 312–313
Shoshone National Forest, Wyoming, 61–62
Sierra Club, 266–267
Snowmass Village, Colorado, 273–274
South Carolina coast, 230–236
Southern Outer Banks, North Carolina, 228
Spirit Lake, Iowa, 25–26
Squam Lake, New Hampshire, 46–47
Stanislaus National Forest, California, 141
Starved Rock Park, Illinois, 313
State park cabins and resorts, 6–7
state by state, 308–327
Stoke State Forest, New Jersey, 320
Suite hotels, 6
Sunrise Camp, California, 90
Superior National Forest, Minnesota, 172–173
Suwanee River, Georgia, 182
Swaha Lodge, Arkansas, 288
Swallow Falls State Park, Maryland, 186–187

Tahoe area, California, 16–17
Texas Guestel, Texas, 277
Tourist offices, list of, 333–336
Train, traveling by, 11
Traveling
by air, 10
by car, 2–3, 9–10
by rail, 11
Trojan Horse AYH Hostel, Vermont, 307

U.S. Tourist Offices, list of, 333–336
Unofficial Guide to Disneyland, 202

Vacation Exchange Club, 4–5
Valley View Lodge, New York, 305
Vashon Island, Washington, 216, 218–219
Virgin River Canyon, Utah, 23–24
Vogelsang Camp, California, 90

Wallops Island, Virginia, 224
Washington, coast of, 219–221
Washington Island, Wisconsin, 175
Western Folklife Center, Nevada, 268–269
Whidbey Island, Washington, 216–218
White Mountains, New Hampshire, 49, 191
Williamsburg, Virginia, 295–296
Wind River, Wyoming, 60–62, 63
Winterbrook Farm, Massachusetts, 302

Yellowstone National Park, Wyoming, 63–64, 81, 109–114, 269–270
Yosemite National Park, California, 85–90, 139–140
Young Naturalist, The, 85

REPLY FORM

Let us know . . .

If, in your travels through the United States with your family, you discover a bargain destination or a vacation that we did not mention in this book, please fill out this form and tell us about it. We will research your suggestion for possible inclusion in future editions of *The Best Bargain Family Vacations in the U.S.A.*

Name and Address of Lodging _____

_____

Date of your visit _____

Age(s) of your children _____

Rates per night or per week _____

What did you and/or your children like about this place? _____

_____

_____

_____

Have any of the places we've recommended changed for better or worse

since this book was written? _____

_____

_____

_____

_____

Your Name _____

Address _____

_____

Phone _____

Send to Laura Sutherland and Valerie Wolf Deutsch
      Best Bargain Family Vacations in the U.S.A.
      c/o St. Martin's Press, Inc.
      175 Fifth Avenue
      New York, New York 10010